Three answers to the question
"What is philosophy?"

Three answers to the question "What is philosophy?"

A comedy in three acts

STUART DALTON

CASCADE *Books* · Eugene, Oregon

THREE ANSWERS TO THE QUESTION "WHAT IS PHILOSOPHY?"
A comedy in three acts

Copyright © 2024 Stuart Dalton. All rights reserved. Except for brief quotations in critical publications or reviews, no part of this book may be reproduced in any manner without prior written permission from the publisher. Write: Permissions, Wipf and Stock Publishers, 199 W. 8th Ave., Suite 3, Eugene, OR 97401.

Cascade Books
An Imprint of Wipf and Stock Publishers
199 W. 8th Ave., Suite 3
Eugene, OR 97401

www.wipfandstock.com

PAPERBACK ISBN: 978-1-6667-7584-6
HARDCOVER ISBN: 978-1-6667-7585-3
EBOOK ISBN: 978-1-6667-7586-0

Cataloguing-in-Publication data:

Names: Dalton, Stuart [Author].

Title: Three answers to the question "what is philosophy?" : a comedy in three acts / Stuart Dalton.

Description: Eugene, OR: Cascade Books, 2024 | Includes bibliographical references and index.

Identifiers: ISBN 978-1-6667-7584-6 (paperback) | ISBN 978-1-6667-7585-3 (hardcover) | ISBN 978-1-6667-7586-0 (ebook)

Subjects: LCSH: Philosophy. | Philosophy—History. | Philosophy—Introductions.

Classification: B72 D35 2024 (paperback) | B72 (ebook)

02/08/24

For my children: Sage, Jackson, and Marcus
and my parents: Sharon and John

Contents

Preface | xi

Acknowledgments | xiii

Introduction: Comedy as a key to understanding what philosophy is and why it matters | xv

How to use this book | xxiii

Part 1: Finding Your Way in a Philosophy Class: Two Practical Guides

Chapter 1: How to be completely miserable in a philosophy class—or how to do the complete opposite | 3

Chapter 2: How to write philosophy papers that no one would ever want to read and create philosophy projects that no one would ever find interesting or useful—or how to do the complete opposite | 11

Part 2: Three answers to the question "What is philosophy?" (a comedy in three acts)

ACT ONE: Philosophy is a conversation that has been going on for over 2,500 years which has been full of comedy from the beginning, and will continue to be funny forever if we do it right

Chapter 3: Ancient philosophy | 25

(Philosophy in its infancy: learning to speak, learning to crawl, getting its head stuck between the stair rails, and nearly getting itself killed in all sorts of interesting and fascinating ways, as all babies do.)

Chapter 4: Medieval philosophy | 72

(Philosophy, now a teenager, rushes into an ill-advised and doomed-to-fail marriage with religion which lasts approximately 1,200 years before it realizes its mistake and asks for a divorce; but like all unhappy marriages this one is very dramatic and interesting and full of creative tension while it lasts.)

Chapter 5: Modern philosophy | 111

(Single again after a long and stifling marriage, philosophy asserts its independence in a rather spectacular way, trying to make up for all the time it lost by wildly experimenting with every idea, argument or theory it can find.)

Chapter 6: Nineteenth- and twentieth-century philosophy | 190

(Now middle-aged and a little bit exhausted after all the crazy experimentation it did during its wild modern years, philosophy settles into a more conventional and less promiscuous lifestyle with a fairly stable job that includes an excellent benefits package, and it's even somewhat respected in polite society; so like all middle-aged people it needs a midlife crisis from time to time to jolt it out of its complacency.)

Chapter 7: Philosophy in the future, which is completely up to you! | 270

ACT TWO: Philosophy is a very awkward business that has always been on the verge of going out of business

Chapter 8: Why all philosophy professors are sophists even though Socrates—the closest thing there is to a founding father or a saint in the history of philosophy—despised sophists and declared that he would sooner die than become one himself | 277

Chapter 9: Ten philosophy departments reinvent themselves to make philosophy a more marketable commodity | 280

ACT THREE: Philosophy is something that makes almost everyone write very badly

Chapter 10: Six different forms of bad philosophical writing, which clarify six important aspects of philosophy (so all this bad writing is actually a good thing!) | 293

Appendix: Some of the authors and texts that were left out of the four history of philosophy chapters | 315

(an incomplete list, but better than nothing I guess)

Bibliography | 319

Index | 325

Preface

THIS BOOK ORIGINATED WITH a disturbing thought: "I don't think my children have any idea what philosophy is or what I've spent much of my life trying to do as a philosophy professor, so I'd like to write something to answer these questions and explain what I did with my life before I drop dead." I began the book with that thought in mind, and then it slowly dawned on me that such a book might also be useful to other people's children who find themselves in a philosophy class and have no idea what they are studying or why.

That was how I felt when I took my first philosophy class. When I started college I had no clue what I wanted to study or what I wanted to do with my life, but these problems were instantly solved for me when—on a whim, in the last term of my freshman year—I signed up for PHI 101: Introduction to Philosophy. The class was so large, with several hundred students, it was held in an auditorium which on weekends doubled as a movie theatre where the classics of 1980s late-night campus cinema were screened: *Rocky Horror Picture Show*; *Harold and Maude*; *Eraserhead*; *Mad Max*; *A Clockwork Orange*; etc. But on Monday and Wednesday mornings I sat in this darkened auditorium along with hundreds of other students and watched the instructor perform something very different called "philosophy." I had no idea what philosophy was until I took that class, but when I found myself in that auditorium watching this show it was love at first sight, and from that moment on I never had any doubt about what I wanted to do with my life. Like all professors everywhere I liked college so much I decided to stay there forever.

I've never changed my mind about the decisions I made in Orson Spencer Hall Auditorium many years ago. I still can't imagine a better job than teaching philosophy. To walk into a classroom full of college students—who are unquestionably the most idealistic and interesting people on earth—and embark with them on a fifteen-week exploration of the many strange and wonderful attempts that the human race has made to understand, through nothing but their own independent thinking, the true nature of reality, knowledge, and values: what could possibly be more fun than that? Every semester in every class I feel like I'm getting away with something, and I expect the police to burst through the door at any moment and arrest me. I've learned something valuable from every one of the students I've been fortunate to teach, and I've been grateful for every moment I've been able to spend exploring philosophy with them.

This book is a celebration of the joy of studying philosophy, and it's an expression of gratitude for the many ways philosophy has enriched my own life. I had a great time writing it and I hope it proves to be a useful and entertaining guide that will persuade everyone who reads it that philosophy is endlessly interesting and endlessly fun.

Acknowledgments

THANKS TO MARCUS DALTON, Wynn Gadkar-Wilcox, Travis Gebing, Amanda Jones, Daniel Thomas Koveleski, Anna Malavisi, Nick Nalbatian, Brian Oberg, Wayne Pomerleau, and Stephenie Swindle for many great suggestions to improve this book, and thanks to Teresa Saunders for terrific assistance with all library matters.

Thanks to my editor, Robin Parry, and everyone else at Cascade Books for their guidance and assistance. I'm so happy to have found such a friendly and supportive publisher.

Parts of chapters 8 and 9 appeared in this essay: "10 Philosophy Departments Reinvent Themselves: An Essay and a Story." *Agathos: An International Review of the Humanities and Social Sciences* 12.1 (2021) 21–39. I thank the editors for permission to include this material.

Introduction

Comedy as a key to understanding what philosophy is and why it matters

PHILOSOPHY IS OFTEN QUITE funny and this is almost never deliberate, almost never the result of trying to be funny; the comedy is almost always unplanned and unintentional. This may seem like an obvious and embarrassing defect and a reason to think the whole enterprise is a joke, but it's actually just the opposite. The fact that philosophy is so often funny without even trying—the fact that it is so good at creating unintentional comedy—is something to be proud of and something we should celebrate. Here's why:

The reason philosophy is so good at creating comedy is because its ideals are so high. Philosophy attempts three things: (1) to discover the ultimate nature of reality, knowledge, and values; (2) to do this completely by means of independent thinking that questions everything and doesn't rely on the supposed authority of any other person, institution, or tradition; (3) to present its theories to the world with good arguments, thus enabling everyone to decide for themselves if these theories are correct and useful. That's it. There aren't many rules in this game but what rules there are set very high standards. By these standards has anyone ever completely succeeded? Probably not. The ideals are so high that perhaps no mortal can ever achieve them, and that's what makes philosophy so good at generating comedy: the distance between its ideals and its imperfect practice by the confused humans here on earth—this distance between the ideal and the actual is an almost perfect comedy-creating machine. We should celebrate every moment of comedy that's created in the gap between philosophy's ideals and its all-too-human practice because it's a reminder of how high those ideals are and how worthy they are of our aspirations, even if our efforts usually fall comically short.

This book has two parts:

Part One
Finding your way in a philosophy class: two practical guides

and

Part Two
Three answers to the question "What is philosophy?"
A comedy in three acts

The two chapters in part 1 are about how to be happy in philosophy classes. The questions philosophy asks—What is real? What is true? What is valuable?—are definitely childish questions, but in an entirely good way. Children are naturally full of wonder and thus see the world as a wonder-ful place. If you allow yourself to have the same sense of wonder and curiosity that children have you'll be able to appreciate how fascinating these questions are and how relevant they are to everyone's life; but if you approach any philosophy class with a closed or uncurious mind nothing will make any sense and you will be deeply unhappy. Chapter 1 provides a prescription for how to be miserable in a philosophy class, so that you can do the exact opposite.

Chapter 2 is a guide to writing philosophy papers and creating other philosophical projects. One of philosophy's greatest strengths and joys is the fact that its ideas can be explored in almost any medium or form. There's nothing wrong with writing a standard argumentative essay—a good one is always a welcome addition to the world—but philosophy is not limited to that medium. From the beginning of its history philosophy experimented with other media and forms beyond argumentative essays. Plato, for example, believed that the best way to explore a philosophical question was through a dialogue, and the thirty-five dialogues that he wrote around 2,400 years ago have proven so enduringly fascinating that (as someone said) the whole history of philosophy can be seen as nothing but a series of footnotes to Plato.[1] Plato's dialogues are scripts that

---

1. Whitehead, *Process*, 39.

call for philosophy to be performed, with a plot, multiple characters, and multiple points of view; and when philosophy is performed in this way it can be much more fun and much more educational than a standard argumentative essay in which you get only one voice and one point of view: sort of like the difference between listening to a long, boring lecture and watching an absorbing and thought-provoking movie. This is just one example of how philosophy isn't limited to argumentative essays and how more indirect forms of communication can be a highly effective means of exploring philosophical questions and presenting philosophical arguments. Chapter 3 provides a detailed prescription for how to write philosophy papers that no one would ever want to read, or create other philosophy projects that no one would ever find interesting or useful, so that you can do the complete opposite.

The rest of the book is a three-act comedy composed of three answers to the question "What is philosophy?" The first act is about the comedy in philosophy's history (four chapters on that since it's a long history) and philosophy's future (only one chapter on that since it hasn't happened yet). The history of philosophy is filled with comedy, and if we continue to do it right (which is up to you, philosophers of the future) it will continue to be hilarious. Philosophy began about 2,500 years ago, and these 2,500 years can be divided into four stages that are remarkably similar to stages in the lifespan of a typical human who lives perhaps three score and fifteen years (that's seventy-five years if you're keeping score at home). So you can think of the history of philosophy as the history of a 2,500-year-old person who developed very slowly and also made some extremely strange choices in her lifetime (as, thankfully, almost everyone does; otherwise we would all die of boredom).

Chapter 3 presents an outline of ancient philosophy, which is the period of philosophy's infancy. Like all babies, philosophy was incredibly cute. In addition to being almost unbearably cute, babies are extremely fast learners for two reasons: first because they're motivated by uninhibited wonder and curiosity; secondly because they don't worry about avoiding mistakes, and when they do make mistakes they don't waste any time being embarrassed. In its childhood, philosophy made many interesting and important mistakes, such as confusing itself with religion, business, and sophistry; but these are mistakes that it needed to make, and the sooner the better, because they helped it discover its true identity. Like a toddler who charges ahead boldly on her little legs—tripping, falling, crashing into furniture, and tumbling to the ground, but always springing right back up and toddling off again in search of more adventure and excitement—philosophy develops very quickly during its childhood, and by the end of this period it has developed into a rather confident and even cocky teenager, secure in its own identity and ready to sally forth boldly to make many more foolish mistakes.

Chapter 4 is all about medieval philosophy, which is defined mostly by one truly spectacular mistake that philosophy made after it emerged from its childhood: it decided to get married to religion. This is remarkable because one of the most important discoveries philosophy made in its childhood is that it plays by different rules than religion, and one of those rules is the requirement that it must think independently—so it can never be the subordinate or employee of an institution such as religion without contradicting a core principle of its identity. Religion and philosophy don't have to be enemies but they are different games with different standards, goals, and rules; so while there is no reason why they can't be friends it was definitely a mistake for them to get married. The medieval marriage of philosophy and religion was a contradiction from the start but it still lasted over 1,200 years, and such a long and tension-filled marriage was bound to be full of drama and intrigue—far from being dreary, dull, or boring in any way, which unfortunately is how the Middle Ages are often understood. As Tolstoy wrote: "All happy families are alike; each unhappy family is unhappy in its own way,"[2] which is why stories about happy families are boring and no one wants to read them. Medieval philosophy is never boring if you study it with one eye focused on the tensions and outright contradictions that are a constant subtext in this marriage of philosophy and religion. The medieval period generated over 1,200 years-worth of creative tension that was just waiting to explode when this marriage finally came to an end.

Chapter 5 is about modern philosophy, which is when this creative explosion took place. This is the most rowdy, raucous, and riotous period in the history of philosophy by far. When philosophy emerges from the medieval period all the creative tension that had been accumulating for the previous 1,200 years bursts forth in an explosion of new ideas and theories. In the modern period philosophy seems determined to make up for lost time. The books from this period are notoriously excessive and overwritten, as if the authors had gone days without sleep, keeping themselves awake on a diet of black coffee and cigarettes. Modern philosophy

---

2. Tolstoy, *Anna Karenina*, 1.

has a manic, over-caffeinated tempo as it races to recover its full creative potential, much of which was suppressed and compromised during the years it spent trying to be a responsible spouse in its ill-conceived marriage to religion; now it seems delighted that it no longer has to behave responsibly. In the sixteenth, seventeenth, and eighteenth centuries philosophy embarks on a period of wild experimentation, something like a three-hundred-year-long bender, and it's enormous fun to go along for the ride as modern philosophers see how fast they can drive this car.

Chapter 6 is focused on nineteenth- and twentieth-century philosophy, which is as far as we'll go in this history. What exactly divides modern philosophy from nineteenth- and twentieth-century philosophy other than a purely arbitrary date such as the beginning of a new century? The lines that divide the first three periods are quite obvious because medieval philosophy was such an aberration. The marriage of philosophy and religion in the Middle Ages is an anomaly that interrupts what perhaps could have been a calm and constant development. But just as most people's lives are not calm and constant, since most of us make mistakes and pursue detours and dead ends and then have to backtrack or start over, philosophy did likewise. Medieval philosophy had the effect of breaking the early history of philosophy into three pieces—before, during, and after—and it led directly to the frenetic spirit that animated modern philosophy when it reasserted its independence in a manic explosion of creativity. But the off-the-hook party that was modern philosophy had to end sometime, if for no other reason than sheer exhaustion. As everyone discovers when they reach their forties, eventually all those sleepless nights will catch up to you and staying up for days is just no longer an option. There's a noticeable difference between modern philosophy and nineteenth- and twentieth-century philosophy in this regard; but more important than this is the fact that by the time philosophy reaches the nineteenth century it has become somewhat successful, accepted, and part of the establishment rather than a rebel or an outlaw. Philosophy settles down somewhat in the nineteenth and twentieth centuries in part because it is exhausted after all the wild experimentation of the modern period, but also as a result of its own success. It now has the option to relax somewhat and just regale its audience with a repetition of theories and stories from its past: replaying its greatest hits rather than creating new material. This is philosophy's middle age, and like all middle-aged people the best thing that can happen to it is a midlife crisis that will shake it out of its complacency and startle it into a burst of creativity. The best philosophy in the nineteenth and twentieth centuries is the result of midlife crises that cause philosophy to wake up in alarm and conclude that its whole life so far has been a mistake and therefore it must blow everything up and start over from the beginning. (We should all be so lucky to experience a middle age like this: full of creative disruptions that prevent us from relaxing into idleness and irrelevance.)

To summarize this Philosophy-Is-Just-Like-Any-Other-2,500-Year-Old-Person-Going-through-Predictable-and-Unsurprising-Stages-of-Life-Model-for-Making-Sense-of-the-History-of-Philosophy (the PIJLAO2500YOPGTPAUSOLMFMSOTHOP model, if you want an easy-to-remember acronym), the four stages (so far) in the history of philosophy are:

1. Ancient Philosophy: Philosophy's Infancy. (Philosophy is born and spends its childhood doing all the cute things babies do. Everyone agrees this baby is adorable.)
2. Medieval Philosophy: Philosophy's teenage marriage to religion. (This was a mistake, but a very educational mistake, so for that we should be grateful.)
3. Modern philosophy: Philosophy's post-divorce period of wild experimentation. (Buckle up and enjoy the ride!)
4. Nineteenth- and twentieth-century philosophy: Philosophy's middle age. (Fortunately this middle age is filled with many midlife crises.)

Philosophy, however, is not dead yet, and that's why there's one more chapter in this first act. Chapter 7 is about philosophy in the future, which is completely up to you.

Act 2 is about the comedy generated by the business of philosophy: a very awkward business that has always been on the verge of going out of business. Chapter 8 considers one hilarious fact that is true of all philosophy professors. When philosophy was in its infancy it defined itself with great zeal in opposition to sophistry, and yet every philosophy professor who has ever lived has been completely willing to become a sophist in at least one respect: they've all been willing to get paid to teach philosophy. In the entire history of philosophy only Socrates was willing to teach for free and even willing to die for philosophy; every philosophy professor since Socrates has declined to follow his example, and so every philosophy professor—who teaches a discipline that defined itself in its infancy as the opposite of sophistry—is in fact a sophist himself in at least this one respect. However, we should note that since Socrates (who refused even to be called a teacher, so much did he loath that profession), philosophy has continued on earth largely because it has been willing to compromise this particular ideal somewhat and allow itself to become something of a business with paid employees. Plato and Aristotle both started philosophy schools, and though these schools and the instructors employed by them were no doubt less than ideal, perhaps the compromise that started there was a good one to make since it allowed philosophy to spread beyond just the fortunate few who were able to engage in conversations with Socrates before he died as a glorious martyr. But the fact that all philosophy professors are sophists has certainly introduced a tension into the business, and this has greater potential to be a creative and constructive tension if we are willing to acknowledge it and laugh at it.

Chapter 9 focuses on the business that all philosophy professors must keep going if they want to keep their jobs: the business of philosophy departments, which must find a way to sell philosophy to college students if they want to avoid going out of business. This is inevitably an awkward and difficult commercial transaction since it involves selling a product that is quite resistant to being commodified, so every philosophy department on earth has struggled to reinvent itself in order to survive in this strange marketplace, and that has led to lots of comedy.

The last act of this three-act comedy focuses on one very funny aspect of philosophy: the fact that it is something that makes almost everyone write very badly. The final chapter finally addresses the very first question that everyone wants to ask when they pick up a philosophy book and try to read it: "Why is this writing so bad?" Almost all philosophy is badly written, but it's badly written in at least six different ways, and these six forms of bad writing clarify six important aspects of philosophy—so all of this bad writing is actually a good thing and we should be grateful for it.

These ten chapters don't pretend to constitute an exhaustive catalog of philosophy's enormous comic output, but hopefully they are enough to convince everyone that philosophy is very good at creating comedy and this comedy is something we should celebrate.

Since this book aims to explore the comic output of the entire history of philosophy from the beginning, one question that obviously needs to be answered before the book can begin is this: When exactly did the history of philosophy begin? Any answer to this question is bound to be controversial, as it should be, and I'm delighted that I can contribute to this controversy right now. Traditionally Thales is recognized as the first of the pre-Socratics: the warm-up act before Socrates took the stage, which included Pythagoras, Heraclitus, Parmenides, Zeno, Xenophanes, and several dudes whose names began with "Anax" (Anaximander, Anaximenes, Anaxagoras) who were therefore destined to be mixed up by philosophy students and philosophy professors for the rest of time. Our understanding of the pre-Socratic philosophers is incomplete and fragmentary but fortunately there's one moment in the life of Thales that was perfectly preserved by Plato. This moment, I propose, should be designated as philosophy's official beginning simply because it captures so perfectly the comic distance between its ideals and its actuality:

> They say Thales was studying the stars, Theodorus, and gazing aloft, when he fell into a well; and a witty and amusing Thracian servant-girl made fun of him because, she said, he was wild to know about what was up in the sky but failed to see what was in front of him and under his feet.[3]

This witty and amusing Thracian servant-girl is one of the great unsung heroes in the history of philosophy. She was the first to notice how funny philosophy can be because the philosophers who attempt to achieve its high ideals are still mere mortals who live and breathe on Planet Earth: a planet that contains many gopher holes, manholes, sinkholes, mineshafts, and wells (among other things) that merely-human philosophers can easily fall into when they are trying to figure out the ultimate nature of reality, knowledge, and values. When Thales fell into a well this was a moment of perfect comedy—physical and intellectual comedy combined: something for everyone. This is the moment when philosophy really began.

This book is an exploration of some of the comedy that philosophy has created in its long and wonderful history as philosophers have followed in Thales's footsteps—and sometimes also followed him down a well. The history of philosophy has been full of comedy like this, and that's something to celebrate.

---

3. Plato, *Theaetetus*, 174a.

How to use this book

PHILOSOPHY IS LIKE A party that started over 2,500 years ago and is still going strong. When you take a philosophy class you're invited to join this party; but walking into a party 2,500 years late can feel a little awkward. This book is meant to solve that problem.

The best way to feel welcome at this party is to focus on how funny philosophy is, simply because its ideals are so high that humans almost never manage to reach them. Laughing at philosophy brings it down to earth where it belongs and where it can do some good. Everyone at this party is just trying to make sense of the strange existence we all fell into, so of course you are more than welcome even though the party started thousands of years ago: everyone has been waiting for you and everyone is thrilled that you're here.

Think of this book as something like a buffet with an assortment of dishes to give you the energy you need to make the most of this party. I suggest you use the practical guides in chapters 1 and 2 as appetizers to get the party started, and then for the main course I recommend the five chapters on the history and future of philosophy (chapters 3–7). Any particular topic, or period, or author in philosophy makes more sense in the context of the entire history of philosophy.

Chapters 8 and 9 are snacks to revive you if your philosophy class ever feels like it's taking itself too seriously. Chapter 8 points out that every philosophy professor on earth is a sophist, which is pretty funny for a discipline that defined itself in its childhood as the opposite of sophistry. Chapter 9 explores the business of selling philosophy here on Planet

Earth—a very awkward business that is constantly threatened with going out of business. To avoid this fate all philosophy departments have tried to reinvent themselves to make their very old discipline attractive to very young college students who have many other forms of entertainment available.

The final chapter is intended as dessert you can turn to whenever you feel like there's nothing good to eat at this party. This last chapter is actually the first one I wrote because I do think that the best way to answer the question "What is philosophy anyway?" is by answering a different question instead: "Why is all this philosophy so badly written?" There are many different forms of bad philosophical writing; this chapter originally included fourteen varieties but I thought that was probably more dessert than anyone needed. I settled for just these six forms of bad writing because they are probably the most common and the most helpful in terms of clarifying important aspects of philosophy and thus indirectly answering the question "What is philosophy anyway?" Please visit the dessert table whenever you encounter some philosophy that is very badly written (which is almost all of it), and hopefully after a little dessert you'll be ready to return to that text and see the good ideas in it even though the writing is terrible.

PART 1

Finding Your Way in a Philosophy Class

Two Practical Guides

Chapter 1

How to be completely miserable in a philosophy class—or how to do the complete opposite

It would be difficult to imagine a more effective way of torturing someone than a semester-long philosophy class, if the person you want to torture has no curiosity or wonder and is therefore unwilling to see human existence as wonder-ful. If your goal is to make such a person thoroughly miserable, any course in philosophy would be an absolutely state-of-the-art, cutting-edge way to accomplish this. If someone has already decided that the three questions philosophy asks—What is real? What is true? What is valuable?—are stupid, pointless, worthless questions, what could possibly be more awful than spending fifteen weeks doing nothing but asking and trying to answer these very questions? If a committee of evil geniuses somewhere in the universe set out to devise an absolutely perfect form of torment for the uncurious and close-minded humans here on Planet Earth I don't think they could improve on this simple plan: sign those people up for a semester-long philosophy class.

Though philosophy classes can work extremely well as instruments of torture, they actually were not created for that purpose. (This may surprise you.) The ancient Greeks who created philosophy all agreed on a few things, one of which was this: "philosophy begins in wonder." Some version of this line can be found in the writing of almost all the first philosophers (even those for whom very little of what they wrote remains). They all agreed that one prerequisite for studying philosophy is wonder. Since philosophy begins in wonder, if you refuse to allow yourself to wonder philosophy will never begin for you—and that fact very effectively summarizes the peculiar suffering experienced by someone who enrolls in a philosophy class but remains stubbornly and steadfastly allergic to wonder: the class will never begin for such a person, no matter how long he sits in the classroom waiting. It will be like sitting on a bench at a bus stop that was abandoned long ago, waiting an entire semester for a bus that will never arrive.

One other thing that all the first philosophers agreed on is this: philosophy is a kind of love. This fact is built right into the name that they chose to describe what they were doing: *philo-sophia*, the love of wisdom. If philosophy is the love of wisdom then no one can really study philosophy unless they too fall in love with wisdom. As we all know from personal experience (and as almost every poem or story or song about love ever written also attests), being in love is the most powerful and wonderful (there's that word again) experience that humans can have. Being in love is a way of experiencing the world; it's not just an abstract attitude that you can adopt like an observer who remains on the outside looking in. If you really want to understand what love is you have to fall in love yourself, so this is the second prerequisite for the study of philosophy: you must fall in love with wisdom.

These are very strange prerequisites for a college course, but they are in fact the prerequisites for every philosophy class: (1) you must allow yourself to wonder, like a little child, about the ultimate nature of reality, knowledge, and values; and (2) you must fall in love with wisdom. These prerequisites ought to be published in the college catalog, and also inscribed over the doorway of every classroom where a philosophy class is taught. If we took these prerequisites seriously, as the first philosophers did, philosophy classes could no longer function as instruments of torture. When these prerequisites are met studying philosophy will be a joyous experience, as it should be. (If falling in love were unpleasant we would have stopped doing it a long time ago.)

Of course the first philosophers weren't also taking five or six courses every semester, including courses in a wide variety of fields that have very different prerequisites than philosophy. This fact of life for a contemporary college student is a source of much of the confusion that leaves them baffled, bewildered, and perhaps even miserable in their philosophy classes. College students today are expected to be something like world travelers who, on any given day, must cross back and forth repeatedly over the borders between the natural sciences, the social sciences, the arts, and the humanities—all of which have radically different cultures and effectively speak different languages. Like a good world traveler, if you want to enjoy your travels and learn as much as possible from every place you visit you have to accept that all cultures have value and that you can learn from all of them. If you can't do this as a college student you will feel like you are a stranger stranded in a strange land where you don't speak the language and therefore have no idea what is going on.

Aristotle is a good example of someone who was very good at moving between all four of these academic cultures, and a few thousand years ago he provided an excellent guide for twenty-first-century college students when he said this: "It is the mark of an educated person not to expect greater precision than the subject matter allows."[1] He made this remark in a book about ethics because he wanted to make it clear that ethics is not precise in the same way that logic or mathematics are precise, and an educated person must recognize this fact and adapt to these differences. Ethics has just as much value as the sciences, and if you dismiss ethics because it's not as precise as the sciences you're simply not an educated person. In the roughly 2,400 years since Aristotle died the power of the sciences has dramatically increased so that today it's very common for people to think that only science counts as knowledge and therefore it's the only academic pursuit that matters, but this is not an educated opinion. Science is certainly good at what it does but it doesn't do everything: for example, science can never tell us what it means to live a good life (that's a question for ethics), it isn't interested in creating or explaining beauty (that's the province of art and aesthetics), and it doesn't even attempt to answer questions about the ultimate nature of reality (that's metaphysics) or knowledge (that's epistemology). The mistake of believing that only science can provide knowledge or value is called "scientism," and like many other words that end in "ism" ("racism," "sexism," "elitism," etc.) it names a serious and dangerous prejudice.

The prejudice of scientism is responsible for a lot of unnecessary suffering on college campuses today, especially the suffering of students who feel disoriented and even angry in humanities classes because they've been conditioned to believe that such classes are a waste of time. The truth is that the natural sciences, the social sciences, the arts, and the humanities all contribute to knowledge and a truly educated person

---

1. Aristotle, *Nicomachean Ethics*, 1094b25.

wants to learn from all of them. Each of these fields is valid and valuable in its own way, just like every culture and every language in the world is valid and valuable. Anyone who is convinced that only his own language and culture are good is a bigot and he will be very unhappy if he ever has to leave the bubble where he is so content and comfortable. But the whole point of college is to eliminate bigotry and ignorance, and that's why college students are required to be world travelers. You can be happy in your daily travels between the different languages and cultures of the arts, the humanities, the social sciences, and the natural sciences if you adopt the cosmopolitan spirit of Aristotle and learn to appreciate each of these worlds on its own terms.

Philosophy shares in the overall cultural milieu of the humanities, but it also has its own idiosyncratic cultural quirks. First of all, while falling in love with any discipline is never against the rules in any field, in philosophy it is quite literally a requirement. If you don't approach philosophy in a spirit of love your philosophy class will be a big disappointment. There are many different aspects of love, but one of them is definitely desire. Loving philosophy means, among other things, truly desiring to know the answers to the questions that philosophy investigates. As Aristotle (yes him again) famously said in the very first line of his *Metaphysics*: "All people by nature desire to know."[2] As a description this is obviously false, since most people on earth clearly do not desire to know, and some may even actively desire not to know; but as a prescription for how to fall in love with philosophy it's perfect. If you don't walk into every philosophy class with a true desire to know, you are guaranteed to have a miserable experience—sort of like going on a date with someone you don't like at all.

Secondly, while obviously the study of any topic will benefit if you approach it with genuine curiosity, philosophy again makes this a requirement, and also demands a form of curiosity that's so extreme it can only be described as wonder. All of us were filled with wonder when we were children, but unfortunately as we grew older most of us came to believe that there's something embarrassing and even indecent about an adult who allows herself to wonder. Even though it's widely believed that being a responsible adult requires one to put away all childish things, including wonder, this is simply an unexamined prejudice that's obviously ridiculous as soon as you look it in the eye. Being a responsible adult does

---

2. Aristotle, *Metaphysics*, 980a25.

not require that you become allergic to wonder—that you run away from any thought about the ultimate nature of reality, knowledge, or values as if such thoughts were shameful or obscene. The truth is that everyone can do both: you can be a responsible adult and also allow yourself to wonder about the ultimate nature of things and to love the pursuit of this wisdom; and if you don't allow yourself to do both you're simply imposing artificial limits on yourself and cutting yourself off from an essential part of your humanity.

One other aspect of philosophy that makes it accessible and fun and relevant for everyone is this: the rules of the game stipulate that it is and always will be an amateur sport and a do-it-yourself activity. Since the only authority in philosophy is the authority of a good idea, the people who play the philosophy game can never become authorities themselves and thus everyone who plays the game remains in the minor leagues forever and no one ever advances to Major League Philosophy—because it doesn't exist. It's true that people often defer to famous figures in the history of philosophy as if they were authorities, but that's just a mistake. The name of any famous author in the history of philosophy (e.g., Aristotle, Kant, Sartre) is really just shorthand for a collection of ideas, which may be good or bad ideas, and the strength of those ideas is the only possible authority in this game. This means that anyone can jump in and play the game at any time. Philosophy is like an endless game of pick-up basketball in which the strength of anyone's game comes entirely from the strength of the ideas they bring onto the court. So if you bring some good ideas you can beat Hegel on a fast break, or block a shot from Plato, or beat Simone de Beauvoir off the dribble, or dunk on Sartre (which shouldn't be hard since he was only five feet tall)—all of which is great fun and also great exercise, so you'll definitely want to keep coming back every day to play philosophy at the very highest level of the game, which is the amateur level.

There's one other aspect of philosophy that can only be practiced in a group setting, such as a class that meets for seventy-five minutes twice a week. To continue the excellent basketball analogy: while you can certainly practice and improve your free throws and your jump shot, practicing alone in your driveway, some aspects of your game can never improve unless you practice with other people. This is because we all have intellectual blind spots that we can never discover by ourselves; someone else has to point them out to us or we will remain ignorant of them forever.

In a purely physical sense a blind spot is a deficiency in the machinery of our senses that we don't know about. The limits of our senses that we do know about we never call blind spots: I know that my eyesight isn't powerful enough to see what's happening right now on the moon, so I don't think of that as a blind spot, just a limit. But whenever I believe I can see/hear/feel/smell/taste everything there is to see/hear/feel/smell/taste, when in fact I can't, that's a blind spot in a purely physical sense. For example, everyone has a blind spot in their field of vision because a small patch of retina, where the optic nerve leaves the eye on its way to the brain, contains no photoreceptors. To experience this, close your left eye and look at the cross below. Hold the page away from you at arm's length and then slowly move it toward you. Focus on the cross but notice in your peripheral vision what happens to the dot. When the dot falls on your blind spot it will disappear.

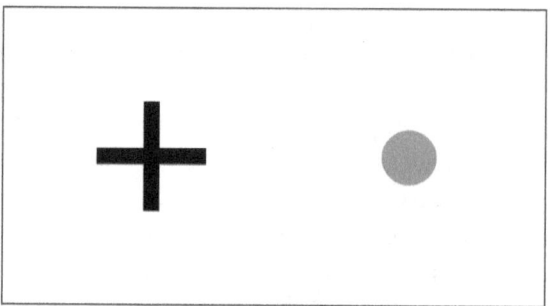

We are oblivious to this blind spot because whenever visual input from the eye is interrupted it is replaced by an interpretation supplied by the mind. The interpretation is always: "I think it's probably just more of the same," so whatever surrounds the blind spot will be used to fill in the blind spot. Notice what happens when the surrounding background is black:

When we talk about "blind spots" in philosophy it's a metaphorical extension of physical blind spots. We all have numerous blind spots in our thinking, usually because we've accepted assumptions and prejudices from the culture we fell into as if they were "just obvious." For example, many of the men in philosophy's history fell into a world which believed it was "just obvious" that women were inferior to men and were born to serve men, and very few of these men managed to discover and correct this blind spot. Philosophers, of course, have hardly been alone in harboring this particular prejudice during most of the world's history, but when such an obvious mistake is committed by philosophers—who claim to be searching for the truth using only their own independent thinking and never deferring to the supposed authority of any culture or tradition—the mistake is particularly glaring. The fact that this blind spot persisted for so long in the history of philosophy is mostly due to the fact that philosophy was limited to a conversation between men: just men talking to other men; women were not invited to the party. When men only talk to other men any blind spots that a woman could easily point out to them could go unnoticed for several thousand years, and that's exactly what happened in the case of this particular mistake. It wasn't until quite recently that women were finally acknowledged and allowed to participate in the dialogue/party/basketball game that is philosophy.

When a philosopher has an obvious blind spot that's obviously quite embarrassing, and philosophy may be particularly susceptible to blind spots because it demands that you think for yourself, but blind spots always need to be pointed out by someone else: you will never find them on your own. So blind spots may be a particular occupational hazard in philosophy, and this is one more reason why philosophy requires everyone to present their arguments to the world instead of just keeping them to themselves, and why everyone can benefit from the team practice that you get in a philosophy class: it gives you the opportunity to have any blind spots in your thinking that you can't see yourself pointed out to you by others.

To summarize, this is how to be happy in a philosophy class:

- Allow yourself to be just a curious as you were as a child and to wonder about the ultimate nature of reality, knowledge, and values. Then the world will become wonder-ful, and so will your philosophy class. If you don't allow yourself to wonder, philosophy can never begin for you, and then you will spend the entire semester waiting for a bus that is not coming.

- Allow yourself to fall in love with philosophy and to desire to know the answers to the questions it's trying to answer. Every student in every philosophy class should fall in love with the love of wisdom; if you are not having a love affair in your philosophy class something has gone horribly wrong.

- Be a good world traveler who recognizes that the cultures and languages of the arts, the humanities, the natural sciences, and the social sciences are all good and valuable. If you don't have this cosmopolitan attitude, instead of enjoying your daily travels between these different worlds you will feel like you are being kidnapped and held hostage against your will, which is certainly no fun, and you will also fail to learn all the interesting and important things that you can learn from each of these academic cultures.

- Recognize that philosophy has always been and always will be an amateur sport and a DIY activity in which the only authorities are good ideas—so there's no reason for you to stand on the sidelines just watching this game: get in there and play (because good ideas are all that's required to play, and you definitely have lots of those).

- Use the time that you have in your classes to correct your own blind spots, since you will never be able to do this on your own. Every philosophy class can be like a team practice where you get a chance to learn from others and they get a chance to learn from you—and also it's just a lot of fun to play this game as a team.

Or, on the other hand, if you would prefer to be confused and miserable for an entire semester in your philosophy class, here's how you can accomplish that goal: just do exactly the opposite of all of the above.

Chapter 2

How to write philosophy papers that no one would ever want to read and create philosophy projects that no one would ever find interesting or useful—or how to do the complete opposite

In any philosophy class you'll have the opportunity to write a paper or create some other kind of project. This chapter will explain how to do this very badly, so that it is a thoroughly unpleasant experience for you and the work you create will be so awful that any sane person would flee from it in terror since there will be nothing that anyone could learn from it and trying to wring some value from this mess will only result in disappointment and sorrow. If you want your philosophy paper or project to be an utterly miserable experience both for you and your audience, then please reverse all of the following instructions and do just exactly the opposite: that will guarantee that both you and everyone else who comes into contact with your paper or project will be deeply unhappy, and no one will learn anything at all other than this: "I never want to do that again!" Or, if you would prefer to have a good time while you write a philosophy paper or create a philosophy project in some other form, and if you'd like your work to be both educational and enjoyable for other people as well, then here's how that's possible.

The most typical assignment in a philosophy class is an argumentative essay, and there is nothing wrong with that. To be able to write clearly, precisely, and directly, as an argumentative essay requires, is an important skill that one can always improve, and every well-written argumentative essay makes the world a better place. However you have no doubt already had many opportunities to write argumentative essays in your life, and you'll no doubt have many more opportunities since this is a form of writing that's not at all limited to philosophy classes; so it's possible that your instructor may give you the chance to create a philosophical project in some other form. One of the things that makes philosophy so much fun and capable of so many surprises is the fact that you can explore philosophical questions and present philosophical arguments in almost any medium or form, and people have been doing this for as long as philosophy has existed. So I'll offer some suggestions for that type of project as well—for a philosophy project that's not an argumentative essay—but first let's talk about our old friend the argumentative essay.

The basic rule of any argumentative essay is this: everything should be explicit and direct; nothing should be hidden or subtle. An argumentative essay is a machine with one very specific job: to convey us by means of clear and explicit arguments to a conclusion announced clearly and explicitly at the beginning by the most direct route possible. Back in ancient times when people didn't just ask their phones to take them wherever they wanted to go, humans used to give each other directions or make little maps to explain how to go someplace. (I know this is hard to believe.) If I invited you to a party at my house, for example, I would also provide directions that you could follow to get to my house, and when you arrived hopefully the first thing you would say is: "Those were excellent directions not only because they worked—they did indeed get me to your house—but along the way I always knew exactly where I was and I never got confused or disoriented. Thanks Bro, you are awesome!" This is exactly what we want from an argumentative essay: tell us right at the start exactly where we're going (the conclusion you will lead us to), and then take us there in a perfectly clear and efficient way so that we always know exactly where we are at any point along the way and we always have a clear sense of how every single word in the essay is helping to get us there. This last requirement means there should not be anything in an argumentative essay that doesn't move this car/bicycle/skateboard/donkey/camel (however you want to picture this vehicle) to its destination. Any indirection or subtle artistry in the essay that doesn't move the car forward will only make us nervous and annoyed because rule #1 in the rule book for argumentative essays is this: everything should be explicit and direct; nothing should be hidden or subtle. There are many other forms of writing and certainly many other forms of art that do not play by this rule and therefore are not constrained to be perfectly efficient machines that do nothing but take their passengers to their promised destination in the most clear and obvious way possible, but argumentative essays do not have that luxury. The drama and excitement in a good argumentative essay should come completely from the argument itself: the fact that the argument proposes to change our mind about something and then succeeds in doing this. That's the movement that occurs in a good argument: movement from disagreement to agreement by means of nothing other than good, convincing reasons. But during this journey there should be no in-flight entertainment, or sightseeing, or stopping to visit an old friend, or snakes getting loose on the plane, or any other distractions of any kind. A good argumentative essay tells us clearly and explicitly where it plans to take us, and then it takes us there with maximum efficiency without wasting time or energy on anything else, and that's all it does.

It's often forgotten that the destination of an argumentative essay should be someplace interesting; otherwise why would anyone want to go there? What this means in terms of the logic of arguments is: an argument requires a controversial conclusion—a conclusion that the reader does not agree with at first, but then a successful argument changes her mind by providing good reasons that she can use to change her own mind. That's why a logical argument is the only form of persuasion that is truly respectful: because it just gives you reasons for you to evaluate on your own and then it gets out of your way so that you can decide for yourself. It respects your autonomy and allows you to convince yourself. But this requires that the audience to whom this argument is directed must initially disagree, or else the writer does not have the opportunity to change their minds. So an argumentative essay that argues for an obvious and not at all controversial conclusion that I probably already accept is actually not an argument, because an argument requires a controversial and interesting conclusion. Such an "argument" blows itself up right from the start by failing to start with a controversial and interesting conclusion that the audience cares about.

An argumentative essay can be any length (one paragraph; five paragraphs; five thousand paragraphs) but the same basic rules always apply regardless of how long or how short it is:

- Announce clearly right at the beginning where you intend to take us, and make sure this is an interesting place (in other words make sure that you are arguing for a conclusion that we don't already accept because otherwise it's impossible for you to take us anywhere: we're already there).

- Then take us there with maximum efficiency and by the most direct route, and don't waste our time or confuse us along the way with anything that doesn't directly contribute to the argument—anything that doesn't help to move this car as efficiently as possible to the intended destination.

- Once we arrive at the destination tell us we've arrived and then you're done, so don't try to do anything else because there's nothing more for you to do. If the arguments you gave us were convincing then you've effectively made yourself vanish, because you gave us the opportunity to convince ourselves with the reasons that you supplied—so you are no longer needed. That's the ideal for a good argumentative essay: for the author to make herself unnecessary and thus disappear.

That's really all there is to writing an argumentative essay, and it's essential to preserve the simple and straightforward nature of this type of writing so I'll resist the temptation to amplify or embellish these requirements. A good argumentative essay is like a good Uber driver: she gets you to your destination as quickly and efficiently as possible and doesn't try to entertain you along the way with jokes, or funny stories, or unrequested political opinions, or juggling bowling pins with one hand while steering with the other, or any other form of distraction. She knows that all you want from an Uber driver is good driving—quick, efficient, knowledgeable, safe driving—so she does that very well and doesn't even try to do anything else. That's all there is to it, so in the simple and straightforward spirit of a good argumentative essay I will now shut up about argumentative essays.

If you have the opportunity in your philosophy class to create a project in some form other than an argumentative essay here are a few thoughts on what's possible and how this can be extremely interesting, fun, and educational. One of the great strengths of philosophy is the fact that it can be investigated and explored in almost any medium or form. Argumentative essays may be the dominant and traditional form for works of philosophy, but philosophy is definitely not limited to that form and from the very beginning philosophers have recognized this fact. Many of the earliest pre-Socratic philosophers chose to write in poetry; Socrates chose to perform philosophy in the streets through confrontations and conversations with his fellow Athenians; and both Plato and Aristotle thought that the best way to present philosophical arguments was in the form of highly theatrical dialogues with multiple characters each with their own point of view and their own theories, something like a plot, and often no resolution or closure to the discussion—it simply ends because everyone has to go home.[1] Other possible media that can work very well to explore a philosophical idea or argument include all of the following:

- a story in any form (writing, graphic novel, film, video, etc.)
- an artwork in any form (painting, music, sculpture, etc.)
- a performance in any form (theatre, dance, music, etc.)

This is far from a complete list; it's just meant to get you thinking about the possibilities. If there are any limits on how philosophy can be explored and expressed those limits are impossible to define and there's no point in even trying. The situation is analogous to trying to define the limits of art: whenever anyone attempts such a definition it only motivates some artist somewhere to prove the definition wrong, and then a new kind of art gets created that does just that. Any medium or form that you can use to accomplish these three objectives can work great for a philosophy project:

- Be educational. Your project should teach us something new, interesting, and important about philosophy.
- Be topical. Your project should apply to at least one of the three areas of philosophy: metaphysics (What is real?), epistemology (What is true?), axiology (What is valuable?).
- Be insightful, not just informative. Information is more accessible today than ever before in the history of the world but insight is just as hard to come by as ever, and a philosophy class is all about insight. Your project should give us new and important insights into any of the three questions that philosophy poses.

1. These characteristics are abundantly evident in the thirty-five dialogues that Plato wrote, which—lucky for us—managed to survive into the present day. The dialogues that Aristotle wrote unfortunately all got lost, but we do know that Aristotle wrote dialogues just like his teacher Plato. The writings of Aristotle that did survive are lecture notes written by Aristotle's students or in some cases by Aristotle himself.

Whatever medium or form you use for your project, if it is educational, topical, and insightful then you obviously found one that works.

A philosophy project that's not an argumentative essay is free from the strict constraints that govern all argumentative essays, but the ultimate purpose of the project is still to argue for a conclusion. The point of any philosophy project is always to argue for an interesting and controversial conclusion and to give its audience a chance to learn something new and valuable. If you write an argumentative essay that fact is completely obvious, because a good argumentative essay argues for its conclusion explicitly and directly and does exactly nothing else. A philosophy project in some form other than an argumentative essay is still an argument for a conclusion, but unlike an argumentative essay it's allowed to present its argument indirectly. Indirection can be a good way to make the audience do some work on their own. Good art does this: it forces its audience to work through the various questions, perspectives, and other interpretative puzzles the artist has built into the art in order to decide for themselves the meaning and value of the work. A philosophical project must argue for a conclusion, but that argument can be presented indirectly in a way that requires its audience to become a contributor and collaborator to complete the work. This work of collaboration can make the argument implicit in the work more meaningful, because the audience is involved and invested in the argument's creation. There are an infinite variety of different ways of drawing in and involving the audience so the possibilities for artistry and creativity are limitless.

In order to stay focused on the fact that beneath any indirection and artistry every philosophy project is fundamentally an argument for an interesting and controversial conclusion, I recommend that if you do an indirect philosophy project (meaning any form other than a traditional argumentative essay) you also write a short argumentative essay which presents in a perfectly explicit and direct form the argument that's presented implicitly and indirectly in your project. This will help you keep your eye on the philosophical core of your project and not forget it while you also add layers of indirection and artistry that will make the audience contribute and collaborate with their own interpretive work. Your instructor may require that you write a short and straightforward essay like this to accompany your indirect project, but even if it's not a requirement it will be very beneficial for you to write an essay like this and use it to anchor your project so that you never lose sight of its primary and fundamental purpose: to make a case through indirection and artistry for the same interesting and controversial conclusion that you argued for directly and bluntly in your argumentative essay. Don't use this short argumentative essay to repeat what you already did in your project; instead use it to make explicit the argument that was implicit in your work, and to extend and clarify that argument.

Whether you write an argumentative essay, or create a project in some other form, the most important thing is to have something to say. We all know what it's like to write a paper, or create anything else, when we have nothing to say: no ideas waiting to be put into words or brought to life in some other form. We all know that even when you really, truly have nothing at all to say it's entirely possible to fill up five, ten, fifteen pages or more with words. Here's how to do it:

- Make completely obvious statements that no sane person would ever say out loud since there is absolutely no need to say them—then repeat all of these statements again many, many times.

- Write in such a vague way that no one could possibly understand what you mean, even though your writing consists of words that are found in the dictionary and it is grammatical—then repeat everything vague and inscrutable that you have written many, many times.

- Pack your writing with formulas and clichés that are well known and generally regarded as meaningful, even though they actually have no meaning at all and are just empty verbal shells with no content—then repeat all of these formulas and clichés again many, many times.

- Use all the resources offered by modern computer typography to make a very short paper appear, miraculously, much longer than it really is: four-inch margins; 118-point fonts; triple or even quadruple line spacing; etc.

- Since you have no ideas of your own to put in your paper, steal some ideas from someone else. This is obviously plagiarism, and it's the one and only technique of the many that are used to say something when you have nothing to say that is regarded as a crime; but really all the techniques in this list should be thought of as crimes since every one of them is essentially an attempt to commit fraud: they are all attempts to pretend to have something to say when in fact you have nothing to say. This is the fundamental crime committed by plagiarism, but it's also the crime committed by making obvious statements that have no need at all to be said, or writing in a deliberately vague and inscrutable way in order to fill up the page with words that have no content, and every other technique that people use to create the illusion that they have ideas of their own that are worth communicating to other people when in fact they have none.

Every one of us has written papers like this, so we all know what a painful and pointless exercise it is. Writing (or any other form of creation) that doesn't start with having something to say—something important and valuable that needs to be said—is perhaps the most egregious and unnecessary waste of time that has ever been perpetrated by the human race, so please do yourself and your audience a terrific favor and don't even begin to write a paper, or create a project in any other form, until you first have something to say. First get some ideas of your own that deserve to be expressed, and then think about the best way to express them.

To summarize, this is how to write philosophy papers that people will actually want to read, and create philosophy projects that people will find interesting and useful:

- If your assignment is to write an argumentative essay, remember that the ideal argumentative essay is a machine that tells the reader clearly where they are going and then takes them to that destination with perfect efficiency and no distractions whatsoever. A good argumentative essay is single-minded and direct: it announces that it intends to prove an interesting and controversial conclusion—the more interesting and controversial the better—and then it does exactly what it promised and nothing else. An argumentative essay is the paradigm of direct communication: nothing is hidden, subtle, or mysterious; everything is explicit, and every word contributes to the ultimate goal of persuading the reader to accept an interesting and controversial conclusion that she didn't accept when the essay began. An argumentative essay changes a reader's mind with good evidence and logical arguments, and that's all it does.

- If you have the opportunity to create a philosophy project in some form other than an argumentative essay—in a form that allows for indirection, subtlety, and artistry—then make the most of whatever indirect medium you choose to explore a philosophical topic and present (indirectly) a philosophical argument. Philosophy can translate well into almost any medium or form, and it would be crazy not to take advantage of the abundance of creative possibilities that are available.

- Whether you write an argumentative essay or create a project in some other form, the first step is always to get some ideas of your own that are interesting and important enough that they deserve to be expressed. First have something to say—something that needs to be said—before you start talking (or writing, or creating in whatever medium you've chosen), or you will just say a lot of nonsense. If you start creating something without first having original and interesting ideas of your own you will only succeed in making yourself (and everyone who tries to make sense of your creation) miserable; your only accomplishment will be to increase the total quantity of misery in the world.

Or, on the other hand, if you would prefer to write philosophy papers that no one would ever want to read or create philosophy projects that no one would ever find interesting or useful, here's how you can achieve that goal: just do exactly the opposite.

PART 2

Three answers to the question "What is philosophy?"

(a comedy in three acts)

Act One

Philosophy is a conversation that has been going on for over 2,500 years which has been full of comedy from the beginning, and will continue to be funny forever if we do it right

Chapter 3

Ancient philosophy

(Philosophy in its infancy: learning to speak, learning to crawl, getting its head stuck between the stair rails, and nearly getting itself killed in all sorts of interesting and fascinating ways, as all babies do.)

If you are looking for a thorough and exhaustive summary of the history of philosophy the next four chapters will deeply disappoint you. It's not my goal to disappoint anyone so please don't read these chapters expecting to find something that isn't here. These chapters paint the history of philosophy with a very, very broad brush. How broad is this brush? It's perhaps the world's broadest brush, broad enough to reduce lifetimes of sincere and meticulous thought by sincere and meticulous thinkers to a few paragraphs on a single page, and hundreds of years of painstaking theorizing to short chapters that can easily be read in less than an hour while you sip your favorite drink and relax on your favorite air mattress while floating in your favorite swimming pool.

"Excuse me," anyone paying attention will rightly say at this point, "but that was a very bad analogy because this is not at all what paintbrushes do. It sounds like you're comparing your writing to some sort of reducing and condensing machine, like a garbage compactor, and not the world's biggest paintbrush." You're right, of course, and thank you for paying attention. Since my paintbrush analogy has run amok—like a truck with no brakes crashing through the guardrails of a winding mountain road and sailing off a cliff at ninety miles an hour—I'll now choose a new analogy that doesn't involve either paintbrushes or trucks with no brakes driving on precarious mountain roads. The new analogy is: a love letter. Please think of the next four chapters as love letters to the history of philosophy. When you read a love letter you expect to find joy, gratitude, happiness, and an enthusiastic, exuberant tone that is certainly excessive but nevertheless tolerated in this particular context, not a somber and precise cataloguing of somber and precise facts. If you received a love letter that was nothing but a somber and precise cataloguing of somber and precise facts you would likely send it back, after first scribbling in the margins in bright red ink: "This is not a very good love letter. I'm giving it an F. Please rewrite it and this time make it less somber and precise and more enthusiastic and joyful." The following four chapters on the history of philosophy should be judged by the grading criteria you would apply to a love letter because they are love letters to the history of philosophy, no matter how inappropriate and indecent that may sound.

"Yes but reading other people's love letters is usually a nauseating experience," say the handful of readers who haven't yet given up on this train wreck of an introduction, "so why should we read your love letters to the history of philosophy if they are likely to make us vomit?" This is also an excellent question, and thank you again for paying attention; but here I will clarify that these are not private love letters to a private party full of private details which certainly can make anyone who is not part of this private relationship quite nauseous if they chance to stumble upon this private correspondence; these are public love letters about something that is the public property of all humans who fall into life on Planet Earth. The history of philosophy belongs to everyone; it is one of the great treasures and accomplishments of humanity, and everyone can and should fall in love with it. My goal in the next four chapters is to seduce you to fall in love with the history of philosophy; therefore please prepare to be seduced! If these chapters succeed, you too will fall head over heels in love with the history of philosophy—the strange and wonderful story of humanity's attempt to figure out the ultimate nature of reality, knowledge, and values using only their own wits.

But perhaps in spite of all my efforts to reassure you that these particular love letters will not be nauseating or obscene in any way, you're still wary of my love letter analogy and you don't want to read any love letters at all unless they are addressed specifically to you! In that case don't despair because I have yet another analogy to offer you, and here it is: these next four chapters on the history of philosophy are intended to be an appetizer, and not the main course. A good appetizer is incomplete, or else it displaces the whole meal and is therefore a real wolf in sheep's clothing: an appetite-assassin rather than an appetite-inducer. If you ordered an appetizer at your favorite restaurant and it turned out to be so enormous and exhaustive that after you finished eating it you found that you had no appetite at all for the rest of the meal THAT YOU HAD ALREADY PAID FOR, and that this so-called "appetizer" was therefore really a destroyer of appetites, you would rightly judge such an appetizer to be a failure, and also a real swindle. If you received this appetizer at your table you would likely send it back to the kitchen, asking the waiter to tell the cook: "This is not a very good appetizer. I'm giving it an F. Please remake it and this time make it less filling and overwhelming and more inviting; in other words: MORE APPETIZING!" What we want from an appetizer is incompleteness—something much less than the main course but nevertheless something very good at preparing you and even (dare I say it?) seducing you to get excited for the main course. In other words, we want an appetizer to be fragmentary, scrappy, and crumby in the best possible way. The crumbiness of a good appetizer is a form of incompleteness that we value because it leads to a more complete appreciation and enjoyment of the meal itself. In that spirit my goal is to write four extremely incomplete and fragmentary chapters on the four main periods of the history of philosophy in order to entice you to continue to the main course—which is a much deeper and more thorough exploration of each of these periods of philosophy's history—rather than calling for the check and heading for the door after you've only eaten the appetizer. So if you think that the next four chapters are crumby then I am delighted and will take this as the highest praise, because crumbiness is exactly what I'm going for. On the other hand if you are looking for a complete and comprehensive account of the history of philosophy then please look elsewhere because you won't find anything like that here, and please don't shoot the messenger (or the waiter). These chapters on the history of philosophy are intended to be fragmentary, scrappy, sketchy, and crumby so that you will want to read much more than just these chapters.

And now, after thoroughly abusing several innocent and undeserving analogies involving paintbrushes, trucks, love letters, train wrecks, and restaurant appetizers, I hereby renounce all analogies. There will be no more analogies from this point on; I give you my word, which is as unshakable as the Rock of Gibraltar. And now that we've gotten all of those unpleasant analogies out of the way, let's finally talk about ancient philosophy.

Ancient philosophy is the period of philosophy's infancy, and this makes it very easy to love. When philosophy was a baby it was adorable, as all babies are. It's enormous fun to observe and study children, especially when you have no obligation to feed them or dress them or chase them around the room to stop them from biting each other or sticking forks into electrical outlets or doing all manner of other potentially dangerous and destructive (but always highly creative and entertaining!) things. Children are endlessly interesting not just because they are so cute, toddling about on their little legs, but also because they are driven by pure curiosity, undiluted by embarrassment or fear of non-conformity or any of the other self-imposed limitations that afflict adults. Aristotle wrote (in the very first line of his *Metaphysics*) "All people by nature desire to know," and it would certainly be wonderful if he had been right about this, but clearly he was not. Sadly many adults lose the desire to know, and even actively cultivate a desire not to know—to remain blissfully ignorant. However all children without exception fit Aristotle's description perfectly. Children are driven by a boundless desire to know, and this is why they learn so quickly and their lives are filled with adventure. The key to enjoying ancient philosophy and appreciating all of its many accomplishments is to remember that you're observing an adorable infant as it learns to walk, talk, figure out who it is, and begins to make its way in the world.

Before we consider the first philosophers here's a quick thought on the world they fell into which may help to explain why philosophy got started in this particular time and in this particular place. Why did philosophy begin in ancient Greece? This is a question that historians, anthropologists, and other specialists who are far smarter than I am can debate endlessly, but I will contribute one humble idea to this discussion.

The world that the first philosophers fell into was a world that was thought to be full of Gods who were for the most part not rational or moral and who didn't particularly care about humans, though they would gladly destroy any human who annoyed them—or maybe just for fun. Today we are accustomed to thinking of this worldview as "mythology," but it wasn't mythology to the people who lived in that world; for them it was the truth. If you'll reconsider all the "Greek mythology" you've studied in that light it quickly becomes clear that the world within which philosophy was born included a great deal of uncertainty and dread.[1] In this world irrational, arbitrary, and capricious Gods might at any moment demand that you do something truly awful, such as sacrificing your own child (see the Iphegenia story), or they might torment and destroy you at any time just for the fun of it (see almost any other Greek "myth"). Historians and anthropologists will no doubt roll their eyes and let out a long, exasperated sigh when they hear my very simple theory, but nevertheless I do think this aspect of the ancient Greek world helps to explain why philosophy started when and where it did. In the Greek worldview humans were clearly no match for the Gods in physical power, but they could still exceed at least some of the Gods intellectually. Most of the Greek Gods were not particularly bright and didn't much value intelligence or independent thinking, preferring instead the spectacle and terror occasioned by hurling bolts of lightning or causing other natural catastrophes. These Gods were like extremely powerful babies, and humans who were willing to think for themselves were able to outwit these Gods and gain some control over their own lives. For anyone who fell into the world of ancient Greece and was paying attention the message was quite clear: the one and only asset you have which distinguishes you from most of the Gods, and gives you some chance of surviving in the world that they govern in such a childish and petulant fashion, is your own intelligence; and you shouldn't expect to find any other reliable authorities or guides in this universe, especially not in the realm of religion since the Gods are generally the worst possible role models. Philosophy (the attempt to figure out the true nature of reality, knowledge, and values through independent thinking alone) would be particularly valuable in such a world, and it would be regarded as a thoroughly useful skill and not just an idle or abstract pastime.

Probably you are not very impressed by my very meek and modest theory about why philosophy was born in ancient Greece, but whatever you think of that theory the fact is that philosophy was born at that time and place in quite spectacular fashion with an eclectic and fascinating group of independent thinkers, so from this point on I'll focus just on the ideas that these thinkers created and no longer speculate on matters of historical causation (which I am definitely not smart enough to figure out).

For the most part in these history of philosophy chapters I won't even try to include every author who could possibly be included in any

---

[1]. Hesiod's *Theogony* summarizes this worldview succinctly, and his *Works and Days* is a wonderful example of a very non-philosophical response to such a world.

particular period (because the goal is to write a crumby appetizer that doesn't pretend to be as good as the main course), but right at the very beginning of philosophy's history I'll make a bit of an exception. It's useful to consider almost all of that extremely motley crew of thinkers who are generally lumped together in one big bucket labeled "Pre-Socratic Philosophers" because they demonstrate several very important mistakes and discoveries that philosophy made quite quickly after it was born. In the same book in which he said that all people desire to know (a claim which is obviously false but which nevertheless expresses a very noble and admirable aspiration) Aristotle also noted quite correctly that philosophy began with wonder.[2] The first philosophers were wonder-ful in every way. There's nothing orthodox, normal, or boring about any of the pre-Socratics. They were unafraid to think independently, and they were willing to question the most basic nature of knowledge, reality, and value. They were also willing to give arguments to support their theories, although we often have to rely on the word of people like Plato and Aristotle that these authors did in fact give reasons for their theories because for the most part we don't have their arguments, we only have bits and pieces of their conclusions. But even though what has survived from the philosophy of the pre-Socratics is fragmentary there is still enough to show how quickly philosophy developed during its childhood. Something radically new came into the world with the pre-Socratic philosophers, and like all infants they learned mostly by making mistakes, and their language was imperfect and sometimes incoherent or almost impossibly obscure, but also profound. Here's a brief overview of some of the most important pre-Socratic philosophers and some of the most important questions, ideas, and theories that they explored.

The beginnings of metaphysics and materialism: Thales, Anaximander, Anaximenes

What unites this first group is their conviction that some material substance is the ultimate reality, the ultimate building block of the universe, as Aristotle explained:

> Of the first philosophers, then, most thought the principles which were of the nature of matter were the only principles of all things. That of which all things that are consist, the first from

---

2. Aristotle, *Metaphysics*, 982b10.

which they come to be, the last into which they are resolved (the substance remaining, but changing in its modifications), this they say is the element and this the principle of things, and therefore they think nothing is either generated or destroyed, since this sort of entity is always conserved, as we say Socrates neither comes to be absolutely when he comes to be beautiful or musical, nor ceases to be when loses these characteristics, because the substratum, Socrates himself remains. Just so they say nothing else comes to be or ceases to be; for there must be some entity—either one or more than one—from which all other things come to be, it being conserved. Yet they do not all agree as to the number and the nature of these principles. Thales, the founder of this type of philosophy, says the principle is water....[3]

These first philosophers all attempted a naturalistic, materialistic, and therefore "scientific" explanation of the physical world. Even Anaximander's idea of "the indefinite" (*apeiron*) is still a form of materialism because it was infinite and boundless material stuff, a kind of unitary, basic material element out of which every other thing is derived. Atomism, as we'll see shortly, will develop this idea even further. It's easy to laugh at these early pre-Socratic theories of reality and dismiss them as outdated and irrelevant, but in some ways they're still cutting-edge because they mark a two-part paradigm shift that could be called the beginning of a scientific attitude: (1) the idea that all of nature can be explained by underlying principles or laws, and (2) that there are basic, elemental building blocks that make up the world in all its complexity. So while it's easy to laugh at Thales, for example, when he argues that water is the basic building block of the universe, the more important innovations made by the first pre-Socratics such as Thales, which we still take very seriously, are the more general ideas that there are some basic building blocks for the universe along with some basic principles or natural laws, and that it's possible for humans to figure all of this out relying solely on our own wits.

---

3. Aristotle, *Metaphysics*, 983b5.

Philosophy attempting to explain or to deny change: Parmenides, Zeno, Heraclitus

Parmenides chose to present his arguments through poetry (why not!) and his philosophy contains exactly one VERY BIG idea: true reality is a single, unchanging, complete whole. Nothing changes, nothing is incomplete, all of reality is a single unified whole, and everything that looks like evidence to the contrary is just an illusion. Parmenides argues that anything else is unthinkable and unsayable, and in his poem the Goddess proves this point by asking her young student to just try to say or think what is not, as opposed to what is—and look, she says, you can't do it! Ergo, "what is not" is simply meaningless, and only what is, is, in the form of a completely unified and unchanging whole. This is the first example in philosophy's history of monism: the theory that everything is one in spite of all appearances to the contrary.[4]

Zeno was Parmenides's number one fan, and he took the logic of Parmenides's monism and ran with it. (That was perhaps the best joke about pre-Socratic philosophy ever, as you will soon see.) Zeno's arguments in support of Parmenides's theory (that even though the world appears to be full of diverse and differentiated individual items everything is actually a unified and unitary whole) are classic *reductio ad absurdum* proofs: you assume the opposite of what you want to prove is true, then demonstrate that absurd consequences follow from this assumption, thereby proving that what you assumed to be true is actually false. For example, Zeno agrees with Parmenides that motion is an illusion, since motion would only be possible if change were possible and if reality were not a unified and complete whole. To prove that motion is an illusion he says: imagine Achilles racing a tortoise. Since Achilles is the fastest human on earth the wily tortoise begs for a head start, and Achilles of course agrees, thinking that he can easily catch the tortoise even if he naps for three days. So after his nap Achilles wakes up and sees that the wheezing and exhausted tortoise is ten feet ahead of him; however (Zeno says) he'll never be able to catch the tortoise now because to go ten feet he'll first have to go half that distance, and in order to go five feet he'll first have to go half that distance, and in order to go two and a half feet he'll have to go half that distance—and so on *ad infinitum*. Now, says Zeno, behold what just happened: when you start with the assumption that motion is possible you end with the obviously absurd conclusion that speedy

4. DK 28B1, 28B2.

Achilles can't even catch up to a tortoise![5] Zeno claims that this absurdity reveals that motion, like every form of change or incompleteness, is incoherent and unthinkable. Zeno gives several other clever *reductio* proofs that follow the same pattern: assume the opposite of what Parmenides claimed about the true nature of reality and then demonstrate how absurd consequences follow from this assumption, thereby proving that the assumption is false and Parmenides was right![6]

Heraclitus is generally thought of as the guy who disagreed with Parmenides and Zeno on all questions of permanence and change, and that's all he did; but fortunately for us Heraclitus (who was also known as "Heraclitus the Obscure") has an even more interesting and complicated legacy than that. Heraclitus uses the Greek word *logos* a lot so it's important to figure out what this means for him. *Logos* means, among other things, reason or logic. Understood in this way when Heraclitus says, "Don't listen to me, listen to the *logos*," it's just a charmingly obscure way of saying: "Ignore me, Heraclitus the Obscure, and instead just focus on the reasons and arguments I'm giving you. In other words: listen to the message but ignore the messenger." This expresses very nicely two crucial ideas in philosophy: that everyone must think independently, and that the only legitimate authority is the authority of your own reason. Heraclitus has a lot to say along these lines: criticism of most people who do not think for themselves, do not listen to the *logos*, and instead just thoughtlessly follow tradition and custom. Heraclitus thus inaugurates another great tradition in the history of philosophy: deliberately writing in a way that's mysterious or obscure so that you, the reader, will have to figure out on your own what he meant. In other words, perhaps he was trying to help you by being obscure; perhaps he thought it would be a disservice to you to make his ideas easy to understand. Nature and the truth both love to hide, Heraclitus argues,[7] because it will be good for you to make the effort required to find them.

Sometimes Heraclitus actually sounds kind of like Parmenides, arguing that everything is one and nothing changes;[8] other times he seems to argue exactly the opposite very emphatically: that there is no unity or stability in the universe and everything is constantly changing, as in his

---

5. DK 29A26.
6. Plato, *Parmenides*, 127b–128d.
7. DK 22B123.
8. DK 22B57, 22B50.

famous lines about the impossibility of stepping in the same river twice.[9] One way to understand this apparent contradiction is that when he talks about the *logos* he means reason: the one thing that's unified and never changes in the universe and which is available to everyone, so everyone who tunes in to this singular rational frequency can share the singular understanding of what's really going on in the universe: which is that everything is constantly changing. The deeper understanding of the universe revealed to you by the *logos* is that nothing ever stays the same, everything changes, so even though a river may have the same name it's actually a different river every time you step in it.

Atomism: Democritus and Leucippus

Atomism is the ultimate reductive theory: the entire universe can be reduced to atoms and void (empty space): basically just atoms and some space for them to bump into each other. "Atoms" are conceptual creations, not empirical discoveries (in Greek the word "atom" simply means "a thing which can't be cut"), and that's still the case today: even the most advanced contemporary physics has yet to discover an atom in the original Greek sense of something that cannot be cut or taken apart. To the question, "How many atoms are there?" the atomists answer: "As many as you need." There's no limit to the number or the variety of atoms, and everything that exists and everything that happens in the universe can be explained by these atoms bumping into each other and sometimes connecting with each other.[10] This is a purely materialistic theory that never went away; atomism made the transition from philosophy to science so successfully that most people are unaware that it ever had anything to do with philosophy.

Later atomism will combine with hedonism to create a much more complete philosophy that finally has something to say about ethics too.[11] This was a real vacuum in pre-Socratic philosophy: at first almost no one has anything to say about how to live. But questions about value are just as basic as questions about reality and knowledge, so philosophy was bound to expand to include those questions. The sophists, who come on

---

9. DK 22B12, 22B91, 22B49a.
10. Aristotle, *Metaphysics*, 985b4–20.
11. E.g., Lucretius, *On the Nature of Things*.

the scene shortly and set the stage for Socrates and Plato, respond to the pent-up demand for ethical theory.

More monism! Anaxagoras

Anaxagoras makes a good contrast with Empedocles (whom we'll meet shortly) because like Empedocles he's clearly borrowing ideas from others, but unlike Empedocles he also adds some truly innovative ideas of his own to the mix and creates something new and improved rather than just a uncreative mash-up. The main contribution of Anaxagoras is his theory of *Nous*, which means mind, as in some particular mind, or you're out of your mind—but Anaxagoras argues that any particular mind is just one part or aspect of a larger mind: a rational force that governs the complete universe.[12] This is a real innovation because it requires a conception of the universe that is both physical and mental: a universe that is permeated by mind. The atomistic theory of Leucippus and Democritus presents a random and pluralistic picture of the universe that probably seems very contemporary since atomism is now one of the fundamental paradigms of the sciences. The philosophy of Anaxagoras, on the other hand, presents a vision of the universe that is neither random nor pluralistic: the universe has a goal and everything that appears to be diverse and pluralistic is actually unified in a single whole (another version of monism). Today this worldview probably seems very remote and mystical and therefore outdated, but actually both of these philosophies are alive and well in various contemporary forms; neither one of them ever went away. It's easiest to study them together since they are almost perfect opposites. Atomism argues that the way to understand the universe is to take it apart, to analyze it down to its most basic elements, which are atoms, and that everything that has ever happened, or ever will happen, is the result of random collisions of atoms as they fall through the void; there's no guiding plan or teleological purpose. Anaxagoras argues for opposing conclusions: that the universe can only be understood through a synthetic operation, that ultimately everything is connected and every being and every event is directed by *Nous*. (In the nineteenth century Hegel will revive many of Anaxagoras's ideas and extend them into an elaborate system.) Which of these two theories has greater explanatory

---

12. DK 59B12.

power? That's an ongoing argument that can trace its origins all the way back to philosophy's childhood.

Philosophy learning to distinguish itself from religion: Pythagoras and his followers

Right at the beginning of its young life philosophy has to struggle to differentiate itself from three other things that can easily be confused with philosophy: religion, business, and sophistry. Pythagoras and his followers (such as Philolaus and Xenophanes) are good case studies in the challenge of separating philosophy and religion. (We'll get to business and sophistry shortly.) Soon after Thales, Anaximander, and Anaximenes produced the first theories of materialism, Pythagoras showed up with the first version of the metaphysical theory which is materialism's polar opposite and eternal enemy: idealism. Ideas are the true and ultimate reality, Pythagoras argued, especially those ideas that we call numbers. Aristotle explained Pythagorean idealism like this:

> Those called Pythagoreans took hold of mathematics and were the first to advance that study; and being brought up in it, they believed that its principles were the principles of all things that are. Since numbers are naturally first among these, and in numbers they thought they observed many resemblances to things that are and that come to be... and since they saw the attributes and ratios of musical scales in numbers, and other things seemed to be made in the likeness of numbers in their entire nature, and numbers seemed to be primary in all nature, they supposed the elements of numbers to be the elements of all things that are.[13]

Pythagoras argued that math isn't just a system to count or organize reality, it is reality. Numbers are pure and perfect ideas that do not grow old, or tired, or lose their youthful muscle tone and good looks, or fall into mud puddles, or get chased and possibly eaten by bears, or sometimes get confused and forget where they were going or what they were supposed to buy at the grocery store, or sometimes get gloomy, or depressed, or nostalgic, or anxious, or giddy, or surly, like all the poor, pathetic, imperfect, dirty, decaying things in the world of our experience. Numbers have far more reality than the things that are numbered, so if you're looking for true reality don't waste your time wandering around outside picking

13. Aristotle, *Metaphysics* 985b23–28.

up material things and studying them as if they were interesting in any way or as if you might learn something from them; go back to your room, shut the door, and study mathematics. (All mathematicians are, in their secret hearts, deeply committed idealists who regard the material world as a pale and pathetic imitation of the true world which contains only numbers and other mathematical concepts—though they will only say this out loud when they are all together at math conferences and the ballroom doors are closed and they know that no non-mathematicians can hear them, because they don't want to be thought of as crazy philosophers.)

One of the things you can do with idealism, if you want, is turn it into a religion, and Pythagoras promptly did just that. He created a mystical cult of mathematics with super-secret dogmas and rituals—so secret that most of them are still unknown even today. "What he said to his associates, no one is able to say with certainty, for they kept no ordinary silence among themselves."[14] There are numerous stories of Pythagoreans who chose to bite off their own tongues rather than reveal the arcana of their faith, so we can be confident that most of these secrets never got out; but enough of the mysteries of Pythagoreanism were leaked that it's now very easy to laugh at it. The dogma for which Pythagoreans have been most widely lampooned is their great worship, or fear (it's hard to tell the difference) of beans. There are multiple stories of how Pythagoras died but they all involve him refusing to cross a field of beans when he was being chased by enemies. In every variation of this story Pythagoras declares, with true religious fervor, that he would rather die than step into this field of beans.[15] Pythagoras's martyrdom inspired Diogenes Laertius to write this truly unforgettable piece of verse:

> Woe! Woe! Whence, Pythagoras, this deep reverence for beans?
> Why did he fall in the midst of his disciples? A bean-field there
> was he durst not cross; sooner than trample on it, he endured to
> be slain at the cross-roads by the men of Acragas.[16]

There's a philosophical idea in Pythagoreanism for sure. Idealism is a profound philosophical theory, like materialism, which has never gone away and never will. But instead of trying to liberate this philosophical theory from the dogmas, rituals, and authoritarian structure of religion, Pythagoras did just the opposite: he built a new religion around this theory.

---

14. DK 14.8a.
15. Critchley, *Dead Philosophers*, 9.
16. Diogenes Laertius, *Lives*, 8.45.

As soon as he did that his version of idealism ceased to be a philosophy because it abandoned the second and third rules of the philosophy game. Pythagoras gave up on independent, autonomous thinking and even became openly hostile to it, and he also made no attempt to present his insights to the world; instead he cloaked them in mystery and tried to conceal them from the unclean, bean-eating masses. There's never a great distance between philosophy and religion at the starting point, since both of them claim metaphysics, epistemology, and axiology as their territory, but after that philosophy and religion play by completely different rules. Pythagoras was the first person in the history of philosophy to demonstrate how quickly and easily philosophy can give up on philosophy and try to cash in by reinventing itself as a religion.

Philosophy learning to distinguish itself from business: Empedocles

Empedocles's philosophy is a very eclectic collections of ideas, including some elements of religion, but the fundamental principle or motivation that seems to drive it is business: it aims to package and commodify philosophy so that it can be sold. As soon as that happens the love of wisdom and the desire to know become secondary to marketing and the demands of the marketplace are ultimately in charge. Turning philosophy into a business effectively kills all the philosophy, and the pre-Socratic philosophers had to learn to recognize and resist that temptation quickly if philosophy was going to survive. Empedocles is an example of philosophy succumbing to the forces of marketing and business and abandoning its task of creating something new.

Since Empedocles wasted none of his time or energy on creating new ideas he was able to devote himself completely to a relentless marketing campaign. He was an extreme power dresser, famous for always appearing in public wearing an ostentatious purple robe, a golden diadem, and his signature bronze sandals (which must have been very uncomfortable). Dressed in this God-like fashion Empedocles took the logical and inevitable next step according to the time-honored rules of self-promotion: he announced that he was an immortal God. This fact was included in Empedocles's routine trumpet blasts of self-promotion in such a nonchalant manner that you might even miss it. Here are two representative samples:

> Friends who dwell in the great city on the yellow Acragas on the heights of the citadel, you whose care is good deeds, respectful havens for strangers, untouched by evil hail! I go about among you, an immortal god, no longer mortal, honored among all, as it seems, wreathed with headbands and blooming garlands. Wherever I go to the flourishing cities, I am revered by all—men and women. And they follow together in tens of thousands, inquiring where lies the path to profit, some in need of prophecy, while others, pierced for a long time with harsh pains, asked to hear the voice of healing for all diseases.[17]
>
> But why do I insist on these matters as if I were accomplishing something great, if I am superior to mortal humans who perish many times?[18]

Sadly this relentless self-promotion led to an unhappy end for Empedocles, since he concluded that he had no choice but to throw himself into a volcano in order to prove that he was in fact immortal. Perhaps a skeptical customer called his bluff, or perhaps he realized that the logic of self-promotion requires such an ending (since once you have proclaimed yourself an immortal God there really is no place left to go). So Empedocles did what logic or the skeptical consuming public required of him and dutifully threw himself into a volcano; and it was reported that one of his bronze sandals was later disgorged from the lava so his fans were left with something to remember him. The difference between philosophy and business is something that philosophy had to figure out in its infancy, and Empedocles helped everyone learn this lesson by doing it completely wrong.

Philosophy learning to distinguish itself from sophistry: the sophists (Protagoras, Gorgias, Prodicus, Hippias, Antiphon, etc.) and their biggest critic: Socrates

Right after philosophy was born sophistry was also born as philosophy's evil twin. Sophistry wears a mask that makes it look a lot like philosophy, but it uses this disguise to commit all sorts of crimes that go completely against everything philosophy stands for. Philosophy is supposed to be an honest search for the ultimate nature of reality, knowledge, and

---

17. Diogenes Laertius, *Lives*, 8.61–2.
18. DK 31B113.

values; sophistry pretends to care about all of this but actually does not. Instead it impersonates philosophy in order to be taken seriously but then focuses completely on other selfish activities—like making money, becoming famous, winning contests, and gaining political power. It takes logical reasoning (the basic tool of philosophy) and turns it into rhetoric, which emphasizes style over substance, looking good rather than getting it right. Philosophers often look silly as they stumble around trying to make sense of the world, like children fumbling in the dark. Sophists never allow themselves to look silly; looking good is rule #1 in the sophistry rule book. Philosophy doesn't guarantee anyone success or fame because wisdom is supposed to be an end in itself, so no other reward is necessary; but a sophist who isn't rich, famous, and successful according to worldly standards would be regarded as a complete failure. Sophistry takes all of philosophy's highest values and subverts them, turns them into something that will probably make you much more rich, admired, and "successful" than philosophy ever could, but it isn't philosophy anymore; it's an imposter.

"Sophist" and "philosopher" share the same root: the Greek word *sophia* which just means "wisdom," yet the history of philosophy ever since Socrates has regarded sophistry as the polar opposite and the mortal enemy of genuine philosophy. Socrates and Plato thought the sophists were horrible frauds because they had no real interest in the truth; they were only interested in money and fame. The sophists were the first professional teachers, which helps to explain why teaching has always been regarded as a dishonorable occupation: the founding fathers of the profession were scoundrels. They were willing to teach anything for a fee, and they emphasized style at the expense of substance. In other words, they taught people how to use bullshit to get whatever they wanted. For example, Aristotle says that Protagoras "made the weaker argument the stronger" which (he said) was very annoying.[19] Protagoras, in his "Twofold Arguments," demonstrates how you can use rhetoric to argue successfully for anything: true/false; good/bad; just/unjust; etc., which is an excellent example of the relativism and disinterest in objective truth that were characteristic of sophistry.[20]

One practical application of the bullshitting skills that the sophists taught was defending yourself in court. In Athens and other Greek city

---

19. Aristotle, *Rhetoric*, 1402a24–26.
20. DK 90, 4.

states when you were charged with a crime you could not hire someone else to defend you; defending yourself was your only option. This was panic-inducing for many Greeks since the typical citizen had to defend himself in court quite often, and in every trial you could potentially be punished with banishment or even execution. This created a great demand for the Sophists's services since for a fee they would teach you what to say in court to win your freedom, even if you were guilty. Socrates is one of the many Athenians who had to defend himself in court when he was charged at the end of his life with (among other things) "corrupting the youth."[21] Socrates's trial is the best place to start to understand what Socrates stood for and his many contributions to the history of philosophy.

Plato tells the story of Socrates's trial in his *Apology*. This title comes from the Greek *apologia* which means "defense," not apology in the sense of "I'm sorry." Apologizing is something a sophist would suggest you should do when you're on trial, but Socrates does just the opposite. In fact, not only does he not apologize, he actually insults the jury when he suggests that the "penalty" he deserves is free room and board in the Prytaneum (where Olympic athletes were allowed to live free of charge after a victory at the games) because of the "gadfly" service he provides for the city. Another part of Socrates's defense that a sophist would say was ill-advised: he actually adds to the list of charges against him. Before he responds to the charges brought against him by three particular Athenians, Socrates says: "Actually I have a generally horrible reputation, so it's as if the whole city had charged me with a crime; so first I'll respond to those charges." These are all examples of Socrates doing things in his trial which any sophist would say were terrible strategic mistakes, but because Socrates despises sophistry he is proud of handling his defense in a way that scandalizes the sophists. Not surprisingly this goes over very badly with the jury, who find Socrates guilty of the absurd crimes he was accused of committing and then sentence him to death. Really Socrates could not have done a better job of advertising for the sophists and generating more demand for their services, since he demonstrated that if you made the foolish mistake of defending yourself with rational arguments rather than purely emotional rhetoric there was a very real risk that you might be put to death. So all the sophists in Athens probably wanted to send a fruit basket to Socrates in prison to thank him for all

---

21. Plato, *Apology*, 19c.

the business he sent their way; but from Socrates's perspective it was all worth it: better to die as a philosopher than live as a sophist!

Plato dedicates several other dialogues to demonstrating how much Socrates loathed the sophists, and how persistent Socrates was in arguing that sophistry is nothing but a counterfeit of philosophy. For example, in *Gorgias* Socrates takes on not just the famous sophist Gorgias but also two of his disciples: Polus, and Callicles. He defeats them all and at the end of the dialogue, after they have all surrendered, Socrates is still going full steam ahead as if he were hoping that another sophist might wander by so that he could go one more round. The action gets underway when Socrates asks Gorgias an apparently innocent question: "What exactly do you do? What do you create?" Gorgias says he's an orator which means he can talk knowledgably about anything and answer any questions. Socrates immediately lasers in on the relationship between oratory and knowledge. What does an orator know? Does oratory persuade with the truth or something else? Gorgias claims that oratory could only be used in the service of what is good and just, but later admits that oratory could just as easily be used in support of injustice—an obvious contradiction, and when Socrates points this out Polus swoops in to defend the honor of his idol Gorgias.

Polus says contradictions don't really mean anything, and it's rude to point them out; then he turns the tables on Socrates: you tell me what oratory is. Socrates's answer: it's one of four types of flattery which are all counterfeits of something good. Here's a complete system of all the forms that flattery can take, according to Socrates:[22]

> In politics:
> Oratory = counterfeit of genuine justice/morality/ethics
> Sophistry = counterfeit of good legislation based on real knowledge (philosophy)
>
> In health:
> Pastry baking (candy, junk food) = counterfeit of medicine/nutrition
> Cosmetics (anything to make you appear more healthy than you actually are) = counterfeit of exercise

Tellingly Polus responds to this elaborate argument about flattery just as he responded when Socrates pointed out that Gorgias had contradicted

---

22. Plato, *Gorgias*, 464a–465d.

himself: with a shrug. It doesn't matter, he says, because orators are powerful—the most powerful people in a state, just as powerful as tyrants (apparently he thinks this is a good thing). Socrates responds by arguing for the opposite conclusion: actually orators and tyrants are the least powerful people when they do evil things because they only harm themselves. Socrates gets Polus to take the position that if oratory, or tyranny, or anything else gave you the power to victimize other people without being victimized yourself that would be AWESOME! As long as you don't get punished this would be the best possible life, Polus agrees. We all want to be like the tyrant Archelaus, who did just that. The position Polus takes suggests that what we call "morality" or "ethics" or "justice" is just a big smokescreen or camouflage for what we really want and what we really believe: that if we could just victimize other people all the time without ever being victimized ourselves that would be the best possible life. A more elaborate version of this argument is presented in *Republic* book 2 by Plato's brother Glaucon, who challenges Socrates to prove that if someone had access to a magic ring that made her invisible and thus able to get away with anything she should still go on acting morally, thereby proving that morality is an end in itself and not just a way to avoid getting punished. In *Gorgias* Socrates argues that the life of Archelaus would be the worst possible life, even if you thought you were having a great time, as Archelaus did. So awful is such a life that if you really hate someone you should try to get them to live this way and then do everything in your power to prevent them from getting caught and punished, because this would inflict the maximum amount of pain and suffering on them.

The punch line of the argument, which Socrates has been building toward from the beginning, is this: if all of this is true what good is oratory, since oratory seems to have no other purpose than to make injustice and immorality appear to be something they're not. Both Polus and Gorgias claim that they can talk about anything and answer any question, thus either claiming to be omniscient, or simply not caring about knowledge at all. And when Socrates argued that oratory is just a form of flattery, on the same level as pastry baking, the only thing that mattered to Polus is that this implies orators are not respected—he only cares about the reputation or power that oratory confers. Polus doesn't hesitate to compare oratory to tyranny: for him it's just a way to have power over other people and get what you want. He repeatedly uses the appeal to the majority fallacy: whatever most people accept as true is in fact true, which forces Socrates to point out to him that questions of morality are never decided by voting.

Once the differences between philosophy and sophistry had been clarified by Socrates (and Plato devoted several more dialogues to demonstrating how thoroughly Socrates did this), philosophy transitioned into a more advanced, more developed stage of its childhood; something like adolescence. It was essential for philosophy to get clear about how it differed from religion, business, and sophistry and of those three possible confusions sophistry is the most insidious and dangerous challenge because it's a masked or counterfeit version of philosophy. Religion and business are just different activities or games, and philosophy needs to understand how it differs from these games, but there's no reason to regard them as enemies; however sophistry presents an actual threat to philosophy because it undermines everything philosophy stands for, so philosophy must regard it as a mortal enemy. The fact that Socrates was willing to be a martyr for the cause of exposing and opposing sophistry is one of the reasons he's so important in the history of philosophy.

Socrates, Plato, and Aristotle: the not-at-all-holy trinity of ancient philosophy

Philosophy's adolescent period was dominated by three people who were like the three most popular and admired kids in junior high: Socrates, who officially had no students at all but still had a lot of people who admired him, learned from him, and followed him around—one of whom was Plato, who started his own school (The Academy) and therefore did officially have quite a few students—the most important of whom was Aristotle, who, after graduating from Plato's Academy and also teaching there for quite a few years, started his own school in Athens: The Lyceum. Socrates, Plato, and Aristotle are the three undisputed superstars of philosophy's childhood. We've already met Socrates—philosophy's first and arguably its only martyr, who was willing to die for the cause of distinguishing philosophy from sophistry—so now it's time to meet Plato and Aristotle.

Plato

There's a long history of characterizing the remainder of ancient philosophy as a debate between Plato and Aristotle in which the differences between them can be summarized very simply. Raphael demonstrated this in his famous painting called *The School of Athens* in which Plato and

Aristotle are positioned right in the middle and are therefore obviously the most popular kids at this school, and the differences between their philosophy are summarized simply by having Plato point up to the sky and Aristotle point down to the earth.

Raphael, *The School of Athens*, fresco, 1509–11

Close up of Plato and Aristotle

This is a fair and very useful characterization of the contrast between the general style of Aristotle's approach to philosophy and the most famous theory in Plato's writing, which is generally called Platonic Idealism or the Theory of Forms. But Platonic Idealism is just one of many different theories and many different voices that can be found in Plato's writing. Plato's dialogues all had a variety of different characters expressing a variety of different ideas. Socrates appears in almost all of them, and there are a few other characters who make repeat appearances, but one character who never appears and never speaks even once is Plato himself. In a letter that Plato wrote to explain why his attempts to transform the tyrant Dionysus of Syracuse into a virtuous Philosopher King did not succeed (that's a long and fascinating story, but no time for that now!), he declared that he never had written, and never would write, what he actually believed:

> No sensible man will venture to express his deepest thoughts in words, especially in a form which is unchangeable, as is true of written outlines. . . . Anyone who is seriously studying high matters will be the last to write about them and thus expose his thought to the envy and criticism of men. . . . Whenever we see a book . . . we can be sure that if the author is really serious, this book does not contain his best thoughts; they are stored away with the fairest of his possessions. And if he has committed these serious thoughts to writing, it is because men, not the Gods, "have taken his wits away."[23]

Of course we only know about this argument against writing what one truly believes because Plato wrote it down, and as you contemplate the implications of this fact, if you now feel like you have stepped into a hall of mirrors, then congratulations, I think you've understood exactly what should be understood from Plato's self-reflexive style of writing, which is: it's not going to be possible to find the author here so we will have to make our own way without an author-ity to guide us. If you're now thinking maybe Socrates can be our guide since Plato refused the job, I'm sorry but that's not going to work either. Though Socrates appears in almost all of Plato's dialogues Socrates himself never wrote anything and in one dialogue (*Phaedrus*) Plato has Socrates explain that he was opposed to writing because any time spent writing is time not spent in conversation with other people, which is the highest and best activity so it would be crazy to waste time doing anything else. But here again we only know

---

23. Plato, *7th Letter*, 343a, 344c.

about this argument because Plato wrote it down. In fact, most of what we think we know about Socrates comes from Plato's writing because Plato made him the star of most of his dialogues, but in those dialogues the character named "Socrates" expresses a wide range of different ideas and arguments, and actually appears to be a whole bunch of different people who all happen to be named "Socrates."

This excellent undecidability is one part of Plato's marvelous textual legacy. All of Plato's dialogues contain a cacophony of different voices which express different perspectives, and this is entirely a good thing because it gives the lucky reader (that's us!) the chance to think for ourselves and critically evaluate these many different theories without tripping over some author-ity in the process. Much later in philosophy's history Søren Kierkegaard summarized this approach to reading philosophy very succinctly when he wrote, in a review of one of his own books (the review was written under the delightful pseudonym "A. F. . . . . .") called "Who Is the Author of *Either/Or*?":

> Most people, including the author of this article, think it is not worth the trouble to be concerned about who the author is. They are happy not to know his identity, for then they have only the book to deal with, without being bothered or distracted by his personality.[24]

Plato did just about everything he could to give us the opportunity to read his dialogues in this way: focusing entirely on the contents of the book and not caring about the author or his personality, and if such an approach had been adopted throughout the history of philosophy some of the saddest moments in that history (such as scholasticism and its unhappy legacy) could have been avoided. Trying to respect the true diversity of ideas and arguments that are expressed in Plato's dialogues certainly makes it more difficult to summarize Plato's thinking, but I will do my best here. (If Raphael had tried to do this more accurately in *The School of Athens* it would have resulted in Plato pointing not just up but in every possible direction, his arm moving like a crazy windmill on a broken axle, threatening to fly off at any moment and poke you right in the eye, which would have been a truly strange and terrifying painting.) In that spirit I'll note that Platonic Idealism was certainly one of Plato's most famous and consequential ideas, but I hope that you'll remember that this chapter is just an appetizer,

---

24. Kierkegaard, *Corsair*, 16.

and that when you actually read Plato's dialogues there are so many more delicious ideas waiting for you there.

Here's one way to organize some of the most important dialogues Plato wrote:

> Early dialogues: these are Socratic and "aporetic" in nature, meaning they end without reaching a decisive conclusion.

Alcibiades
Apology
Charmides
Clitophon
Euthyphro
Hippias Major
Hippias Minor
Ion
Laches
Lysis

Transitional dialogues: in these some Socratic style remains but Plato seems to be experimenting with going beyond Socrates and creating ideas and theories of his own.

Crito
Euthydemus
Gorgias
Menexenus
Meno
Protagoras

Middle dialogues: in these Socratic ignorance and *aporia* have disappeared, replaced by what appears to be more confident and decisive theories, especially Plato's theory of Forms ("Platonic Idealism").

Cratylus
Phaedo
Phaedrus
Republic
Symposium

Late dialogues: in these Plato seems to become self-critical and perhaps even abandons the theories of his middle period to returns to the Socratic, aporetic style with which he began.

Critias
Laws
Philebus
Sophist
Statesman
Thaetetus
Timaeus
Parmenides

Apology and *Gorgias* have already been briefly outlined, and since there isn't time in this ancient philosophy appetizer to explore all of Plato's dialogues I'll discuss just one more, and hopefully that will be enough to make you want to read them all. Here's a brief summary of *Symposium*, a middle dialogue that contains one version of Plato's famous theory of Idealism.

In *Symposium* six men at a party compete to present the best theory of love. The party lasts all night, and by morning everyone has collapsed in a drunken stupor except for Socrates, who goes off to the gymnasium to exercise while everyone else sleeps off their hangover. All of the theories of love that are presented are also about sex to one extent or another, and then in the end Alcibiades crashes the party and talks about nothing but sex when he tells the story of how he has tried for years, unsuccessfully, to get Socrates to have sex with him, even resorting to sleepover parties and naked wrestling. *Symposium* is a wonderful example of the multitude of voices and theories that abound in all of Plato's dialogues, and it also contains a wonderful and very memorable version of Plato's theory of Forms or Ideals: the theory that the world of our experience is just a pale shadow or imitation of true reality which is someplace else—in a transcendent world that can only be discovered by leaving behind the world of physical sensation and entering a space of pure Ideas. (Plato did not call this space "heaven," and he presented his theory of Idealism as a purely intellectual activity that didn't have anything to do with religion, but obviously it isn't hard to spin Platonic Idealism as a religious story, and during the medieval period that happened very quickly.) Socrates is in this dialogue too, but this version of Socrates is quite different from the Socrates we met in *Apology*. This Socrates claims to know a thing or two (actually quite a few things), and he doesn't hesitate to say so; but before Socrates presents his own theory there are five other theories of love that precede him. Here's a summary of all seven theories of love that are offered in *Symposium*.

The first to speak is Phaedrus.[25] The relationship that most of these men refer to is one between an older man and a younger boy, which was understood as, among other things, a kind of apprenticeship, and Phaedrus focuses on that. This is the best way, he thinks, for the young to learn from the old. Love brings out the best qualities in everyone, it makes them want to be their best in each other's presence. When you love someone you try to show her only the best side of your personality. Thus, all other virtues are augmented by love. Phaedrus is the one who wanted to talk about love, the one who is supposed to be obsessed by the topic, but he turns out to have the least to say. (He does get his very own dialogue though later, and he will have quite a lot to say about love there.)

Pausanias speaks next,[26] and he focuses on distinguishing love that has good effects from love that has bad effects. The most interesting part of his speech is the discussion of cultural rules that regulate love. Tyrannical states are afraid of love, along with sports and philosophy, because all of them foster independent thinking and this makes them a threat to the government. Consequently all tyrannies condemn love and try to eliminate it. On the other hand cultures that are not intellectually developed sanction all love with no restrictions at all. Pausanias thinks both of these extremes—absolutely condemning love and absolutely sanctioning it—are wrong. The truth is that love is complicated, and so it should be governed by complicated rules which both encourage and discourage relationships. Intelligent societies establish rules and traditions that turn love into a kind of competition or test: one has to win the competition or pass the test in order to prove worthy of another's love, worthy of the relationship. This is necessary because love is always a kind of submission, a way of making yourself subservient to another, and this is dishonorable unless the other proves worthy.

Eryximachus follows.[27] He's a doctor (so Aristophanes asks him to cure his hiccups). Eryximachus takes Pausanias's idea about good and bad love and runs with it. He says that distinction can explain the whole universe; in medicine, for example, it explains health and disease, and he also gives examples from poetry, farming, and especially music. Is this an example of going over the top—making love into everything, so that the concept is no longer useful to explain anything? Or is Eryximachus on to

---

25. Plato, *Symposium*, 178b–180c.
26. Plato, *Symposium*, 180c–185c.
27. Plato, *Symposium*, 185c–189a.

something? Is love a concept that can explain even science? (As a medical doctor Eryximachus is the closest thing to a scientist at this party.)

Aristophanes[28] was a comic playwright who wrote several very funny plays, such as *The Clouds* and *Lysistrata*. Aristophanes outlines a theory of love that has now become commonplace: that you have exactly one soulmate and you must spend your life searching for her/him. It's possible he meant this as a joke (he was a comedian), but it's still a profound and interesting theory. Love "calls back the halves of our original nature together, it tries to make one out of two and heal the wound of human nature." This theory also helps to explain why it is that people can't articulate exactly what they want from love. It has to be more than sex, because some people stay together forever, long after they stop caring about sex, "and still cannot say what it is they want from one another."[29] As Aristophanes explains it, love is the ultimate form of selfishness, even though it's directed toward another person.

Agathon, the host of this party, promises to reveal the true nature of love itself.[30] The theories so far have just been self-congratulation on behalf of people in love, he says, not an attempt to understand the thing itself. This puts Agathon right on Socrates's turf: he claims to be able to answer the sort of question Socrates loves to ask, but, as we see later on, Socrates is not impressed[31] and Agathon has to admit that he had no idea what he was talking about. Agathon's speech turns out to be a pure rhetorical explosion: someone using beautiful words and claiming to answer the biggest questions without understanding anything. He describes love as a very simple ideal, not complicated at all, and in very superficial terms. Love is perfect in every way: perfectly beautiful, has perfect skin, always peaceful, never violent, etc. By the time you get to Agathon there's a clear sense of competition—each speaker trying to describe love in the most grandiose terms, trying to praise love the most lavishly—and it results in this kind of thoughtless and over-the-top speech.

Finally it's Socrates's turn to speak,[32] but he immediately announces that everything he has to say about love he learned from a mysterious woman named Diotima, so in effect there is one more person at this party. Diotima is the only female voice in all the Platonic dialogues, and

---

28. Plato, *Symposium*, 189a–193e.
29. Plato, *Symposium*, 192d.
30. Plato, *Symposium*, 195a–198a.
31. Plato, *Symposium*, 198b–201d.
32. Plato, *Symposium*, 198b–212c.

also the only person that Socrates claims to have learned from. (It's too bad she wasn't invited to the party so that she could speak for herself.)

Socrates begins by laughing at Agathon's rhetoric, and he says he'll do what Agathon promised to do: reveal the essential truth about love itself. What we need to know about love is what is its object. What does love love; what is it trying to accomplish? Love desires its object, therefore it can't already have it. This means love can't be beautiful, wise, etc., since it desires those things. This sets up the very interesting idea that love is always in between, incomplete, in process. Because it's incomplete, love can't be the perfect ideal that Agathon described. Instead, Socrates idealizes the object of love. Love is a spirit that acts as a messenger between humans and the Gods; it's like a philosopher, a lover of wisdom: always underway, in process of becoming, in love with wisdom because she doesn't have it yet.

What's the point of love? What good is it? What goal does it aim for? These questions structure the rest of Socrates's speech. Beauty is the most obvious starting place to answer these questions. We love beauty and want to possess it, but why? What do we think we possess when we possess beauty? Socrates says we're only interested in the beautiful as a way to get to the good. We want to possess the good forever, but that's not possible because humans are mortal. The closest we can get to immortality is through reproduction. Socrates starts with physical reproduction (which everyone understands) and then expands the idea to include intellectual reproduction—giving birth to ideas, which he regards as far superior to giving birth to children. Both forms of reproduction require beauty: beautiful bodies or beautiful ideas. Reproduction can't take place in the presence of ugliness. Through reproduction love is trying to achieve immortality and permanence. Human life is constantly in flux, and we hate that, so all reproduction, both physical and intellectual, is motivated by the desire to escape from this flux, to transcend to a world of stability and permanence.

Socrates now describes the stages of real love: how love develops into a true quest for immortality.[33]

1. love of one particular beautiful body
2. love of all beautiful bodies
3. love of souls—the ideas hidden behind the bodies

33. Plato, *Symposium*, 210a–d.

4. love of all beautiful activities and principles
5. love of all beautiful ideas or Ideals

True beauty, which is beautiful ideas, has the following characteristics:[34] it's permanent, universal, intellectual rather than physical, and it's a singular Form, an Ideal that all beautiful things partake of. So true love, according to Socrates, starts with physical bodies but eventually abandons them completely. In its highest form it is only interested in ideas, because they offer the permanence and universality that love seeks. (What we call "Platonic love" today captures just the first part of Plato's theory of true love—the "no sex" part—but ignores the rest of Plato's theory—the "fall in love with ideas" part.)

At this point Alcibiades bursts uninvited into the party, and loudly proclaims: "Good evening gentlemen, I'm drunk!" When he realizes that Socrates is there he launches into an account of his many unsuccessful attempts to seduce him,[35] and this account effectively contains one more theory of love. It's clear that Alcibiades doesn't understand Socrates's theory at all, and Socrates says as much to Alcibiades but he says it ironically so Alcibiades doesn't get it.[36] Alcibiades has tried everything to seduce Socrates, even naked wrestling, but Socrates isn't interested in him physically because he's only interested in ideas. Alcibiades is still at the very lowest level of love, still obsessed with superficial beauty, while Socrates is way beyond that.

Plato's theory of Forms—one version of which is presented in *Symposium*, and which Alcibiades either does not understand or doesn't care about at all—is certainly Plato's most famous theory and the one that has had the greatest impact on the history of philosophy, but hopefully this crumby introduction to Plato has convinced you that there was much more than this going on in Plato's delightfully chaotic dialogues. Perhaps one reason Plato's theory of Forms went viral is because Plato presented it with such striking and memorable imagery, such as in his account of the different stages of love in *Symposium*, or even more famously the "Allegory of the Cave" in book 7 of *Republic*—probably the most famous thing that Plato ever wrote, but according to the very theory of Idealism that the Allegory of the Cave is trying to present it's still not perfect: there's always a better, more ideal allegory to explain Platonic Idealism that remains to be written.

34. Plato, *Symposium*, 211a–b.
35. Plato, *Symposium*, 212c.
36. Plato, *Symposium*, 217a, 219c.

Aristotle

The most obvious difference between Aristotle and Plato is the difference in their style of writing. Aristotle wrote dialogues just like Plato, but unfortunately all those dialogues are lost now and all we have left from Aristotle are lecture notes that were written either by him or by his students at the Lyceum. Those lucky souls who were able to read Aristotle's dialogues before they all vanished reported that they were much better than these lecture notes, which sound very much like lecture notes: they contain lots of repetitions, asides, circling back to make amendments, exploration of dead ends, and various other tangents. They are exactly as messy and inefficient as you would expect from transcriptions of someone thinking out loud. Aristotle also liked to walk around while he lectured, and thus his students and followers acquired the title of "peripatetic philosophers," meaning "the dudes who like to walk around while they philosophize; the philosophers who won't sit still." All of this is helpful to keep in mind as you read Aristotle so that you're not surprised or offended by the inefficiencies of his texts. There are many moments of great brilliance and profound ideas in Aristotle's writing but to reach them you need to be prepared to do some walking around, some peripatetic wandering as Aristotle thinks out loud, putting on a show for his students. Unlike Plato's dialogues, which contain a menagerie of diverse characters and voices, Aristotle's writing contains only Aristotle's voice, but that voice is best understood as the voice of someone walking and talking and thinking out loud; a teacher trying out new material to see how well it goes over with his students.

Aristotle was a student at Plato's Academy, then stayed on as an instructor—and perhaps he might have stayed there forever if he had not been fired when Plato died and Plato's nephew Speusippus took over the Academy. After he lost his job at the Academy he decamped to the island of Lesbos to study fish and other marine life, and that particular career move reveals a lot about the nature of Aristotle's thinking. More than anyone else Aristotle embodied the ideal of philosophy that is built into the Greek world *philosophia*: the love of all wisdom with no boundaries whatsoever. Today philosophy professors are thought to concern themselves with only a very small slice of the academic pie but in Aristotle's time and in Aristotle's mind to study philosophy was to study . . . everything. The original meaning of *philosophia* as simply the love of all wisdom, without any disciplinary limits or any other artificial boundaries, is preserved in the PhD degree (*Philosophiae Doctor*), which is why today even a chemistry or communication professor who never took a single philosophy class and perhaps regards the fact that philosophy still exists as a scandal is nevertheless stuck with the title "Doctor of Philosophy," which must be extremely irritating.

Much of Aristotle's prodigious output would today be classified as natural science, including the following titles:

> *Physics*
> *On the Heavens*
> *On Generation and Corruption*
> *Meteorology*
> *On Memory*
> *On Sleep*
> *On Length and Shortness of Life*
> *On Youth, Old Age, Life and Death, and Respiration*
> *History of Animals*
> *Parts of Animals*
> *Movement of Animals*
> *Progression of Animals*
> *Generation of Animals*

The content of these works is philosophical in the broader sense of philosophy as the love of all wisdom, but ever since the natural sciences emerged as specialized fields works such as these by Aristotle have been regarded as part of the ancient history of biology, physics, etc. Actually almost every modern academic discipline, including the social sciences and the humanities, could argue that their genealogy can be traced back to Aristotle. Philosophy has been very good at creating and then spinning off new disciplines and Aristotle's work is clearly the single best example of that. The core of philosophy that will always remain, that will never be spun off into a subsidiary, consists of those three questions that are fundamentally theoretical in nature: what is the true and ultimate nature of reality, knowledge, and values? Aristotle's works that are squarely within the boundaries of these three questions and are therefore still very much a part of the philosophy game include the following titles:

> *Categories*
> *On Interpretation*
> *Prior Analytics*
> *Posterior Analytics*
> *Topics*

Sophistical Refutations
Metaphysics
Nicomachean Ethics
Eudemian Ethics
Politics
Rhetoric
Poetics

In these works there is more than enough to create a complete philosophical system in Aristotle's name, which is what scholasticism did in the Middle Ages; but the pernicious consequences of that impulse to build a closed and dogmatic system out of Aristotle's work can't be blamed on Aristotle; he was just an extremely curious person who liked to walk and talk and propose theories about everything. The style of Aristotle's lecture notes constantly reminds us that these are works in progress, thoughts that are in motion in every possible way, and nothing like settled or systematic dogma, so it's best to approach Aristotle's philosophy with the same spirit of childish wonder and adventure that we observed in the pre-Socratic philosophers. Aristotle did not think that philosophy ended with him; he understood that it was just getting started. In that spirit, here is a very incomplete and fragmentary walk through a few of Aristotle's ideas and theories in the peripatetic style that characterized Aristotle's thinking which I hope will persuade you to do more walking around and exploring in the extensive and fascinating territory of Aristotle's philosophy.

Most of Aristotle's disagreements with Plato are disagreements with Plato's theory of Forms. Aristotle never hesitated to point out when he thought that Plato, his former teacher, was wrong. The general spirit of Aristotle's disagreement with Plato's theory of Forms was captured quite correctly by Raphael in *The School of Athens* where we see Plato pointing straight up emphatically and unequivocally as if to say "the truth is up there in the world of the Forms, not down here among the shadows," and in response we see Aristotle not exactly pointing down, which in Raphael's time might have seemed like an endorsement of hell over heaven, but rather spreading his hand out and sort of pressing down, as if he were trying to keep a lid on Plato's wild, transcendent exuberance. In direct contrast with Plato's theory of Forms Aristotle insists that the truth is always down here, on Planet Earth, in the world of our experience—among the fishes and other marine life of Lesbos for example and not in some transcendent realm of pure Ideas. That is a consistent theme that runs throughout all of Aristotle's philosophy, and it's evident in all of the following examples of his thought.

Among his many other accomplishments, Aristotle was the first person to create an organized system of logic. No one can claim with a straight face to have created logic itself, since logic is built into language and is therefore something that everyone learns when they learn a language. (The ancient Greeks understood this fact well and expressed it in their word *logos*, which means both language and logic, thereby recognizing that the two are inextricable.) So Aristotle definitely didn't create logic, but he did do an excellent job of organizing and systematizing it so that this collection of concepts could be more quickly and efficiently used. Aristotle's work on logic is found in several different texts, including *Categories*, *Topics*, *Prior Analytics*, *Posterior Analytics*, and *On Interpretation*.

In *On Interpretation* Aristotle begins by explaining how logic can only work with statements, which are the parts of language that are either true or false. But then in section 9 he acknowledges that there has to be an exception to this rule. Statements about the future cannot be considered true or false because that would eliminate human freedom. If the statement "There will be a sea battle tomorrow" is true right now, or if it is false right now, it would follow that humans have no freedom to affect the future. If it's true that there will be a sea battle tomorrow I can't do anything about it: I can't choose to stop this sea battle. So even though as logicians we would like to be able to say that all statements without exception are true or false, as humans we must acknowledge that this would be absurd and therefore unacceptable because such a logical principle would negate human freedom. Logic, rather than free choices, would control the future, which is an outcome that everyone should consider absurd. This is one of the fascinating moments when Aristotle acknowledges one of the limits of logic.

Aristotle's approach to ethics is generally called "virtue ethics," but this introduces an unfortunate confusion right from the start because "virtue" has a much narrower and more exotic meaning than Aristotle ever intended. Aristotle wants to talk about "practical wisdom" (*phronesis*) in a way that everyone will understand because it immediately connects with their own experience. Whenever you read the word "virtue" in English translation keep in mind that Aristotle's word was *areté*, which simply means "excellence." The fundamental question Aristotle wants to answer is "What does it mean to be excellent in everything you do?" This makes ethics as broad as it can possibly be and makes it immediately applicable to everyone. Approaching ethics in this way, one of the first things Aristotle clarifies is that if you try to be too precise about ethics you'll blow up the whole thing right from the start. Ethics isn't a precise science, and though we might prefer that there be a rule book for how to live an excellent life that we could follow, that just isn't the case; instead, we have to learn from our own messy experience, mostly by getting it wrong. Aristotle says that most kinds of practical excellence are means between extremes, but this isn't a mean in the mathematically precise sense; ethics is never that precise. There are many forms of excellence that can be understood as a mean between extremes, but there are other forms of excellence that can't be understood that way. For example, Aristotle says that in the case of adultery, "rightness and wrongness do not depend on committing it with the right woman at the right time and in the right manner, but the mere fact of committing such action at all is to do wrong."[37] (This was perhaps Aristotle's best joke—perhaps also his only joke—so I hope you enjoyed it!)

Aristotle's political theory assumes his ethical theory and builds on it. Here's an easy way to make sense of Aristotle's political theory: take Plato's political theory and stand it on its head. Early in *Republic* Plato is given the chance to discuss ethics but turns it down. Instead, he changes the subject and says: if you want to know what makes a good person, first create a good state, because a good state will necessarily have good people in it. Aristotle does just the inverse. He argues: if you want to know what makes a good state, first figure out what it means to be a good person, because good people will naturally and necessarily create a good state to live in. In his *Politics* Aristotle demonstrates how his political theory is the inverse of Plato's. Plato's state is dictated from the top down: Plato's Philosopher King leaves the cave, discovers true reality in the realm of the Forms, and then returns to Earth to build a state following the Ideal pattern dictated by the Forms. Aristotle inverts this and reimagines the state as a sort of organic, living thing, like a plant growing up from the ground. Aristotle was a botanist among other things, and his political theory sounds a lot like a botany book. It's all about how the state naturally grows up from its natural roots in human nature. It's all nature, nature, nature. Aristotle presents political science as very much like natural science. It's just a matter of reading the book of nature to discover the facts of human nature, and how those facts manifest themselves first in families and then in communities. This is a very appealing picture of politics. Wouldn't it

---

37. Aristotle, *Nicomachean Ethics*, 1107a15.

be nice if politics were a kind of science in the same way that botany is a science? Wouldn't all political disagreements and victimization immediately vanish if politics had the same objective standards as botany?

To accomplish the transformation of politics into political science Aristotle argues that what most people think of as values are actually facts. The natural sciences deal with facts, not values, and that's what makes so much agreement and progress possible in the natural sciences. Aristotle tries to accomplish the same thing in his political science by taking what appear to be values and reconceptualizing them as facts. That, in a nutshell, is natural law theory, which has had an enormous impact on the history of philosophy and on human history generally. It flourished in the Middle Ages (Thomas Aquinas was a big fan), and it is still very much alive and kicking today. The long life and legacy of natural law theory is even more surprising when you consider that in his *Politics* Aristotle uses it to justify slavery, discrimination against women and children, and basically any oppression you like against anyone other than Greek men, since Greek men are by nature in charge. Given this baggage you might imagine that no one would have the audacity to advocate natural law theory today, but that isn't what has happened at all. The promise of replacing messy and murky values with clear objective facts continues to make natural law theory appealing to many today, thousands of years after Aristotle proposed it.

Psychology is one of the many disciplines that could trace its genealogy back to Aristotle if it wanted, specifically to Aristotle's text called *On the Soul* (or *De Anima* in Latin). It remains very much an open question what Aristotle is talking about in this book. The Greek title is "About the Psyche," but what is that? Psychology is the study of the psyche, but most psychologists would slap you right in the face if you told them that they study souls. (Aristotle also says that plants have a psyche, so you should probably not mention this fact to a botanist, who will probably slap you again.) Whatever "psyche" means to us today it seems to have a very different meaning for Aristotle. One clue that may be helpful: all of Aristotle's works were given Latin names in the Middle Ages but *De Anima* still sticks to this text today, perhaps because it does a better job of capturing what the text is about for contemporary readers. *Anima* means soul, but it also suggests life in general, as in "animating force" or "that angry psychologist was very animated when he slapped me in the face!" *Anima* seems to get closer to the idea of whatever it is that separates the living from the dead, or living things from all the other things we find on Planet Earth. Much of Aristotle's writing now fits squarely in the natural sciences (physics, meteorology, etc.), while other writing remains squarely within philosophy (metaphysics, logic, ethics, etc.) or within other branches of the humanities (poetics, rhetoric, etc.); but there are a few works of Aristotle that today seem just weird: they don't really seem to fit anywhere. *De Anima* is one of those works. The particular topics Aristotle addresses in this work have all been appropriated by different fields: psychology took a little; botany and zoology took a little; theology took a little, etc.; but no one bought the whole package that Aristotle was selling. That just makes this book even more interesting, and to fully appreciate Aristotle we ought to consider some of the aspects of his thought that remain mysterious and didn't feed directly and neatly into some new discipline or science as so much of his work did. There's a wonderful naïve quality to *On the Soul* that reminds us that philosophy is still a young child at this point and still driven (as it always must be) by childish wonder. At the most basic level it seems like Aristotle is just trying to answer the question: "What is it that makes all living things different from non-living things? Whatever that is, that's what I mean by a soul."

At this point you're probably thinking that what I promised would be a relaxed peripatetic stroll through Aristotle's philosophy has in fact turned out to be more like a frantic and breathless sprint—as if we were running for our lives from a pack of hungry wolves or a gang of very fit peripatetic philosophers—and for that I apologize; but since this chapter is meant to be merely a tantalizing appetizer or a short and seductive love letter, incompleteness is unavoidable, especially when considering someone like Aristotle who explored just about every conceivable topic and set a standard for philosophical omnivorousness that no one since has matched. To compensate somewhat for the very fragmentary quality of this survey of Aristotle's philosophy I'll conclude with a more thorough summary of book 1 of *Metaphysics*. This is a good coda because in book 1 Aristotle also offers his own summary of the history of philosophy so far and explains how he has (he believes) corrected the mistakes of all the philosophers who preceded him. Here are some of the highlights of *Metaphysics* book 1:

In the very first sentence of the book Aristotle writes: "All people by nature desire to know"—a beautiful line that I've already cited several times. Here's that sentence in Greek in case you decide to make it your next tattoo (which I highly recommend). Just tear this page out of the book and take it to your favorite tattoo parlor:

πάντες ἄνθρωποι τοῦ εἰδέναι ὀρέγονται φύσει.

What does Aristotle mean by "metaphysics"? The book is about knowledge of "first causes and the principles of things"; in other words, knowledge of the true and ultimate nature of reality. Aristotle focuses on "causes" simply because his own metaphysical theory is all about causes. You also see right from the start Aristotle's commitment to basing knowledge on our own senses, to remaining here within the world of our experience and resisting the temptation to explain things by positing a world beyond. The second line of the book, after the eminently tattooable opening sentence, says: "If you want proof that everyone desires knowledge, just consider how much we all enjoy our senses; obviously that's because we love the fact that our senses bring us knowledge." Then in section 2 we get a defense of philosophy as an end in itself, and not just a means to an end, and motivated by nothing more than wonder: the desire to know. These first two sections constitute a marvelous prelude. They set the stage and the tone for the rest of the argument that follows.

In section 3 Aristotle gets down to the business of selling his own theory of metaphysics, which is: there are four fundamental and foundational realities for everything that is, or as he prefers to put it, four causes:

1. The material cause (the matter of everything that is)
2. The formal cause (the form or pattern of everything that is) (Aristotle also uses the word "substance" to describe this cause, but don't let that throw you; he means substance in the sense of essence, not in a material sense)
3. The efficient cause (the start or catalyst of everything that is)
4. The final cause (the goal or *telos* of everything that is)

One of the things that Aristotle does to sell his four-cause theory is review the history of philosophy so far in order to show how his metaphysical theory is better than everyone else's—how other philosophers may have recognized one or two of these causes but only he got them all. We should be grateful that Aristotle decided to market his theory in this way because it results in one of the best sources we now have for the ideas and arguments of the pre-Socratic philosophers. Section 4 continues this project with lots of great material about how (according to Aristotle) the pre-Socratics only got part of the complete four-cause picture, and even then they didn't really understand what they were saying.

In section 5 Aristotle argues that the Pythagoreans were the first to recognize a formal cause (numbers), but not in a way that actually worked to explain the world. This section seems to serve mainly to set up the critique of Plato in section 6, where Aristotle claims that Plato was motivated to create an idealistic metaphysical theory because he believed Heraclitus's argument that everything in the sensible world is constantly in flux and therefore no real knowledge is possible in this world; you have to look to the intelligible world to find lasting truth. Plato was more sophisticated and dialectical than the pre-Socratics but didn't create anything new, according to Aristotle. Plato's theory of Forms at most recognizes only partially the formal and material cause of things.

After section 6 there's a bit of an intermission in sections 7 and 8 where Aristotle returns to his marketing campaign that he is the first person in the history of philosophy to recognize and understand all four forms of causation. Then in section 9 he returns to his criticism of Plato, and this time he doesn't hold back. We see how opposed he was to Plato's theory of Forms and also how much he views it as a competitor with his own theory. His criticisms include:

- The Forms just double the number of things that need to be explained, so Plato just kicked the can down the road and didn't really explain anything.
- Plato never proves to us that Forms actually exist. We're asked to accept them on faith, which is supposed to be against the rules in philosophy.
- Forms destroy or overshadow what we should really care about: the real things right here in front of us in the world of our experience.
- The Forms are good for nothing: they explain nothing, they do no work. How do Forms cause or create anything? This seems to be nothing but a metaphor or poetry.
- What's the efficient cause of the Forms? How did they come to be? This needs to be explained.
- Most of all: in his theory of Forms Plato turns his back on the real world and annihilates the study of nature. Real learning and knowledge must start here on the ground, not in Plato's transcendent world of the Forms. This, Aristotle argues, was Plato's fundamental error.

Finally, section 10 wraps up Aristotle's sales pitch for his own metaphysical theory and also provides a very fitting conclusion for our own relaxed stroll (or frantic sprint) through Aristotle's thought: the whole history of philosophy so far, he says, is like a stammering, childish, uncritical and uncomprehending attempt to grasp what he (Aristotle) actually did grasp with his own theory of causes; and for this, Aristotle says, you are all welcome.

Hellenistic Philosophy: Stoicism and Epicureanism

We've almost reached the finish line of this super-seductive and super-scrappy ancient philosophy appetizer! The not-at-all-holy trinity of Socrates, Plato, and Aristotle put on quite a spectacular show that would be a tough act for anyone to follow, so the ancient philosophers who came after Aristotle have sometimes been overlooked—obscured as they were by the rather long shadows of the Socrates/Plato/Aristotle triumvirate. But in the shade cast by these three quite a few interesting philosophers were still at work creating quite a lot of interesting ideas and arguments. Ancient philosophy after Aristotle is often labeled "Hellenistic" philosophy, because even though the people involved were mostly Romans they remained very much under the spell of classical Greek philosophy; so even though this was not exactly Greek philosophy it was still very much Greek-ish. Roman/Hellenistic philosophy is particularly noteworthy for the ethical theories that it created, and there are two ethical theories that dominate the Hellenistic contribution to ancient philosophy: stoicism and hedonism (also called Epicureanism in honor of a particularly enthusiastic advocate of hedonism named Epicurus). These two ethical theories may seem like polar opposites, but they actually have a great deal in common. Both theories were radical (in every sense of the word), but at the same time they were utterly pragmatic. They are both best understood as attempts to give people a way to stay in control of their lives in spite of the increasingly chaotic and out-of-control nature of the Roman world, and obviously everyone still wants to do that today, so these ethical theories are no less relevant now than they were in classical Rome.

Today when someone is praised for being a good stoic it usually means: "Here's someone who has suffered an absolute catastrophe in her life, something that would have overwhelmed everyone else I know, but somehow she managed not to be overwhelmed. I don't know how she did it because it seems impossible, so the name I'm going to give to this sort of incomprehensible endurance is stoicism." This way of thinking about stoicism makes it impossible to be a stoic except in the most extreme and extraordinary circumstances. A tragedy is a necessary prerequisite, and stoicism becomes possible only as a response to the sort of disaster that no one ever wants to experience. When stoicism is understood in this way it's reduced to a kind of emergency ethics, like a fire extinguisher kept behind glass to be broken only if the building is on fire and your life is in immediate peril; at all other times it's supposed to stay there behind the glass, and we all truly hope that we'll never have to use it. We admire someone who acts stoically but we hope that we'll never have to do it ourselves, and we don't believe that it's even possible to be a stoic all the time.

Similarly, hedonism is generally regarded today as a good and entirely appropriate way to live only in extremely lucky circumstances that are the polar-opposite of the extremely unlucky circumstances that make stoicism possible. Most people think that if you get extraordinarily lucky (for example: you win the lottery, or you find yourself on an all-expenses-paid vacation in Las Vegas) then you should definitely be a hedonist, dedicating your every waking moment to nothing but the pursuit of pleasure. But again, it's understood that this is a temporary response to a temporary condition and certainly not at all how one should live all the time. This is the "what-happens-in-Vegas-stays-in-Vegas" version of hedonism that thrives today, and even though it sounds like a lot more fun than the break-glass-only-in-case-of-emergency version of stoicism it turns hedonism into another ethical theory that applies to extreme and special situations only, and not to one's entire life.

That's the big difference between how stoicism and hedonism are generally understood today and how they were understood by the original stoic and Epicurean philosophers who created them. The founding stoics and hedonists presented their ethical theories as a complete guide to living, a set of principles that apply all the time to everyone with no exceptions. Today most of us think: "I really hope I never have to be a stoic; and if I get a chance to be a hedonist that would be awesome but it better not be for too long or else it will kill me." But the original stoics and Epicureans argued that if you weren't a stoic or an Epicurean all the time you were doing it wrong and hadn't really understood their ethical theories, so clearly we're going to have to make an effort to understand stoicism and Epicureanism as they were originally understood. Fortunately both ethical theories are very easy to understand, and that's by design. They both want to be ethical theories for everyone, easy to understand so that all your effort can go into applying the simple principles of these theories and not wasted on wrestling with abstract concepts. Both stoicism and Epicureanism argue that we should see the world through the lens of a single idea or principle, they just disagree on what that principle is.

For hedonism the principle is advertised right in the name of the theory. *Hedone* in Greek means pleasure, and the singular principle of hedonism is simply that pleasure is good and pain is bad. In nineteenth-century Victorian England this ethical theory was assigned the less scandalous name of "utilitarianism," but behind the name change was exactly the same ethical paradigm: an action that produces pleasure is good, and an action that produces pain is bad; simple as that. Stoicism comes from the Greek word *stoa*, which means porch, because apparently the stoic philosophers liked to hang out on porches, and also because whoever had the job of naming this ethical theory was extremely lazy and put no effort into his work at all; so stoicism doesn't advertise its guiding principle right in its name like hedonism but you don't have to look very far to find it. The singular principle of stoicism is simply that the only things that belong to us are our interpretations of our experience; everything else that we're inclined to think of as ours—such as our many material possessions (houses and cars and bicycles, etc.), our bodies, and our family and friends—none of that actually belongs to us at all. Stoicism argues that it's possible to stay in control of your life all the time, no matter what happens to you, if you focus exclusively on controlling the one and only thing you can control—your interpretation of the world—and don't allow yourself to get distracted by anything else. This will be hard work, but the principle behind it is very easy to understand. Similarly hedonism argues that it's possible to stay in control of your life all the time, no matter what happens to you, if you focus exclusively on controlling the one and only thing you can control—maximizing pleasure and minimizing pain—and don't get distracted by anything else. This too is a very simple principle, easy to understand, but applying it in every moment and every situation of your life will be hard work because you must constantly perform an honest calculation of both the short-term and long-term pleasure and pain created by every action, and this constant calculation results in a form of hedonism that is extremely unextreme and is best characterized by a word that today is almost never associated with hedonism: prudence.

The stoic principle that the only things that really belong to you are your interpretations and everything else is an accident is wonderfully clarified by the external, accidental circumstances of the two most famous stoic philosophers: Epictetus, who was a slave, and Marcus Aurelius, who was an emperor of Rome. It seems impossible to imagine two people who were more different from each other in terms of wealth, power, privilege, social status, etc.—all the things that stoicism says are accidents that don't belong to you at all. That's exactly how Epictetus and Marcus Aurelius understood the accidents of their lives, so while their circumstances were very different their philosophy was virtually identical. Try picking up a text by Epictetus or Marcus Aurelius and guessing, based only on the ideas, who was the author; I don't think you'll be able to do it. From a stoic perspective being born into a life full of accidents that don't belong to you at all and that you can't control, as Marcus Aurelius was when he became emperor of Rome, just makes it harder to be a good stoic since there's more noise around you and more possibilities to be distracted and to believe that these accidents are your property. As soon as you start believing that anything other than your interpretations belong to you that's when you become a slave in the only sense that matters, according to stoicism, so Marcus Aurelius arguably had more opportunities to become a slave than Epictetus, even though Epictetus was born into slavery.

Stoicism instructs you to look within yourself for the solution to every challenge, and it informs you that you have almost superhuman powers as an individual. There's absolutely nothing that the world can throw at you that you can't handle while still remaining tranquil and serene. This includes natural disasters, war, all other forms of bad fortune, illness, and even death. You have within yourself everything you need to avoid any real harm in your life, no matter what happens to you. "But," you may ask, "if I have all this power as an individual, and if the solution to every problem is always within me, why should I even bother trying to work with other people?" This tension is especially pronounced in Marcus Aurelius's philosophy because he was a stoic philosopher who also happened to be emperor of Rome. He was in charge of the largest organization in the world at the time. The *Meditations* were written while he was trying to get things done in this very unwieldy and complicated bureaucracy and this required constantly working with other people, most of whom were not stoic philosophers. The very first entry in *Meditations* (after he thanks all the people who have helped him in his life) shows this emphasis on applying stoicism to working with difficult people:

> When you wake up in the morning, tell yourself: The people I deal with today will be meddling, ungrateful, arrogant, dishonest, jealous, and surly. They are like this because they can't tell

good from evil. But I have seen the beauty of good, and the ugliness of evil, and have recognized that the wrongdoer has a nature related to my own—not of the same blood or birth, but the same mind, and possessing a share of the divine. And so none of them can hurt me. No one can implicate me in ugliness. Nor can I feel angry at my relative, or hate him. We were born to work together like feet, hands, and eyes, like the two rows of teeth, upper and lower. To obstruct each other is unnatural. To feel anger at someone, to turn your back on him: these are obstructions.[38]

The *Meditations* are best understood as Marcus Aurelius getting himself in the right state of mind every morning to go to work, where he will constantly be surprised. It demonstrates very effectively that the ideas of stoicism are quite simple, but the application of those ideas is very challenging. Marcus Aurelius and all the other founding stoics did not believe that they had the luxury to be stoics just in extreme moments of emergency, when really there was no other option. Instead they thought it was their duty to be stoics all the time and in every possible situation. Epictetus explains that even something as apparently trivial as bathing at the public baths can be done ethically, or unethically—which means losing control over your own life and becoming a slave to people and things that you can't control:

> When you are about to undertake some action, remind yourself what sort of action it is. If you are going out for a bath, put before your mind what happens at baths—there are people who splash, people who jostle, people who are insulting, people who steal. And you will undertake the action more securely if from the start you say of it, "I want to take a bath and to keep my choices in accord with nature;" and likewise for each action. For that way if something happens to interfere with your bathing you will be ready to say, "Oh, well, I wanted not only this but also to keep my choices in accord with nature, and I cannot do that if I am annoyed with things that happen."[39]

The original version of hedonism taught by philosophers like Epicurus and Lucretius was also an ethical theory that required great discipline since it had to be applied to every moment and every situation of one's life, even the most mundane. Consequently most people are shocked to discover how boring it is. Epicurus agreed with the founding principle

---

38. Marcus Aurelius, *Meditations*, 17.
39. Epictetus, *Handbook*, 12–13.

of hedonism: pleasure is good and pain is bad, but he insisted on a very prudent and careful long-term calculation of all the pleasures and pains that follow from any given action, which entails a lifestyle that would be deeply disappointing to most people who come running as soon as they hear the word "hedonism," wearing a toga and carrying a keg of beer, because they thought this would be the best party ever. As Epicurus wrote:

> No pleasure is a bad thing in itself, but the things which produce certain pleasures entail disturbances many times greater than the pleasures themselves. . . . If the things that produce the pleasures of profligate men really freed them from fears of the mind concerning celestial and atmospheric phenomena, the fear of death, and the fear of pain; if, further, they taught them to limit their desires, we should never have any fault to find with such persons, for they would then be filled with pleasures from every source and would never have pain of body or mind, which is what is bad.[40]

Such a careful and calculating approach to hedonism rules out almost all of the pleasures of the "what-happens-in-Vegas-stays-in-Vegas" version of hedonism, so today a true hedonist in the Epicurean mold can pursue pleasure prudently and probably never be recognized as a hedonist because this original version of hedonism has been almost completely forgotten.

In the classical Roman world stoicism and Epicureanism flourished side by side. This was a world in which philosophical theories were part of popular culture and were even actively discussed at parties. Here's an account from Cicero of one such party:

> The topic of the immortal gods was made the subject of a very searching and thorough discussion at the house of my friend Gaius Cotta. It was the Latin Festival, and I had come at Cotta's express invitation to pay him a visit. I found him sitting in an alcove, engaged in a debate with Gaius Velleius, a Member of the Senate, accounted by the Epicureans as their chief Roman adherent at the time. With them was Quintus Lucilius Balbus, who was so accomplished a student of Stoicism as to rank with the leading Greek exponents of that system.[41]

Cicero says that this was the best party ever! And it was not at all unusual in Rome. This demonstrates how seriously both of these ethical theories were taken in the ancient world, and it also shows that stoics and

---

40. Epicurus, "Principal Doctrines," 32–33.
41. Greenblatt, Swerve, 69.

Epicureans understood that their theories actually had a great deal in common, so they had a lot to say to each other. That party at Gaius Cotta's house, where stoics and Epicureans enthusiastically debated how to live based on philosophical theories they took very seriously, is an excellent final scene for this story of ancient philosophy.

The end of ancient philosophy is the end of philosophy's childhood. Philosophy had a truly wonder-ful childhood, and now, like an eager and overly confident teenager, it's about to sally forth and make a truly spectacular mistake.

Mini-appendix to this first chapter on the history of philosophy concerning what the history of philosophy has generally excluded or ignored

Before getting to that spectacular mistake, I want to conclude this first history chapter by acknowledging everything that wasn't here. My approach to the history of philosophy is to focus on the ideas and arguments that have gotten the most attention and have generated the biggest response. These works are the "classics" simply because they have had the greatest impact, and that's a quantitative rather than qualitative judgment: it focuses exclusively on the quantity of responses a work has generated and not the quality of its ideas. Since this approach focuses on authors who were the most widely known and widely read it necessarily excludes many people who were kept out of the conversation and therefore were mostly unknown in their time even if they had remarkable and excellent ideas. For much of its history philosophy made the mistake of excluding or simply ignoring whole classes of people, such as women and others who (according to the prejudices of the time, which unfortunately most philosophers did not question) were thought to be incapable of understanding this conversation or contributing anything interesting to it. Women were not the only people that philosophy ignored through most of its history, but the exclusion of women is perhaps the most obvious and instructive example of a truly egregious blind spot that has limited philosophy's progress.

Until very recently philosophy has consisted almost exclusively of men talking to other men and ignoring women—as if it were completely obvious that not a single woman on earth had a single interesting idea or theory that was worth considering. In the history of the world almost every discipline, institution, activity, or tradition of every kind has suffered from this same ridiculous prejudice, but philosophy has more reason to be embarrassed about harboring and tolerating this blind spot because it claimed to be better than this. From its beginning philosophy defined itself as independent thinking that would not defer to any supposed authority as it pursued the truth, so it's particularly embarrassing that in spite of these lofty ideals philosophy too (for the most part and until very recently) accepted uncritically the authority of this very thoughtless and stupid tradition, and the fact that most philosophers have been just as willing as everyone else in the history of the world to accept this prejudice is really quite embarrassing.

Or you could think of it this way: it's really quite hilarious. The guiding idea of this book is that the ideals of philosophy are so high there is inevitably an immense gap between those ideals and the actual practice of philosophy, and also that it's best to laugh at this incongruity rather than to cry or be ashamed. In philosophy's history there's probably no more obvious and hilarious failure to live up to its ideals than the failure of men to question the traditions of the world that they fell into with regard to their supposed intellectual superiority, and because until very recently philosophy was primarily just men talking to other men, as if women simply didn't exist, philosophy handicapped itself for thousands of years through an inability to do what it was supposed to be so good at doing: questioning all supposed authorities, including the authority of tradition. That's very sad, but also very funny.

This self-inflicted handicap didn't begin to be recognized on a large scale until the late eighteenth century when philosophers such as Mary Wollstonecraft (who wrote *A Vindication of the Rights of Woman* in 1792) finally managed to get men to listen to them and take them seriously. But in the thousands of years that preceded philosophy finally awakening from its embarrassing and hilarious dogmatic slumbers there were several extraordinary and exceptional women who still managed to break into the philosophical conversation in spite of all the prejudices and other obstacles that were placed in their way. In order to be heard by men who had already decided that women had nothing interesting to say all of these women had to be subversive and sneaky in truly creative ways. It's also likely that we are only aware of a very small selection of the many interesting ideas that these women had to offer, since that's all that survived of their thinking. (In many cases their ideas are preserved only in letters they wrote, since they didn't have the time or any of the other resources that are required to write and publish a book.)

For all of these reasons there are many gaps and absences in the history of philosophy caused by people being excluded from the conversation, or their ideas being ignored and neglected or other accidents of time and nature that led to written texts getting lost. In this book I will follow a quantitative paradigm when telling the story of the history of philosophy, but I'll also try to acknowledge the limitations and flaws of such an approach—and if anyone asked me to defend my method here's what I would say:

> Greetings, Dear Reader! I offer here my report of the conversation called "philosophy" that has been underway for more than 2,500 years. Like most human conversations this one has been far from perfect. Many mistakes have been made and many blind spots have been manifest, and it's also certainly true that the conversation could have been greatly improved if more people had been let into the room and allowed to participate. Women, for example, were turned away at the front door until quite recently, because unfortunately philosophy was not immune to the same thoughtless prejudices that have plagued all of human history, so the few women who did manage to join the conversation had to find a way to sneak in—perhaps through a window or by disguising themselves as part of the catering staff for this party. But I don't think the fact that the long conversation has not been perfect is a good reason to reject and discard the whole thing. In spite of its obvious blind spots and incompleteness the history of philosophy still includes many marvelous and wonderful ideas, and I'll do my best to report this history to you without evaluating or endorsing any of it so that you can decide for yourself what was good and what was bad and what got left out completely. And here's the best news: philosophy isn't over, so there's no reason why the mistakes and blind spots of the past can't be corrected in the future.

I'll attempt to acknowledge the many gaps in my recounting of the history of philosophy by including, in an appendix, a partial list of the many people I've left out. There is an ongoing project to recover the many voices that have been ignored or forgotten in the history of philosophy, so the task of expanding these lists and understanding these authors better is part of philosophy in the future (see chapter 7!) to which you are invited to contribute.

Chapter 4

Medieval philosophy

(Philosophy, now a teenager, rushes into an ill-advised and doomed-to-fail marriage with religion which lasts approximately 1,200 years before it realizes its mistake and asks for a divorce; but like all unhappy marriages this one is very dramatic and interesting and full of creative tension while it lasts.)

If you're interested in religion and theology, studying medieval philosophy will be pure ecstasy for you and you'll need to be careful not to burst into song while you're reading your medieval philosophy books lest someone call the campus police to have you arrested for disturbing the peace or behaving indecently. But if you're not interested in religion or theology medieval philosophy can make you feel confused, disoriented, frustrated, or even a little bit angry. If that happens, studying medieval philosophy won't be much fun for you, which means that something has gone horribly wrong because studying philosophy should always be fun. The main purpose of this chapter is to make sure that your trip through medieval philosophy is both fascinating and fun, as it ought to be, in spite of the challenges that this period poses. Even if you're very interested in religion, if you're going to study philosophy in the Middle Ages—as opposed to religion and theology—then you'll have to do some careful sorting and editing to separate philosophy and religion since the two are so thoroughly mixed up with each other in this period; but this too is a fun and fascinating challenge.

The best way to avoid confusion and frustration when you study medieval philosophy is to start with a clear understanding of how truly weird this period is. Medieval philosophy ought to have something like the content warning that appears before every movie or TV show which allows you to avoid the extremely awkward experience of inviting your parents to watch a movie with you and then discovering that the film is full of nudity from beginning to end—in fact, the whole movie takes place on a planet where clothes have not yet been invented and so all the action in the film (including a very long and dramatic snowmobile chase, a festive community square dance, a spirited debate between seven candidates for mayor, an intense game of rugby between teams with a long and fierce rivalry, a hang-gliding expedition that starts well but ends badly, and a final climactic bicycle race that includes several category 1 climbs and ends in a field sprint) takes place completely in the nude; and although both you and your parents will of course sit nonchalantly on the couch and watch the entire two hours and twenty minutes of this movie together because you want to pretend that the nudity is no big deal and of course you watch movies all the time in which all the actors are nude, in fact you are terrifically embarrassed for the entire two hours and twenty minutes and wish that you had investigated this movie more carefully before you invited your parents to watch it with you. This is why we all appreciate content warnings before movies and TV shows, and a similar warning attached to medieval philosophy can spare everyone a lot of awkwardness and unhappiness.

There isn't much nudity in medieval philosophy (none, to be precise: all medieval philosophers remain fully clothed at all times, except for maybe Abelard and Heloise), but there is quite a lot of other shocking and scandalous content about which you should be warned. Here's the content warning I would attach to the extremely long (approximately 1,200 years) movie called *Medieval Philosophy*:

Rated OXC (Often Extremely Confused) for many moments in which philosophy seems to forget what it learned in its childhood, as if it just got hit on the head by a rock or an air conditioner that fell from the sky and then developed an extreme case of amnesia that led it to engage in strange behavior for over a thousand years.

To be more specific, here are three weird, shocking, and scandalous aspects of medieval philosophy for which you should be prepared before you sit down to watch this movie, either alone or with your parents:

- Suddenly religion and philosophy are completely mixed up with each other, like some sort of strange philosophy and religion stew. This is quite disorienting since one of the greatest accomplishments of ancient philosophy was figuring out how philosophy is distinct from religion. During its childhood philosophy learned to distinguish itself from sophistry and business and religion and it established its own identity apart from all three of them, but now suddenly it seems to have forgotten what should have been the easiest and most obvious of those hard-won lessons: that philosophy and religion are different games that are played according to different rules.

- Suddenly philosophy is taking orders from a higher authority, from a boss, like a teenager who's thrilled to get a summer job at Burger King; and it seems perfectly content with this arrangement, as if it would be happy to go on working at this fast-food joint forever. This is weird, of course, because in its childhood philosophy formed its own distinct identity around the core principles of thinking for itself and not deferring to any other supposed authority in any form, including the supposed authority of religion, but again philosophy seems to forget this lesson during the Middle Ages.

- Suddenly everyone's a saint. Well not everyone; that's a slight exaggeration, but there are quite a few medieval philosophers (including some of the most important and influential, such as Saint Augustine, Saint Bonaventure, Saint Anselm, Saint Thomas Aquinas, etc.) who have attained sainthood and therefore (according to the official story) are in heaven now, gazing down upon you and passing judgment as you read their books. This is certainly weird. There were no saints in the history of philosophy before the medieval period, and there are none after it. There's nothing wrong with being a saint, of course, and if you too, Honored Reader, happen to be a saint, then I take my hat off to you and say, "God bless you!" (which is a completely unnecessary thing to say to a saint, but I couldn't think of anything else to say since I've never been in the presence of a saint before). But it is certainly jarring to read philosophical texts, which are supposed to rest entirely on the strength of their own arguments, while also being aware that the authors of these texts are supposedly now in heaven working as consultants and advisors to The Almighty. You have to go through this disorienting and disconcerting experience a lot when you study medieval philosophy, since almost all medieval philosophers are either saints or something close to that: almost every medieval philosopher is highly venerated and regarded as an authority in their respective religious traditions.

Everything that's weird and confusing in medieval philosophy is due to the fact that this is one of the strangest marriages ever. Many marriages are weird, confused, and dysfunctional, and whenever we encounter a couple who seem unhappily married and we can't make any sense of why they got married in the first place or why they have stayed together in spite of their obvious differences and unhappiness, we say to ourselves: "I'm so glad that's not me!" and then we go on our way rejoicing. We never hesitate to stare at any dysfunctional marriage we encounter in a blatantly voyeuristic fashion because it's undeniably great fun and we also feel entitled to do this because we had the good sense not to make such poor choices ourselves. Observing and studying an unhappy marriage in this manner is something everyone loves because it gives us a feeling of catharsis and moral superiority, and I recommend that you study medieval philosophy with the very same attitude of self-satisfied voyeurism. It's perfectly appropriate to approach medieval philosophy with the understanding that you're about to study a flawed marriage based on a foundation of numerous misunderstandings, but which nevertheless persisted for over a thousand years. When you do this you put yourself in a position to learn what really matters from medieval philosophy and not get distracted or confused by all the weirdness that results from this dysfunctional marriage. Despite the many mistakes and confusions, philosophy did not cease during the Middle Ages and medieval philosophy is not just the history of an error. When this strange marriage finally dissolved, philosophy was wiser because of what it went through in the Middle Ages.

Though it's impossible to know the thinking and the motivation behind the strange marriage of philosophy and religion in the medieval period, should we let that deter us from wildly speculating? I think not, so here's some wild speculation. What was really going on in the weird medieval marriage of philosophy and religion? Here are at least two possibilities:

- Philosophy was seduced, co-opted, or enslaved by religion. However you want to spin it, these are all ways of understanding medieval philosophy as a period when philosophy was victimized by religion: religion was the big bully, flush with money, power, and authority, that took advantage of poor little philosophy.

- It's also possible that philosophy was nobody's victim. During this period many religions had an almost insatiable demand for everything that philosophy was selling and they went on a wild philosophical shopping spree. Perhaps philosophy (being at heart a wily opportunist) did nothing more than take advantage of this opportunity that fell into its lap.

The philosophy-as-victim and the philosophy-as-wily-opportunist interpretations of medieval philosophy are just two possibilities worth keeping in mind. According to the philosophy-as-wily-opportunist view, philosophers in the Middle Ages quickly deduced that religion was the best available distribution system available at the time for their theories about metaphysics, epistemology, and axiology, so they packaged their theories in a religious wrapper and thus managed to get them shipped out into the world (and they also managed to get paid—something that has never been easy for philosophers). This is certainly one viable interpretation of why philosophy entered into a partnership with religion in the Middle Ages, and I recommend this interpretation to anyone who finds it hard to care about medieval philosophy because it seems like philosophy isn't doing anything except trying to defend various religions like a public relations officer. If you feel this disdain or disinterest try the philosophy-as-wily-opportunist interpretation: then medieval philosophy becomes an adventure story in which those clever medieval philosophers were just trying to keep philosophy alive at a time when religion controlled the world. On this reading medieval philosophy was a subversive and sneaky activity that managed to get a lot of very interesting philosophical ideas and arguments into the world using religion as the delivery mechanism, sort of like a sneaky parent hiding healthy vegetables in a delicious muffin or bowl of soup, so that the child eats them even though he doesn't like vegetables.

In order to study the philosophy in medieval philosophy you have to separate philosophy from religion constantly. This is not very difficult, as we saw in the previous chapter: philosophy figured out how to make this distinction during its childhood. Once you take the religion out of medieval philosophy, or translate the religious arguments into philosophical arguments, you're left with hundreds of years of fascinating philosophical creations, and it would be tragic to overlook or ignore these creations just because philosophy happened to be mixed up in a rather confused marriage at the time. That's the spirit that I will follow in this overview of medieval philosophy, which once again will be a fragmentary, scrappy, and incomplete appetizer and not an attempt to tell the whole story. I won't attempt to present all of the many, many authors who managed to sneak some philosophy into the world during the more than 1,200 years of medieval philosophy since that would try everyone's patience and likely make this book 1,200 pages long and therefore impossible to take with you everywhere you go to impress your friends and intimidate your enemies (which is the primary purpose of any book). Instead, I'll focus on just a handful of authors who are particularly useful guides through this weirdest and longest of all the periods of philosophy's history, and the first of these is Augustine.

Augustine

Later in his life Augustine will become Saint Augustine, but he was by his own account definitely not a saint in his youth, which he spent studying Greek philosophy and committing an impressive number of sins. That's what makes Augustine such a useful guide through the transformations that philosophy underwent as it shifted from the ancient to the medieval world: he was thoroughly familiar with Greek philosophy and he spent roughly the first half of his life living like a committed hedonist, but then he converted to Christianity at age thirty-one and brought all that Greek philosophy with him and put it to work in the service of Christian theology. Augustine's story is thus a microcosm of the whole macrocosm of medieval philosophy in which philosophy was transformed into the servant of religion. Augustine blazed the trail that the rest of medieval philosophy followed, and he seemed fully aware of how instructive his life story could be so he didn't hesitate to offer it to the world (including a very detailed analysis of his sinful youth) as an example of how philosophy and religion could form a partnership in the service of The Almighty. Augustine gives us an almost too-good-to-be-true case study of the paradigm shift that takes place when philosophy transitions from the ancient to the medieval period both on the level of ideas, but also on a very personal level.

Augustine maintained that it was his intensive study of Greek philosophy that made it possible for him to understand Christianity and thus enabled him finally to become a Christian at age thirty-one. He explains this in his *Confessions*, which is written as a conversation with God:

> By reading these books of the Platonists I had been prompted to look for truth as something incorporeal, and I *caught sight of your invisible nature, as it is known through your* creatures. . . . I believe that it was by your will that I came across these books before I studied the scriptures, because you wished me always to remember the impression that had made on me.[1]

In other words Augustine proclaims to the world: "Thank God (literally!) that I studied Greek philosophy (especially Plato!) before I tried to understand Christianity, because it never would have made any sense to me unless I could see it through the lens of Greek philosophy. Philosophy prepared the way for Christianity, so if you really want to understand Christianity and be a good Christian you should follow my example and start with an intensive study of Greek philosophy!"

Already Augustine has clarified for us two important aspects of medieval philosophy. First, though Christianity is not the only religion that proposes marriage to philosophy during the medieval period it is the religion that figures most prominently in the history of medieval philosophy. Islam and Judaism also take an interest in philosophy during the Middle Ages but for both that interest didn't really stick, and therefore Islamic and Jewish philosophy both have rather short shelf lives. Christianity, on the other hand, had a voracious appetite for philosophy right from its beginning which it never lost. The sentiment expressed by Augustine—that Greek philosophy was a gift from God to prepare the way for Christianity—really caught on in the Christian world. Consequently when you study medieval philosophy most of the authors you read are in the Christian tradition and they are trying to use philosophy to support Christianity. (Most of these authors were also employed by the Christian Church in some capacity, as priests, bishops, monks, abbots, etc., and many of them will later become enshrined as Christian saints, so their connections to the institutions of the Christian religion are about as deep as they could possibly be.)

---

1. Augustine, *Confessions*, 154. (Any emphasis in any quotations is always the author's own—never added by me.)

The medieval Christian attitude toward philosophy is nicely captured in that same painting that I mentioned in the previous chapter: Raphael's *School of Athens*. Raphael was commissioned by the Catholic Church to paint this ancient philosophy class picture on one of the walls of the Vatican's Apostolic Palace, which was where the pope lived at the time. It's hard to imagine a more emphatic and enthusiastic endorsement of philosophy by a religion than this. Christianity has never hidden its love for Greek philosophy or the extensive use that it has made of Greek philosophy in the construction of its theology, and this painting celebrates that history. Why Christianity was more interested in shopping at the philosophy store than any other religion during the Middle Ages is certainly an interesting question, but not a question that's relevant to philosophy. When you study medieval philosophy you always have to separate the philosophy from the religion, no matter what religion that happens to be. In some medieval philosophy that religion is Islam or Judaism, but most of the time it's Christianity; however, from a philosophical perspective that's all just an accident. Even if the religion were Scientology or Mormonism or Pastafarianism or any other more recent religious creation it wouldn't matter; whatever the religion happens to be it must be separated from the philosophy if you want to study philosophy.

Secondly, Christianity's interest in Greek philosophy was first of all an interest in Plato's philosophy, which was very easy to translate into theology. Later Aristotle becomes even more important than Plato in the Christian tradition, and also in the Islamic and Jewish traditions, but at the beginning of the Middle Ages it was all Plato all the time, and Augustine's passion for Plato is a perfect example of this.

The Plato connection in medieval philosophy is worth exploring further right here at the outset, so let's put Augustine on hold for a moment and go back to our old friend Plato to consider how easy and natural it was for Christianity or any other religion to give Plato's theory of Forms a religious spin. In the beginning of the medieval period there was Plato, whose philosophy was not at all difficult to transpose into a religious key, and Augustine was the first to do so on a truly grand scale.

Take, for example, Plato's *Symposium*, which we explored in the previous chapter. Recall that this dialogue presents a competition to see who can present the best theory of love, and all of the theories of love are also about sex to some extent, especially the last account of love by Alcibiades who talks about nothing but sex when he tells the story of trying for years to seduce Socrates. Clearly this drunken party of horny men is hardly a pious gathering, but even a dialogue like this proved to be irresistible catnip to various religions in the Middle Ages because in the midst of all the comedy and lewd behavior in *Symposium* there's a wonderful summary of Plato's theory of Forms: the theory that the world of our experience is just a pale shadow of true reality which is someplace else—in a transcendent world that can only be discovered by leaving behind the world of physical sensation and entering a space of pure Ideas. Plato did not call this space "heaven," he presented his theory of Idealism as a purely intellectual activity that didn't have anything to do with religion; but obviously it isn't hard to spin Platonic Idealism as a religious story if that's what you want to do. This is exactly what many medieval religions did, starting with Christianity. They argued that Plato was telling a story about God even if he didn't realize it at the time. The ease with which Plato could be turned into an unconscious and unintentional Christian really got the ball rolling in medieval philosophy. Early Christian theologians, who were looking for a way to explain their new religion and differentiate it from the competition in the religious marketplace of the time, decided to go shopping at the Greek philosophy store for ideas, arguments, and theories they could use; and they were delighted to find that the shelves were quite well stocked with possibilities.

When he converts to Christianity at age thirty-one Augustine brings Plato with him. Did Plato want to take this trip? Did he want to become a Christian, or did he want his theory of Forms to be put to work in the theology of this new religion? Plato was not around to express his opinion on these questions, but it's clear that his philosophy was given a new life in the Middle Ages first when it was appropriated by Christian theologians. Plato, who was clearly one of the superstars of ancient philosophy, enjoyed a kind of resurrection because of the enthusiasm of Augustine (and others) for his philosophy, and thus became one of the superstars of medieval philosophy as well.

Augustine put Plato's theory of Forms to work in Christian theology wherever he could, but he also impacted medieval philosophy in other ways that couldn't be traced back to Plato or that were radically divergent from Plato's thought. Augustine's willingness to use Plato's philosophy in the service of Christian theology, but also to depart completely from Plato's philosophy when he believed that Christian theology required it, is demonstrated nicely by his response to the problem of evil.

The "problem" posed by the problem of evil is the challenge of explaining why a God would allow the world to be such a mess. "Evil" in this case just means whatever we don't like. There's almost universal agreement that certain things are unpleasant, such as falling off a cliff into a lake of fire, having all your limbs chewed off by hungry bears, or being called on in class to explain the problem of evil. Those are all easy examples, but evil isn't limited to those; it includes anything and everything we don't like about the world. The basic question is simply this: if a perfect God made the world why didn't she/he/it make the world without all of these imperfections? This is only a problem for a religion that asserts there's only one God and this God is perfect in every way: perfectly good, perfectly powerful, perfectly knowing, etc.

One of the religions that was quite popular in Augustine's time was Manichaeism, based on the teachings of the prophet Mani, who maintained that there are exactly two Gods in the universe: one good and one bad, but both equally powerful and eternally at war with each other. These two Gods fight over everything, and the imperfect world we find ourselves in is just one of the consequences of this endless fight—like parents who despise each other, but still stay together in the ultimate nightmare of a passive-aggressive relationship, and one night they have a terrible fight and totally trash the house: that's the house you live in now, and that's all the explanation you need for why the world is such a mess. (Thanks, Mom and Dad!) The Manichaean solution to the problem of evil is: "God is not omnipotent, so you can't blame God for the evil in the world. There are actually two Gods—a good God and an evil God—and they have exactly the same amount of power so they are constantly fighting each other and the history of the world is the history of their battle. Sorry, that's just the way things are in this world that you fell into, and you'll have to deal with it, but at least theologians don't have to worry about solving the problem of evil any more." When Augustine was a student in Carthage, Manichaeism was far more popular than Christianity, and he himself was a big fan for several years before he converted to Christianity. Manichaeism was later designated by Christianity as a heresy, and Manichaeism as a religion has almost entirely disappeared, but the Manichaean worldview never went away. It's alive and well, for example, in the Marvel Cinematic Universe because a world in which good and evil forces are equally matched is perfect for keeping movie franchises going for eternity.

Manichaean theology completely eliminates the problem of evil, and that's probably one of its features that appealed to Augustine; but later, when he converted to Christianity (which maintains that there is exactly one God with unlimited power and no competition in the universe), Augustine had to come up with a solution to the problem of evil. He does this in three steps.

(1) First, he breaks evil down into two types: natural evil and moral evil.

(2) Natural evil is everything that we don't like about the natural world, such as earthquakes, floods, alligators, sharks and other animals that would be delighted to eat us, diseases such as cancer and athlete's foot, forest fires, and excessive humidity. Since a perfect God created the natural world it seems perfectly appropriate to ask: "Why didn't God do a better job? Why did God include all this stuff we don't like?" This question is one that we ask ourselves in some form probably every day so it's far from being an abstract or trivial theological question. For example, right now in the mountains of Montana, Erastus McUmber is being chased by four very hungry bears, one for each of his four limbs, and thinking to himself, "Why did God make bears who want to eat me? If I had created the world I would have left out the bears!"

Augustine solves the problem of natural evil with a stiff shot of pure Platonic Idealism. "If you complain about natural evil you are simply wrong," Augustine says. "There just isn't any; what you think is natural evil is only an illusion. As Plato explained, everything we think is real in the world of our experience is actually just a pale shadow and an imitation of the Forms, which are the true reality and which are beyond the world of our experience. If we complain about natural evil we are just like the poor idiots chained inside the cave who watch a parade of shadows all day and think they know what's real. Just as they are wrong, we are wrong if we think there's natural evil in the world that God created. In reality there's no evil at all in this world, there's only more or less good, and the fact that we can't see this is just one more symptom of our pathetic mortal condition and one more reason to convert to Christianity so that we can someday be rescued from this cave of ignorance and see things as they really are." And just like that (according to Augustine) all the natural evil we thought was in the world vanishes, and half of the problem of evil has been solved. (Thank you, Plato!)

(3) Moral evil is everything in the world we don't like that is the result of the choices and behavior of our fellow humans, for example: when one person chooses to insult or rob or murder another person or when the government of one country decides to send its citizens into battle or when a truly wicked person cuts right in front of me to steal

my parking place at Burger King. Augustine's solution to the problem of moral evil is closely connected to another big question that preoccupied him throughout his life: the nature of lust.

The first thing Augustine says about Carthage (where he went to college) is that it was a "hissing cauldron of lust"[2] (a description that could be applied to most college towns). Augustine was preoccupied with lust throughout his life; in fact, he says that he would have converted to Christianity much sooner if he had been willing to give up sex, but it was quite a while before he was willing to do that. He recounts how he would often pray, "Lord, grant me chastity and continence, but not yet."[3] *Confessions* book 2 is a good example of how Augustine connected the problem of lust with the problem of moral evil. Book 2 focuses on two things that happened when Augustine was sixteen years old: (1) he was a very lusty dude at this age—"the frenzy gripped me and I surrendered myself entirely to lust,"[4] he writes, and (2) he spends a lot of time analyzing a time when he and his gang of ne'er-do-well friends went out at night and stole a bunch of pears from a neighbor's tree. Augustine really wants to get to the bottom of this pear-stealing episode because he thinks it contains some important truths about the nature of all moral evil. He and his friends were not hungry when they stole the pears (they just threw them away), so why did they lust after these pears?

Augustine connects his own act of fruit-theft with another immoral act involving fruit: Eve's choice to eat the fruit from the Tree of Life in the garden of Eden even though God told her and Adam very clearly not to do this. This is the nature of all moral evil, Augustine concludes: it's simply disobedience. So what does this have to do with lust—the other topic that he analyzes at length in book 2, and in many other places in his writing? Lust, he argues, is the body refusing to obey the mind, and the experience of lust is meant to remind us of the fundamental nature of all moral evil: it comes from humans refusing to obey God. Lust is the body disobeying the mind, just like Adam and Eve disobeyed God in the garden of Eden, and just like everyone else disobeys God when they do something immoral. Augustine's solution to the problem of moral evil entails an ethical theory that's simply divine command morality: whatever God commands is right so ethics is simply obedience to God, just doing what God has told you to do; simple as that. This part of Augustine's

---

2. Augustine, *Confessions*, 55.
3. Augustine, *Confessions*, 169.
4. Augustine, *Confessions*, 44.

solution to the problem of evil was very much out of step with Plato. In his dialogue *Euthyphro* Plato has Socrates argue against divine command morality in such a convincing way that poor Euthyphro, who began the dialogue with perfect confidence in this theory, runs away in a panic after contradicting himself repeatedly. So Augustine's solution to the problem of natural evil (there isn't any, you're just perceiving the world wrong) is as Platonic as it could be, but his explanation of moral evil (there's a lot more than you thought, all of it caused by humans disobeying God, and the experience of lust is meant to remind us of this fact) is a complete divergence from Plato.

Augustine's *Confessions* is a terrific example of how philosophy and religion are entangled during the Middle Ages, and how they can be disentangled by a careful reader, such as you! The entire book is written as if in conversation with God, and much of the text is given over to the confession of what Augustine regards as a multitude of sins; but in the midst of all this there is also plenty of metaphysics, epistemology, and axiology. Book 11 is a good example of this. Here Augustine shows off his philosophy chops by creating his own theory of time. The argument for this theory is presented, as usual, in the form of a conversation with God (though it's not much of a conversation since Augustine does all the talking and God never replies), and in the end Augustine doesn't hesitate to extract a religious moral from his theory, but when you take away those two features of the presentation you're left with a straight-up theory of temporality that probably would have made Plato very happy.

Augustine begins with this simple question: "Where is there any duration or extension in our experience of time?" His answer: "Nowhere." Time only exists for humans in the present moment, and that moment is so fleeting it has no duration or extension at all. The past and future only exist as projections of the present moment (in the form of memory or anticipation), so although we like to think of ourselves as possessing all of our past and all of our future in a totality that feels like eternity (an illusion reinforced by every kind of clock ever invented, since clocks only measure space, not time), the truth is that all we have of time is a present moment that is so fleeting that it has no duration whatsoever. This is really pitiful and frankly an embarrassment, especially since humans find anything less than eternal, unchanging, permanence to be unsatisfactory (as Plato pointed out). This is where Augustine cashes in his theory of time for a religious payout: the time of mortality is a total disappointment to us, and the only solution to this problem is to convert to Christianity and thus eventually escape from time into eternity, which is what we really want.

Augustine's theory of time in *Confessions* book 11 is one example of a larger theme of his philosophy, which is his use of philosophy to argue that mortal life is a disaster. For example, when the city of Rome was successfully invaded by the Visigoths in AD 410 it demonstrated that the Roman Empire was clearly no longer the dominant superpower it had been for hundreds of years, and many people blamed this decline on Christianity, which had become the official religion of Rome in 380. Augustine wrote an entire book (*The City of God*) to defend Christianity against these attacks. The argument of the book, in a nutshell, is that the sack of Rome or any other calamity that occurs on Planet Earth is just a reminder that all of human life is one big calamity, and this is not Christianity's fault. On the contrary, Christianity should be thanked for revealing the truth of the human condition and explaining that no real happiness is possible as long as one is alive, and we should all be grateful for that clarification. Thus, the whole book is a sustained argument for philosophical pessimism. It's not that hard to be an average, everyday, lazy pessimist: just be cranky and start saying that everything sucks—congratulations, you're a pessimist. But to be a philosophical pessimist is harder work because you have to give philosophical arguments to support all your pessimistic conclusions, and these arguments can be based only on human experience and human reason: no revelations or any other appeals to authority allowed. Philosophical pessimism requires rational arguments, not just a bad mood.

Augustine's arguments for pessimism are presented in four stages in *The City of God*:

1. He summarizes some arguments from Greek and Roman philosophers that were explicitly pessimistic and agrees with these arguments completely.

2. He presents other arguments from Greek and Roman philosophers what were implicitly pessimistic, and then he extends and amplifies these arguments further.

3. He adds his own arguments for pessimism, which are mostly philosophical, though as usual in medieval philosophy there a few religious/theological assumptions and arguments tossed into the mix that we have to sort out.

4. As we should expect from someone whose day job is working as the Bishop of Hippo and who isn't getting paid to write philosophy books, Augustine will always find a way to extract a religious conclusion from any philosophical argument he creates, so the argument ends with a sales pitch directed at non-Christians arguing that even though no one can expect true and lasting happiness while they are alive, Christians can at least achieve something like peace. (We saw this with his theory of time in *Confessions* 11 too: even for a metaphysical theory concerning the true nature of time the moral of the story is going to be religious in nature—another argument for converting to Christianity, as Augustine himself did.)

Augustine experienced the transition from ancient to medieval philosophy in his own life and he practically begs us to adopt him as a tour guide to the strange world of medieval philosophy, so it seems crazy not to accept that invitation. Beginning a discussion of medieval philosophy with anyone other than Augustine is hard to imagine, but after Augustine it's entirely appropriate to jump around wildly within the 1,200 years of the Middle Ages, focusing on themes and arguments and not feeling constrained at all by linear time. So I'll begin doing that now, jumping from Augustine (354–430) to the story of Peter Abelard (1079–1142) and his student/girlfriend/wife/employee (in that order) Heloise d'Argenteuil (1100–1163).

Heloise and Abelard

Heloise and Abelard are both philosophers who created important philosophical theories, but those philosophical creations have been almost entirely upstaged by the story of their infamous teacher-student love affair. I'll recount that story because we can learn a lot from it about the challenges for both women and men who tried to think independently during the Middle Ages, and it also provides essential background for understanding the ideas of Abelard and Heloise. In addition to these decent and respectable pedagogical values it's also (let's be honest) just a truly awesome and entertaining story that's both comical and tragic: one of the best-known love stories of all time.

The most interesting person in this story is Heloise, and (as I'm sure you've noticed) she is also the first woman who has appeared so far in this summary of the history of philosophy because of the hilarious blind spot that philosophy tolerated for thousands of years: the bizarre idea that only men are capable of creating and understanding philosophical theories. The exclusion of women from philosophy is another example of comedy resulting from the distance between philosophy's ideal aspirations and its actual practice, and the case of Heloise demonstrates this comedy perfectly. What little we have of her very original thinking is preserved in letters that she wrote to Abelard, who was first her teacher, then her lover, then her husband, then her boss when they both became employees of the church. Heloise was one of the few women who managed to break through and have at least some of her ideas inscribed in the history of philosophy, and that's just one reason why this is such an awesome story—and here (finally) is that story, in very broad strokes.

Heloise was unusual first in that she was one of the few women in twelfth-century France who had a chance to get an advanced education. Her family sent her to Paris to live with her uncle Fulbert so that she would have access to the best possible tutors. Fulbert recruited Peter Abelard (age thirty-seven) for the job of tutoring his niece (age sixteen), and this probably had everything to do with the fact that at the time Abelard was the most famous philosopher in town. Fulbert does not seem to have been a deep thinker himself; his only thought seemed to be, "How can I capitalize on the intelligence of my niece to make myself and my family more respected and famous?" Since Abelard seemed to be the hottest commodity on the market at the time (a time when it was not completely ridiculous to refer to philosophers as hot commodities) Fulbert decided that he was the man for the job. Abelard accepted the job on the condition that he also be allowed to live in Fulbert's house, where Heloise also lived, so that it would be easier for him to (ahem) give lessons to his young student. This apparently raised no red flags in the mind of Fulbert, who we can now confidently say was definitely not a deep thinker since he agreed to this plan enthusiastically. Then, to absolutely no one's surprise (except perhaps Fulbert), Abelard promptly began to tutor Heloise not in philosophy but rather in sex, and began boasting about his hot new girlfriend who was twenty-one years younger than him, and started showing up to teach his classes exhausted and unprepared because he had been busy all night having sex with Heloise.

After a few months of this routine Heloise became pregnant and Abelard snuck her away to stay with his sister, where she gave birth to a son they named "Astralabe"—the name of a cutting-edge scientific instrument of the times which was used to measure the height of celestial bodies (sort of the twelfth-century equivalent of parents naming their child "iPhone" or "Large Hadron Particle Accelerator"). Fulbert apparently already knew about the affair before the child was born having walked in on Abelard and Heloise *in flagrante delicto* while they were (ahem) studying, and it seems like he wasn't particularly surprised and may have even been quite pleased since he thought this would guarantee that his niece would now become the wife of the famous Peter Abelard, thus securing for him and his family the fame that he craved; so when Heloise and Abelard did not make any move toward getting hitched only then did he get upset. (The opposition to marriage actually came entirely from Heloise, as we'll see later.) The couple finally did get married but they tried to keep the marriage a secret—and this was the last straw for Fulbert, because what's the point of your niece being married to a celebrity IF YOU HAVE TO KEEP IT A SECRET! This is when Fulbert decided that he had been so wronged by Abelard that the only way he could possibly get even was to send a gang of armed men into Abelard's bedroom while he slept to castrate him. Thus, Abelard explained, "they cut off the parts of my body with which I committed the wrong they complained of."[5]

Abelard's castration brought his affair with Heloise to an emphatic and unambiguous end, after which he entered a monastery as a monk and Heloise entered a monastery as a nun, and both of them remained in monasteries for the rest of their lives, but they also remained married to each other. Later in their monastic careers Abelard became Heloise's boss when the group of nuns that she led moved to a monastery that Abelard supervised, but they never met face to face again. They did, however, write a series of letters to each other fifteen years after their affair ended. This correspondence was catalyzed by a long letter that Abelard wrote to a friend ostensibly to console him when he had some problems, but Abelard decided that the best way to do this was to explain in detail how his own life had been much harder than his friend's, and so he composed a delightfully self-absorbed text called *The Calamities of Peter Abelard* which contained an account of his affair with Heloise and how that affair led to the loss of his testicles and (more importantly in his mind) his fame. The text of this letter become well known far and wide, which Peter Abelard did not exactly discourage. Eventually Heloise got her hands on a copy, and then wrote to Abelard to complain that his version of the

---

5. Abelard and Heloise, *Letters*, 18.

story was incomplete and inaccurate. This initiated a series of seven letters between the two which became one of the most famous he said/she said conversations of all time and also the source of everything we know about Heloise's thinking.

The story of Abelard and Heloise is certainly wild and raucous, full of sex and violence and kids named after scientific instruments, but beyond its purely sensational value what can we learn from it about philosophy in the Middle Ages? Here are just two noteworthy lessons:

(1) It is truly astounding to see how vain Peter Abelard was. He boasts about everything: his good looks, his vast intelligence, and even the extent of the calamities he suffered in his life. Apparently everything that happened was always all about him. Here's the gist of his affair with Heloise, according to him: He and Heloise had almost nonstop sex—because how could she resist him?—and his students were greatly disappointed because he started showing up for classes unprepared and exhausted, which deprived them of the opportunity to bask in his vast intelligence. He writes the following in *The Calamities of Peter Abelard*:

> There was in Paris a young woman by the name of Heloise. She was niece of one of the canons there called Fulbert, who doted on her and did everything he could to further her education. In her looks she was not the least of women, but in her learning she was supreme. As a gift for learning is so rare in a woman, it added all the more to her appeal and had already made her famous throughout the whole kingdom of France. Now, having carefully considered all the things that usually serve to attract a lover, I concluded that she was the best one to bring to my bed. I was sure it would be easy: I was famous myself at the time, young, and exceptionally good-looking, and could not imagine that any woman I thought worthy of my love would turn me down. But I thought that this particular girl would be even more likely to give in because of her knowledge and love of letters.[6]
>
> What more do I need to say? First we were joined in one house, then in one heart. Under the pretext of study, we had all our time free for love, and in our classroom all the seclusion love could ever want. With our books open before us, we exchanged more words of love than of lessons, more kisses than concepts. My hands wandered more to her breasts than our books, and love turned our eyes to each other more than reading kept them on the page. . . .

---

6. Abelard and Heloise, *Letters*, 10–11.

> But the more I was taken up with these pleasures, the less time I had for philosophy or teaching.... My lectures became lukewarm and slack, relying now on my past practice and not on my intelligence at all. I did everything by rote, repeating only what had been new years before. All my new work, such as it was, now went into writing love songs and not the mysteries of philosophy. Many of these songs are still popular, as you know, and are sung throughout the country, especially by those who like the sort of life I myself was living then. But what of my students? It is hard even to imagine their misery, their sorrow, their wails of lamentation when they understood what was preoccupying, or I should say, what was deranging my mind.[7]

Abelard was clearly a very intelligent dude, and he did make some important contributions particularly in the field of logic, but for someone studying philosophy today he's far more useful as a case study of a walking, talking blind spot. His vanity and his uncritical acceptance of the life of privilege he fell into as a man in a position of power in the world of institutional Christianity seemed to blind him to the inequalities inherent in his relationship with Heloise and also the strength of her ideas—some of which I'll summarize now.[8]

(2) All of the truly radical ideas that emerge as Heloise and Abelard discuss their affair and try to make sense of their lives come from Heloise. Abelard, in spite of his claim to be extraordinary in everything, espouses utterly conventional, predictable, and self-serving ideas about how to live, while Heloise is willing to question conventional thinking in every respect; so it's Heloise far more than Abelard who demonstrates what true philosophy looks like and how it survived in the Middle Ages in spite of all the prohibitions and limitations that made her own life so difficult. Here are just three of her truly radical arguments.

First, she argues that true love doesn't require the institutional authorization of marriage, that a relationship is best when it's an independent and individual creation rather than just a repetition of traditional norms.

> I never wanted anything in you
> but you alone,

---

7. Abelard and Heloise, *Letters*, 12.

8. Abelard's last words were "I don't know." This may have been the only time in his life that he said these words. (Davies, *Europe*, 687.)

> nothing of what you have
> but you yourself,
> never a marriage, never a dowry,
> never any pleasure, any purpose of my own—
> as you well know—
> but only yours.
> The name of wife may have the advantages
> of sanctity and safety, but to me
> the sweeter name will always be *lover*
> or, if your dignity can bear it,
> *concubine* or *whore*.[9]

Heloise points out that Abelard left out most of her arguments against marriage when he summarized the "calamaties" of his life. Her arguments fundamentally boiled down to this one foundational idea: "I preferred love over marriage, freedom over a chain."[10] She remained faithful to Abelard throughout her life, she writes, but she did this as a continuing free choice and not because she feared defying some institutional or traditional norm. So when she says she would rather be Abelard's "concubine or whore" rather than his wife it's not an argument for promiscuity; it's an argument in a very existential spirit for creating meaning and value with completely free choices.

Second, she's willing to criticize institutional religion even when she depends on it for her survival. Philosophy, of course, is not the sworn enemy of religion and there's nothing about any critique of religion that makes it automatically philosophical, but in Heloise's case there are good reasons for regarding her critique of Christianity as an impressive display of independent philosophical thinking. After her affair with Abelard she entered a monastery and lived the rest of her life as a nun, depending on the church for everything. However, this did not stop her from thinking critically about the principles and the traditions of the religion that employed her and certainly had the ability to destroy her life. Even though it was extremely imprudent to do so, she argued that God was neither consistent nor just in the punishments inflicted on them:

> O, the ungodly savagery of God, if I may say it!
> The mercilessness of his mercy![11]

---

9. Abelard and Heloise, *Letters*, 55.
10. Abelard and Heloise, *Letters*, 56.
11. Abelard and Heloise, *Letters*, 74.

> When we were still pursuing the joys of love
> and—to use an ugly but a more expressive phrase—abandoning
> ourselves to fornication,
> God spared us his hard judgment.
> But when we took steps to correct what we had done,
> to cover the illicit with the licit
> and repair our fornication with the proper rites of marriage, the
> Lord raised up an angry hand against us
> and struck our now-chaste bed when he had winked
> at our unchaste bed for so long before.[12]

She also argued that Christianity seems terrified of women and depicts them as the natural enemy of men. She expresses this criticism in a decidedly ironic tone:

> But *me*—
> Was it my sorry birthright to become the cause of evil,
> the well-known curse of womankind
> to lead the greatest men to greatest ruin?[13]
>
> Oh yes,
> the great Seducer in his cunning
> knew one thing well, and that from long experience:
> the easiest path to ruin for men
> is always through their wives.
> So, when he would extend his well-known malice
> to our own time and found a man
> he could not bring down through fornication,
> he tempted him with marriage instead,
> using good to work his evil,
> now that evil was denied him for the purpose.[14]

Again, this criticism is philosophical not because it's directed against religion but because it demonstrates independent thinking and bravery. Heloise isn't intimidated into accepting institutional Christianity as an authority that cannot be questioned even though institutional Christianity did have almost complete power over her own life at the time.

Third, she's willing to question the assumption—firmly established in both the religion and the general culture of the time—that the mind and the body are completely at odds and the body is the enemy in this

---

12. Abelard and Heloise, *Letters*, 75.
13. Abelard and Heloise, *Letters*, 76.
14. Abelard and Heloise, *Letters*, 77–78.

perpetual war. Abelard explains in his second letter to Heloise that getting castrated was the best thing that happened to him. God did him a great favor when He relieved him of his testicles:

> I was lessened in that part of my body where lust had its dominion and desire its root cause, to become a greater man in many ways. What justice that those organs should lament all they had done to us and expiate in pain when they had sinned in taking pleasure, cutting me off from the loathsome filth in which I had been sunk to leave me circumcised in mind as well as body. It then would make me only the more fit to approach the altar of God with no stain of pollution in my flesh to call me back again. ... I was purged, not deprived, of those organs—so vile they are called the parts of shame for what they do and have no proper name of their own—and the grace of God did nothing else but rid me of corruption to leave me purified and clean.[15]

All wise men, Abelard argues, long to be castrated, and some (such as Origen) even do the job themselves.[16]

Abelard's conviction that his body was the enemy of his soul is an extreme example of mind-body dualism, a metaphysical theory that was certainly not limited to the Middle Ages. In those rare moments when women were allowed to speak in the early history of philosophy they often criticized this theory, and Heloise is one example of this. A more nuanced view of how the mind and body relate to each other is possible, Heloise suggests. Writing to her now-castrated husband (a monk who lives in a monastery) Heloise (a nun who also lives in a monastery) has the audacity to say to him that she wishes he had not been castrated and that they could still have sex, and also that she doesn't think sex and spirituality are incompatible in any way:

> For me,
> the pleasures we shared in love were sweet,
> so sweet
> they cannot displease me now,
> and rarely are they ever out of mind.
> Wherever I turn, they are there before my eyes
> with all their old desires.
> I see their images even in my sleep.
> During Holy Mass itself,

---

15. Abelard and Heloise, *Letters*, 95–96.
16. Abelard and Heloise, *Letters*, 96.

> when prayer should be its purest,
> unholy fantasies of pleasure so enslave my wretched soul that
> my devotion is to *them* and not my prayers: when I ought to
> groan for what I have done,
> I sigh for what I have lost.[17]

Heloise was not allowed to develop her thinking on these topics any further since Abelard—her husband and her boss—chastised her and told her not to say another word about them, so once again philosophy missed out on an opportunity to expand its horizons and correct one of its blind spots because women were not allowed to join the conversation. This is sad, and also very funny. The supremely self-confident Peter Abelard, who thought his student/girlfriend/wife/employee had no interesting ideas, is one of the most comical figures in the history of philosophy.

Islamic Philosophy (especially Al-Ghazali and Averroes)

Thus far in this very fragmentary summary of medieval philosophy we've discussed only philosophers in the Christian tradition. Although Christianity was certainly the religion most interested in shopping at the philosophy store during the Middle Ages and the majority of medieval philosophers did come from the Christian tradition, Christianity was not the only game in town. Both the Islamic and the Jewish traditions also developed an infatuation with philosophy during the Middle Ages, though in both cases it turns out to be a passing crush that fades away after a few hundred years whereas Christianity's love affair with philosophy persists throughout the Middle Ages and into the present day. So we'll come back to the Christian tradition later in this chapter but for now let's give Christianity a rest and consider the Islamic and Jewish traditions. In both of these philosophy flourishes for a few hundred years before it loses its appeal, and in that time there are interesting debates about the correct balance between faith and reason. In the Islamic tradition perhaps the most interesting and entertaining of these debates takes place between Al-Ghazali and Averroes.

Islam arrives on the scene about six hundred years after Christianity and the Islamic world doesn't start to take an interest in philosophy until the ninth and tenth centuries. By that time Aristotle had surpassed Plato as the superstar of the medieval philosophy world throughout

17. Abelard and Heloise, *Letters*, 79–80.

every religious tradition, including Islam; so when Al-Ghazali attacks philosophy in his delightfully titled *The Incoherence of the Philosophers* and Averroes defends philosophy against Al-Ghazali's criticisms in his even more delightfully titled *The Incoherence of the Incoherence*, they are mostly arguing for and against Aristotle's philosophy.

Al-Ghazali's approach is to argue that Aristotle broke his own rules. If Aristotle had written a rule book for philosophy the first two rules would be:

> Rule #1: Argue for everything—give good reasons to support every conclusion.

> Rule #2: In your arguments don't contradict yourself. (Aristotle called this "the principle of excluded middle," meaning statements are true, or they're false, and there's no middle ground between the two.)

In *The Incoherence of the Philosophers* Al-Ghazali argues that all philosophers, and especially Aristotle, break these simple rules. All philosophers contradict themselves and are therefore incoherent, which is pretty much the most serious crime that a philosopher could commit. Al-Ghazali believes that philosophy poses a serious threat to Islam and he calls upon all Muslims to band together to gang up on philosophy and send it back to Greece. Averroes on the other hand argues that philosophy is so essential to religion that God commands all good Muslims to study philosophy. (That would certainly make a great marketing campaign for any philosophy department: "God commands you to take this class!") So Averroes is the polar opposite of Al-Ghazali in his attitude toward philosophy: he not only loves it, he thinks it's essential.

This twelfth-century debate about the place of philosophy within Islam may seem dated and irrelevant but it remains about as good as it gets in terms of clarifying the fundamental issues for anyone interested in a possible partnership between faith and reason. Al-Ghazali gives reasoned arguments and not just an angry rant for his conclusion that philosophy is not just distasteful, or unpleasant, or lacking in dignity, but actually incoherent. Coherence and good arguments matter to philosophy, so if he can prove with good arguments that philosophy is incoherent, then philosophy will have been hoisted by its own petard! Averroes on the other hand argues that not only is philosophy compatible with Islam, studying philosophy is actually a requirement of Islam. There was certainly much more to Islamic philosophy than just this debate between Al-Ghazali and Averroes but their arguments about the compatibility of philosophy and religion remain very valuable because they transcend the limits of any particular religion.

It's also interesting to note that the Islamic tradition voted decisively on the side of Al-Ghazali and the brief period in which Islam showed an interest in philosophy came to an end shortly after Al-Ghazali and Averroes fired off their respective charges of incoherence at each other. But Averroes remained important in the Christian tradition even after Islam lost its interest in philosophy. His commentaries on the texts of Aristotle were so highly esteemed that Thomas Aquinas refers to him simply as "The Commentator," just he refers to Aristotle as "The Philosopher," and in each case everyone knew exactly who he was talking about.

Jewish Philosophy (especially Moses Maimonides)

In the Jewish tradition, as in the Islamic world, an interest in philosophy appeared relatively late in the Middle Ages and didn't persist. The most famous Jewish philosopher was Moses Maimonides, and his most famous work was another book with a delightful and unforgettable title: *The Guide for the Perplexed*. In this book Maimonides tries to reconcile the three sources of knowledge that often seemed totally at odds with each other in his time: divine revelation (through scripture and prophecy); human reason (which includes philosophy); human experience (Maimonides was a medical doctor and he has great respect for empirical data and science). Trying to reconcile these was a rather heroic task, and to make it even more interesting Maimonides thought that the best way to do this was through a method of indirect communication. He believed that the ultimate truths of both Judaism and philosophy were esoteric truths and therefore needed to be communicated in a sort of code rather than in plain and simple exoteric language that everyone could understand. For example, parts of *The Guide for the Perplexed* directly contradicted other parts of the book—something that Maimonides fully acknowledged. Religion and science and philosophy are all completely compatible he argues, but the pathway that will lead you to discover their compatibility cannot be communicated directly without destroying it, so it can only be communicated indirectly in a kind of code.

One aspect of this esoteric presentation is Maimonides's argument that any attributes of God can only be named negatively. In other words, we can only say what God is not; we can't say what God is. It's impossible to summarize in a direct, exoteric way any esoteric work; the whole idea is that the reader must wrestle with the text on her own in order to extract whatever secrets it contains. But Maimonides's famous arguments for negative theology are perhaps a good hint at the way this particular guide for the perplexed is supposed to work: the book will show you not what the correct balance of religion, science and philosophy is, but only what it is not, and that will enable you to discover the higher esoteric truth on your own. Effectively *The Guide for the Perplexed* says to the reader: "So you think you're perplexed now? Great! Read me and I'll make you even more perplexed by showing you what you are not looking for; but this experience will be good for you because if you master this secret code you will be enabled to emerge from your perplexity and discover the higher, esoteric truth about the perfect compatibility of philosophy, religion, and science for yourself!"

Mysticism, and a few women who managed to make themselves heard: Bonaventure, Hildegard of Bingen, Teresa of Avila

An esoteric approach such as Maimonides adopted in *The Guide for the Perplexed* isn't mysticism, but it may seem very close to it. Maimonides didn't inform his readers that they would be required to have some kind of mystical experience before his conclusions would make sense to them; instead he simply wrote his arguments in a way that required the reader to do additional purely rational and non-mystical work on her own. In this way esoteric writing such as *The Guide for the Perplexed* continues to follow all the rules of the philosophy game, one of which is: present your arguments in a way that enables everyone to understand them purely through their own independent thinking. Mysticism breaks this rule because it imposes an additional requirement that goes beyond rational, independent thinking: now a mystical experience is required to make sense of the ideas and arguments presented. Since philosophy was already breaking one of its cardinal rules in the Middle Ages when it allowed itself to become the subordinate and employee of religion it's not surprising that there was a willingness to look the other way when some mysticism also began to creep into medieval philosophy—just one more mistake that philosophy tolerated in the Middle Ages.

The ideas, practices, and experiences of mysticism are not limited to religion; they can be applied to love, justice, forgiveness, and basically all questions of meaning and value. To make things easier on ourselves we'll limit our study of medieval mysticism to just one author: Bonaventure, but this one author makes it clear that there are many varieties of mysticism and therefore many possibilities for mystics to misunderstand each other. Bonaventure outlines six different versions of mysticism, which are not limited to religion; they are, for example, quite prevalent in human relationships where they lead to all sorts of misunderstandings between people. Bonaventure says there are six versions of mysticism, which correspond to the six stages in his book *The Mind's Journey into God*, and he argues that you should use these six stages like rungs on a ladder to climb up to the final mystical union with God; but especially in the world of love and relationships people often camp out at one of these stages instead of continuing to climb.

1. "Sense/sensation": falling in love with particular physical properties of particular physical things in the physical world. For example: "I love your toes, your nose, your shoes, your stamp collection, your flat-screen TV, your kitchen, your microwave oven."

2. "Imagination": abstracting and generalizing from the properties of particular physical things to fall in love with general properties of many physical things. For example: "I love all toes, all noses, all shoes, all stamp collections, all flat-screen TVs, all kitchens that are bright yellow, all Panasonic microwave ovens." (These first two stages are focused on the external, physical world.)

3. "Reason": the basic rules of logic, and the ability to follow an argument. For example: "I love the principle of non-contradiction! I love formal logic! I love math!" (This is a very nerdy kind of love. Instead of focusing on the world of physical things it focuses on the internal operations of thought, especially the most basic operations that allow for certainty.)

4. "Understanding": reason in a more complete and diversified sense, everything that thought is capable of, not just its most basic operations. For example: "I love informal logic! I love social, political, and aesthetic theories! I love theoretical discussions of art and politics

and all other values even if they don't lead to perfect certainty!" (Stages 3 and 4 turn away from the world into the mind itself.)

The last two stages focus outward and upward to a higher, transcendent reality. For Bonaventure this higher reality is God, but it could also be another person as long as that person is idealized, understood as something much more than a physical body, or it could be an idea or some other reality as long as it's understood as a transcendent ideal of perfection, like God.

5. "Intelligence": the first stage of contemplating another person, or some other idea or thing, as a transcendent and perfect ideal. For example: "I love you because you are perfect in every way, and any appearance of imperfection is simply an illusion."

6. "The summit of the mind": this form of idealism is so extreme that it leaves language behind, so we can only say what it is not. Bonaventure's example is the mystery of the Trinity: understanding that God is both One and Three. In normal human language this is incoherent, but at this super-elevated level of idealism it makes perfect sense.

There's an obvious Platonic inspiration for Bonaventure's mystical ladder, and no doubt you were immediately reminded of the theory of love Plato presented in *Symposium* when you read the six steps above. But this is a good time to remind ourselves that Plato himself was not a mystic, just as he was not a Christian. Medieval philosophy that spins Plato's philosophy as mysticism is just one more interpretation and appropriation of Plato's philosophy, and obviously it doesn't take much imagination to do this—which is why Plato's philosophy was such a hot commodity in the Middle Ages.

Mysticism clearly breaks one of the rules of the philosophy game, but arguably all of medieval philosophy breaks at least one of these rules so it's best to study all of it with a charitable spirit and try to learn what we can from it in spite of its rule-breaking, outlaw character. In this spirit one charitable interpretation of why mysticism flourished in medieval philosophy is that it provided a means for people who had been excluded from philosophy to make their voices heard. This seems especially relevant in the case of several women who used mysticism to break into the philosophical conversation, and two particularly interesting case studies of this phenomenon are Hildegard of Bingen and Teresa of Avila. Both of these women were nuns, living in monasteries, and both of them reported having mystical experiences that were revelatory. In other words, their mystical experiences communicated ideas to them—they claimed to have learned important truths from these experiences and they sought to teach these truths to others. People listened to them because they claimed that their ideas were revealed to them through mystical experiences. Would anyone have listened to the ideas of these two women if they had not said anything about mystical experience and revelation, if they had simply said: "Here are some interesting and insightful philosophical theories that we—two people who happen to be women—have created on our own"? That seems unlikely. So one possible explanation for some medieval mysticism is that some clever women recognized that it was a way to make themselves heard—it was a way to become visible during a time when philosophy was handicapped by a massive blind spot which made women invisible.

In the history of philosophy every time a woman manages to be heard she points out some enormous blind spots that the men who were running the show totally ignored. For example: unlike pretty much all medieval philosophers before them (except for Heloise), Hildegard and Teresa argued for the integration of mind and body, and also reason and emotion. All the men in medieval philosophy were profoundly allergic to the human body and to all human emotions (except perhaps arrogance and self-satisfaction), and wanted nothing to do with either. Hildegard and Teresa, however, argue that both mind and body and emotion and reason can work together in a complementary and harmonious fashion, which shows much they were willing to depart from the (male) mainstream in their ideas about the perennial questions concerning the relationship between body and mind, and feeling and thinking.

Back to the Christian Tradition: Anselm

In what remains of this very scrappy summary of medieval philosophy we'll return to where we started: philosophy deployed in the service of Christianity. This was by far the dominant strain of medieval philosophy from beginning to end. All of medieval philosophy is characterized by the attempt to make philosophy a tool and a servant of religion and Christianity was not the only religion that attempted this marriage, but it was the first to do so and also the most persistent. As you've no doubt noticed, philosophy in the Christian tradition was practiced mostly by bishops, priests, monks, and other full-time employees of the church, and one very common practice (you might even call it a hobby) of these church employees was to use philosophy to prove the existence of God. (This could be seen as the ultimate expression of gratitude to their employer.) Many different proofs for the existence of God were proposed in the Christian tradition, but certainly one of the most interesting and memorable proofs was the one proposed by Anslem, who was employed by the church as the Archbishop of Canterbury.

Anselm proposed a proof for the existence of God based purely on *a priori* logic. The "prior" in "*a priori*" means that it uses only evidence that's prior to experience. Throughout the Middle Ages there are also numerous attempts to prove the existence of God in an *a posteriori* way too, which is just a sexy way of saying "based on evidence that occurs after (posterior to) experience"—in other words, empiricism. That's what Aquinas will try to do, as we'll see shortly, because (like the good Aristotelian that he is) he thinks that's the best approach to everything. What exactly is prior to experience, you may ask? A truly committed empiricist (when you read the next chapter on modern philosophy, you'll meet a lot of them) would reply: "Absolutely nothing, you dumbass." But Anselm is no empiricist, so he would not reply in such a rude and obnoxious manner. Anselm thinks you can create a complete and thoroughly convincing proof for the existence of The Lord God Almighty that does not require any empirical evidence whatsoever and therefore should be compelling for everyone based on nothing more than self-evident logic. That's the great appeal of *a priori* arguments: they allow you to say, triumphantly, "If you are not convinced by this argument you are just stupid." *A priori* arguments can also be very attractive because they appeal to the laziness in all of us: an *a priori* proof can be done completely in your head as you lie comfortably in bed with your eyes closed and your head resting on your favorite pillow. There's no need to get out of bed on a cold morning in January, stumble into your clothes and venture out into the bleak and unwelcoming physical world to gather empirical evidence; *a priori* proofs can be done entirely within the warm and comfortable space of your own mind.

Here's how you can prove the existence of God without lifting a finger or opening an eye and using nothing but logic, according to Anselm:

No doubt you've got all sorts of thoughts in your head that I don't know about but here's one thought that I'm sure you have in your personal collection: God is that than which nothing greater can be conceived. This is nothing more than the correct definition of God, according to Christian theology, so if you don't possess this thought then I must say it's hard for me to imagine how you pulled that off while living in a Christian country in Europe in the eleventh century, which is when I came up with this proof. But if you did somehow manage to make it through life so far without acquiring this thought, then we can easily correct that now. Here you go: God is that than which nothing greater can be conceived. Now you have the thought in your mind too and as soon as you do have that thought this *a priori* proof of God's existence is effectively already over, because obviously the greatest conceivable being necessarily exists. A being which is quite awesome in many ways and yet does not actually exist, like the unicorn I'm thinking about right now which can speak seven languages and is also proficient in trigonometry and can dance the tarantella—that's a truly awesome unicorn; however, this unicorn does not exist, so it's obviously not the greatest conceivable unicorn. And remember, according to the thought which you yourself now have in your head, God is not just quite awesome or more impressive than a very well-educated unicorn; God is BY DEFINITION the greatest conceivable being among ALL beings. In this way the existence of God can be proven by simple logic: all you need is the correct definition of God, which Christianity has graciously provided for you, and then any logical person can easily deduce that God necessarily exists.[18]

It should be noted that Anselm's proof is perhaps the greatest conceivable demonstration of the gap between an abstract, philosophical argument about God and the way that almost every human being who believes in God understands and experiences their faith. In Christianity and every other religion faith for the truly faithful has everything to do with emotion and personal spiritual experiences and almost exactly nothing to do with abstract reasoning. Anselm presents a proof for the existence of God that's purely a logical exercise, but for almost everyone in the history of the world religious faith is developed through emotional and spiritual experiences that are carefully crafted by religious authorities

---

18. Actually that was entirely me talking, doing my best to paraphrase Anselm's argument. See Anselm's *Monologion* and *Proslogion* for his own words.

and by the families that people happen to fall into. Medieval philosophy mostly connects with religion at the very extreme edges of purely logical or rational approaches to faith, and Anselm's proof is a marvelous example of that. Anselm seems to suggest that anyone who reads his proof would immediately say: "Well I'll be goddamned. I thought I didn't believe in God but now I understand that atheism would make me illogical, and I certainly don't want to be illogical, so I guess I do actually believe in God—or I should say, I don't just believe that God exists, I know it—so don't you dare call me irrational!" Has anyone ever, in the history of the world, experienced this sort of conversion through pure logic? It seems unlikely. At any rate, Anselm's proof demonstrates how much fun medieval philosophers had applying philosophy to theology, and also how irrelevant these arguments could be to the actual lived religious experience of the faithful.

Thomas Aquinas

Just as it's hard to imagine beginning an outline of medieval philosophy with anyone other than Augustine, it also seems inconceivable not to end with anyone other than Aquinas. More than any other author in the medieval period Aquinas manifests the firm conviction that the marriage of philosophy and religion can not only be saved—this marriage can flourish! "Philosophy and religion really can live happily ever after," Aquinas effectively proclaims, "and if you want proof, just look at my *Summa Theologica*, where I solved every possible theological problem using philosophy and religion in a perfect and powerful partnership: truly a demonstration of what an ideal marriage looks like!"

Aquinas was audacious enough to claim that he had in fact written "the sum of all theology": a complete catalog of every possible theological question, along with a decisive and authoritative answer to each. Throughout *Summa Theologica* he demonstrates the greatest confidence in reason and philosophy by starting every question with the strongest possible arguments against his own conclusion; then he doesn't just refute those opposing arguments, he effectively makes them disappear by showing how any arguments that seem to be opposed to his own theory actually are not at all opposed if you just understand them correctly. In this way Aquinas attempts to create a grand synthesis of all the authorities that medieval philosophy wants to hold onto: Greek philosophers;

church authorities; revealed scripture; and also his own fantastic intelligence: God's gift to humanity. Aquinas creates a version of religion that is about as philosophical as it could possibly be: the knowledge of God is attained through an operation of the speculative intellect, and the highest form of human happiness is contemplation, just like Aristotle said. This is a religion where philosophers will feel right at home, and it's a reminder of how philosophy during the Middle Ages was more powerful than it had ever been before or ever would be again. (If you were looking for a job in philosophy there was no better time to be alive.)

The *Summa Theologica* is a very big book (over three thousand pages if it's printed in a font that remains legible to humans), and Aquinas also wrote several other big books to go along with it, so clearly he gave us plenty of material to choose from; but his arguments on just two topics are enough to capture the style and the spirit of his philosophy (which is all this extremely fragmentary and scrappy summary of medieval philosophy is trying to accomplish). So instead of trudging through all of the 512 questions that Aquinas claims to answer definitively in the *Summa*, we'll just look at two.

(1) Question: Can the existence of God be proven? Answer: Yes! But only with the right kind of proof.

Not surprisingly, Aquinas has his own proof of God's existence—or more accurately five proofs, since he's a bit of a show-off. But before he presents his proofs he first takes time to argue against the method of proving God's existence through logic alone, which we saw in Anselm. Like the true disciple of Aristotle that he is (throughout his writing he refers to Aristotle with the shorthand "The Philosopher," making no effort at all to conceal which team he is on), Aquinas insists that the only way to prove the existence of God is through the *a posteriori* effects of God's existence and not through any sort of *a priori* close-your-eyes-and-just-use-logic approach. You can't prove that God exists using logic alone, Aquinas argues, but you can prove God's existence if you reason from the effects of that existence; and those effects are so plentiful that you can easily crank out at least five different proofs that God exists without breaking a sweat, which is exactly what he does. All of these proofs follow the same pattern and the same logic: there are abundant phenomena abundantly available in the world that can only be explained as the effects of a very particular cause, and this cause (everyone understands) is God.

This pattern of reasoning is borrowed directly from Aristotle, who of course was not a Christian and never made any attempt to prove the existence of any God, but who did emphatically believe that an infinite regress of causes was absurd and consequently there had to be a first cause to explain the numerous phenomena that fill our everyday experience. For example, every movement that we have ever observed we understand to have been caused by some previous movement, but that movement also had to be caused by some previous movement, so to explain the existence of movement—which must be explained since it obviously exists—you can posit an infinite regress of one movement causing another movement (which Aristotle believes is patently absurd, as are all infinite regresses), or there must be an original first mover which starts the chain of causation that results in every other movement but is itself unmoved. Thus, Aristotle concludes, reasoning from observable effects backwards to the necessary causes that those effects require, there is necessarily an unmoved mover. QED. All Aquinas has to do to turn this proof of an unmoved mover into a proof for the existence of God is add: "And this everyone understands to be God." Aristotle's unmoved mover becomes the Unmoved Mover (aka God) of Christian theology. Of course such a proof tells you nothing about the qualities or attributes of God, just that God exists; "but," Aquinas says, "I never claimed to prove anything more than that." God must exist because that's the only possible explanation for the existence of movement, which obviously exists because we observe it constantly. Aquinas finds this method of proving God's existence to be almost embarrassingly easy and so he tosses off four more proofs using the same logic and gives every indication that he could easily toss of fifty-nine more in the same style while standing on his head, but chooses not to out of decency.

Numerous medieval philosophers offered proofs of God's existence; the proofs authored by Anselm and Aquinas were probably the most famous but they were not the only ones. The very idea that the existence of God can be proven using philosophical arguments, and doesn't have to remain a matter of faith, shows how much medieval theologians had faith in philosophy, and how committed they were to the idea that philosophy should be used to solve theological problems. The belief that God wanted humans to use philosophy whenever it was enough to answer a question (such as "Does God exist?") or solve a problem (like the problem of evil), and that in those cases God would not provide a revelation or any other divine assistance to help us lazy humans who are perfectly capable of working things out on our own just using our own wits—it was this conviction more than any other that kept the Christian tradition coming back to philosophy throughout the Middle Ages. Aquinas was profoundly influenced by Aristotle and not particularly impressed by Plato, while Augustine was deeply in love with Plato's philosophy and didn't much care for Aristotle; but aside from the particular tastes in Greek philosophy that these two thinkers at the beginning and the end of the medieval period harbored, they and every other medieval philosopher in the Christian tradition believed that philosophy was a tool God wanted them to use whenever they could, and they used that tool enthusiastically and confidently, even to the point of claiming that they could prove the existence of God and thus make faith in God unnecessary.

(2) Question: Are the laws of morality so perfectly rational that they are inscribed right in the book of nature itself, so any rational person can simply read the laws of good and bad conduct for himself, and no faith at all is required? Answer: Yes!

"Natural law" is a natural extension of "natural theology": the idea that God doesn't have to reveal a thing (in this area at least) because you can figure it all out just using your own mind. Natural law extends this paradigm into the secular/social/political sphere, where religious faith is not a requirement. All natural law is written in the book of nature, just waiting for you to read it. No religious faith is required to read this book; it makes perfect sense to everyone. Natural law theory began with Aristotle, but after Aquinas this theory really takes off and it could be the area where Aquinas has had the most impact on the secular world. This theory claims to transform what most people thought was an inherently subjective business—creating laws that reflect all important human values and that are fair and just to everyone—into something more objective, much more like a natural science. The idea is that human laws don't need to be created, they just need to be discovered; they are already there inscribed in the book of nature just like all the laws of the physical sciences. If that's true it would certainly make the business of government much easier and much more confidence-inspiring for everyone, since legislation would be just as objective as physics, or biology, or chemistry. But is it true?

Natural law certainly sounds appealing since it claims to turn ethics into something like a natural science, and thereby eliminate all the conflict and controversy in the sphere of ethics—which is where all conflict and controversy always reside. Just like physics, biology, and chemistry produce objective results about objective facts in the objective universe simply by reading carefully the book of nature, ethics could now do likewise. Wouldn't that be wonderful! This vision of an uncontroversial, objective ethics has animated fans of natural law theory ever since the time of Aristotle, but it's only fair to balance this theoretical enthusiasm by noting that ever since the time of Aristotle natural law theory has in practice been used to support and justify some profoundly terrible beliefs and practices. Aristotle, for example, casually and confidently asserted in his *Politics* that there are obviously natural differences between different classes of people: for example, that Greek men were suited by nature to be in charge of everyone else, including women, children, and non-Greek humans who were by nature slaves. This was all so completely obvious and self-evident, Aristotle thought, that it didn't even require any argument, thereby demonstrating the great Achilles heel of natural law theory: it has proven to be extremely difficult for humans to distinguish between what is truly natural and what is merely traditional. The social stratification and rigid class structure that Aristotle argued was an objective fact of the natural world just happened to be exactly the social stratification and rigid class structure that Aristotle fell into when he was born as a Greek man, and he just happened to benefit from that same social stratification and rigid class structure immensely since it stipulated that everyone worked for him, including his wife and his household slaves. Thus, natural law theory has in practice often been put to work to defend an obviously oppressive and unjust status quo. Aquinas seemed to think that any practical failures in the application of natural law theory do not detract from the truth of the theory itself, so his enthusiasm for natural law theory remained undiminished almost 1,500 years after Aristotle first proposed the theory. But after reviewing natural law theory's checkered history of defending the indefensible one could also conclude that it's simply based on faulty assumptions such as the assumption that values are objective facts that are capable of being inscribed in the objective book of nature.

Boethius

Even though Aquinas is clearly the most obvious choice if you're looking for something like an apex or a culmination of medieval philosophy, and even though just a few pages ago I said that it's inconceivable to end a survey of medieval philosophy with any other author, nevertheless I'm going to do just that. I'm going to give the very last word to an author from much earlier in the Middle Ages—all the way back to AD 523, not very long after Augustine died (in AD 430). I've jumped around in a very casual and carefree manner in this very fragmentary and incomplete outline since my goal was only to capture the style and spirit of medieval philosophy and thus hopefully inspire you to study this period more deeply on your own. With that goal in mind I'll conclude this chapter with Boethius, because if someone put a gun to my head and demanded: "Tell me right now which one book captures best the strange and wonderful quality of philosophy in the Middle Ages or I will shoot you dead!" (this did actually happen to me once; it's quite an interesting story . . .)—the answer I would give without a moment's hesitation is: *The Consolation of Philosophy* by Boethius.

Boethius wrote *The Consolation of Philosophy* while he was in prison for a crime (treason) that he didn't commit, and it was the last book he wrote because he was found guilty of the crime that he didn't commit and then executed. Boethius died in his mid-forties but he still managed to accomplish quite a bit in his short life, including serving as a Roman senator and several other high offices in the Roman government, including consul, and he also wrote four other philosophy books. The most impressive and revealing fact of his life, however, is the goal he set for himself of demonstrating that the philosophies of Plato and Aristotle and the theology of Christianity were all totally in harmony with each other. He didn't live to realize this lofty ambition, but just the fact that he thought it was possible and made it his goal captures so perfectly the spirit of medieval philosophy that drove Boethius and many others to attempt such a grand synthesis and reconciliation.

When he finds himself in prison and likely expected that at the end of his imprisonment he would be executed (apparently he had made himself very unpopular in the Roman court by speaking out against the rampant corruption of government officials), Boethius decides that this is the perfect time to write a philosophy book. In *The Consolation of Philosophy* he tells the story of being visited in prison by Lady Philosophy:

philosophy personified and embodied in the form of a woman—so here we have one more woman who managed to sneak into medieval philosophy, and arguably the most spectacular example![19] Lady Philosophy and Boethius spend the entire book in philosophical conversation inside Boethius's prison cell. This is all described in such a matter-of-fact manner that it seems plausible that Boethius wanted readers to understand these conversations not as works of imagination but rather as a dialogue that really happened—because it is possible to engage in a conversation with philosophy even while you are completely alone in a prison cell since philosophy is nothing more than thinking for yourself about the ultimate nature of reality, knowledge, and values. Boethius and Lady Philosophy devote their conversation to applying philosophy to the injustices and disappointments of his life (lots of classic Greek and Roman stoicism here), and also to solving and unravelling complicated knots in Christian theology such as the problem of evil and the apparent incompatibility of human free will and divine foreknowledge. In brief, Boethius finds consolation in philosophy first because philosophy explains to him how he can remain calm and in control of his life even now while he's in prison awaiting execution, and second because philosophy can resolve even the most difficult questions and problems presented by Christian theology. All of this is consoling, reassuring, and empowering, even to someone in prison waiting to die. In *The Consolation of Philosophy* we see Boethius doing on a small scale what he aspired to do on a much grander scale if he had had the chance to live a little longer: demonstrate that the philosophies of Plato and Aristotle and the theology of Christianity were all in harmony with each other; that they could all work together to resolve the mysteries of life and provide consolation and confidence as one neared death. I can't imagine a better picture of the style and spirit of medieval philosophy than that.

The confidence in the medieval marriage of philosophy and religion that Boethius expressed in AD 523 was still very much alive and kicking in the thirteenth century when Thomas Aquinas used philosophy as his chief tool for solving (according to him) every theological problem that there was. Medieval philosophy was permeated by the belief that the marriage of philosophy and religion could work and that this couple could live happily ever after. For more than 1,200 years philosophy and religion attempted to make this marriage work, but eventually and inevitably

---

19. Boethius, *Consolation*, 2.

it had to come to an end. This is not to say that religion—or any other institution, or discipline, or human project in any form—should be prohibited from using philosophy as a tool to achieve its own unique ends, but when that happens strictly speaking it isn't philosophy any longer if philosophy is required to take orders from someone else or if it is compelled to recognize some other authority besides its own independent thinking. In the Middle Ages that's pretty much all there was of philosophy: philosophy working for religion and compelled to recognize it as the ultimate authority which would always get the last word in this marriage.

Not surprisingly, after about 1,200 years of this philosophy grew tired of this marriage and asked for a divorce; and as it walked out the door this is what it said to religion: "See you later, baby! You're welcome to any of the stuff I'm leaving behind. Go ahead and use any of my ideas and arguments as much as you like, but I would like to be single again, a free agent, like I was at first—free to experiment wildly without anyone else telling me what to do; free to try everything and make my own stupid mistakes again. This marriage was fun while it lasted, and it also created so much pent-up demand in me for experimentation and extreme living that I'll probably spend the next three hundred years or so frantically trying to make up for lost time, so I'm looking forward to that!"

You can read all about this next stage in philosophy's weird and wonderful life, a stage of wild experimentation and free thought, in the next chapter.

Chapter 5

Modern philosophy

(Single again after a long and stifling marriage, philosophy asserts its independence in a rather spectacular way, trying to make up for all the time it lost by wildly experimenting with every idea, argument, or theory it can find.)

Modern philosophy begins in the sixteenth century, and if your first thought when you hear this is: "What a scam! I signed up for this class because I wanted to study current, cutting-edge, super-sexy philosophy that was written yesterday, or maybe a week ago, but certainly not five hundred years ago! This is fraud, and I'm going to sue!"—then don't drop the class or file a lawsuit just yet because I think this is going to be the perfect class for you. While it's true that the "modern" in "modern philosophy" refers to a conceptual shift that took place in the sixteenth, seventeenth, and eighteenth centuries—the period when many of the ideas and arguments that we now recognize as essential components of modernity are born—and therefore modern philosophy isn't modern in the sense of being recent or new, it's also true that this is still the wildest period in the history of philosophy by far: so if you're looking for a good show and a wild ride you've come to the right place.

Though modern philosophy is not the most recent period in philosophy's history, it is still the most radical. This is when philosophy reclaims its independence after a long marriage to religion that required it to do as it was told and to make itself subservient to the authority of the church. Doing what it's told and deferring to any other authority, whether it's religion or anything else, is not in philosophy's nature. Philosophy survived during the Middle Ages, it didn't disappear, but it did get distorted as it departed from many of its defining principles. Its dysfunctional marriage to religion allowed philosophy to persist, albeit in a rather contorted form, and it also created an enormous amount of creative tension that was waiting to explode in a spectacular fireworks show of independent thinking and radical experimentation. The modern period is when this explosion happened. Philosophy reasserts its autonomy and seems determined to make up for over a thousand years of lost time; this is what gives modern philosophy its accelerated, even hyperactive quality. The ideals that created philosophy in the beginning and animated it throughout its infancy—truly independent thinking with no deference to any supposed authority, and a determination to understand the ultimate nature of reality, knowledge, and values and not just as much as religion says it's appropriate to understand—these ideals didn't disappear, they were just dormant; and when they woke up during the modern period they were very well-rested and ready to go on a wild road trip.

My main goal in this chapter is to capture the joyous, experimental, creative, and promiscuous (in the best possible sense) spirit of modern philosophy. The sixteenth, seventeenth, and eighteenth centuries were a period of rebirth and regeneration in the history of philosophy that produced many revolutionary ideas, and they were also a period of wild experimental excess and eccentricity. It's much easier to appreciate the revolutionary ideas if you can also appreciate the excess and eccentricity as a feature and not a bug. Experimentation in any field requires excess: to get any meaningful results the experimenter must overdo it—trying out all sorts of ideas and theories that will not work in order to discover something that does. That's what happens during the modern period: after philosophy quits its job working for religion it runs back home to its own laboratory and starts wildly experimenting with all sorts of new ideas and theories, some of which are bound to blow up or turn into something very different from what the experimenter imagined. As philosophy emerged from almost 1,300 years when thinking independently about the ultimate nature of reality, knowledge, and values was considered anathema (because those topics were thought to be were reserved for Gods, or their representatives) it's bound to appear a little bit wild and crazy at times; but what's the alternative? The only other option is to let someone else think for you, and every philosopher in the modern period agreed they didn't want that. It was time to reassert the principles that got philosophy started in the first place: humans can think for themselves about the ultimate nature of things, and the only authority that should be respected is the authority of a good idea.

As with the two previous chapters, this summary of modern philosophy will necessarily be fragmentary, scrappy, and crumby. My goal in this scrappy summary is not to pretend to cover everything that happened in the sixteenth, seventeenth, and eighteenth centuries; I just want to give you enough of a taste of the philosophy of this period that you'll want to study it more completely on your own. In other words, I just want to put on a good show! It seems to me that the best format to capture the manic, joyous energy of modern philosophy is something like a Gilbert and Sullivan comic operetta such as *Pirates of Penzance* or *H.M.S. Pinafore*. The operetta performed in this chapter will have an overture, three acts, and a curtain call:

> Overture: a warm-up act to clarify the radical and experimental spirit of modern philosophy featuring some modern political philosophy, which was in every way revolutionary.
>
> Act 1: the epistemological duel between rationalism and empiricism, which is like a play within the play—a mini drama/comedy which plays out in three scenes: (1) rationalism pushes its own assumptions and arguments as far is they can go and hoists itself by its own petard; (2) empiricism pushes its own assumptions and arguments as far is they can go and hoists itself by its own petard; (3) Immanuel Kant rides to the rescue with his own theory that uses both rationalism and empiricism and offers to provide a *deus ex machina* resolution to the rationalism vs. empiricism debate.
>
> Act 2: While rationalism and empiricism do battle throughout the sixteenth, seventeenth, and eighteenth centuries other theories are created that don't fit neatly into that narrative, such as the weird and wonderful creation that Leibniz called "monadology" and the theory of everything that Spinoza called simply "Ethics." These wildly creative philosophical systems are perhaps the best demonstrations of the experimental spirit of philosophy in the modern period.

Act 3: speaking of ethics, there were a few theories about that too in the modern period; and here too Kant would like to clean up the mess that everyone else made.

Curtain Call: A final moment of revolutionary social and political philosophy at the end of the eighteenth century: the birth of feminism.

I hope you enjoy the show!

Overture: a quick overview of modern political philosophy, which was in every way revolutionary

The chief obsession of modern philosophy was epistemology: trying to answer the question "How is knowledge possible?" This obsession probably had a lot to do with how science was making obvious and startling progress; philosophy did not want to get left behind. It probably was also driven by not wanting to depend on religion any longer as the ultimate epistemological authority. Both of these factors likely motivated the interest in epistemology; but whatever was driving it epistemology was definitely the dominant concern of modern philosophers so that will be the first act of this chapter. But these arguments about epistemology will make much more sense if we first spend some time getting into the irreverent, experimental, and promiscuous spirit of modern philosophy with a survey of political theory. In this area the revolutionary nature of modern philosophy is particularly obvious. I'll quickly summarize just a few of the most influential political theories of modern philosophy that exemplify the radical and revolutionary spirit of the whole period.

Thomas Hobbes

Hobbes is an important figure in British empiricism so we'll return to him later when we turn to that topic, but he remains most famous for his political philosophy, especially the wild and wonderful book called *Leviathan*. In this book he attempts a completely naturalistic explanation of how societies get organized, states come to be, and justice gets done. His theory is revolutionary because in the past the norm was to appeal to the supernatural to explain all of those things. Hobbes is a hardcore empiricist (as we'll see later when we return to other parts of *Leviathan* where he declares his conviction that empiricism is the only legitimate basis for knowledge), but his revolutionary political theory is based on a thought experiment that is entirely non-empirical: imagining what life is like in the state of nature. No one has any experience of life in the state of nature because we all fell into a world that was organized with a government and various other social structures such as families, and obviously humans only survive on Planet Earth if they have parents who take care of them. So the state of nature that founds Hobbes's political theory is completely counter-factual and non-empirical but it's still very useful to Hobbes because it allows him to explain how the creation of a state is already a revolutionary act, and how this revolution is a purely human creation.

Life in the state of nature is, Hobbes says, "solitary, poor, nasty, brutish, and short,"[1] and the reason it's so unpleasant is because ethics and law are entirely human creations. There is nothing natural about them; they don't exist until humans create them through a social contract. Consequently in the state of nature there's no reason for anyone not to kill or otherwise victimize anyone else, and in fact that's the smart thing to do because anyone I kill is someone who can't kill me, and there's no reason for anyone not to kill me if I don't kill them first. Consequently the only intelligent thing to do in the state of nature is to live in constant anxiety, in "continual fear and danger of violent death."[2] The complete absence of both morality and law in the state of nature is only solved when humans create a government in the form of an "artificial man" which is composed of all the people in the state—that's the only way a state can be created, Hobbes argues, and he is so serious about this that he made sure to include a picture of this artificial man on the cover of *Leviathan*. In this picture the body of the sovereign is composed of the bodies of all the sovereign's subjects: the sovereign is quite literally composed of all the individuals who chose to leave the state of nature and subject themselves to a new power that they created. A sovereign is an "artificial man" which is a materialistic and mechanistic machine that's nothing more than an extension of the human body, which is also a materialistic and mechanistic machine.

---

1. Hobbes, *Leviathan*, 89.
2. Hobbes, *Leviathan*, 89.

The state of nature is completely intolerable, Hobbes says, but there is a way out provided by our natural passions and our natural, self-interested reason.

Natural passions:
- we're all afraid to die
- we all want a comfortable, anxiety-free life
- we all want to be able to realize such a life through our own work

Natural, self-interested reason:
- we all hate the state of nature and therefore it's in our best interest to do everything we can to escape from it
- to escape from the state of nature we must be willing to surrender the right we have in the state of nature to do whatever we want—our natural right to all things, which sounds awesome but actually isn't because it entails an unbearable war of all against all
- it's in our best interest, and therefore it's a law of nature, that we should make covenants to escape from the state of nature and then keep all of these covenants, because otherwise we'll be thrown back into the state of nature and we definitely don't want that

(Though Hobbes calls these three principles "laws of nature" they are nothing more than conclusions about individual self-interest—descriptions of what a rational person would do to protect herself in the state of nature, not prescriptive laws concerning how people should treat each other in society since such laws can only be created by a government and in the state of nature there is no government.)

These three passions and three laws of nature provide a natural exit ramp from the state of nature. There's no God in Hobbes's account of justice and government except for the god that we create ourselves in the form of an artificial man. Hobbes explains human governments, human laws, and human morality as entirely human creations.

John Locke

Since Hobbes imagines the state of nature to be horrific and completely absent of morality or rights his political theory provides no justification for overthrowing and replacing an existing government. If a government is dissolved humanity would be thrown back into the state of nature, and for Hobbes that would never make sense because no government could be worse than the "war of all against all" in the state of nature. But because the state of nature is necessarily a work of imagination it's possible to take the basic features of Hobbes's social contract theory and reconceptualize them to get a political theory that could justify overthrowing one government and creating a new one to take its place.

Such a political theory was provided by John Locke in his *Second Treatise of Government*. Like Hobbes, Locke was a committed empiricist so we'll have more to say about him later when the focus shifts to epistemology. But even though Locke, like Hobbes, argued that the only legitimate basis for knowledge is empiricism, this didn't stop either of them from arguing that the only legitimate basis for political philosophy is the completely non-empirical idea of the state of nature. People have experienced many different forms of government but no one has ever experienced a world in which there's no government, and the very idea of humans existing in a state of nature is obviously completely counter to human biology since it requires us to imagine that people somehow fall from the sky fully formed and developed as individual adults capable of taking care of themselves. So Locke really has no choice but to imagine what life would be like if humans somehow did live on their own in a world with no government, and he imagines it very differently from how Hobbes imagines it.

Locke agrees with Hobbes that the only legitimate basis for any government is a social contract in which everyone agrees to leave the state of nature behind and subject themselves to the rules of a government that is their own creation, but he disagrees with Hobbes on just about everything else. The differences between Locke's view of the state of nature and Hobbes's are about as great as they could possibly be and this has numerous consequences. Locke's political philosophy was one of the things that made the American Revolution possible. This was a revolution of ideas that began with lots of philosophical debate. The American colonies first had to convince themselves that they had a natural right to declare "that these United Colonies are, and of Right ought to be, Free and Independent States" before they could begin the fight that made this theoretical independence a political reality. Locke's political theory was not the only theory that was used to arrive at this conclusion, but it was one of the most important voices in that debate.

For Locke, life in the state of nature is not "solitary, poor, nasty, brutish, and short"; it's actually quite awesome. Locke argues that the state of nature comes fully stocked with everything humans need to flourish and be happy, including plenty of resources for all and a complete set of moral principles that make it possible for everyone to live together in peace and prosperity with no government whatsoever.[3] While Locke agrees with Hobbes that human governments are human creations that do not fall from the sky and do not require divine intervention in any form, he doesn't agree that morality and law are nonexistent until a government creates them. In the state of nature, Locke argues, everyone knows it's their duty to treat everyone else with decency and respect, and they also understand perfectly that they must respect other people's property. (The natural law that governs the acquisition of property is simply this: when you mix your labor with any natural resource that thing becomes yours; it's now your property.)[4] So for Locke the state of nature is a kind of paradise, the complete antithesis of "a war of all against all," and there's no reason at all to leave it behind except for one inconvenience: even though the laws of morality are natural laws that are plainly obvious to everyone, people are still free and therefore they can still break these laws, and when they do it becomes the responsibility of everyone to enforce the laws of nature. Because in the state of nature there's no police, or courts, or any other government institution or apparatus to enforce the laws, every law-abiding person in the state of nature must take on this responsibility.[5] For example: if some rogue comes to my house and steals some of the apples that I've picked, or some of the rocks and sticks and flowers that I gathered for a very interesting artwork that I'm planning to make, even though it's completely obvious that all of these things belong to me by natural law since I mixed my labor with them when I went out and gathered them up, then I must stop whatever I'm doing to arrest and punish this law-breaker myself. I'm fully empowered and entitled to do so, Locke argues, but it's still inconvenient and rather annoying that I have to interrupt my plans to spend the evening eating my delicious apples and constructing my very interesting artwork because now I have to arrest and punish this outlaw. We therefore naturally come to the conclusion that it would be better to form a government, by means of a social contract, because we're tired of having to enforce the laws of nature

3. Locke, *Second*, 269–270.
4. Locke, *Second*, 285–302.
5. Locke, *Second*, 271–272.

ourselves all the time; but we can certainly dissolve this government any time and return to the state of nature if we conclude that the government we created has become more oppressive than the inconvenience of having to enforce the laws of nature ourselves.

Locke's version of social contract theory provides excellent arguments to justify a political breakup in the real world, and the spirit of the *Second Treatise of Government* can be plainly heard in the Declaration of Independence, the document that the theorists of the American Revolution thought it was only good and proper to present to the world to explain what they were doing:

> We hold these truths to be self-evident, that all men are created equal, that they are endowed by their Creator with certain unalienable Rights, that among these are Life, Liberty and the pursuit of Happiness.—That to secure these rights, Governments are instituted among Men, deriving their just powers from the consent of the governed,—That whenever any Form of Government becomes destructive of these ends, it is the Right of the People to alter or to abolish it, and to institute new Government, laying its foundation on such principles and organizing its powers in such form, as to them shall seem most likely to effect their Safety and Happiness.

Edmund Burke

There are many other examples of modern political philosophies that are radical and revolutionary, such as Rousseau's version of social contract theory (which influenced the French Revolution), but in order to bring this appetizing introduction to modern philosophy to a conclusion and get on to the main course I'll mention just one more political theorist, in this case someone who was radical in his arguments for conservatism: Edmund Burke. Burke's *Reflections on the Revolution in France* is written in the form of a letter addressed to an unnamed person in France and it sounds a lot like a real conversation. It also sounds very much like an intervention: Burke is trying to save his French friend from what he considers to be the mistakes of the French Revolution much like someone trying to save a friend with a drug problem. His anonymous French friend, along with almost all of France at the time, is addicted to the wrong political philosophy Burke thinks, and he's trying to show where this addiction leads before it's too late. Burke argues that history, tradition, and culture are all that any society has to work with, so they must be treated with care as the precious and fragile things they are rather than being casually discarded or overthrown. In its own way this too is a revolutionary political theory: a revolutionary reassessment of the value of the basic elements of community (history, tradition, and culture) that are easily taken for granted and cast aside, as if they had no value at all. Conservative political philosophy argues that it's naïve to believe that communities can be manufactured as easily as social contract theories claim, as if they were nothing more than folding chairs or plastic sporks or some other simple human artifact, and these arguments against flippant and thoughtless political revolution have become central to modern conservatism.

That's the end of the overture; on to act 1!

Act 1: The epistemological duel between rationalism and empiricism, which plays out in three scenes.

The fundamental difference between the rationalist and empiricist approaches to epistemology is encapsulated in two Latin terms that you're bound to encounter often when you read modern philosophy: *a priori* and *a posteriori*. These terms simply mean before or prior to (that's *a priori*) and after or posterior to (that's *a posteriori*); so they are just sexy ways or saying before and after. But before and after what? The answer is: sensory experience. An *a posteriori* approach to epistemology argues that knowledge can come only after and as a consequence of sensory experience, while an *a priori* approach argues that sensory experience is just a lot of noise and confusion that gets in the way of knowledge, a lot of sound and fury that ultimately signifies nothing if what you're looking for is the certainty we want from knowledge. Rationalism and empiricism stake out these two different locations on the timeline of sensory experience and there they set up camp, both convinced that the other side is wasting its time by looking for knowledge (and perhaps also love, to quote an old country western song)[6] in all the wrong places.

Early in the seventeenth century Descartes climbed behind the wheel of the Rationalism-Mobile and drove the car as far and as fast as he

---

6. The 1980 country western song "Looking for love in all the wrong places" by Johnny Lee, which was in the film *Urban Cowboy*, would make a good soundtrack to play in the background while you study the rationalism vs. empiricism debate in modern philosophy.

could, pushing the machinery of rationalism right to the breaking point. After the dust had cleared from Descartes's wild ride it was not at all clear how knowledge is possible based exclusively on rationalist assumptions, and it was also not clear how everything that Descartes took apart in his search for certainty (minds and bodies, thinking and feeling, reason and imagination, etc.) can be put back together again. This is the pattern that plays out in both of the first two scenes of this duel between rationalism and empiricism: both teams end up hoisting themselves by their own petards (as they say in Utah) when they insist they are the only game in town—the only legitimate way to answer the question "How is knowledge possible?" Descartes got this party started when he went all in on rationalism, and thereby demonstrated the many surprises that follow when you try to blow up all of our accumulated beliefs and start over on a purely rationalist foundation. This demolition and reconstruction project will be scene 1 in this drama/comedy/play within the play.

In the case of empiricism the same process played out more gradually and multiple authors took turns in something like a 500-meter relay, pushing empiricism to its logical limits and in the end undermining the very possibility of knowing anything. Empiricism presents itself as a commonsense epistemology; it doesn't argue for blowing up anything, but it ends up being just as explosive as rationalism. To see this progression from a very intuitive and commonsense theory of knowledge to a very surprising and counterintuitive approach to epistemology that calls into question the possibility of knowing anything at all we'll need to consider five different authors: Bacon, Hobbes, Locke, Berkeley, Hume—and that's where we will go next in scene 2.

Scene 3 is (according to Immanuel Kant at least) the happy ending of this story in the form of a grand synthesis of both rationalism and empiricism. Kant happened to propose this climactic conclusion to the rationalism vs. empiricism drama almost exactly at the end of the eighteenth century and so it's been difficult ever since then not to regard Kant's spectacular epistemological synthesis as the climactic conclusion of all of modern philosophy. Whether or not the *deus ex machina* ending that Kant proposed succeeded in settling the many disagreements between rationalism and empiricism and making both teams perfectly happy will be up to you to decide, but the audacity and creativity of Kant's epistemological theory is impossible to deny. (And by the way, epistemology is not the only area of philosophy that Kant claimed to clean up and systematize once and for all: he also proposed complete systems of ethics and aesthetics, which we'll get to later.)

Scene 1: rationalism throws down the gauntlet and challenges empiricism to a duel, and then it proceeds to push its own assumptions and arguments as far is they can go and effectively hoist itself by its own petard

René Descartes

Descartes may be the figure in modern philosophy who represents better than anyone else what this period is all about and how it differs from the period that came before. In this respect he occupies a place like that of Socrates in ancient philosophy and Augustine in medieval philosophy. These authors stand out because of the major contribution they made to the paradigm shift that brought philosophy into a new era and gave it a new focus. Socrates more than anyone else brought about the initial revolution that created philosophy in the first place. Augustine was thoroughly steeped in Greek philosophy when he converted to Christianity in the middle of his life, and he decided that philosophy was created so that it could contribute to Christian theology. He spent the rest of his life demonstrating to the world what this new paradigm of philosophy-is-a-tool-for-religion looks like, and this became the model that defined philosophy throughout the medieval period. Like Augustine, Descartes had one foot in the past period of philosophy and the other in the new paradigm that came to define his own age. The transition from the medieval model of philosophy as a servant of religion to the modern paradigm of philosophy as once again a free agent (as it was originally during its childhood) was not easy or immediate. In the sixteenth, seventeenth, and eighteenth centuries religion was still very much the dominant power and was still widely regarded as the ultimate authority on everything, so anyone who wanted to argue that philosophy could be a free agent again, no longer taking orders from religion, had to be very careful and creative in how they presented their arguments. Modern philosophers generally undersold how radical their theories were, not wanting to incite unwanted attention from the religious authorities who could make their lives miserable. Many modern philosophers also lived rather itinerant and eclectic lives, wandering throughout the world and working in *ad hoc* positions that gave them freedom to think and write and also kept them off the radar of anyone who might not be pleased with their unorthodox ideas. In this respect, and in many others, Descartes is a model of the most important goals and strategies that drove philosophy into modernity, so it's worth spending a disproportionate amount of time on his theories because they clarify not just what an extreme rationalist approach to epistemology looks like but also much of what was new and unique and radical about modern philosophy generally.

A good place to start is Descartes's *Discourse on Method*, which is actually a very personal story about something to which everyone can relate: the moment you realized that most of what you'd been taught wasn't true. Descartes explains how he came to the conclusion that he couldn't be certain of anything, and how he responded to this discovery by formulating a method that he believes will allow him to avoid making any mistakes in the future. The basic pattern that Descartes follows is one that all of us could also easily duplicate: tell the story of your life that led to your discovery that so much of what you thought you knew for sure is actually uncertain, and then create a method of your own to correct the mistakes you've discovered and to avoid making mistakes in the future. This is all that he does in the *Discourse on Method*, and it's a good place to start to appreciate better the human dimension of his philosophy: how all of us would like to have certainty.

Effectively the motto of the *Discourse on Method* is: "We won't get fooled again!" Descartes wanted to provide a rule book everyone could follow to be confident of always being in the right: never again misinformed or misled. It turns out to be a surprisingly short rule book. There are only four mental rules and four moral rules.

The mental rules:[7]

1. Accept as true only what is clearly and obviously true.
2. Divide large challenges into small, manageable problems, and thus divide and conquer them.
3. Follow an orderly process by starting with the simplest elements.
4. Review your work and make sure you didn't leave anything out.

---

7. Descartes, *Discourse*, 120.

The moral rules:[8]

1. Just follow the rules of whatever state, culture, and religion you're in.
2. Be firm and resolute!
3. Just focus on yourself; don't try to save the world.
4. Find a good job!

Between the mental rules and the moral rules we can see how narrowly focused Descartes was on matters of epistemology and how profoundly disinterested he was in thinking critically and skeptically about social, political, or ethical questions. His moral rules basically amount to: accept all the moral rules of whatever world you fell into and don't waste your time questioning or trying to change any of them because you've got more important things to do. The one moral rule that does stand out is number 3. In all of Descartes's philosophy the focus is strictly on the single individual: the intentionally isolated and insulated I. All groups, institutions, or people are immediately suspect for Descartes because they could potentially deceive you, and you need to devote all your energy and attention to avoid being deceived yourself so there's nothing left to give to anyone else. Descartes's singular focus on single individuals is an extremely important part of his legacy so it's a good idea to keep an eye on the assumptions that underlie it right from the start.

Descartes says he was very pleased with his method, and he applied it thus to his own life: "Throughout the following nine years I did nothing but roam about in the world, trying to be a spectator rather than an actor in all the comedies that played out there."[9] But as he wandered and watched he continued to think about the problem that motivated him to write the *Discourse on Method*: how is it possible to avoid all deception and be completely certain in a world in which we're so often deceived by others, and even by ourselves? He gave his most famous answer to this question a few years later in the book he called *Meditations on First Philosophy*. He seemed particularly proud of this work, so much that he sent copies to many famous intellectuals and asked them to write back with their questions and objections. Not all of these recipients were as impressed as Descartes was; for example, Thomas Hobbes was one person Descartes chose to review the *Meditations*, and since he was a committed

---

8. Descartes, *Discourse*, 122–24.
9. Descartes, *Discourse*, 125.

empiricist he thought that Descartes's distrust of the senses (more on that shortly) was simply a mistake, so he sent back a rather sarcastic review that dismissed the whole book as a mistake. Nevertheless, Descartes wanted Hobbes's criticisms (along with his own response) to be included in all published editions of the *Meditations*, which demonstrates how strongly he believed the book's arguments were sound and could resist any criticism. It should also be noted that Descartes made quite an effort to tell a good story in the *Meditations*. The book has a clear narrative arc, even something like a dramatic plot. It's a philosophical page-turner, with each of the six meditations ending on a suspenseful note that makes you want to keep reading to see how the challenge gets overcome or the dilemma gets resolved. Just as he did in the *Discourse on Method* Descartes tries to make his philosophical arguments personal rather than mere abstractions with no obvious relevance to the reader.

The dedication of the *Meditations* is often overlooked as readers race right past it to get to the action of meditation 1, but that's unfortunate because it can teach us a lot about modern philosophy as a whole: the context and the challenges of this particular period. Descartes dedicates the *Meditations* to "those most learned and distinguished men, the Dean and Doctors of the Sacred Faculty of Theology in Paris,"[10] and the dedication is written as if it were a very personal letter (or confession) to these church officials. Descartes promises them that the book's only purpose is to prove the existence of God and the immortality of the human soul. In other words, Descartes swears to these religious authorities that he's written nothing more than a very traditional work of medieval philosophy which accepts philosophy's place as a servant of religion and is focused exclusively on solving theological problems and saving men's souls. In case anyone didn't get the message from this dedication, Descartes includes the theological purpose of the *Meditations* right in the full title of the book, making the title so long that it's almost never cited in its entirety: *Meditations on First Philosophy, in Which Is Proved the Existence of God and the Immortality of the Soul*. If this lengthy title were in fact a completely accurate description of the *Meditations*' contents the book would be nothing but a strange vestigial echo from the Middle Ages and there would be no reason at all to discuss it in connection with modern philosophy. Though Descartes does say a few things about the existence of God and the immortality of the human soul in the *Meditations*, there

---

10. Descartes, *Meditations*, 3.

is much more in the book that he didn't advertise in the title or in the dedication.

That the arguments in the *Meditations* are actually much more extensive and radical than Descartes acknowledged or advertised becomes clear very quickly in meditation 1. Here is the very first paragraph:

> Some years ago I was struck by the large number of falsehoods that I had accepted as true in my childhood, and by the highly doubtful nature of the whole edifice that I had subsequently based on them. I realized that it was necessary, once in the course of my life, to demolish everything completely and start again right from the foundations if I wanted to establish anything at all in the sciences that was stable and likely to last. But the task looked an enormous one, and I began to wait until I should reach a mature enough age to ensure that no subsequent time of life would be more suitable for tackling such inquiries. This led me to put the project off for so long that I would now be to blame if by pondering over it any further I wasted the time still left for carrying it out. So today I have expressly rid my mind of all worries and arranged for myself a clear stretch of free time. I am here quite alone, and at last I will devote myself sincerely and without reservation to the general demolition of my opinions.[11]

In order to discover some idea that can't be doubted Descartes decides to follow a method of hyperbolic or radical doubt: he will doubt everything that can be doubted until he finds a belief that's impossible to doubt. Since the goal is to find an idea that's absolutely certain, all that this method of doubt requires to disqualify an idea that presents itself as a candidate for the job is anything less than certainty: some possibility that we may be wrong, that we may be deceived if we believe this idea is true. Applying this method Descartes disqualifies every belief derived from the senses before the end of the first page. There are numerous reasons why any belief based on the empirical evidence of the five senses could be false, such as:

- The senses are imperfect instruments that give us imperfect data (e.g., optical illusions and other tricks our senses play on us, plus the obvious limitations of all five senses: I can only see a few hundred feet with my glasses on, and if I take them off, I can barely see at all).

11. Descartes, *Meditations*, 17.

- If that's not enough for you, consider that you could be dreaming (in dreams we are completely convinced that we're perceiving the real world when in fact we're just lying in bed with our eyes closed, and thus we can never be certain that we're not dreaming: you may think that you are awake and reading this book right now but in fact you're simply having a really bad dream).
- If that's not enough for you, consider that you might be on drugs right now (and so again you think you're perceiving reality when in fact you're just high).
- If that's not enough for you, consider that you might be playing a very good virtual reality game right now—you get the picture . . .

(Descartes actually only gave the first two arguments to prove that empirical data is useless in the quest for certainty, but you could easily imagine many more scenarios in which your senses deceive you, such as drugs and virtual reality. For Descartes's method of doubt all it takes is one possibility of deception, but it's a lot of fun to imagine more.)

Beliefs based on sensory experience constitute almost all our beliefs, so if you call all of those beliefs into question (as Descartes does immediately in meditation 1) what's left? There are a few other ideas in our heads that are not based on sensory experience. These include beliefs that are analytic or true by definition such as "all squares have four sides" or "all philosophy classes are extremely fun." Descartes (who was, among other things, quite an accomplished mathematician) does not hesitate to include all of mathematics in this category. The truths of mathematics don't require empirical confirmation; they don't depend on our senses in any way. They are purely conceptual relationships that remain true in the interior world of the mind even if we can't see, hear, taste, smell, or feel the external world in any way. $7 + 5 = 12$ even if your eyesight is very bad, and even if you're dreaming or on drugs or immersed in a virtual reality game. So it looks like Descartes has found what he was looking for: a collection of beliefs that are indubitable—impossible to doubt, no matter how hard you try (and how convenient too, since mathematics already serves as the foundational, common language of the sciences).

This is the moment in the *Meditations* when Descartes demonstrates two things emphatically: (1) he really meant it when he promised to doubt anything that can be doubted, and (2) this is definitely not a work of medieval philosophy, in spite of what he said in the dedication. In order to argue that even mathematics is uncertain and can be doubted

Descartes introduces a new and very memorable character in this story: the Evil Genius. Where did Descartes get this idea? He doesn't hide the fact that he borrowed it from Christianity:

> And yet firmly rooted in my mind is the long-standing opinion that there is an omnipotent God who made me the kind of creature that I am. How do I know that he has not brought it about that there is no earth, no sky, no extended thing, no shape, no size, no place, while at the same time ensuring that all these things appear to me to exist just as they do now? What is more, just as I consider that others sometimes go astray in cases where they think they have the most perfect knowledge, how do I know that God has not brought it about that I too go wrong every time I add two and three or count the sides of a square, or in some even simpler matter, if that is imaginable?[12]

Descartes simply takes the Christian dogma that God is perfect in every way and makes one slight modification: imagine that this all-powerful being is *not* good, and therefore enjoys nothing more than deceiving us about concepts and conceptual relationships that we think are indubitable, such as mathematics. This may not seem very likely, since an all-powerful being would presumably have better things to do than spending all its time feeding into our minds the belief that $7 + 5 = 12$ when in fact $7 + 5 = 37$, or 93, or 4, but it is possible that there is such a diabolically single-minded being who has deceived every math teacher and math class throughout human history, and therefore we can't be certain even about mathematics.

In a few short pages Descartes's method of radical doubt has left us completely uncertain of everything, and Descartes—like a practiced writer of dramatic pulp fiction—ends the first meditation on a suspenseful note:

> I will suppose therefore that not God, who is supremely good and the source of truth, but rather some malicious demon of the utmost power and cunning has employed all his energies in order to deceive me. I shall think that the sky, the air, the earth, colors, shapes, sounds and all external things are merely the delusions of dreams which he has devised to ensnare my judgment. I shall consider myself as not having hands or eyes, or flesh, or blood or senses, but as falsely believing that I have all these things. I shall stubbornly and firmly persist in this

12. Descartes, *Meditations*, 14.

> meditation; and, even if it is not in my power to know any truth, I shall at least do what is in my power, that is, resolutely guard against assenting to any falsehoods, so that the deceiver, however powerful and cunning he may be, will be unable to impose on me in the slightest degree. But this is an arduous undertaking, and a kind of laziness brings me back to normal life. I am like a prisoner who is enjoying an imaginary freedom while asleep; as he begins to suspect that he is asleep, he dreads being woken up, and goes along with the pleasant illusion as long as he can.[13]

In the second meditation Descartes finds what he was looking for: an idea that is impossible to doubt, but it comes in a very surprising form. What is needed is a belief that can withstand even the Evil Genius who works nonstop to deceive me at all times. Descartes's insight is basically this: even if I'm deceived all the time about everything, there must be some "I" that exists that is constantly getting deceived. This is something I can be certain of all the time.

> But there is a deceiver of supreme power and cunning who is deliberately and constantly deceiving me. In that case I too undoubtedly exist, if he is deceiving me; and let him deceive me as much as he can, he will never bring it about that I am nothing so long as I think that I am something. So after considering everything very thoroughly, I must finally conclude that this proposition, I am, I exist, is necessarily true whenever it is put forward by me or conceived in my mind.[14]

The more popular version of this argument, that you are likely to find in some form inscribed on black T-shirts worn by hipster philosophy majors, is: "I think, therefore I am" (or in Latin: *cogito ergo sum*), but the argument could also be worded as: "I am deceived, therefore I am," because the core of the argument is that even if I'm deceived about everything, all of that deception still constitutes thinking, and if I'm thinking obviously I exist! Descartes claims this is impossible to doubt. It's a loophole that the Evil Genius cannot close, an absolutely indubitable idea that leaves the Evil Genius shaking its evil fist in frustration, and upon the bedrock of "I think, therefore I am" he proposes to rebuild everything that he's torn down and get the whole world back.

That project of reconstruction begins immediately in meditation 2 with Descartes admitting that even though he's proven beyond any

13. Descartes, *Meditations*, 15.
14. Descartes, *Meditations*, 17.

possible doubt that he exists he still has no idea what he is. Since radical doubt is still in operation he can't understand himself as a body, since every idea we have of bodies is based on nothing but sensory experience and the Evil Genius (or drugs or a dream or a hot new virtual reality game) can easily deceive us about that. What can I say with certainty about what I am? Only that I'm a thing that thinks; a thinking thing (or, in Latin, if you're looking for new black T-shirt to impress your friends: *res cogitans*). So by the end of meditation 2 Descartes claims to have found the firm and lasting foundation for the sciences that he was looking for, and he also (rather casually) has completely divided the mind and the body. (But don't worry, he says; he's going to put everything back together by the end of the book.)

Meditations 1 and 2 tend to get most of the attention but the other four meditations are no less important. Here's a quick tour of the last four sections of the book.

Meditation 3: This is the medieval meditation. Descartes uses a lot of medieval assumptions and logic to bring God back into the world so that he's not alone. In paragraph 2 probably the most decisive argument of the whole book is introduced with no fanfare so it's easy to miss: *cogito ergo sum* is true because it's a clear and distinct idea, therefore all clear and distinct ideas are true; I can trust all of them. Really this one argument would be enough to get the whole world back, so the *Meditations* could end right here, but Descartes the *raconteur* draws it out for four more chapters. The rest of this meditation is dedicated to proving that God exists using the ontological proof, which was most famously championed by Saint Anselm in the eleventh century. The argument is: God is by definition that than which nothing greater can be conceived, and it's better to exist than not to exist, therefore God necessarily exists. This is supposed to be a proof that you can do with your eyes closed: no sensory data is required; it's just logic, so it's fitting that Descartes uses it because he still doesn't trust his senses. Along the way he argues that both the idea of God and the idea of *cogito ergo sum* are innate ideas: we were born with them; we didn't have to discover them in the world with our senses. (Innate ideas are embraced by all rationalists and rejected by all empiricists.) From this point on Descartes will use these two ideas to reassure you at every turn that it's safe to come out of your hole and climb back into the sunlight: any idea that is clear and distinct is necessarily true; and God exists and is perfectly good so he would never deceive you. Either one of these claims, if it were indubitable, would be enough to get the world back, so again Descartes could just stop right here, but he uses the rest of the *Meditations* to make moral arguments.

Meditation 4: This is the problem of evil meditation; again a very medieval theme. The problem of evil is a problem for any religion, like Christianity, that maintains that God is perfectly good: why would a perfectly good God allow evil (anything I don't like) in the world? Since Descartes has just proven that God exists he now wants to answer the question: "Why does God allow me to be deceived?" His answer mirrors Augustine's from the fourth century: there is no natural evil at all, it's just an illusion or a misunderstanding, and all moral evil is your fault. You have the ability to resist the temptation of any ideas that are not clear and distinct, so if you don't do that you're to blame, not God. Descartes comes back to this cautionary theme especially in the last meditation.

Meditation 5: This is the meditation on math, Descartes's favorite subject (after philosophy of course). Descartes brings all of mathematics back because it's all composed of clear and distinct ideas, and also God would never deceive you about math because God loves math too. Much of the meditation is spent discussing the wonderful things you can do with math, anticipating the role that math will play as the common language of the natural sciences.

Meditation 6: This is where you officially get the whole world back, with lots of warnings about how to avoid mistakes in the future: don't trust your imagination, be wary of your senses and remember that they are never the ultimate source of knowledge, remember that your mind is completely different from your body. (We no longer have to doubt that we have a body, but we now know that the mind is independent and fundamentally different from the body.)

Before we leave the *Meditations* it's worth noting one more time how hard Descartes tried to make the book suspenseful, dramatic, and engaging. All six meditations are written in a very cinematic style, and I have no doubt that if Descartes were writing them today he would pitch the project to a movie studio. Without much effort you can easily think of numerous TV shows and films you've seen or stories you've read that are structured around the same ideas that Descartes presents in meditation 1: that everything we thought we knew may be a complete deception; that beliefs based on both perception and pure reason may be mistakes; that perhaps there is no way to have certain knowledge of anything, etc. This proves how much we're fascinated by the questions Descartes is exploring in this book, and how much we're all haunted by the absence of certainty in our own lives.

Meditation 1 may have some of the flashiest arguments in the book, which are just waiting for a filmmaker with a large special effects budget to bring to life, but the cinematic potential of the book doesn't stop there. Here are three more possibilities for cool films that could be based on other arguments in the book, and I'm sure that you can easily think of more:

- Right after discovering that it's impossible to doubt that he exists, Descartes declares that he still doesn't know what he is. The rest of meditation 2 is dedicated to answering this question: what we can know about ourselves with certainty (because remember the Evil Genius is still out there trying to deceive us). Along the way Descartes says that we can't be certain yet that we have bodies, but we can at least be certain that we are essentially "thinking things." What is it like to be a "thinking thing" that isn't at all certain if it has a body? This too would make an excellent movie, and I hope that one of you will make this film very soon so that I can see it before I die.

- While trying to answer the question of what we can know about ourselves when the Evil Genius is out there trying to deceive us, Descartes gives an extended argument about wax. He argues that we know "the same wax remains" in spite of all the apparent changes that wax can undergo (gathered from a beehive, formed into a candle, melted into a puddle, etc.) because we have a mental intuition or insight into the true nature of the wax which doesn't depend on eyesight or any other of the five senses. This is a fascinating argument that could also serve as the basis of an engrossing film. (A movie about wax would be very boring, so you would have to come up with an idea for a more exciting story that advances the same argument that Descartes makes using wax, but I'm sure you can do it.)

- In meditations 3–6 Descartes claims to recover everything that was lost in the first two meditations, but now (he claims) everything rests on a foundation of absolute certainty so doubt is no longer possible. However, the Evil Genius that he created as part of his method of doubt back in meditation 1 may not be so easily conquered. Is it possible the Evil Genius is still deceiving Descartes in meditations 3–6? If so, even though Descartes thinks he's in control and has found a way to get the whole world back, really he hasn't;

the Evil Genius could still be running the show and still deceiving Descartes about everything. You could make a very interesting film exploring this possibility, perhaps from the perspective of the Evil Genius so that we can see how funny it is that Descartes thinks he's defeated him.

Beyond its potential for a really terrific movie, this last scenario is certainly worth thinking about further. Descartes's game plan in the *Meditations* is basically this: doubt everything that can be doubted in order to discover something that can't be doubted, and once you've found that indubitable idea use it as the foundation on which you can reconstruct the whole world and recover every idea and belief that matters. In this way he claims it's possible to establish "a firm and lasting foundation for the sciences." But is it really possible to stop doubting once you have resolved to doubt everything that can be doubted? Is there really a natural conclusion to doubt, as Descartes argues, or does the Evil Genius of doubt always win once you've turned it loose? The only way to test Descartes's engineering is to try to blow up the building that he erected. He claims he constructed a new, modern edifice of absolute certainty that's beyond any possible doubt, but what he actually accomplished may have been something quite different. Descartes's real legacy may be that he demonstrated quite decisively that when one begins doubting everything that can be doubted there's no possible way to stop doubting; that doubt can only lead to more doubt and never to certainty. That is not at all the result that Descartes intended, but it may be one of his most important inadvertent accomplishments.

Another part of Descartes's legacy that seems completely unintentional is mind-body dualism. Just as it proves difficult (and perhaps even impossible) to find a way to turn off the machine of hyperbolic doubt once you've turned it on, it's also quite difficult to reconnect the mind and body once they've been disconnected. Dividing the mind and body was not part of Descartes's agenda when he began the *Meditations*, he just wanted to find a firm and lasting foundation for the sciences; but the method of hyperbolic doubt that he follows to accomplish that goal leads to the conclusion that the mind and body are completely separate and independent entities since Descartes can only be certain that he exists as a mind—as a thinking thing—and not as a body since bodies are known only through the senses. This fundamental fissure of mind and body is today often called "Cartesian dualism" in recognition of how much this division is a part of Descartes's legacy, but clearly this isn't a legacy that Descartes was seeking. It was an incidental but necessary consequence of what he was seeking, which was simply: certainty. It turns out that for Descartes certainty can be purchased only at the price of uncertainty about how the mind and body connect or interact with each other.

The difficulty of putting the mind and body back together again once they've been conceptualized as fundamentally different things is brought to life quite wonderfully in Descartes's correspondence with Princess Elisabeth of Bohemia. This is one of the rare moments in modern philosophy (and in the history of philosophy as a whole) when a woman gets to talk, and these moments are always fascinating. Their correspondence contains many truly hilarious lines, such as when Descartes says to Elisabeth: "Seeing superhuman discourse issue from a body similar to those painters give to angels, I would have been overwhelmed in the same way as those must be, I should think, who, coming from earth, are just entering into heaven."[15] In other words: "How can you be so good looking and also so smart?" That's a seventeenth-century attempt at a pickup line, but it seems to have little effect on Elisabeth, who reminds Descartes that she is a princess and therefore grew up "in a place where the ordinary way of conversing accustomed me to hearing people incapable of giving true praise."[16] (In other words: it's not the first time some dude tried to flatter her.) But while Descartes is trying very hard to flirt with Elisabeth she's trying to get some straight answers from him about how a mind or soul that is immaterial can interact in any way with a body that is material. Descartes proposes several different answers to this excellent question, and these answers seem to be increasingly desperate:

- The union of the mind and body is an innate idea that only seems confusing when you try to apply other innate ideas to it, such as those we have of the body alone and those we have of the mind alone. Each of these three distinct types of innate ideas must stay in its own lane; then there's no confusion.
- If you're still confused, just use your senses to verify the union of the mind and body; then it's completely obvious. "As a result, those who never philosophize and who only use their senses do not doubt that

---

15. Descartes, "Correspondence," 94.
16. Descartes, "Correspondence," 96.

the soul moves the body and that the body acts on the soul; but they consider the one and the other as a single thing."[17]
- Actually we're not really capable of understanding the union of mind and body, and if you think too hard about it you'll just get confused, so please stop thinking about it so much.

In response to Descartes's inability to answer her question Elisabeth tactfully says, "I think there are some properties of the soul unknown to us, which could perhaps overturn what your *Metaphysical Meditations* persuaded me of."[18] Descartes may not realize it, but Elisabeth has just informed him that she finds his response to the mind–body problem that his philosophy created to be severely lacking.

Descartes's *Meditations* can be read as, among other things, the story of a very nasty breakup, followed by an attempted reconciliation. In his quest for certainty Descartes quickly concludes that his body is just getting in the way, so it's one of the first things to go in meditation 1. The great discovery in meditation 2 that *cogito ergo sum* is the foundation of all knowledge is only possible because of this. "Am I so tied to a body and to the senses that I cannot exist without them?" Descartes concludes that there is a deeper "I" that has nothing to do with his body, and the existence of that "I" is in fact the most certain thing in the world. Descartes, who has concluded that he is fundamentally a "thinking thing," proceeds to rebuild the world on the foundation of this idea. By the time you resurface in meditation 6 he claims to have recovered the whole world: everything that was put into doubt at the beginning when he started excavating, including his own body. So after throwing his own body under the bus because it was getting in the way of his pursuit of certain knowledge, Descartes invites it to come back home again as if nothing had ever happened. But maybe this reconciliation will not be quite as easy as he imagines. Maybe his body will not forgive and forget the way it was kicked to the curb. Perhaps their relationship will be filled with tension from this point on. That tension is apparent in the conversation between Descartes and Princess Elisabeth. Elisabeth asks Descartes what seems like a very simple question: "How does this marriage work? If the mind and body are completely different how are they able to do anything together?" Descartes seems unable to answer this question, and the fact that this is revealed in the course of a conversation between a woman and

17. Descartes, "Correspondence," 97.
18. Descartes, "Correspondence," 98.

a man that's filled with all the tension and misunderstanding that such interactions can have (e.g., Descartes flirting with Elisabeth and trying to get her to stop talking about philosophy; Elisabeth trying to get Descartes to focus on her mind and not her body, etc.) just makes this conversation about minds and bodies even richer. What emerges from this conversation is a picture of a couple that clearly needs some marriage counseling. That couple is Descartes's mind and his body (not Descartes and Elisabeth—that's never going to happen; sorry René). Descartes insists that everything is just fine in this marriage but Elisabeth knows better. She recognizes that this marriage is clearly on the rocks. The obvious next step would be for Descartes to take his mind and his body (the strangest couple ever) to see a marriage counselor, and Elisabeth seems perfect for that job. This marriage counseling would also make a great movie: it has perhaps the greatest cinematic potential of all the ideas in *Meditations on First Philosophy*.

All of the excellent movies that have been, or could have been, inspired by Descartes's philosophy are a fine demonstration of how many questions Descartes managed to raise—and how much uncertainty he managed to create—in his quest for certainty. This is not at all what he wanted. He wanted to provide a secure and lasting foundation for the sciences, and he wanted to make philosophy just as confident and as certain as the sciences, but that isn't what happened. Descartes raised more questions than he ever answered, and he demonstrated the difficulty (or impossibility) of stopping hyperbolic doubt once it has started.

Scene 2: Empiricism insists that sensory experience of the world gives us knowledge of the world, which seems like a perfectly reasonable and commonsense theory of knowledge, but after it pushes its own assumptions and arguments as far is they can go it calls into question how knowledge is possible at all; and thus empiricism—like rationalism—ends up hoisting itself by its own petard.

One reason Descartes is so important to modern philosophy is because he so clearly and distinctly presents the underlying assumptions of rationalism, which insists that knowledge is only possible if it's independent of the senses. The very first thing Descartes does in meditation 1 after he launches the project of doubting everything that can be doubted is set aside any evidence based on the senses as potentially false and therefore completely useless in the search for certainty. Everyone on Team Empiricism thinks that Descartes made a fundamental mistake when he did that because they believe that cutting yourself off from your senses cuts you off from the only source of knowledge that humans have.

Francis Bacon

Bacon's arguments for empiricism are a good place to start to get a sense of why empiricists do not distrust the senses as Descartes does. Bacon offers a radically different explanation for all the mistakes that humans make that exonerates the five senses completely. He argues that knowledge is inhibited not by the senses, but by what we do with the data our senses give us. In the marvelous book that Bacon called *The New Organon* (as opposed to the old *Organon*, which is the one that Aristotle wrote almost two thousand years earlier) he focuses on social or psychological factors that limit human knowledge. He calls these "idols," and they are like viruses of the mind for which we need an inoculation.[19] He diagnoses four of these idols that limit and distort knowledge:

- Idols of the tribe, which result from human nature generally—the many fears and foibles that afflict the human species as a whole.

- Idols of the cave, which are individual idiosyncrasies—the particular caves of prejudice and ignorance that individuals choose to make their homes.

- Idols of the marketplace, which are the intellectual diseases we catch from each other—the misconceptions and false beliefs that we pass around like the flu or the latest rhinovirus, infecting each other every time we gather in groups.

- Idols of the theatre, which are the bad ideas that are performed like so many bad musicals by so many so-called experts—like a bad movie that nevertheless sells a lot of tickets and finds its way into everyday conversation and pop culture.

Bacon argues that these four human weaknesses are all we need to explain every breakdown and failure of human understanding. The five senses do their job perfectly, supplying the mind with perfect information but then the mind limits itself under the influence of these four

---

19. Bacon, *New Organon*, 40–42.

idols, like a member of a cult who thoughtlessly idolizes a charismatic leader and thus allows himself to be manipulated and controlled like a little child. Bacon argues that human psychology is to blame for all of our epistemological shortcomings, not the senses. He wanted to rebuild the natural sciences on a better foundation (that should sound familiar), but arguably he made a major contribution to the social sciences along the way with these insights into the psychology and sociology of knowledge. The tone of his book suggests that part of the proper cure is laughter: we need to put these idols of the mind on stage under a spotlight so that we can see how ridiculous each one is, and thus we can be cured of our compulsion to worship such ridiculous gods. Responding to this condition as Descartes does—by throwing the senses under the bus and isolating ourselves within our own minds—will succeed only in preventing us from knowing anything about the world, because our senses are the only access we have to the world.

Thomas Hobbes (again)

All empiricists want to be empiricists all the time about everything, and a quick return visit to our old friend Thomas Hobbes is a good chance to observe this. Hobbes's book *Leviathan* is famous for its naturalistic and materialistic political theory that makes human government a purely human creation, so it's revealing that he thought it was essential to make the first part of that book a primer on empiricist epistemology. Hobbes wanted to connect empiricism in epistemology to materialism in science (including the new science he was in the process of creating called political science). He devoted the first part of *Leviathan* to taking us on a tour of the purely empirical world within which he wanted to situate his political theory. This is an excellent reminder that both rationalism and empiricism call for a complete transformation of one's worldview that's very much like visiting another country or even another planet, and learning the language of this world is the best way to learn the culture.

John Locke (again)

Bacon and Hobbes are both important voices in the world of British empiricism, but the person who did the most to define the culture and values of this world was John Locke. We've already encountered Locke's political philosophy, and we noted the stark contrast between his description of the state of nature as a kind of paradise and Hobbes's insistence that life in the state of nature is "solitary, poor, nasty, brutish, and short"; so it's interesting to note that even though Hobbes and Locke disagreed in their political theory Locke was just as committed to empiricism as Hobbes was. The fact that these two devout empiricists could disagree so completely about the nature of the state of nature is a reminder that there's nothing empirical about the state of nature: no one has ever experienced it, so any accounts of it can be nothing but works of imagination based on completely non-empirical assumptions. The radical differences between Hobbes's and Locke's political theories also clarify that agreement on what seem to be completely intuitive and "common sense" principles of empiricism doesn't preclude thoroughly surprising and counterintuitive results from emerging later on when the logic of common sense is pushed to its limits. (That was some awesome foreshadowing right there, as you'll soon see!)

Hobbes made the first part of *Leviathan* something like an empiricist manifesto because he wanted to make it perfectly clear that the new science of politics he was presenting was based on a purely mechanical and material model of nature. Locke, on the other hand, wrote a much longer book devoted to nothing but empiricist epistemology. Clocking in at nearly eight hundred pages, *An Essay Concerning Human Understanding* effectively codified the principles of empiricism and came to be regarded as something like the constitution governing Planet Empiricism. Locke attempted to clarify all the principles of empiricism and also to work out all the implications of these principles. Like almost all revolutionary and paradigm-shifting works in the history of philosophy this book is overwritten, repetitive, and excessive in every way, but as we'll see later in this story both Berkeley and Hume think that Locke still didn't go far enough—that he stopped short of recognizing everything that follows from a thorough and consistent empiricism, and they extend Locke's arguments to conclusions that he himself never considered.

Locke was a medical doctor who also practiced philosophy,[20] and like a good physician he treats epistemology as a collection of illnesses that need to be cured. The prescription he offers throughout this massive

---

20. Like many modern philosophers, Locke made a living by bouncing around between different professional gigs. He was trained as a medical doctor and did in fact practice medicine, but he also had numerous other jobs, including personal secretary and political advisor.

book is always the same: acknowledge that the only legitimate basis for human knowledge is the evidence offered by the senses, that the physical senses are the only access we have to the physical world and the only basis for ideas that are not complete nonsense, but this is not cause for despair because they give us more than enough material to work with, more than enough to know everything that can be known and everything we need to know. Doctor Locke argues that if we follow this prescription we can expect better epistemological health in two ways:

1. We won't waste our time pursuing impossible knowledge.

> If by this inquiry into the nature of the understanding, I can discover the powers thereof, how far they reach, to what things they are in any degree proportionate, and where they fail us, I suppose it may be of use to prevail with the busy mind of man to be more cautious in meddling with things exceeding its comprehension, to stop when it is at the utmost extent of its tether, and to sit down in a quiet ignorance of those things which, upon examination, are found to be beyond the reach of our capacities.[21]

2. We will be confident that everything we need to know can in fact be known.

> We shall not have much reason to complain of the narrowness of our minds, if we will only employ them about what may be of use to us; for of that they are very capable. And it will be an unpardonable, as well as childish peevishness, if we undervalue the advantages of our knowledge and neglect to improve it to the ends for which it was given us, because there are some things that are set out of reach of it.... If we will disbelieve everything because we cannot certainly know all things, we shall do quite as wisely as he who would not use his legs, but sit still and perish, because he had no wings to fly.[22]

The *Essay Concerning Human Understanding* begins with a tirade against innate ideas. This, Locke believes, is the best way to begin a book about how knowledge is possible: "The first thing we do, let's kill all the innate ideas." (To appreciate this truly excellent joke see *Henry VI*, part 2, act 4, scene 2.) He devotes almost one hundred pages to denouncing and

---

21. Locke, *Essay*, 3.
22. Locke, *Essay*, 4–5.

ridiculing innate ideas, which shows how much Locke (and all empiricists) despise the very idea of innate ideas. Really all the arguments in this section boil down to one central claim: we just don't need innate ideas. We can know everything that can be known if the mind is a blank slate (*tabula rasa*) that is simply waiting to be written on by the senses as they bring us the joyous news about what's going on out there in the external world. Then, after doing his utmost in book 1 to exterminate innate ideas, Locke goes on in book 2 to present his own theory that every single idea we can ever have comes from the senses; but as soon as he tries to develop this rough and ready commonsense philosophy into a more systematic and comprehensive theory of knowledge he confronts a few challenges that are not easy to resolve, including the following:

- How do we explain all the ideas we have which obviously have no empirical basis? Right at this very moment, for example, I have in my head an idea of a leprechaun who spends his days writing excellent biographies of modern philosophers, including a Pulitzer Prize-winning book on John Locke, and every evening goes out bowling with his three friends: a horse who paints enormous recreations of battles from the Civil War; a lobster who does consulting work for the World Bank; and a United States senator whose service is motivated entirely by love of country and humanity. Sadly I have no experience of any of these creatures, but I still have no difficulty imagining the four of them as they make their way through all sorts of adventures. How is this possible? Where did these ideas come from, and how should a good empiricist make sense of them?

- One of the attractions of empiricism is that it seems to offer a clear and commonsense way to make human knowledge objective. If the only legitimate basis for knowledge is the senses, and sensory data comes to us directly from the external, objective world, then it seems like our knowledge can be tethered to the objective world in a way that keeps us from disconnecting from reality and spinning off this planet into a world of pure nonsense. Empiricism holds out the promise of a connection between the objective world of objective facts and the subjective world of consciousness—a way to overcome the gap that separates knowing subjects and known objects; but how well does this connection hold up under closer scrutiny? How much can we really, honestly claim to know about the objective "thing in itself"?

To respond to these two challenges Locke deploys the following conceptual machinery:

- It's possible, he argues, to have ideas that are not derived from sensory experience, but those ideas are illegitimate and therefore should not be recognized as real ideas. These so-called "ideas" need to be called out for what they are: nonsense, because there is literally no sense—no sensory experience—behind them, and sensory experience is the only legitimate source of meaning. (This begins a long tradition, which continues in all iterations of empiricism including logical positivism in the twentieth century and still persists today, of empiricists assuming the role of a referee or police officer and blowing a whistle whenever anyone presents an idea that doesn't have empirical data behind it—and humans do generate a lot of these ideas so there's never a shortage of crimes for a good empiricist police officer to investigate.)

- Of the legitimate ideas that remain after the illegitimate nonsense ideas are removed, some are simple and some are complex. The simple ideas are directly connected to sensory experience, so they are the tether to the objective world that makes it possible for knowledge to be objective. Complex ideas are composed of simple ideas, and anything is possible once you start mashing up and recombining simple ideas—which helps to explain why we can have so many ideas that clearly do not directly reflect the realities of the objective world.

- Some of the qualities we perceive in objects are primary, and others are secondary. Primary qualities are actually present in the objects of the objective world, while secondary qualities are not. Locke argues that the objective basis for secondary qualities is a power in objects that is able to generate the experience or perception of secondary qualities within subjects, but the quality itself is not within objects as primary qualities are. Primary qualities are "utterly inseparable from the body, whatever state it is in. Qualities of this kind are the ones that a body doesn't lose, however much it alters."[23] Secondary qualities are not inherent in things themselves so they can change. If you want some examples of secondary qualities, Locke says: "colors,

---

23. Locke, *Essay*, 119.

sounds, tastes, and so on."[24] He doesn't attempt to give a complete catalogue of primary and secondary qualities because it's really just the idea that matters: if the qualities of an object never change then those are primary qualities, and if they do change then those are secondary qualities; that's really all you need to know.

With these three pieces of conceptual machinery Locke attempts to preserve a direct connection between knowledge and the objective world but at the same time explain how we can have all sorts of ideas that are not direct reflections or perfect replicas of the external world. So if you come to Doctor Locke's office complaining of any epistemological illnesses, wondering if perhaps you are entertaining mad ideas that are disconnected from reality, he now has three possible diagnoses he can offer:

- If the ideas you're entertaining have no connection at all to the external world, then yes they are nonsense and the cure is quite simple: Stop thinking nonsense!
- If the ideas in your head are complex ideas that have been assembled by shifting and combining the many simple ideas that you've stored up in the warehouse of your mind, then have no fear: these are still legitimate ideas because they have a genealogy which traces back to simple ideas directly connected to the objective world. As long as you recall that these complex ideas are not direct reflections of the external world you'll be fine; don't worry that you have a serious epistemological illness. (There's actually only one such disease: the one called "nonsense" that Locke diagnosed above.)
- If the ideas in your head are of secondary qualities, have no fear: these too are legitimate ideas that maintain a connection to the objective world. Even though secondary qualities are not actually present in objects (as primary qualities are) they're still caused by certain powers in objects that have the ability to produce the experience of these qualities. So here again Doctor Locke would say, "You're not ill as long as you recall that these secondary qualities you are perceiving are not really in objects themselves. You're still tethered to the external world so you're still a healthy and objective subject."

The concepts that Locke introduced to make these diagnoses possible seem quite innocuous at first, but they end up leading to some very

24. Locke, *Essay*, 120.

surprising results and perhaps only widening the gulf between subjects and objects—the gulf that empiricism was trying to close. Most of these surprising results were not worked out until later, most notably by Berkeley and Hume, but already in Locke's *Essay Concerning Human Understanding* there are lots of surprises that Locke is happy to embrace. It turns out that pure empiricism, which denies the possibility of innate ideas or any other legitimate source for ideas besides sensory experience, leads to some very surprising and counterintuitive results.

One noteworthy example of Locke's willingness to follow the logic of empiricism wherever it leads is his theory of human identity, which is summarized in book 2, chapter 27: "Of Identity and Diversity." Here Locke argues that you are not your body, and in fact your identity has nothing at all to do with your body. This is an interesting argument for a physician to make. According to this argument, if you take your body to a doctor (such as Doctor John Locke) to get it repaired, the doctor is only dealing with you as a "man" (or, to use less sexist language, "human" or "guy" or "dude"—in the sense in which all interesting and thoughtful people are obviously "dudes" regardless of their gender), not as a "person." To arrive at this conclusion Locke begins with the simplest form of identity: the identity of a "substance." Think of a rock or any other inanimate object: it's easy to understand that it's the same thing over time because this physical substance continues to occupy the same space and time. But as soon as you try to make sense of the identity of anything that lives and grows (such as an oak tree or a weasel or a human) you need a more sophisticated theory of identity that allows for the thing to change over time yet still retain its core identity. Plants and animals are like machines, with lots of moving parts and changes over time, but it's still possible to understand their identity strictly in terms of their physical bodies. This is what Locke means by the identity of a "man": having the same "living, organized body." This is a very superficial understanding of identity but for the most part we settle for this in the human world: when we say something like "that's the same guy" it's a judgment based entirely on the outward appearance of someone's body. But, Locke argues, this superficial version of identity doesn't reflect the true, deeper identity that everyone has as a "person," which is 100 percent a function of one's consciousness. Consciousness alone is what gives humans the only identity that really matters, the form of identity that sets us apart from oak trees and weasels.

It follows that if you or anyone else on earth has at this moment all of the memories and every other part of the consciousness of John Locke dating all the way back to his birth in 1632, then you are without a doubt the "person" John Locke in the only sense that matters; and by the same logic if you or I ever lose possession of our memories and all the other aspects of our current consciousness that define us as the persons we are today, then we're no longer those persons, regardless of the body we happen to be using at the moment. Locke's theory of identity as nothing more or less than consciousness is alive and well today in one of the many technologies that we use to prove our own identity and prevent others from stealing it (and along with it all of our money): passwords. The whole idea of a password is that you remember it, that it exists only in your unique and private consciousness, and thus every time you remember a password you're proving that you still have the same consciousness and are thus the same person.

Locke's theory of identity maintains that since consciousness is the only thing that determines identity it's completely possible for one identity to occupy multiple bodies, or for multiple identities to occupy a single body. Empiricism is supposed to be a down-to-earth, commonsense approach to philosophy so it's surprising that it leads to this rather bizarre result, but it does because Locke emphasizes that all we really know about our own personal identity from our own experience is that consciousness is both a necessary and a sufficient condition for it: everything else about personal identity is a mystery to us. So in this case a consistent empirical method leads us to embrace empirical evidence to which we alone have access: the experience of our own consciousness, and reject the empirical data that's available to everyone else: the appearance of our bodies. An honest and complete empiricism leads us to acknowledge that knowledge of anyone else's identity other than our own is impossible; individuals can only be certain of their own identity and can't pretend to know anything about anyone else's identity. Locke's willingness to embrace this surprising result is a good preface to the many other surprises his empiricism will occasion.

George Berkeley

In his *Essay Concerning Human Understanding* Locke tried gamely to prove that empiricism keeps us connected us to the objective world outside our heads, and also keeps the thoughts in our heads connected to each other in a coherent manner. Because these connections are preserved, he argued, empiricism can cure all our epistemological illnesses. However, the next two athletes to take the baton in the British Empiricism 500-meter relay claimed that the principles of Locke's *Essay*, if taken to their natural conclusion, actually undermined both of these connections which Locke insisted were necessary to make knowledge possible and to defeat nonsense. Berkeley began by arguing that Locke's empiricism actually severed any connection to an external, objective world—that it actually made the very idea of such a world nonsensical; and then Hume followed by arguing that a thorough and consistent empiricism has to acknowledge that there are no necessary connections at all between the ideas in our head—that here too an honest empirical observation of our thoughts reveals that nothing holds them together except custom and convention. So the connections that Locke worked so hard to establish in his *Essay* end up getting dissolved not by enemies or opponents of empiricism but rather by its most ardent defenders.

To set the stage for Berkeley please consider how, in spite of Locke's best efforts, his empiricism seems to open up a gulf between subject and object rather than closing that gap. Locke labored diligently to establish a connection between the subjective ideas in our head and the objective reality of things in the world, but in order to preserve that connection and also explain the wide variety of thoughts we actually have in our heads he had to allow that in addition to simple ideas (directly connected to objective reality) there are also complex ideas (recombinations of simple ideas that are no longer directly tethered to objective reality), and in addition to primary qualities (which are built right into the things themselves) there are also secondary qualities (which are somehow provoked by objective things but not actually present in them, so these ideas too are not directly tethered to the objective world). Locke was honest enough to acknowledge that when he was done the connection he'd established between our thoughts and the world was tenuous at best and that the objective world which is the basis of all legitimate knowledge, according to empiricism, can only be thought of as a "something I know not what."[25] "But," Locke says, "at least we know it's there!" We can at least be confident that there is an objective external world that is the origin of all our ideas even if we can't know everything about it, and Locke thinks that is good enough.

25. Locke, *Essay*, 424.

This is the moment when George Berkeley interrupts and says: "Actually if you really want to be a consistent empiricist, the time has come to acknowledge that the idea of an external, objective world that is the origin of all our empirical ideas is complete nonsense—it's the most nonsensical idea of all. A real empiricist realizes that the external, objective world is just as irrelevant to human knowledge as innate ideas: both of them are completely nonsensical and unnecessary to explain how knowledge is possible." Berkeley argues that objects don't exist independently of our perceiving them because "to be is to be perceived." To get to this startling conclusion—that one necessary consequence of empiricism is that there is no empirical world—Berkeley simply followed Locke's arguments to their logical conclusion. More specifically, Berkeley latched onto Locke's claim that secondary qualities are not in the objects themselves and extended the logic of that argument to cover all of our ideas: none of them are in objects themselves, he argued. There is in fact no lifeline, no tether, between the ideas in our heads and the world of objective things outside our heads, because there is no objective, external world outside our heads.

Before we go any further we should note that Berkeley did not think the loss of the external world is in any way a calamity. This is because Berkeley is in some ways the last of the medieval philosophers: the last person to attempt to put philosophy to work for the purpose of saving our souls. Berkeley argues that Locke and the other British empiricists who preceded him were sort of like Plato in that they created an excellent philosophical argument but were oblivious to the awesome theological potential that it possessed. The theory of pure empiricism that Locke codified and systematized is actually a marvelous missionary tool, Berkeley thinks, because it clarifies that human knowledge is only possible if God constantly intervenes. Thus empiricism proves the existence of God, and thus it can save the souls of all unbelievers. Like so many of the medieval philosophers in whose footsteps he is following, Berkeley was employed by the Christian Church (he is often referred to as "Bishop Berkeley" since he was the Anglican Bishop of Cloyne), and he wrote works of philosophy that always had an explicitly Christian purpose. In one of his most interesting and entertaining works—a conversation between "Hylas," who is so benighted that he still believes that there is an external world, and the more enlightened "Philonous," who is a convert to Berkeley's true version of empiricism—Berkeley made the religious purpose explicit right in the book's title: *Three Dialogues between Hylas and Philonous in Opposition to Sceptics and Atheists*. Berkeley argues that his version of empiricism makes it impossible to be a skeptic, because skeptics are skeptical that our human ideas conform to objective reality but in his theory there is no external world to be disconnected from (and thus skepticism is eliminated forever), and also impossible to be an atheist, because according to his theory the only possible source for the ideas that we do in fact have is the Lord God Almighty, and thank God for that (quite literally) because otherwise it would be impossible for us to know anything.

Berkeley argues that the only possible explanation for our perception of the world is that what we call "reality" is actually more like virtual reality. Human experience is effectively one enormous virtual reality video game that is run by God. God keeps the game running at all times and coordinates all of our perceptions so that we all experience the same (virtual) reality and thus we all naively think that there's a material, substantial world out there that supplies us with all our ideas when actually there isn't: the game is just that good. Though this theory may seem like the complete rejection of everything empiricism stands for Berkeley argues that it's actually just the next step in a consistent empiricist theory—just a matter of taking Locke seriously. Here's why:

First we need to acknowledge that the only thing we ever experience is ideas, and ideas can only resemble other ideas. This is what honest empirical observation of our experience reveals. Since we only experience ideas, and since ideas can only connect to other ideas, the notion of some sort of necessary connection (or tether) between the ideas in our minds and objective things outside our minds is just incoherent: a classic example of the sort of nonsense that empiricism condemns. It follows from this that to be is simply to be perceived, and therefore everything we think has an existence independent of our perception in the material world actually does not: it exists only as an idea in our minds.

> All the choir in heaven and furniture of the earth, in a word all those bodies that compose the mighty structure of the world, have no existence outside a mind; for them to exist is for them to be perceived or known; consequently so long as they aren't actually perceived by myself or any other created spirit, they must have either no existence at all or else in the mind of some eternal spirit; because it makes no sense—and involves all the absurdities of abstraction—to attribute to any such thing an existence independent of a spirit.[26]

26. Berkeley, *Principles*, 89.

Berkeley invites everyone to try as hard as they like to imagine an external world that's independent of your mind—so go ahead, try that right now. Finished? Ok now please consider: what did you accomplish? Samuel Johnson famously claimed to have refuted Berkeley's theory by kicking a large rock ("I refute him thus!" he said), but Berkeley would say that Johnson only succeeded in hurting his foot and didn't harm his epistemological theory at all, because the rock, his foot, and the pain in his foot—all of these exist only as ideas in Samuel Johnson's mind so all he did was create more ideas that can only connect with other ideas and can never connect in any way with "an external world." Like Samuel Johnson, when you did your little thought experiment just now Berkeley would say that you only created more evidence to support his theory because no matter how intricate and detailed you imagined the external, objective world to be it still remained nothing but ideas in your mind—ideas that exist only in your mind and that can only resemble or connect in some way with other ideas. So congratulations, Berkeley would say, you just proved his point: the connection that Locke insisted upon between ideas and objects simply doesn't exist.

Like every good empiricist Berkeley insists that all ideas originate with our senses, but that our senses actually sense an external, material world and have their ideas impressed upon them by this external world—that part of Locke's theory is incoherent nonsense. We all do have regular and orderly ideas of an external world but Berkeley argues that the only possible explanation for this fact is that God is constantly supplying all these ideas to everyone's minds and thus creating for us the experience of a persistent and orderly material world. What we think of as reality is actually more like virtual reality: we're all absorbed in the most amazing video game ever and God keeps the game running glitch-free forever. This is where pure empiricism takes you, Berkeley argues, if you're willing to follow its principles all the way: to the conclusion that there is no external, objective world, and that all the ideas that come to us through our senses are dispatched to us by God in the greatest virtual reality game ever created. (Berkeley's empiricism uses something like the perfect opposite of Descartes's Evil Genius, who is effectively the Christian God run amok. Whereas Descartes argues it's possible that an omnipotent Evil Genius is devoting all of its power and time to deceiving us, even going as far as feeding into our minds completely false concepts of mathematics such as $5 + 7 = 12$, Berkeley insists that what God is really doing all the time is supplying our senses with a constant stream of ideas that creates the same virtual reality experience for everyone alive—which is certainly a proof that God is very good and also quite a genius: a very good genius.)

This worldview is not cause for confusion or despair, Berkeley argues: actually just the opposite. It will cure both your skepticism and your atheism and send you on your way rejoicing. This is the main point he wanted to make in *Three Dialogues between Hylas and Philonous in Opposition to Sceptics and Atheists*. This dialogue is like an intervention in three acts. Philonous is trying to save his friend Hylas, who has a serious substance-abuse problem: he is addicted to the belief that material, unthinking substances exist, and that they—not God—are the source and the cause of all our ideas. Philonous wants Hylas to see that his addiction is ruining his life because it has turned him into a skeptic for sure, and possibly even an atheist. So Philonous stages a three-day intervention to rescue his friend from his substance-abuse problem, his philosophical addiction, and as in any intervention the addict puts up lots of resistance and there's a lot of screaming and yelling and the same arguments get repeated over and over, but in the end it works and Hylas is cured. Over the course of this three-day dialogue as Hylas is gradually converted to the truth that "to be is to be perceived" he feels confused and disoriented, wondering how to get his bearings in a world that he now recognizes as a virtual reality world; but the enlightened Philonous reassures his friend that nothing has been lost: everything that charmed us about the world before when we thought that it had a material existence independent of our perception is only more charming now that we realize it's all a video game—that just makes it even more impressive and leads us to adore and worship the Game Maker. Philonous wakes up every morning practically singing and delights in the amazing detail and regularity of the virtual world that God supplies to him, and everyone else, in the form of nonstop sensory ideas; he only enjoys and appreciates it more now that he knows that this "reality" is actually virtual reality. Here's how Philonous greets Hylas as they begin their dialogue outside in a garden:

> Can there be a pleasanter time of the day, or a more delightful season of the year? That purple sky, those wild but sweet notes of birds, the fragrant bloom upon the trees and flowers, the gentle influence of the rising sun, these and a thousand nameless beauties of nature inspire the soul with secret transports. . . .[27]

It takes a full three days of therapy to get Hylas to see that one can celebrate the natural world with this sort of rapture while still understanding

27. Berkeley, *Three Dialogues*, 151.

that there really is no natural world—that what you're experiencing is nothing but a virtual reality in a truly impressive video game created and maintained by God.

One of Berkeley's most interesting accomplishments is that he managed to get a particular part of the objective, external world (which he believed did not exist) named after him. In 1866 when the trustees of the College of California were wondering what to call the place where they had chosen to locate the College one of them recalled this poem that Berkeley wrote in 1726 called "Verses on the Prospect of Planting Arts and Learning in America":

> The Muse, disgusted at an age and clime
> Barren of every glorious theme,
> In distant lands now waits a better time,
> Producing subjects worthy fame.
>
> In happy climes, where from the genial sun
> And virgin earth such scenes ensue,
> The force of art by nature seems outdone,
> And fancied beauties by the true;
>
> In happy climes, the seat of innocence,
> Where nature guides and virtue rules,
> Where men shall not impose for truth and sense
> The pedantry of courts and schools:
>
> There shall be sung another golden age,
> The rise of empire and of arts,
> The good and great inspiring epic rage,
> The wisest heads and noblest hearts.
>
> Not such as Europe breeds in her decay;
> Such as she bred when fresh and young,
> When heavenly flame did animate her clay,
> By future poets shall be sung.
>
> Westward the course of empire takes its way;
> The first four acts already past,
> A fifth shall close the drama with the day;
> Time's noblest offspring is the last.

They liked this poem so much they decided to call the location of the future University of California "Berkeley" in honor of its author. Of course

George Berkeley would say that what they named after him was just a collection of ideas that are uniformly and consistently conveyed to every human mind by God, and certainly not an actual place in the physical world, since that would be completely incoherent.

David Hume

After Berkeley undermined Locke's claim that there are necessary connections between ideas in our minds and objective, material things in the world, Hume followed with an argument that there are also no necessary connections between any of the ideas in our minds. Hume, like Berkeley, is a proponent of empiricism, not an opponent; but like Berkeley he thinks that the full implications of empiricism have not been acknowledged. The two massive epistemology books that Hume wrote begin by arguing that empiricism is obviously the only legitimate foundation for knowledge, but by the end of each book it's not at all clear how it's possible to know anything at all based on this foundation.

Hume started writing the first of these books, *A Treatise of Human Nature*, when he was only twenty-three years old and finished it three years later. When that book went almost completely unnoticed (the book fell "stillborn from the press" Hume wrote in his characteristically droll fashion), he wrote another book (*An Enquiry Concerning Human Understanding*) to try to say the same things in a more succinct and accessible way. There's really just one big epistemological idea that both of these books are trying to express, and the fact that Hume struggled and stammered through two books and several hundred pages to express this one big idea is actually a very useful demonstration of that very idea, which is this: things fall apart; ideas disintegrate; there's nothing holding them together; no necessary connections at all between one idea and another. This is, Hume argues, a truth that empiricism reveals; it's a natural consequence of taking the founding principles of empiricism seriously. The fact that the two long books that Hume wrote to express this idea often seem fragmentary and disjointed demonstrates quite effectively the very idea that he's struggling to express in these books.

In fairness we should acknowledge that anyone trying to say something radically new, whether that person is an artist, a scientist, a philosopher, or anyone else, often stammers and stutters and says too much, circling around and around the idea they're trying to express and trying out every possible way of saying it. As Hume circles his own big idea one metaphor that he tries out is particularly useful:

> And by this means we may, perhaps, attain a new microscope or species of optics by which, in the moral sciences, the most minute and most simple ideas may be so enlarged as to fall readily under our apprehension and be equally known with the grossest and most sensible ideas that can be the object of our enquiry.[28]

Hume's basic insight is that if you really want to be an empiricist all the way and all the time you have to treat your own ideas as empirical data too, and you have to give an honest and accurate empirical description of what you find there. Take any moment of experience and freeze it—like a picture, a snapshot—and then put that moment of experience under a microscope and enlarge it so that you can look at it more closely and see what's really there. When we do this what we thought was a coherent and unified experience disintegrates: it atomizes, fracturing into particular ideas and impressions that have no necessary connections that hold them together. Today it's much easier to appreciate the empirical result Hume was describing because digital technology enables us to do exactly what Hume and his readers could only imagine. Take, for example, a digital photograph (which is a nice representation of a moment or snapshot of experience) and just keep enlarging it on your screen. Very quickly the photograph pixelates and you can begin to see the individual bits of color that compose the overall image. You may have to enlarge it several times but eventually every digital image will disintegrate when you put it under this microscope because that's the basic nature of all digital media: it's just lots of individual bits of data that have no necessary connection to each other. You can do the same thing with a movie or piece of music or anything else that has been digitized: when you put it under a microscope and enlarge it until you can see it at the most basic and fundamental level what you find is just a string of bits (ones and zeros ultimately) that have no necessary connection to each other at all. This is what honest empirical observation of our own ideas reveals to us.

Of course when you listen to digital music or watch a digital movie you experience it as a completeness, a wholeness, and not a fractured string of arbitrary numbers or bits, and the same is true of any piece of our experience. Right now as you read this book, for example, you're no doubt thinking: "This chapter is a truly excellent account of modern philosophy,

---

28. Hume, *Enquiry*, 62.

and really the entire book is just outstanding. It's extremely well-written and coherent; every sentence and every word fits into the larger narrative perfectly to form a thoroughly rewarding and edifying reading experience. I certainly got my money's worth when I bought this book; I don't regret buying it at all!" This is what the experience of reading the book feels like on the surface, but a good empiricist can't settle for a merely superficial understanding of reality. Beneath the surface of any experience is a booming, buzzing confusion of the individual atoms of perception that have no necessary connection with each other at all. When we look at any experience honestly, under the microscope of empirical analysis, everything falls apart. So why does all of our experience feel unified and coherent even though at its most basic level it's fractured and disjointed? Because we add something to the empirical data that smooths it out and makes the bits appear to stick together, namely: custom and convention. Obviously this breaks rule 1 in the Empiricism Rule Book: don't allow anything that isn't actual sensory experience to sneak into your mind and pretend that it's legitimate. That's the cause of all the epistemological illnesses that Doctor John Locke diagnosed and it's the basic idea that allows empiricism to present itself as common sense, but Hume has revealed that even the most committed empiricist relies on the habits of custom and convention to keep the bits of his sensory experience glued together.

Hume provided a very useful application of his fundamental insight in his analysis of human identity. Recall that when Locke turned his own empirical theory on the question of the self the results were quite startling, with Locke arguing that consciousness alone constitutes a self and that the objects we call "human bodies" have nothing to do with it. Locke's conclusion about identity is surprising, but not nearly as surprising as Hume's conclusion, which is that an honest empiricist must admit there really is no self. When you put the notion of the self under a microscope and enlarge it you discover that it's nothing more than a "bundle of perceptions" with no necessary connections that unify these bits of empirical data. Locke's version of the self as consciousness was supposed to be immune to the change and disintegration that's so obvious in the human body (everyone's body is constantly changing, mostly for the worse, and generally falling apart); but if you put your consciousness under a microscope, Hume argues, it falls apart just as obviously as your body does. What we actually find when we strip away all the customs and conventions that are built into our thinking about selves is simply:

> Nothing but a bundle or collection of different perceptions which succeed each other with an inconceivable rapidity and are in a perpetual flux and movement. . . . The mind is a kind of theatre where several perceptions successively make their appearance, pass, repass, glide away, and mingle in an infinite variety of postures and situations. There is properly no *simplicity* in it at one time nor *identity* in different, whatever natural propensity we may have to imagine that simplicity and identity.[29]

When this same analysis is applied across the board to all of our experience everything that we thought we knew disintegrates. One notable casualty is the concept of cause and effect, which is quite important to science or any other effort to make sense of the world. If you put any experience we confidently call cause and effect under a microscope what you actually see there is just one damn thing after another with no necessary connection whatsoever between all these damn things. To use Hume's most famous example: imagine playing billiards. You hit the cue ball and it rolls across the table and bumps the eight ball, sending it into the side pocket, causing you to win this nationally televised round of the World Series of Billiards and causing your fans to erupt in wild applause. It looks like there's a lot of causation going on here, but what do we actually observe, empirically, when we put all of this under a microscope? When the cue ball hits the eight ball and then the eight ball starts rolling toward the side pocket everyone agrees that the cue ball caused this movement, but what do we actually observe? The cue ball rolls across the table, it strikes the eight ball, then the eight ball starts rolling; that's all there is in terms of empirical data. Nowhere among all the atoms of this experience is there any experience of causation. Causation is just a convention that we apply to situations like this, it's a non-empirical custom or habit that we add to the bits of our experience to smooth them out and make them seem to fit together in some way when actually they don't. So every time we say that one thing caused another thing we break the first rule of the Empiricist Rule Book: we add something completely non-empirical to our experience and pretend that this non-empirical impostor is legitimate.

Like Berkeley, Hume takes empiricism to a place that Locke never imagined. The *Enquiry Concerning Human Understanding* ends on a dramatic note with Hume commanding everyone to "commit to the flames" most of what's in the philosophy section of the library, because the vast

---

29. Hume, *Treatise*, 165.

majority of it is "nothing but sophistry and illusion."[30] What's left of philosophy after Hume is done with it? Very little; almost nothing. Hume agrees with all the other British empiricists that empiricism is the correct approach to epistemology, but he claims that a thorough and honest empiricism leads unavoidably to the conclusion that most of what we call knowledge is actually just custom and convention: basically just a habit or a tradition that works for us, so we keep doing it.

Perhaps the most surprising part of Hume's empiricism is that he doesn't find any of this very concerning. Hume seems to regard philosophy as something like a disease that needs to be cured so that the wisdom of common life can reassert its true authority, and therefore he wrote several long and complicated philosophy books to persuade philosophy to commit suicide. For Hume philosophy is useful to reveal the limits of philosophy, but once those limits have been clarified a greatly humbled philosophy should stop pretending to know so much. Berkeley takes the founding principles of Locke's empiricism and argues that they lead to the startling and counterintuitive conclusion that empiricism proves there is no objective, empirical world, but he regards this discovery as a terrific missionary tool that can save the souls of skeptics and atheists. There are no necessary connections between our ideas and objects in the world, Berkeley argues, but that's just fine—in fact its cause for celebration (and worship), because it shows how true philosophy leads to true religion. Hume isn't interested in using philosophy to support religion but in his own way he does present his arguments on epistemology as a sort of missionary tool. The conversion experience Hume offers is a reaffirmation of the wisdom of custom and convention, common sense and common life. An honest empirical accounting of the ideas that make up our experience reveals there are no necessary connections between any of them and only pragmatic conventions hold them together. This, however, is not a disaster, because the pragmatic conventions of common life are more than enough. So chill out dude, Hume argues, because nothing is lost when philosophy accepts its greatly demoted status and slinks back home in humility. Go play some billiards; hang out with your friends; go with the flow; stop worrying so much about whether or not knowledge is possible. This is the religion of common life that Hume offers his readers, and he's quite content with it.

30. Hume, *Enquiry*, 165.

We should note, however, what a huge step down this is from the original epistemological aspirations of modern philosophy. Descartes wanted to use philosophy to provide a secure and lasting foundation for the sciences that were making such obvious and rapid progress in the sixteenth and seventeenth centuries, and he claimed that he succeeded. The first British empiricists thought that Descartes's rationalist approach was all wrong, but they shared his goal of explaining how knowledge and certainty are possible. Locke attempted to clarify and systematize the basic principles of empiricism and thus cure any lingering doubts about human knowledge; but then Berkeley and Hume took Locke's ideas and used them to show that knowledge is only possible by means of constant divine intervention (Berkeley), or else not really possible at all, unless we're willing to call non-empirical customs and conventions "knowledge" (Hume). By the time Hume is done with philosophy it has been reduced to a very meek and humble status and it's hardly in a position to provide a secure and lasting foundation for anything, especially the sciences. For Hume philosophy is really only useful to demonstrate what philosophy *can't* do.

Hume was perfectly fine with this result, so after writing his two big epistemology books he went off to enjoy himself for the rest of his life. He traveled throughout Europe and became famous as a historian (he published a multivolume *History of England* that was a best-seller in his time) and as a *bon vivant*. But one person who was definitely not okay with Hume's conclusions was a philosophy professor who was famous for not traveling at all, and in fact never once left the city where he was born. This was Immanuel Kant, who now rides onto the stage on a white horse named "Synthetic A Priori Bucephalus" (the significance of which will become clear shortly) to begin scene 3 of this play within a play.

Scene 3: Immanuel Kant rides to the rescue with his own epistemological theory that uses both rationalism and empiricism and offers to provide a deus ex machina resolution to the duel between rationalism and empiricism

Immanuel Kant

One thing that's clear from the debate between rationalism and empiricism that has been our entertainment for much of this chapter: each of these squads regards the other team as deluded and exasperating. Empiricists think it's just obvious that information gained from the senses is the only possible basis for knowledge. The senses are all we've got to work with, they think, so it seems completely insane to refuse to use the senses and even turn against them, as rationalists argue we should. Rationalists, on the other hand, think it's just obvious that the senses are far too limited and imprecise to serve as the foundation for knowledge since what we want from knowledge is absolute certainty. The senses never allow us to be completely certain about anything, and sometimes they very obviously deceive us, so it seems completely insane to waste time on the senses instead of trying to find another source for knowledge that will allow knowledge to be certain. There's something like a cultural divide that separates rationalists and empiricists throughout the modern period, and only at the end of the eighteenth century does Immanuel Kant finally address this divide and try to overcome it with an epistemological theory that acknowledges the insights of both rationalism and empiricism and attempts to integrate the best elements of both into a single theory. As we've seen, both rationalism and empiricism can seem intuitive and commonsensical but when you push the founding assumptions of those theories to their logical conclusion you find yourself in very strange, counterintuitive territory. Kant wants to rescue rationalism and empiricism from the corners they've painted themselves into, and he wants to answer definitively and finally the simple question they both tried to answer: "How is knowledge possible?"

Kant is the obvious choice for last major philosopher of the eighteenth century (he died in 1804, just a few years into the nineteenth century), but what he really wanted was not just to be the last actor to leave the stage but rather the playwright who crafts an ending to the conflict between rationalism and empiricism. He wanted to clean up all the loose ends in this story and bring it to a satisfying conclusion. This will not be at all easy since the rationalists and empiricists of the sixteenth, seventeenth, and eighteenth centuries were all rather wild and crazy extremists who had no interest in cleaning up after themselves, so it's going to require something like a *deus ex machina* ending. *Deus ex machina* means "God from the machine." In some Greek plays this technique was employed to wrap up all the loose ends so that the play could conclude and everyone could go home finally: an actor playing the part of a God was lowered onto the stage in a basket and basically declared: "I hereby fix everything!" This is a good way to understand what Kant is trying to do with the marvelous machinery that he creates to end the duel between rationalism and empiricism for at least two reasons:

- Kant wants to make everyone happy and solve all the problems that both rationalists and empiricists have created for themselves. He wants everyone to go home satisfied that all the questions and conflicts raised in the standoff between rationalism and empiricism have been resolved.

- Kant does create (actually he said he discovered it, inside your head) something like a machine to bring about this happy ending, though it's a much more complicated machine than just a basket attached to a rope and a crank. Kant's machine is like a factory where an army of workers hammer, saw, weld, drill, sand, and polish the raw material of perception until it emerges at the end of the assembly line as knowledge—or you could see it as an immense bureaucracy with many departments, divisions, commissions, agencies, and offices: The Department of Space; The Sub-Division of Time; The Transcendental Port Authority; The Bureau of Categories; The Office of Noumena; The Division of Phenomena; The Archetectonic Agency; The Synthetic *A Priori* Commission, etc. But unlike most bureaucracies this one operates with efficiency and alacrity. A humble bit of perception enters the colossal office building that houses the Ministry of Knowledge, hat in hand and feeling rather intimidated by the immensity and complexity of this bureaucracy, but it is quickly and efficiently led though the many corridors and offices of the enormous building and every form and stamp and signature that it requires is promptly provided, so with remarkable speed and efficiency the raw material of perception is processed and discharged, exiting the building proudly into the bright summer sunshine having been officially certified as knowledge.

Here's the blueprint for the machine that Kant discovered inside your head. The mind has three general faculties, which are like departments in a bureaucracy or stages on an assembly line, and each of them shapes, structures, and processes the raw material of perception with *a priori* forms, concepts, and demands until this raw material is finally transformed into knowledge.

	The Faculty of Sensibility	The Faculty of Understanding	The Faculty of Reason	
The external, objective world (aka *noumena*) supplies empirical input—"the manifold"—to the faculty of sensibility →	Two *a priori* forms of sensibility that make sensation possible: (1) Space (the form of outer sense) (2) Time (the form of inner sense) The manifold, now shaped and structured by the forms of space and time, is passed along to →	Twelve *a priori* categories or concepts that make thinking and knowledge possible: Unity Plurality Totality Reality Negation Limitation Substance Causation Community Possibility Existence Necessity . . . and there's still one more stage →	Three transcendent ideas that transgress the limits of possible experience and thus are undecidable and unknowable: (1) The Psychological Idea (that there is a substantial *psyche*: a self or soul) (2) The Cosmological Idea (four contradictions in which both thesis and antithesis can be proven) (a) the world is finite/infinite (b) everything is simple/complex (c) there is/is not freedom (d) something/nothing is necessary (3) The Theological Idea (that there is a transcendent, infinite God) →	At the end of this process, knowledge (of *phenomena*, not *noumena*) finally emerges into the world!

Here are some design notes to clarify exactly what's going on in this machine and how it combines elements of both rationalism and empiricism.

First: the whole process starts with perception: input from the external world. The raw material that is processed by Kant's machine is perception of the actual, objective world, which Kant insists is still there.

This is the lifeline or tether between objective things and subjective ideas that was so important to Locke's empiricism; but like Locke, Kant acknowledges that this objective, external world is a "something I know not what." Things in themselves or *noumena* remain forever unknowable to us because the machine of thought can only recognize what it has processed: it can only recognize its own output. The noumenal input that supplies the raw material to the machine of thought is *a posteriori* in that it is the consequence and product of sensory experience, but all the forms, concepts, and ideas that structure this raw material from this point on are *a priori*: they are structures that are built into the machinery of the mind itself. These *a priori* structures are subjective but also universal: even though they operate within the private space of individual consciousness they are exactly the same for every individual.

The first of these *a priori* structures are the two basic forms of sensibility: space and time. We are long accustomed to thinking of space and time as features of the objective world, and this is the first mistake that Kant wants to correct. Space and time are templates or filters that we impose on the raw data of perception we derive from the external world, he argues. They are properties of our minds, not properties of the world, and if you want proof do this experiment right now: try to have any thought whatsoever that's not situated within space and time. So how did you do? If you claim to have succeeded in thinking a thought that was completely free of space and time Kant would say, "Try a little harder; look a little closer at the thought you created and see if you can't discern space and time lurking within the frame, always there as the backdrop of any possible idea." There are echoes of Berkeley here in that like Berkeley, Kant instructs us to stop looking out there in the world for these two features of the world because they're not out there; but unlike Berkeley, Kant doesn't resort to divine intervention to explain how these ideas get into your head. If Berkeley's model of epistemology is something like a fantastic virtual reality game controlled by God, Kant's paradigm is more like a simple hardware explanation that doesn't require divine intervention. This is simply the nature of the hardware that we call the human mind, he argues. Space and time are hardwired into this machine, and everyone alive is using the same machinery so everyone necessarily perceives a world that is structured by both space and time.

In the same way Kant also argues that the twelve categories of the understanding (which include causation, necessity, substance, etc.) are properties of our minds, not features of the objective world. These are laws we impose on the objective world, like legislators impose laws on the states that they govern.

> The highest legislation of nature must lie in ourselves, i.e., in our understanding, and . . . we must not seek the universal laws of nature in nature by means of experience, but conversely must seek nature, as to its universal conformity to law, in the conditions of the possibility of experience, which lie in our sensibility and in our understanding.[31]

> *The understanding does not derive its laws (a priori) from, but rather prescribes them to nature.*[32]

This is how Kant proposes to solve the problem Hume discovered when he pushed the principles of empiricism to their logical limits: that everything falls apart when you put it under a microscope; that there are no necessary connections that hold our ideas together. When Hume points out that no one ever perceives anything like causation, for example, Kant agrees, but then he adds: "You're looking for causation in all the wrong places, Herr Hume." Causation is not a feature of the external world that we can perceive, it's a concept that's hardwired into the machinery of the mind (along with eleven other concepts). Because these twelve categories are basic structures of the understanding's machinery we have no access to the world without these filters. So there's no need to fear that cause and effect, or any of the other eleven concepts of the understanding, are illusions or distortions of reality or that perhaps someday we'll wake up and they won't exist any longer. These twelve categories are built into the machinery of every mind, so like space and time they will always be there and it's impossible for us to become disconnected from them.

These first two stages of mental machinery Kant calls the "Transcendental Aesthetic" and the "Transcendental Logic." "Transcendental" has long been a favorite term of philosophers but they often mean completely different things when they use this word. In Kant's case "transcendental" means "the conditions of the possibility of knowledge within the limits of possible experience." This is part of Kant's effort to preserve the connection between the objective world of things and the subjective world of knowledge which was so important to empiricism. Even though the forms of sensibility and the categories of the understanding are hard-wired, *a priori*

---

31. Kant, *Prolegomena*, 80–81.
32. Kant, *Prolegomena*, 82.

features of the mind, they still operate within the limits of possible experience. As soon as the mind tries to go beyond these limits it's attempting something transcendent, not transcendental. Knowledge is possible only within the limits of possible experience, Kant argues; beyond these limits only unknowable and undecidable speculation is possible.

The first two mental faculties that filter and process the raw material of perception respect the limits of possible experience and thus remain strictly transcendental faculties. Really these two faculties alone are all you need to explain how knowledge is possible. But Kant includes a third faculty in his machine that insists on transgressing the limits of possible experience and venturing into the realm of the transcendent where knowledge will no longer be possible. There are three different ways that we attempt transcendent knowledge even though it's impossible. This is a rather crazy, irrational thing to do, so it's truly fascinating that Kant chooses to call this crazy faculty "reason." This final stage of mental processing is something like a capstone class that's the final requirement before you can graduate. The faculty of reason extends itself beyond the limits of possible experience in order to teach two important lessons to every thought before it graduates from this academy of transcendental studies:

- Don't forget that when you venture beyond the limits of possible experience you give up any possibility of knowledge and enter a zone of pure speculation and undecidability where no one can claim to know anything. This is pointless and chaotic and really just a big waste of your time, so don't do it. Resist this temptation. Every human is capable of transcendental knowledge, but no one is capable of transcendent knowledge.

- There is, however, one exception to this rule and that concerns the transcendent ideas that Kant says are necessary for morality. These include the idea that humans have an immortal soul, that God exists, and that our lives are eternal. The truth of these ideas can't possibly be known because they exceed the limits of our mental machinery, but they are "practical postulates of morality"—necessary assumptions that we must make because otherwise there's no reason for us to behave ethically. So this part of the capstone class taught by the Faculty of Reason is a reminder that humans are not merely thinking machines, because we also have an ethical calling that requires us to make certain assumptions on faith. The rather crazy, irrational desire that we have to know the unknowable is in some cases noble because the transcendent ideas which are practical postulates of morality remind us of our true vocation and clear a space for morality. (This is, among other things, a teaser for Kant's next big show, which is all about how ethics is possible. See act 3 of this chapter for more on that!)

Once every thought has learned these two final lessons in the capstone class taught by Reason it's cleared for graduation, and then it can go out into the world and ~~look for a job~~ be recognized as knowledge!

This is the grand finale that Kant proposes for the primary drama/comedy of the modern period: the contest between rationalism and empiricism for the honor of being able to answer the question, "How is knowledge possible anyway?" The resolution that Kant offers is: "It turns out that both rationalism and empiricism are right, at least partially right, because they both prepared the way for my own glorious transcendental synthesis which finally and conclusively explains what's really going on inside our heads when we process the raw data of the noumenal world and transform it into phenomenal (in every sense of the word!) knowledge." Then Kant—still mounted on his excellent horse named Synthetic A Priori Bucephalus—takes a bow, and exits stage left.

Act 2: While rationalism and empiricism do battle throughout the sixteenth, seventeenth, and eighteenth centuries other theories are created which don't fit neatly into that narrative, such as the weird and wonderful creation that Leibniz called "monadology" and the theory of everything that Spinoza called simply "Ethics."

Sometimes modern philosophy is characterized as nothing but a three-hundred-year-long duel between rationalism and empiricism, but that sort of reductive packaging is most likely the product of desperation: a compulsion to clean up and systematize a stage of philosophy's development which is actually quite messy and eclectic. It's true that epistemology was the primary obsession of modern philosophy and it's also true that the debate between empiricism and rationalism was the most prominent aspect of that debate, but that wasn't the only game in town. There are several remarkable philosophical creations in the modern period that can't be reduced to the feud between rationalism and empiricism, such as the utterly unique creation Leibniz called "monadology" and the theory of everything Spinoza called "Ethics." It's true that both of these creations share some characteristics with rationalism, but mainly just in the sense that they are clearly opposed to the rigid limitations demanded by empiricism. They agree with rationalism that philosophy should not be limited only to empirical data; mathematics in some form (which seems like the epitome of a rationalist discipline) is also an inspiration for these authors; and they often adopt a mathematical or geometrical model as the paradigm of certainty and rigor. (Descartes and Leibniz, in addition to being philosophers, were also serious mathematicians, and Spinoza chose to model his magnum opus on Euclid's *Elements*.) Rationalism fights to defend the honor of the *a priori*, which includes the honor of the imagination and every other thought that's possible before the limitations of sensory experience are imposed. So you could call Spinoza and Leibniz rationalists, but only as a way of saying: "Whatever these dudes were doing it definitely wasn't empiricism." But it makes more sense to treat the philosophy of Spinoza and Leibniz as *sui generis:* purely unique creations that don't fit neatly into the empiricism vs. rationalism storyline of modern philosophy. The theories these authors created are perhaps the very best demonstrations of the spirit of radical and joyous experimentation that flourished in the modern period so it would be both crazy and tragic if we allowed their work to be reduced to nothing more than two more moments in the duel between rationalism and empiricism. In this second act of the comic operetta called "Modern Philosophy" I'll do my utmost to present the ideas of Spinoza and Leibniz in a way that does justice to their profound imagination.

Gottfried Wilhelm Leibniz

Leibniz has been described as "the last universal genius," meaning the last person who was actively involved and accomplished in all the intellectual fields that existed in his time, but he could also be understood as the last philosopher who took seriously the idea that philosophy is the love of all wisdom and therefore nothing is off limits. Aristotle, who studied everything from marine biology to psychology and physics, is perhaps the most obvious analogue to Leibniz in this regard. Like Aristotle, Leibniz studied and made contributions to every field in his time, often very important contributions. He and Isaac Newton both independently created calculus; he's often called the first computer scientist because of his work on binary number systems and mechanical calculating machines; he created a breakthrough system of library cataloging—and this list of innovative ideas extends to just about every other intellectual pursuit of the seventeenth century. At that time all of this could be called "philosophy," but the breakthroughs of people like Leibniz and Newton led to a division of philosophy into the many different disciplines that we recognize today. For example, Newton called his most famous book *Mathematical Principles of Natural Philosophy*. Today we call what Newton did "physics," but in Newton's time it was still considered philosophy. The success of the system of natural philosophy that Newton created caused the new science of physics to spin off, and this same dynamic has been repeated many times since then with other natural and social sciences. Leibniz lived at the last moment in human history when every aspect of thought and research was still considered part of philosophy, and perhaps he demonstrated better than anyone, even Aristotle, what such a vision of philosophy looks like in practice.

Of his ideas and arguments that still remain firmly within the bounds of philosophy the cluster of ideas collected under the banner of "Monadology" are Leibniz's most important contribution. Monadology offers its own solution to the debate between rationalism and empiricism, and it also responds to other conflicts and questions raised in modern philosophy such as the gulf between minds and matter that Descartes left in his wake. Leibniz never refined his monadology into anything like a complete system, and its principles are scattered through several different writings, most of which are unfinished. (Almost everything that Leibniz wrote was unfinished—one more reflection of how busy he was working on so many different projects in so many different areas.) This coupled with the fact that the principles of monadology were so unorthodox and surprising made it ripe for parody and misunderstanding, and Voltaire leaped at the opportunity to do both when he made Doctor Pangloss in his novel *Candide* a caricature of Leibniz. *Candide* is certainly a brilliant and hilarious story but no one should rely on it to understand Leibniz's philosophy, which is fascinating and entertaining enough on its own without any help from Voltaire.

Monadology isn't just an attempt to address a particular problem or answer a particular question such as "How is knowledge possible?" It's a theory of everything, and in this respect, as in so many others, Leibniz was ahead of his time since theories of everything don't really take off until the nineteenth century. But there were earlier examples of this genre in the history of philosophy, and one of the first is perhaps the best place to start in order to understand what Leibniz means by monadology. Think back to the classical Greek theory of atomism. Proponents of this theory, such as Leucippus and Democritus, argued that atoms and the void could explain the existence of everything. Later the ethical theory of hedonism (pleasure is good and pain is bad) was grafted onto the metaphysical infrastructure of atomism by Epicurus and his followers to create a true theory of everything that was quite proud of its power and simplicity, so much so that Leucretius confidently titled his poetic summary of atomism *On the Nature of Things*. The atomists claimed that all the questions of all three branches of philosophy could be answered by their theory. Leibniz aspires to the same completeness, and his theory of monadology can look very similar to atomism on the surface, but important differences emerge when we look more closely.

Instead of atoms, Leibniz argues that the basic simple substance of the universe is something he calls a "monad." Monads are "the true atoms of nature,"[33] he says. They are the basic element of existence but that doesn't mean they're the smallest possible things—so small that they can't be cut into anything smaller, which was the defining characteristic of atoms. What matters for Leibniz is not size but completeness and self-sufficiency. Every monad is a self-contained world that doesn't interact in any way with every other self-sufficient monad. He expresses this self-sufficiency with a memorable image: "monads have no windows through which something can enter or leave,"[34] and while you're trying to imagine what a windowless monad looks like you may as well add another feature to your mental picture: each monad "is a perpetual, living mirror of the universe."[35] Monads are windowless in the sense that nothing comes in or goes out of them; they don't interact with any of the other monads, yet they still mirror every other monad in the sense that they appear to be connected and appear to interact with all of them. The apparent interaction that is mirrored in all monads is the consequence of a pre-established harmony created by God. This is like God winding all the monads in the universe as if they were clocks and setting them into perfect synchronicity, but a computer or video game analogy is probably even more apt. Unlike Berkeley's version of empiricism, which is like a universal virtual reality game in which God is busy all the time running the game—making sure that everyone is constantly supplied with the

33. Leibniz, "Monadology," 213.
34. Leibniz, "Monadology," 214.
35. Leibniz, "Monadology," 220.

correct perceptual inputs so that their experience of the virtual world is consistent and uniform—in Leibniz's model of the universe God does all the programming work before the machine is turned on and then gets to sit back and enjoy the show as all the pre-programmed, pre-established harmonies follow their scripts and all the windowless and mirrored monads appear to interact with each other while each one actually remains a completely self-sufficient and self-contained world.

This is probably a good time to pause and remind ourselves what Leibniz is doing. Monadology isn't just a work of imagination, an attempt to create a fictional new world simply because it's beautiful or entertaining or intriguing, like a science fiction story or the latest iteration of the Marvel Cinematic Universe. Leibniz isn't suggesting that the world of monadology is just a possible world; instead he's arguing that this is the best explanation of the world that we all fell into, the world as we actually experience it. To appreciate fully the ideas and arguments that Leibniz chose to include in his monadology we should remind ourselves that he was completely committed to the principle of sufficient reason, which is simply the idea that there's a good explanation for everything.[36] Leibniz applied the same logic of experimentation and explanation to his philosophy of monadology that he applied to the creation of calculus, or a mechanical calculating machine, or a library cataloguing system, or any of the other projects that he worked on throughout his life. If a pre-established harmony of windowless but mirrored monads seems bizarre, Leibniz would say that strangeness is just a reflection of the strangeness of the world as we found it—the strangeness of the human condition. Our experience is so weird that the only possible explanation for it is that the world consists of self-sufficient monads that do not interact in any way but only seem to because the God who created this world of monads synchronized all of them in a perfect and everlasting harmony, thus creating the best of all possible worlds. "This is the best of all possible explanations for this best of all possible worlds," Leibniz would say, "and if you think this explanation is weird don't blame me; I'm just the messenger. If you can come up with a better explanation for the world as we actually experience it, please tell us!" Monadology may look like mysticism or religion, but Leibniz was one of the greatest proponents of rationalism and enlightenment in the history of the world and he doesn't expect us to take any of his ideas on faith. He argues for every claim, and he asks us to

---

36. Leibniz, "Monadology," 217.

open our minds to the possibility that the reality of the universe beneath the surface may be completely different from what we imagined. His philosophy is one of the apexes of the spirit of experimentation in modern philosophy, and it also clarifies some of the most important divisions and disruptions that occurred during this period.

Before we leave Leibniz, if perhaps you are now thinking to yourself, "I believe this monadology would make an awesome TV show which I for one would definitely watch"—then you're in luck! *John from Cincinnati*, which ran for only one season in 2007 on HBO, is surely one of the strangest TV shows ever, but it does seem like a very sincere attempt to perform Leibniz's *Monadology*. The show is built around a mysterious central character named "John Monad," but all of the other characters act like monads as well. They wander through the surfer community of Imperial Beach, California, apparently interacting with each other and affecting each other, but actually just following their own interior nature and qualities. All of the apparent "interactions" that occur between these monads make more sense as the consequence of a pre-established harmony that God created. In the midst of this complicated performance most of the monads/characters have no idea what's going on, which isn't surprising because according to Leibniz most monads are "mere monads" that don't have very distinct perceptions and don't manage to form memories based on their experience. All monads have perceptions, "but when there is a great multitude of small perceptions in which nothing is distinct, we are stupefied. This is similar to when we continually spin in the same direction several times in succession, from which arises a dizziness that can make us faint and does not allow us to distinguish anything."[37] Oh and by the way, this extremely complicated system of windowless monads and minds and bodies which seem to interact with each other, but actually are just following the pre-established harmony created by God, is the best of all possible worlds. The show left everyone who watched it thoroughly puzzled; the number of viewers declined with each episode; and immediately after the final episode of its first season HBO announced that the show was canceled. Apparently the world was still not quite ready for this radical theory of reality from the seventeenth century.

---

37. Leibniz, "Monadology," 216.

Baruch Spinoza

The complete title of Spinoza's most famous book is *Ethics Demonstrated in Geometrical Order* because Spinoza structured the book like a series of geometrical proofs using the conceptual architecture of Euclid's *Elements*, including all of the following:

> "definitions" (the author defines his terms however he likes)
> "axioms" (statements which are supposed to be obviously true and therefore need no arguments)
> "propositions" (statements which are controversial and therefore need to be supported with arguments)
> "demonstrations" (arguments to support each controversial proposition)
> "*scholia*" (plural of *scholium*, wherein Spinoza interrupts the logical march of his arguments to take the reader to school by elaborating on some key concept or argument)
> "corollaries" (any additional propositions that happen to follow from propositions that have already been proven).

There are also "explanations" inserted whenever Spinoza wants to clarify or elaborate; there's a "preface" before parts 2–5; and parts 1 and 4 end with an "appendix" which functions like a long concluding *scholium* to summarize the arguments and results of the book so far. Spinoza's attempt to demonstrate conclusions concerning God, nature, ethics, emotions, and freedom with the same rigor as a geometrical proof about lines, circles, or squares was certainly audacious, and it can be a little disorienting to encounter arguments on these exceedingly humanistic topics expressed in the same dispassionate and clinical tone that Euclid used to argue about the principles of geometry; but whether you think this stylistic choice was brilliant or just a lot of unnecessary noise don't let it get in the way of appreciating the overall argument of the book, which is not dependent on the form of its presentation. Spinoza himself seems aware that his theory of everything could not be easily squeezed into the narrow packaging of geometrical proof, and he often allows his arguments to spill out over the edges in the *scholia*, explanations, and appendices, which are effectively sidebars in which he steps outside the constraints of geometrical proof and speaks directly to the reader in a more down-to-earth and human style.

There's one more adjustment that everyone needs to make if this book is going to make any sense: we need to think of ethics much more broadly than we normally do. In the twenty-first century we increasingly shrink and compartmentalize ethics, often reducing it to a particular rule book that only the members of a particular profession need to worry about and everyone else can safely ignore (e.g., business ethics, medical ethics, legal ethics, etc.), and constricting it to nothing more than the requirements of the law: basically just a rule book for how not to get arrested. Spinoza's approach to ethics is the opposite of this. It is expansive rather than reductive, and it applies to everyone. For Spinoza, God and nature and every aspect of human thought and feeling are connected to ethics. He wants to transform how we understand ethics, which requires a complete transformation of how we see everything else starting with God and nature. In this respect his philosophy is similar to many religious traditions which argue that humans require a revelation or some other mystical experience so that the scales will fall from our eyes and we will finally see things as they really are. As Paul writes in the New Testament, "For now we see through a glass darkly, but then we will see face to face." But whereas a religious tradition may insist that our confusion can only be overcome by divine intervention or a mystical experience, Spinoza tries to change our whole mode of understanding the world by means of logical proofs that require only that you follow the argument and think for yourself. Perhaps that's another reason why he chose to package his theory in the form of a rigorous mathematical proof: to emphasize that everyone can reach this enlightenment on their own, through nothing but independent thinking, and that no mystical experiences are required.

The book has five parts:

Part 1: On God
Part 2: On the Nature and Origin of the Mind
Part 3: On the Origin and Nature of the Emotions
Part 4: On Human Servitude, or, On the Strength of the Emotions
Part 5: On the Power of the Intellect, or, On Human Freedom

In part 1 Spinoza argues that there is only one substance in the universe and everything we think of as separate, distinct, and individual is actually just a different aspect of this one reality. This should sound very familiar for two reasons. First, it's just a more elaborate, metaphysical version of a simple idea that we often hear today: that everything is connected. Secondly, it's not at all a new idea in the history of philosophy. Spinoza is arguing for monism, which was proposed by multiple pre-Socratic philosophers (e.g., Parmenides, Zeno, Anaxagoras) all the way back in philosophy's childhood. He may have chosen the form of deductive proof for the *Ethics* in order to connect his theory to the very first version of monism in the history of philosophy, which was initially presented by Parmenides in the form of a long poem but then more famously defended by Zeno with several *reductio ad absurdum* arguments—a standard method of proof in mathematics, geometry, and formal logic. Zeno claimed that anything other than a monistic metaphysical theory was completely incoherent and therefore would collapse under the weight of its own absurdity as soon as that incoherence was clarified, and Spinoza situates his own version of monism within this same tradition of deductive proof.

Spinoza calls the opening chapter of *Ethics*, where he presents his version of monism, "On God." Since he explains that what he means by "God" is simply the unitary substance of this monistic universe, and so instead of "God" you could just as correctly say "nature" or "substance" or whatever you want as long as you understand the underlying concept: that everything we think of as particular, individual, separate, and distinct are really all just aspects or modes of a single reality. So part 1 could have been called "On Monism" or "On Nature" or "On the Unity of All Things"; but Spinoza chose to call it "On God," which suggests that he wanted to make it very clear that his version of monism is a corrective to any religion which understands God in completely the wrong way. God is not a being separate from nature and from human beings; "God" is just another name for all of nature, which includes human beings and everything else in the world. The idea that God is somehow separate from nature, and able to control nature as he sees fit either to benefit or afflict mankind, is the basic metaphysical mistake at the foundation of every monotheistic religion.

> From this it came about that each person, in accordance with his own way of thinking, thought out different ways of worshipping God, so that God might love them above the rest, and direct the whole of Nature to the advantage of their blind desire and insatiable avarice.[38]

The mistake here is that God is not separate from nature, controlling and directing it from the outside; God is nature, and everything that happens in the natural world, which includes our own lives, is simply

---

38. Spinoza, *Ethics*, 107.

the consequence and realization of God's nature (or you could say Nature's nature—it means the same thing). This account of God/Nature completely undermines any notion of transcendence or mystery and also any claim to religious authority, which Spinoza recognizes is not going to make the people who claim such authority happy:

> Someone who seeks the true causes of miracles, and whose concern it is to understand natural things like a man of learning, and not to marvel at them like a fool, is commonly taken to be heretical and impious, and is proclaimed as such by those whom the mob adores as interpreters of Nature and of the gods. For the latter know that if ignorance is removed, then the wonder which is their sole means of arguing and of protecting their authority is removed also.[39]

Spinoza was excommunicated by his own Jewish congregation in Holland because they deemed his concept of God to be a "God existing in only a philosophical sense," and after he died all of his books were added to the Catholic Church's Index of Banned Books since they were considered dangerous to the faith. I'm certainly no advocate of book banning or excommunication, but it does seem fair to acknowledge that the interpretation of Spinoza's philosophy that motivated these actions was not inaccurate. Spinoza's definition of God removes God from religion, thus making every religion on earth dedicated to the worship of God completely pointless and effectively canceled.

"God" and "Nature" are just two different names for the same reality, according to Spinoza, and yet throughout the book he uses the word "God" almost exclusively to name this reality. This is very helpful in terms of clarifying how his version of monism is a critique of religion, but to clarify all the other implications of the *Ethics* it helps immensely to substitute the word "Nature" for "God" throughout the book. (Spinoza did say they are perfect synonyms, so he invites us to use the words interchangeably.)[40] For example, here is the opening sentence of the appendix to part 1 rewritten in that fashion:

> With this I have explained the nature and properties of Nature, such as that it necessarily exists; that it is unique; that it exists and acts solely by the necessity of its own nature; that it is the

---

39. Spinoza, *Ethics*, 110.

40. In Latin Spinoza expresses this fact as *Deus sive Natura* which can be translated as "God or Nature" or "God or in other words Nature." See *Ethics*, part 4 preface and prop. 4.

> free cause of all things, and in what way; that all things exist in Nature, and depend on it in such a way that without it they can neither exist nor be conceived; and finally that all things were predetermined by Nature, not out of freedom of will, i.e. its absolute good pleasure, but from the absolute nature of Nature, i.e. its infinite power.[41]

So much of the ethical arguments that Spinoza will present in the remainder of the book are contained in just that one sentence, but they are much easier to see when "God" is understood as "Nature" so we're reminded that this is a naturalistic philosophy of everything and not just a critique of religion. Spinoza argues that everything that is and everything that happens in the world follows from the nature of Nature, from the necessity of Nature's nature. This means that everything is necessary: the world is exactly as it must be and there are no free or contingent events. There are four main consequences of this fact that are relevant to ethics, which Spinoza explores in the remaining four parts of the book. (I'll continue to substitute "Nature" for "God" when discussing the remainder of the book.)

In part 2 he argues that it's not just humans that are thinking things (*Res Cogitans*), as Descartes argued; all of Nature is a thinking thing,[42] and each individual human mind is part of the overall infinite mind of Nature.[43] Since everything in Nature happens necessarily it follows that:

> There is in the mind no absolute, i.e. no free will, but the mind is determined to will this or that by a cause, which is again determined by another, and that again by another, and so on to infinity.[44]

In a long *scholium* that concludes part 2 Spinoza insists that when we understand free will is an illusion it will benefit us both individually and collectively because "it makes the mind entirely calm" and "teaches us in what our supreme happiness, or, our blessedness consists: namely, solely in the knowledge of Nature, from which we are led to do only those things which love and piety advise," and it also "contributes to social life, in so far as it teaches us to hate no one, to despise no one, to deride no

---

41. Spinoza, *Ethics*, 106.
42. Spinoza, *Ethics*, 114.
43. Spinoza, *Ethics*, 123.
44. Spinoza, *Ethics*, 155.

one, to be angry with no one, and to envy no one."[45] It is entirely a good thing to recognize that all of us are just part of the much larger whole called Nature (or God, if you prefer), and that everything within this larger whole, including our thoughts, is determined necessarily by the nature of Nature.

In part 2 Spinoza also presents his dual-aspect approach to the mind-body problem that Descartes bequeathed to the world: the mind and body are just two different aspects of the same substance. Given his argument in part 1 that every apparent separation in the world is illusory—that all the apparently individual and distinct things in the universe are actually just different aspects of the same unified substance, this is not at all surprising.

In part 3 he attempts to give a completely naturalistic account of human emotions, taking seriously the idea that all emotions are natural phenomena just like rocks, trees, squirrels, and human minds. "No one," Spinoza writes, "has determined the nature and strength of the emotions."[46] Philosophy has definitely been allergic to the emotions throughout its history and Spinoza is a rare exception to this rule. In part 3 he tries to define all human emotions and explain them in a completely naturalistic way without dismissing or passing judgment on any of them, and this is an impressive application of his naturalistic theory to a topic that philosophy has traditionally regarded as obscene.

The catalog of emotions in part 3 is entirely descriptive. Spinoza treats all human emotions as natural phenomena that can be observed, described, and analyzed just like everything else in nature. But in parts 4 and 5 he shifts from description to prescription to present an elaborate program for controlling and managing emotions in order to avoid servitude and attain freedom. This is certainly an ambitious project, demonstrating once again that Spinoza did not think small thoughts, but it is fundamentally at odds with the arguments of the first three parts of the book which categorically denied that there is any freedom or contingency in the universe since everything that is and everything that happens is the necessary consequence of the nature of God/Nature. In the last two parts of the book Spinoza attempts to graft a very demanding ethical system (which looks a lot like stoicism) onto this monistic and deterministic framework, but it is a very uncomfortable fit—by which I mean: it doesn't

---

45. Spinoza, *Ethics*, 161.
46. Spinoza, *Ethics*, 163.

fit at all. There are many profound ideas and arguments about the nature of particular emotions, and how people can become slaves to their own emotions, but all of this insight and analysis is undermined by the fact that *Ethics* begins by insisting that there is no freedom in the monistic reality we call God or Nature.

This is, however, a very instructive failure and it clarifies wonderfully several issues that will get much more attention in the nineteenth and twentieth centuries when philosophy shifts from a focus primarily on epistemology to questions that are more ethical and existential in nature. Most modern philosophers are so focused on epistemology that they have little or nothing to say about ethics, and Spinoza, to his credit, is an exception to that rule. There is so much more in *Ethics* than a theory of ethics, but ironically it seems like the theory of ethics is the least successful, undermined as it is by the completely deterministic metaphysics which starts the show. One of the first benefits Spinoza claims for his theory that everything in the universe is just a necessary and inevitable aspect of God's or Nature's nature is that "it makes the mind entirely calm." Mental tranquility is certainly a nice thing, but as so many authors in the nineteenth and twentieth centuries will argue, freedom entails anxiety. Spinoza attempts to fuse a monistic metaphysics—wherein we can all relax because everything is exactly as it must be and individuals are absorbed into something much bigger than themselves which is ultimately in control—and an ethical theory of personal liberation and individual responsibility. This doesn't work, but it is such a perfect prelude for so much of nineteenth- and twentieth-century philosophy that we should all be grateful.

Act 3: Speaking of ethics, there were a few theories about that too in the modern period—and here too Kant would like to clean up the mess that everyone else made

As I've noted *ad nauseam* throughout this chapter, the main obsession of modern philosophy was epistemology; but ideas and arguments about the nature of ethics did not vanish from the earth during these three centuries. There are at least three important moments in the history of ethical theory in the modern period.

Hobbes, Locke, and Burke on ethics

First, many modern philosophers argued (either directly or indirectly) that ethics was really just a branch of political philosophy. This was not a new idea: Plato made the same argument in his *Republic* when he said that it's too hard to understand what makes a person good, since people are so small and therefore it's hard to discern anything clearly in them; so if we want to understand goodness we should create an ideal city in thought and then it will be easier to find goodness in that larger reality—so effectively he argued that ethical theory should be subsumed within political theory. Some of the political theorists we considered at the beginning of this chapter could all be understood as making a similar argument, especially Hobbes, who argues that good and bad only exist after a sovereign creates them so ethics is completely meaningless until then. In the state of nature Hobbes claims there is no right or wrong, which is what makes it so intolerable and leads rational people to form a social contract which will allow them to escape from the state of nature by creating a sovereign power which will in turn create morality. The people create the sovereign ("a mortal god") and then the sovereign creates morality; so ethics is completely absorbed within politics for Hobbes. Locke disagrees with Hobbes's idea that the state of nature is an ethical vacuum; he thinks it's a lovely place where all true ethical principles are written right into the book of nature for all to read, and therefore there's no reason to leave the state of nature except the annoying obligation to enforce the law of nature whenever a stupid person refuses to follow it. Locke seems to think that everything about ethics is just so totally obvious in the state of nature that it's kind of boring and there's nothing worth saying about it. So even though he doesn't believe that moral principles are nonexistent until a political power creates them (as Hobbes argues), still in his own way Locke makes ethical theory nothing more than an aspect of political theory. The same argument could apply to other political theorists we considered such as Burke: to the extent they had anything to say about ethical theory it was only indirectly implied in their political theory, and so all of these authors either directly (as in Hobbes's case) or indirectly (as in the case of Locke and others) suggested that ethics was built into politics and therefore it didn't really need its own theory.

There were other voices in the modern period, such as Pascal and Hume, who were wary of the modern urge to systematize and seek certainty for everything and argued that this wouldn't work for ethics. Both

Hume and Pascal agreed that ethics is beyond the limits of the systems they saw being constructed all around them with such enthusiasm.

Pascal on ethics

Blaise Pascal was a mathematical and scientific prodigy from a very young age but his priorities shifted dramatically in 1654 when (at age thirty-one) he had a mystical experience that prompted him to dedicate the rest of his life (though he didn't live much longer; he died at thirty-nine) to defending religion against anyone who criticized faith in the name of reason. Prior to his own mystical conversion Pascal was just such a person, so he knew his opponent well. The spirit of Pascal's approach to religion is captured perfectly by the memento of the mystical experience that changed his life which he sewed inside the lining of his coat so that it would be over his heart for the rest of his life:

> From about half past ten at night until about half past midnight,
> Fire.
> God of Abraham, God of Isaac, God of Jacob, not of the philosophers and of the learned.
> Certitude. Certitude. Feeling. Joy. Peace.
> God of Jesus Christ. My God and your God. Your God will be my God.
> Forgetfulness of the world and of everything, except God.[47]

To clarify that true religion has nothing to do with the theories of philosophers Pascal began writing what he called "A Defense of the Christian Religion." He intended this to be a thorough and systematic book, and it was so thorough that he didn't manage to complete it before his death. The unfinished and very fragmentary manuscript was published after he died with the humble title of *Thoughts of M. Pascal on religion and on some other subjects*, which has since been abbreviated to simply *Thoughts* (*Pensées* in French, and probably because *Pensées* sounds more profound the book is generally known by its French title even outside of France).

Pensées is a beautiful work of literature that contains many haunting pronouncements, such as:

> The eternal silence of these infinite spaces terrifies me.[48]

---

47. Pascal, *Pensées*, xlv.
48. Pascal, *Pensées*, 73.

As a work of philosophy it is first and foremost an argument that religious faith need not apologize or in any way feel ashamed or inferior when confronted by the supposed criticisms of philosophy or science or reason generally. Philosophy needs to back off and realize that it doesn't really understand religion, that the God of Abraham, Isaac, and Jacob is not the God of the philosophers and of the learned. It may seem like a very meek and humble book but really it's more like a warning shot across the bow of all the ambitious philosophy and science that Pascal could see busting out all over during modernity which believed it could systematize everything, including religion. Ethics wasn't Pascal's primary focus but he does seem to think of morality as an inherent part of religion and therefore it too is off limits to philosophy and its systematic pretensions. Ethics is, and ought to be, a matter of faith and a matter of feeling rather than pretending to be rational or systematic in any way. Here are just a few fragments from *Pensées* which advance this argument in an appropriately unsystematic way:

> The heart has its reasons, which reason itself does not know.[49]

> We know the truth not only by means of the reason but also by means of the heart. It is through the heart that we know the first principles, and reason which has no part in this knowledge vainly tries to contest them. . . . The principles are felt, and the propositions are proved, both conclusively, although in different ways, and it is useless and stupid for the heart to demand of reason a feeling of all the propositions it proves, before accepting them. So this powerlessness ought to be used only to humble reason, which would like to be the judge of everything.[50]

> What a figment of the imagination human beings are! What a novelty, what monsters! Chaotic, contradictory, prodigious, judging everything, mindless worms of the earth, storehouse of truth, cesspool of uncertainty and error, glory and reject of the universe. Who will unravel this tangle? It is certainly beyond dogmatism and Pyrrhonism and the whole of human philosophy. Man is beyond man.[51]

The last quote makes it clear that Pascal thinks ethics is just too complex and complicated for feeble humans to understand, and therefore it's

---

49. Pascal, *Pensées*, 158.
50. Pascal, *Pensées*, 35–36.
51. Pascal, *Pensées*, 41–42.

entirely appropriate for morality to remain the province of religion and not philosophy.

Because Pascal presented his arguments against philosophical ethics as just one aspect of a larger defense of religion it wasn't difficult for modern philosophy to dismiss them as merely a reflection of his own zealous devotion to Christianity, and therefore just another vestigial remnant of the Middle Ages. But when David Hume (who was not at all interested in defending religious faith and could not be so easily dismissed as merely an echo from the Middle Ages) put forward essentially the same conclusions about the irrational and unsystematic nature of ethics as Pascal did, the arguments were harder for philosophy to ignore. Kant definitely did not ignore them; like Hume's skepticism concerning the possibility of certain knowledge, his arguments about the non-rational nature of morality could also be said to awaken Kant from his dogmatic slumbers.

Hume on ethics

Hume's theory of ethics was presented alongside his epistemological theory right from the start. He called his first book *A Treatise of Human Nature*—all of human nature—and roughly half of that very long book focused on the "passions" or emotions, and morality. Hume's argument in that half of the book, though it was quite detailed and exhaustive, was still very simple: ethics is a matter of feeling, not thinking, and therefore reason has nothing to do with it. Throughout its history philosophy has been highly prejudiced in favor of reason and has mostly regarded emotion as an embarrassing defect in human nature; but fortunately it's a defect that reason's awesome power can always overcome. This prejudice does not stand up to empirical scrutiny when Hume puts it under a microscope, as he did with the individual bits of perception, and honestly reports what he observes.

> Nothing is more usual in philosophy, and even in common life, than to talk of the combat of passion and reason, to give the preference to reason, and to assert that men are only so far virtuous as they conform themselves to its dictates.... On this method of thinking the greatest part of moral philosophy, ancient and modern, seems to be founded.... In order to show the fallacy of all this philosophy, I shall endeavor to prove *first*, that reason alone

can never be a motive to any action of the will; and *secondly*, that it can never oppose passion in the direction of the will.[52]

We speak not strictly and philosophically when we talk of the combat of passion and of reason. Reason is, and ought only to be the slave of the passions, and can never pretend to any other office than to serve and obey them.[53]

Honest empirical observation reveals that reason and emotion occupy two separate worlds and never once cross paths. They're like two people who speak completely different languages and don't understand each other at all. To the long tradition of moral philosophy this is a shocking and scandalous result, just as Hume's claim that empiricism leads to the conclusion that there is nothing underlying our claims to know anything about the world other than just custom and convention; but in both cases Hume accepts these results with amiable good cheer and sees no reason to panic. Philosophy has once again demonstrated that philosophy can't do very much, but that's fine because now there's more time to play billiards, write history books, and enjoy the rest of the pleasures of common life free from the pretensions of philosophy.

Kant on ethics

Kant sees all of this as another mess left for him to clean up, because he's not willing to hand ethics over to politics and he's also not prepared to give up on the idea that an ethical system and ethical knowledge are possible. In the case of ethics, as in the case of epistemology, Kant is quite alarmed by the conclusions that Hume reached and he's not content to follow Hume down a path that would effectively put philosophy, and philosophy professors (such as himself), out of work.

We've already seen where Hume took epistemology when he ran the last leg in the British Empiricism 500-Meter Relay. He argued that empiricism is obviously the only legitimate basis for knowledge, but because there are no necessary connections between any of our individual ideas and impressions all we can know with certainty are analytic relations of ideas and not synthetic matters of fact. This means that certain knowledge of the empirical world—which is the one thing that we wanted

---

52. Hume, *Treatise*, 265.
53. Hume, *Treatise*, 266.

empiricism to give us—remains out of our reach. Even something as basic as cause and effect can't be known, because when we put the experience of causation under a microscope all we observe there is the same thing we discover when we go looking for our own selves: just a bundle of perceptions with no necessary connections whatsoever. All that holds these perceptions together in our minds is custom and convention, so what we thought was knowledge turns out to be just a bunch of arbitrary habits with no necessary connection to reality. Hume's response to these discoveries was to shrug. "We've done just fine so far living according to custom and convention," he says, "so there's no reason we can't just continue in the same way. So go ahead and commit to the flames most of the books in the library and let's get back to playing billiards, because the wisdom of common life is all we need!"

In case any philosophy professors try to argue that they should not be fired now that philosophy's claim to explain epistemology has been shot down—because they can still teach ethics classes—Hume has more bad news for them. Honest empirical observation of moral behavior reveals that all we do when we make ethical judgments is follow our feelings, and therefore once again there's nothing philosophy can teach us; but once again Hume thinks this is no great loss. A few more worthless library books have been identified that the university can burn to reduce its heating bills, and to save even more money you can go ahead and close the philosophy department now too since there isn't anything left for them to do; all those former philosophy professors can go find jobs that actually make a contribution to society (such as managing billiard parlors), and the world can continue just as it always has since we've done just fine so far following nothing but custom, convention, and feeling.

Kant, however, was not ready to retire, and he's alarmed by the idea that philosophy would so casually be tossed aside like a pair of pants that are out of fashion. He presented his first *Critique* in a way that made it perfectly clear this new epistemological system was meant to fix what everyone else had broken. "Hume woke me from my dogmatic slumbers," Kant says, "and I saw that while I was sleeping this branch of philosophy had nearly died, killed in the crossfire between rationalism and empiricism; but I've brought it back to life by recognizing that both rationalism and empiricism got some things right, and I've combined these elements in a system which demonstrates that philosophy can in fact answer the question 'How is knowledge possible?' instead of just showing us how knowledge is impossible; and therefore philosophy is still relevant and philosophy professors should keep their jobs!" Then Kant followed the *Critique of Pure Reason* with the *Critique of Practical Reason*, and it too was very much an effort to clean up the mess that others had left behind, this time in the area of ethics. However, the ethical system Kant created in the second *Critique* was not ecumenical like his epistemological system was. He doesn't survey all the ethical theories of the sixteenth, seventeenth, and eighteenth centuries, then single out the best ideas from all these theories and combine them in a single system that makes everyone happy. Instead Kant wrenches ethics back from politics and insists that the requirements of ethics are not subjective or mysterious in any way but are in fact completely systematic and clear because morality is really just a subdivision of logic. So if any university administrator (probably the Interim Junior Assistant to the Associate Dean) reads Hume and thinks he has found a good justification to close the philosophy department, thus saving the university about $300, Kant would say: "Not so fast, you trigger happy Interim Junior Assistant to the Associate Dean! Philosophy alone can explain how knowledge is possible (thanks to the awesome epistemological system I created in my first *Critique*), and philosophy alone can also explain how morality is possible (thanks to the awesome ethical system I created in my second *Critique*), so if you close the philosophy department you will eliminate both knowledge and morality from the earth! Are you sure you want that on your CV?"

Here's how Kant argued that ethics was nothing more than a branch of logic, and therefore was undeniably still part of philosophy. In the *Critique of Practical Reason* (and also the *Groundwork of the Metaphysics of Morals*) Kant maintains that ethics is entirely a matter of following preexisting duties—obligations that are in place before we ever showed up, and that these responsibilities are easily discovered by following the basic rules of logic. An ethical person is simply someone who applies logic to her own behavior, someone who behaves in a logical manner. And it's not advanced or esoteric logic that's required here; it's strictly elementary logic that everyone can understand. In fact, Kant argues that ethics requires only that we follow rule 1 in the Logic Rule Book, which is: don't contradict yourself. Here's how every choice and every action can be conceived as a logical transaction in which the possibility of self-contradiction exists but can always be avoided.

The first step is to recognize that nothing happens without a reason; there are no random acts. Whenever we act we do so according to a personal rule that we give ourselves, which Kant calls a "maxim." There's always a maxim behind every choice and every action even if we don't take the time to think about it clearly or to realize fully what it is; but even if we don't make ourselves consciously aware of this maxim we're still responsible for it and it's still the basis for determining if our actions are good or bad. The second step is to apply the first rule of logic to every one of the maxims that are behind our choices and actions. Ethics requires us to be consistent in all of our maxims; in other words never to contradict ourselves by following a maxim we would not want others to follow. Kant calls this the "categorical imperative" and if you want to proclaim its requirements as stiffly and formally as possible, as if you were reading from a scroll like a messenger dispatched by the king, it would sound like this: "*I ought never to act except in such a way that I could also will that my maxim should become a universal law.*"[54] Really all this says is "Don't contradict yourself," but that sounds a lot less impressive. If you personally follow a maxim (and remember every choice and every action has a maxim behind it) that you're not willing to universalize into a rule for everyone, you are contradicting yourself and this makes you unethical.

If you're now thinking to yourself, "This Categorical Imperative sounds suspiciously familiar, in spite of its austere and technical language," then I would completely agree with you. The Categorical Imperative is just a logical formalization of the most basic ethical principle that we were all taught as children: Don't treat other people in a way that you would not want them to treat you. This is often called "the Golden Rule." When Kant transforms the Golden Rule into the Categorical Imperative he makes it a matter of logic that everyone can understand rather than just a directive that we should follow because of faith or feeling or the insistence of our parents. As long as logical arguments have existed there has always been the vague idea that there was something shameful or immoral about being illogical. When we give someone a truly awesome argument but they refuse to be persuaded by it we all feel that this person should be embarrassed, just as they should be ashamed if they were caught stealing a fashionable new pair of pants. Kant would say that our vague feeling that something disgraceful occurs whenever anyone refuses to be logical is a good intuition that's pointing us to the true nature of ethics. Ethics is in fact entirely a matter of logic, and if you go looking anyplace else for an understanding of ethics you will just make morality more confused and complicated than it really is.

---

54. Kant, *Groundwork*, 15.

All of this is clarified very nicely in the way that Kant argues in favor of capital punishment.[55] There are of course many different arguments for and against capital punishment, but Kant's argument is unique and it demonstrates how ethics is entirely a matter of logic for him. Capital punishment is appropriate when someone commits a murder, he argues, because anything else would be an extremely disrespectful way to treat the murderer. If I kill someone the maxim for my action was "It's alright for me to kill another person," and if we apply the Categorical Imperative to that maxim it becomes a universal rule that applies to everyone: "It's alright for everyone to kill another person." When the state executes me it shows me the greatest possible respect by treating me like a rational, logical person. Capital punishment is a way of saying to me: "Surely you are a logical person and therefore you would not have acted on your personal maxim unless you intended that maxim to be universalized, so out of respect for you we will universalize your maxim and apply it to you by killing you—because if we didn't do that we would be announcing that you're not a logical person, and that would be the worst possible insult to you, far more insulting than executing you." According to Kant's ethical theory, capital punishment isn't punishment, it's more like a reward. It's the only way to treat a murderer with respect, as a logical person: by universalizing the maxim the murderer acted upon, because all logical (and therefore ethical) people intend all of their maxims to be universalized. So the last words of every convicted murderer, just before he is executed, ought to be: "Thank you for treating me like a logical person! I would have been deeply insulted if you had not executed me."

Since ethics is a branch of logic for Kant he insists that ethical principles are just as universal and objective as all logical principles. The Categorical Imperative produces categorical results: perfectly clear, precise, and the same for everyone because logic unites everyone on the same common ground regardless of all the other differences between us. Kant is not a great fan of examples because he thinks that if you understand general principles you have no need for them (in the *Critique of Pure Reason* he calls examples "wheelchairs of the understanding,"[56] and seems to regard the idea that someone might need such a wheelchair as laughable). Nevertheless, in chapter 1 of the *Groundwork* Kant does begrudgingly

55. Kant, *Justice*, 102–5.
56. Kant, *Reason*, 178.

provide five ethical case studies which he says are easily resolved when we treat them as matters of logic and simply refuse to contradict ourselves:[57]

- A shopkeeper should not overcharge his customers even when it would be easy.
- No one should kill himself.
- Everyone should be beneficent, a benefactor to humanity, as much as they are able.
- Everyone has a duty to assure their own happiness, even when they don't want to.
- No one should make a promise that she doesn't intend to keep.

That's about all we get for examples of how the Categorical Imperative works in practice, and some of these might not seem totally obvious to you. But if Kant's ethical system really works as advertised there are exactly zero counterexamples, so if you can think of any examples of someone doing the right or the wrong thing that can't be explained by Kant's ethics you will have exposed a fatal weakness in this system, and you should pull that thread and see where it leads you.

In the nineteenth and twentieth centuries ethical theory becomes much more the central focus of philosophy, and all the arguments about ethics that were created in the modern period will make even more sense in that context. We'll return to Kant's ethical theory when we encounter nineteenth-century utilitarianism in the next chapter, since it's the polar opposite of everything that Kantian ethics stands for.

Curtain Call: A final moment of revolutionary social and political philosophy at the end of the eighteenth century—the birth of feminism

So far in this scrappy overview of modern philosophy the only female voice that managed to sneak into the conversation was Princess Elisabeth, whose correspondence with Descartes includes many wonderful insights and challenges to Descartes's assumptions. This is just another sad example of one of the most flagrant, embarrassing, and hilarious blind spots in the history of philosophy that persisted until very recently: forgetting that women exist. Fortunately one of the revolutions that began

57. Kant, *Groundwork*, 11–15.

to take shape in the modern era, this period that was so full of radical and revolutionary experimentation, was the revolution of feminism: the idea that there are no essential differences between women and men. This simple yet revolutionary argument, as presented in Mary Wollstonecraft's *A Vindication of the Rights of Woman*, is a great conclusion to this summary of modern philosophy.

Mary Wollstonecraft

Mary Wollstonecraft wrote *A Vindication of the Rights of Woman* in 1792, right at the end of the eighteenth century, so the title of "Last Philosopher of the Modern Period" which is usually assigned to Kant could just as easily be given to her. Kant probably wins this contest in most people's minds because he lobbied so hard for the job, claiming constantly to have finished everything that modern philosophy started in epistemology, ethics, and even aesthetics. He didn't hesitate to blow his own horn and advertise his revolutionary accomplishments; but Wollstonecraft wasn't very interested in self-promotion, and one reason for this may well have been that she just didn't have time to think about it. Unlike Kant, who famously lived his entire life in the city where he was born, never leaving town even once, and was never troubled by the emotions or obligations of family life since he steadfastly remained a bachelor until he died at age seventy-nine, Wollstonecraft had quite a turbulent and tumultuous life that ended when she was thirty-eight. She died from complications of childbirth eleven days after she gave birth to her second child, who was named Mary like her mother and who later married the poet Percy Bysshe Shelley and wrote the book *Frankenstein*. In the thirty-eight years that she lived Mary Wollstonecraft wrote six other books besides *A Vindication of the Rights of Woman*, including two novels; she spent several years in France as an enthusiastic observer of the French Revolution; she lived in several very unorthodox relationships; and she gave birth to one other child. She was intensely interested and involved in all the social and political events of her time, and her arguments that became foundational for feminism grew out of those interests.

A Vindication of the Rights of Woman was actually written as a sequel to another book she wrote in response to Edmund Burke's *Reflections on the Revolution in France*, which she called *A Vindication of the Rights of Men*. Burke's text is a classic of conservative thought, and the fact that Wollstonecraft was so incensed by it is a good indication of her own political philosophy. In the customs and conventions that governed the world at that time she didn't find much worth defending, and she was happy to see them overthrown. After writing this first book it seems like she recognized that much of her arguments were motivated by the casual way Burke assumed the customs and conventions which governed women's lives in particular were just grand—no need for any changes here! So she decided that a deeper argument was needed, one that called for a revolution in how we think about that half of the human race that has largely been ignored. That's what makes *A Vindication of the Rights of Woman* a philosophy book and not just a work of social and cultural criticism: the fact that Wollstonecraft attempts in this book to go beyond current events and current culture to the deeper assumptions about sex and gender that are fundamentally philosophical in nature. What is the true metaphysical reality of being a woman or a man, how are those roles valued differently, and how does all of this affect how both women and men are educated and empowered to learn and to know? These are philosophical questions that were lurking behind the French Revolution and everything else that was happening in the world at the end of the eighteenth century, so she wrote a philosophy book to address these questions. The argument of the book is essentially this:

> To those of you who say that women are inferior to men, you're right: women in their current state are in fact inferior to men and thoroughly dependent on men, but only because they've been taught to be this way. This has been caused by education, understood in the broadest possible sense which includes formal schooling (or the lack thereof) but also the myriad other ways that women are instructed to assume their roles in families and in society. In other words, there's nothing natural about women's lives in the world today; women have simply become what they have been educated to become. Of course there are differences between women and men, such as the fact that women can give birth and men cannot, but none of these differences are essential. Philosophy has been correct to argue that rationality is the essence of being human, and women have been taught not to be rational; so effectively the education of women has taken their humanity away from them and many unnatural and inhuman characteristics have rushed into the void. And by the way all of these arguments apply just as well to men: their nature has also been distorted by education that has taught them

they are superior to women and that women are their property, and these distortions have done just as much damage in the lives of men as they have in the lives of women. The solution to these problems is obvious: both women and men should be educated—in schools for sure, but also in every other aspect of life—to become fully rational and therefore fully human, which is their true nature.[58]

If these arguments seem rather obvious today that's an excellent measure of how successful they have been in transforming how people think about sex and gender. The fact that it now seems remarkable that anyone would need to write a book called *A Vindication of the Rights of Woman* is a good indication of the effectiveness of the book, because at the end of the eighteenth century Wollstonecraft's conclusions were not at all obvious to most people, including women. While other revolutions were taking place all around them, such as the French and American revolutions, almost no one else thought there was any need for a revolution in education based on the simple (but still revolutionary) idea that women and men are naturally and essentially the same: rational creatures who can only flourish when their rationality is fully respected and fully developed. Wollstonecraft's ideas obviously call for enormous changes in how schools and families and every other institution and social structure on Planet Earth functions, but behind all this activity are fundamentally philosophical arguments about the metaphysics, epistemology, and axiology of gender. For most if its history philosophy ignored not just women but also all sorts of other things that were considered to be "women's work," such as raising and educating children, marriage, and family issues generally, and Wollstonecraft tries to correct all of these long-standing mistakes.

With Wollstonecraft (or with Kant, if you insist) the history of philosophy in the eighteenth century comes to a close, and philosophy—which has now reached middle age and is well-established and even somewhat respected—strides confidently toward the parade of midlife crises that will make its life interesting in the nineteenth and twentieth centuries.

---

58. This paragraph was entirely my own words, my own attempt to paraphrase Wollstonecraft's arguments—and yes I do recognize that this probably looks like the single most tone-deaf instance of mansplaining in the history of the world, but it seemed like the best way to summarize the overall argument of a long and complicated book. (That's my lame excuse.)

Chapter 6

Nineteenth- and twentieth-century philosophy

(Now middle-aged and a little bit exhausted after all the crazy experimentation it did during its wild modern years, philosophy settles into a more conventional and less promiscuous lifestyle with a fairly stable job that includes an excellent benefits package, and it's even somewhat respected in polite society; so like all middle-aged people it needs a midlife crisis from time to time to jolt it out of its complacency.)

"What sets nineteenth- and twentieth-century philosophy apart other than just arbitrary dates? Why should it be recognized as a distinct period in philosophy's history?" These are excellent questions and I'm thrilled that you asked! The massive disruption or aberration called medieval philosophy makes it easy to distinguish the first three periods of philosophy's long history because it's so radically different—religion and philosophy are suddenly intertwined at all times, philosophy is now taking orders from a higher authority, almost everyone's a saint, etc.—so it clearly stands out as a unique and distinct period, and this also has the effect of setting apart the periods that come before and after it as well-defined stages in philosophy's lifespan. But that gives us only three periods in philosophy's history; what grounds are there for tacking on one more? The three periods that precede nineteenth- and twentieth-century philosophy are all defined by an overarching spirit or idea and not just by dates: ancient philosophy is the period of philosophy's childhood when (like all children) philosophy had to figure out its own identity and find its place in the strange world it fell into; medieval philosophy is the period when philosophy leaped into a marriage with religion and experimented with surrendering its ideals of independent thinking in exchange for security and full employment; modern philosophy is the period when philosophy gave up on its marriage to religion and reasserted its own independence in a flurry of wild invention and experimentation which gave birth to modernity. But when the last two hundred years or so of philosophy's history are simply labeled "nineteenth- and twentieth-century philosophy" this may look like a completely arbitrary or even desperate attempt to stretch things out, like giving a term paper three-inch margins and a forty-eight-point font in order to inflate five pages into fifteen. If nothing more than the calendar unifies this last period of philosophy's history that would certainly be disappointing, and out of character given the wild and raucous ride that philosophy took to reach the present day. However, in spite of the lack of a sexy and memorable name, nineteenth- and twentieth-century philosophy is also defined by its own distinct character and personality because there were in fact significant shifts that occurred when philosophy transitioned from the eighteenth to the nineteenth century.

Obviously the human habit of keeping track of minutes, hours, dates, years, decades, centuries, etc., is capricious and idiosyncratic, and the development of ideas (along with the development of everything else) is not impressed by the strange timekeeping habits of our species and pays no attention to them. So it's really just a very lucky break that the history of philosophy developed in such a way that ideas and arguments which appeared right at the end of the eighteenth century and the beginning of the nineteenth century made it possible for humans to say: "Here begins a new period in philosophy's history—and lucky for us this beginning just happens to correspond to the beginning of a new century, so that will make it easier to keep track of things in our tiny brains!" Here are a few of the things that happened at the end of the eighteenth century and the beginning of the nineteenth that made this lucky accident possible:

- Almost exactly at the end of the eighteenth century, Kant happened. Kant published his three *Critiques* in 1781, 1788, and 1790, and then he himself died just a few years into the nineteenth century in 1804. In his three *Critiques* he claimed to have finished pretty much everything that modern philosophy started in the roughly three hundred years that preceded him. He didn't persuade everyone that he succeeded in this venture, but he did at least leave everyone momentarily stunned and speechless. Kant's systems of epistemology, ethics, and aesthetics compelled his readers to learn the new language of transcendental philosophy, and even those who didn't buy what he was selling found it impossible not to be impressed by the audacity of it. To this day Kant's philosophy is considered perhaps the single greatest seismic event in philosophy's history and many histories and anthologies use only the two big buckets of "before Kant" and "after Kant" to organize every author and text from the history of philosophy.[1] Kant also initiated The Age of the Philosophy Professor: the beginning of an era of professionalization when teaching at a university became the standard job track. Before Kant almost no one had this job. Some modern philosophers before him were offered university teaching positions but turned them down, preferring to bounce from one gig to another in their restless and adventurous lives. Kant, on the other hand, lived his entire life in Königsburg, the city he fell into at birth, and only left town when he died and was carried out in a pine box. This is significant not just because the story of Kant never leaving his hometown is funny; the fact that philosophers now routinely got solid middle-class jobs as university professors is one sign that philosophy has entered into a secure and stable middle age where its biggest challenge would be to continue to produce radical and revolutionary ideas and not just settle into a comfortable and respectable life in the suburbs with three kids, a dog, and a riding lawn mower.
- Almost exactly at the beginning of the nineteenth century, Hegel happened. Hegel published *The Phenomenology of Mind* in 1807 and afterward became probably the world's most famous philosophy professor, with students flocking to his standing-room-only lectures at the University of Berlin. Hegel's philosophy was a powerful machine that provoked a powerful response from just about

1. E.g., the recent *Norton Anthology of Western Philosophy* (2017).

everyone who studied it (either they loved it or they hated it), and much of nineteenth-century philosophy consists of attempts to appropriate Hegel's ideas or to find some way to refute them. Hegel too was something like an earthquake (or maybe an explosion is a better analogy) that launched a new form and style in nineteenth-century philosophy.

- An ethical and existential emphasis (or you might say obsession) takes hold of philosophy in the nineteenth and twentieth centuries. This is one of the reasons why it makes sense to think of this period as philosophy's middle age: because suddenly it's very interested in questions about mortality and meaning, and wondering if maybe it has wasted its whole life—just like a middle-aged insurance salesman who one day finds himself behind the wheel of a large automobile, or in a beautiful house, with a beautiful wife, and asks himself, "Well, how did I get here?"[2] (Of course there were several world wars in these centuries that may have had something to do with this shift, as well as the consequences of modernity in the form of industrialization and rapid scientific progress which made the destruction of the entire planet much easier than ever before.)

Since nineteenth- and twentieth-century philosophy, like every other period in philosophy's history, is unified by ideas, interests, questions, and obsessions and not just by arbitrary dates, it really needs a better name. Therefore I propose to rename this period "The Age of Midlife Crises" since that's a much more dramatic and memorable title. A midlife crisis is the best thing that can happen to you when you've reached a respectable and comfortable middle age as a tenured full professor of philosophy and are tempted to drift into mediocrity, or to start repeating yourself—playing your greatest hits to your aging fans while they hold aloft their aging Bic lighters—instead of creating new material. The best philosophy of the nineteenth and twentieth centuries is the product of a midlife crisis that causes philosophy to panic and wonder if its life so far has all been wasted; but hopefully there's still time to come up with a theory that will make sense of the whole weird and wonderful mess, so let's try one more time! That's the unifying spirit of nineteenth- and twentieth-century philosophy, aka The Age of Midlife Crises, and this spirit was expressed wonderfully by Schopenhauer early in the nineteenth century.

2. That was a horrible paraphrase of the Talking Heads song "Once in a Lifetime." I'm sorry.

A very brief preface to philosophical midlife crises by Arthur Schopenhauer

Arthur Schopenhauer's most famous contribution to philosophy was his book *The World as Will and Representation* which he worked on for much of his life. The first edition was published in 1818, then the second edition came twenty-five years later and the third fifteen years after that. With each new edition he added a great deal to the book so that the third edition was more than twice as long as the first, but he also continued to insist that the book really only had one idea. Schopenhauer labored away on this project for much of his life in complete obscurity since his own attempt to be a philosophy professor went very badly and therefore was very brief (more on that later), and his ever-lengthening book did not prove to be a bestseller (to absolutely no one's surprise). But then a few years before the end of his life he published a motley collection of essays with the rather repellent title *Parerga and Paralipomena* (Latin for "fragments and scraps"), and to his astonishment that book became quite popular. Schopenhauer attributed the notoriety at the end of his life to "the comedy of fame,"[3] and one reason he found this so bizarre is because in one essay in this collection he argued that philosophy can never be popular:

> The philosopher's work . . . tries to revolutionize the reader's whole mode of thought. It demands of him that he shall acknowledge as error all that he has hitherto learnt . . . that he shall declare all his time and trouble to be wasted; and that he shall begin again at the beginning.[4]

This is a wonderful description of the whole philosophical enterprise but it applies especially well to philosophy beginning in the nineteenth century, when the haunting thought that perhaps their whole lives had been a mistake caused many philosophers to wake up in a cold sweat and resolve to overthrow all existing systems of thought and start over. That's a good guiding principle to keep in mind as we make our way through philosophy's Age of Midlife Crises starting (unavoidably) with Hegel.

---

3. De Botton, "Schopenhauer Method," 58.
4. Schopenhauer, "Method," 5–6.

Georg Wilhelm Friedrich Hegel

Much of philosophy in the nineteenth century is a response to Hegel: either an attempt to appropriate and extend his philosophy or an attempt to assassinate it, and that's why starting with Hegel is unavoidable. One reason Hegel got everyone's attention is because he claimed that his System (why this word is capitalized should become clear soon) could absorb and assimilate everything: every idea, argument, or theory that ever has existed or ever will. The Hegelian System is thoroughly ecumenical: everyone is welcome and every belief they bring with them is accepted as correct—partially correct, that is, since the complete truth can only be realized when all these fragments of philosophy are brought together in the higher synthesis that Hegel calls "Absolute Mind." Hegel doesn't think fragments or scraps are ever acceptable as the final product of philosophy (so he would definitely not be pleased with the scrappy overview of the history of philosophy that I've offered in these last four chapters). Anything less than the complete and comprehensive whole of reality can't be true, he insists, but his System welcomes every possible incomplete and fragmentary thought as raw material for the dialectic that can fuel the machine and move it closer to that final goal.

And now I'll stop and acknowledge that much of the previous paragraph is probably close to unintelligible if you've never heard of Hegel before, but we had to start somewhere so I elected to dive right into the middle of this ocean and hope that no one drowns. Because Hegel claims his philosophy can comprehend everything, when a mere mortal such as you or I first tries to comprehend these ideas it can feel a lot like getting beaten over the head with a broomstick. To make things less painful a good place to start is with the happy news that we've seen this movie before, or at least a version of it, because Hegel's philosophy is another version of monism. All the way back in the time of the pre-Socratics our old buddy Anaxagoras argued that *Nous* (mind or reason) controls everything in the universe and also is everything in the universe, and this is similar to Hegel's Absolute Mind more than two thousand years before Hegel introduced that character to the world. So Hegel didn't create his system *ex nihilo* (as he might like us to believe); this is just the latest and perhaps most audacious version of a story that is almost as old as philosophy itself.

However, one thing that is quite new in Hegel's version of this story is the claim that every philosophy and indeed every idea that has ever been created is correct. We haven't seen that before. According to the American pragmatist Charles Sanders Peirce, the time-honored method in philosophy is:

> for each professor to seize upon any philosophical position he found unoccupied and which seemed a strong one, to entrench himself in it, and to sally forth from time to time to give battle to the others.[5]

Instead of sallying forth to do battle Hegel waves a white flag and proclaims:

> We are not enemies and I will not fight you! Your idea, argument, or theory is part of the great truth that constitutes the whole, the final synthesis of Absolute Mind. So join us! Bring your fragment of truth and combine it with all the others so that the marvelous machinery of my dialectic can finally lead us to the final synthesis which is complete truth and also complete reality!

Hegel says yes to everything and no to nothing. It's impossible to argue with him because he won't disagree with you. This is something fundamentally new in the history of philosophy, and it creates fundamentally new challenges for anyone who thinks Hegel was wrong and wants to refute him, since Hegel says yes even to those who disagree with him.

Another novelty in Hegel's philosophy is that in his version of monism the unity of everything is not present at the beginning, as in Spinoza's God or Nature; instead it's achieved at the end of a long dialectical process. "Dialectic" is another word that gets used in many different ways by many different philosophers, but for Hegel it's best understood as something like a conversation (a dialogue) in which people are actually listening and responding thoughtfully to each other (which of course isn't true in most conversations); so there will be spontaneity and surprises along the way but there will also be progress and ultimately a final understanding and agreement will be reached. Since the Hegelian System asserts that there are no real contradictions or disagreements this is a conversation in which everyone involved says yes to whatever is said and then adds something more to it. That is also the guiding principle of improv: never say no to anything; whatever your improv partners give you your response is always, "Yes, and . . . ." Hegel isn't particularly funny, and in fact it's not clear if he has any sense of humor at all, but his dialectical

---

5. Peirce, "Clear," 131.

method still works very well to create endless possibilities for both comedy and drama. Actors skilled at improv can take anything they're given and build on it, giving back something more to their partner and ultimately steering the whole conversation toward an interesting conclusion. This is a good way to think of the dialectical process that Hegel says is driving history toward the realization of Absolute Mind: as an excellent improv performance in which each actor says "yes, and . . ." to everything. From the perspective of the Absolute Mind there's no idea that's absolutely false. It's always possible to say, "Yes, this is part of the truth, but there's also much more to it, and only when this dialectical improvisation has reached the finish line and the System is complete will it be true in the fullest sense of truth, since the truth is always comprehensive and complete: a finished System that absorbs every fragment into a larger whole."

Hopefully this introduction to Hegel is starting to feel more agreeable than getting beaten over the head with a broomstick. Hegel's writing has a reputation for being obscure and even incomprehensible, but his philosophy is much easier to understand when you realize that this theory of everything boils down to a few simple ideas. Some of these simple ideas have already been trotted out before you had a chance to put up any resistance, and here are a few more of them now:

- There are no actual contradictions, only apparent contradictions. Every time two claims or ideas seem to contradict each other (we can call these a "thesis" and an "antithesis" even though Hegel didn't use these terms), they can be resolved in a higher synthesis in which there's no contradiction at all. The German word *Aufheben* is essential to Hegel's System since it expresses all three of those moments or stages of the dialectic. *Aufheben* can have three different meanings: (1) to cancel; (2) to preserve; (3) to lift up, and normally it's understood to have just one of those meanings at a time depending on the context, but when Hegel uses the word all three of its meanings apply at once. This one word expresses perfectly the movement of the Hegelian dialectic: a thesis is in one sense or from one perspective canceled (because any particular idea or event is always short of complete reality and truth), but in another sense or from another perspective that incomplete idea or event is preserved (as it is absorbed into the larger whole of the dialectic, which says yes to everything), and in yet another sense and from another perspective all such fragments are lifted up into the higher synthesis of Absolute

Mind as it progresses toward completeness. There are many mistakes and misunderstandings that are built into language, Hegel thinks, but he regards this one word as quite accurate in describing what's really happening in the world.

- Everything is ultimately unified in the Absolute Mind or Spirit (the German word *Geist* means both mind and spirit, so I'll use both words interchangeably). The Absolute Mind absorbs all particular minds, bodies, objects, and moments (such as my mind, my body, this delicious peanut butter sandwich that I'm about to eat for lunch, and this particular moment in time which is called "lunchtime"). All apparent distinctions and differences, such as those between minds and bodies, subjects and objects, past and present, are overcome in the Absolute Mind. (Since Hegel's System claims to be complete, if something important got left out that would be quite a problem, and an embarrassment.)

- This may look like an entirely metaphysical or ontological system but Hegel says, "Epistemology is built into my System too: truth is the agreement of thought with itself, not the agreement of objects and ideas. Truth is also complete and whole: anything particular/individual/fragmentary is false." (And if you're now wondering, "What about ethics? Ethics is also part of philosophy, so where's the ethics in your System Herr Hegel?"—that's an excellent question and we will get to that soon.)

- As you read Hegel—or Kant, or any other German author from this period—remember that the word translated as "science," "scientific," etc., is *Wissenschaft*, which simply means any organized body of knowledge: it's not limited to the natural or social sciences. (The Latin *scientia* from which our word "science" derives also had that same general meaning, so it made perfect sense to talk about the *scientia* of painting or poetry or any human activity whatsoever.) When Hegel uses this word he means something like "genuine knowledge" or "systematic knowledge," which is what he wants philosophy to be.

- The higher synthesis which absorbs everything into the Absolute Mind requires a process, and all of us are caught up in that process. We're all small parts in a very big machine and it doesn't matter if we don't understand the bigger picture and the larger operation which is sweeping us along. This is somewhat analogous to Adam Smith's argument that capitalism's "invisible hand" of the market uses individual selfishness to benefit everyone, except for Hegel there's no necessary benefit or happy ending for everyone involved. The Absolute Mind uses individuals as tools and doesn't care about their happiness. History is driven by the clash and conflict of apparent contradictions, but eventually all of these apparent divisions are overcome. All of us are swept up in this dialectical process whether we like it or not, and Hegel advises us (in the final paragraph of the preface to *The Phenomenology of Mind*) to relax and enjoy the ride:

> For the rest, at a time when the universal nature of spiritual life has become so very much emphasized and strengthened, and the mere individual aspect has become, as it should be, correspondingly a matter of indifference, when, too, that universal aspect holds, by the entire range of its substance, the full measure of the wealth it has built up, and lays claim to it all, the share in the total work of mind that falls to the activity of any particular individual can only be very small. Because this is so, the individual must all the more forget himself, as in fact the very nature of science implies and requires that he should; and he must, moreover, become and do what he can. But all the less must be demanded of him, just as he can expect the less from himself, and may ask the less for himself.[6]

These are all simple ideas but they're challenging to express since they go against beliefs that seem built right into language (such as the belief—widely regarded as "common sense"—that a contradiction is simply nonsense); so Hegel tries to express these ideas in many different ways, sort of like throwing everything against the wall and hoping that something sticks. For example, his claim that the truth is the whole makes it difficult to say or write anything, since speaking and writing are always fragmentary and incomplete; but his response to this challenge is just to say and write more rather than less. In *The Phenomenology of Mind*, which first announced Hegel's dialectical System to the world in 1807, he acknowledges and embraces this apparent contradiction in the very first words of the preface. This is a preface to a system that claims not to need a preface—because if the System is true it's complete, but if you then add a preface to this complete system the preface is outside

6. Hegel, *Mind*, 130.

the system and thus refutes its completeness. Hegel acknowledges this apparent contradiction, and then proceeds to write the preface anyway. When he does this he effectively announces to everyone: "This is something you'll have to get used to if you want to understand my philosophy, because human language can't adequately express my philosophy, built as it is on the mistaken idea that contradictions exist. So first I'm going to announce that my System should not need a preface, and then I'm going to write a preface anyway so that you, Lucky Reader, will have the opportunity to ponder the fact that there are no real contradictions, only apparent contradictions." This may seem like an appeal to mysticism or magic, but that isn't what Hegel is doing or else this would no longer be philosophy. He's trying to use nothing but rational arguments to present his ideas and he's not suggesting that the intervention of a magician or a God is necessary before any of this will make sense. But Hegel is definitely pushing the machinery of human language right to the breaking point, and many of his critics will say there's an excellent reason why it's so hard to make sense of Hegel's arguments and why he has to bend and even break language in his attempts to express them: because they simply don't make sense.

Kant claimed that the real world (the thing in itself or *noumena*) remains forever off limits and unknowable, and that all we can possibly know are *phenomena*. Hegel rejects this separation of the noumenal and the phenomenal. For Hegel there are no limits on the mind, but you have to keep in mind (heh heh) he's not talking about your individual mind or my individual mind, he's talking about the Absolute Mind, of which there is only one, and your mind and consciousness and experience are just puny moments or aspects of this larger reality. All individuals are swallowed up in this much larger whole. And while there are no limits on what the mind can know, its knowledge is only achieved gradually, through a process of the Absolute Mind (which is not separate from the world in any way) gradually coming to know and understand itself. ("The real is the rational and the rational is the real," Hegel writes in one of his many memorable and gnomic couplets which would make excellent tattoos.) For these reasons Hegel argues that all of history is rational. It is not, as Henry Ford said, just "one damn thing after another"; it all fits together in a perfectly coherent whole. Eventually it will be clear how everything fits together (this is called the end of history), but while this process is underway history is something like the diary kept by the Absolute Mind as it gradually comes to understand itself.

One moment of surprising clarity in *The Phenomenology of Mind* that many have clung to like a life raft as they've tried to make sense of the Hegelian dialectic is the section called "Independence and Dependence of Self-Consciousness: Lordship and Bondage."[7] Dialectic or mediation is the process by which the Absolute Mind comes to know itself moving through the process of thesis, antithesis, and synthesis, and that will always be difficult or impossible for our puny individual minds to understand. But in this section Hegel gives a concrete example of that abstract process to which everyone can relate: human relationships. Hegel argues that in the development of our own self-consciousness we use each other as mirrors. When two potential self-consciousnesses meet each other they both demand that the other serve as their mirror: they both demand to be recognized by the other. What follows is a life-and-death struggle for recognition until one person capitulates and becomes the "slave" while the other becomes the "master." Or so it seems. But the person who thinks she has become the master has actually become the slave because she depends on the slave to recognize her, to be the mirror that reflects her status as master, while the person who at first thinks she is the slave eventually learns to realize herself through her own creative work so she doesn't depend on anyone else to be her mirror: and thus the supposed slave attains true freedom through her own creative work while the supposed master loses her freedom and becomes a slave who depends on the recognition of others. The thesis, antithesis, synthesis stages of the dialectic are all apparent in this account of the dynamics of average, everyday human interactions and relationships, and you can probably think of several examples from your own experience where Hegel seems to have captured the life-and-death struggle for recognition that is part of some human relationships quite accurately. (The master/servant dialectic, as it has come to be called, was very important to Marx, and to others who tried to bring the Hegelian dialectic down to earth and apply it to real-world problems.)

Hegel never stopped trying to express his simple yet very difficult-to-express ideas, cranking out book after book in his lifetime, beginning with *The Phenomenology of Mind*, which first announced his dialectical theory of everything to the people of Earth. Much of the rest of nineteenth- and even twentieth-century philosophy can be seen as a response to Hegel's philosophy, either from those who fell in love with it and tried

---

7. Hegel, *Spirit*, 111–19.

to extend, amplify, and apply its concepts in ways that Hegel did not, or from Hegel's critics who either thought that his philosophy was incoherent nonsense, or that it was perfectly coherent but also perfectly dangerous, and therefore needed to be stopped. The most famous and influential people in the camp of Hegel admirers were Karl Marx and Friedrich Engels, and we'll get to them shortly, but first we'll turn to two Hegel critics. Schopenhauer and Kierkegaard are good representatives of the two main critical reactions Hegel provoked: Schopenhauer thinks that Hegel is just a charlatan who mesmerized his admirers with his babble, while Kierkegaard argues that Hegel's philosophy is coherent and understandable but dangerous because it swallows up individual choices and lives and completely falsifies human existence.

William James (more on him later when we get to American pragmatism) wrote a delightful article for the philosophy journal *Mind* in 1882 describing how he finally felt like he understood Hegel when he gave himself a strong dose of nitrous oxide. (James was a medical doctor so he was able to pass this off as medical research.) Much of James's article is worth quoting since it illustrates so well both of the main criticisms of Hegel that Schopenhauer and Kierkegaard will develop further, without any self-medication.

> Some observations of the effects of nitrous oxide gas-intoxication . . . have made me understand better than ever before both the strength and the weakness of Hegel's philosophy. . . . With me, as with every other person of whom I have heard, the keynote of the experience is the tremendously exiting sense of an intense metaphysical illumination. Truth lies open to the view in depth beneath depth of almost blinding evidence. The mind sees all logical relations of being with an apparent subtlety and instantaneity to which its normal consciousness offers no parallel; only as sobriety returns, the feeling of insight fades, and one is left staring vacantly at a few disjointed words and phrases, as one stares at a cadaverous-looking snowpeak from which sunset glow has just fled, or at a black cinder left by an extinguished brand.
>
> The immense emotional sense of reconciliation which characterizes the "maudlin" stage of alcoholic drunkenness . . . is well known. . . . Now this, only a thousandfold enhanced, was the effect upon me of the gas: and its first result was to make peal through me with unutterable power the conviction that Hegelism was true after all, and that the deepest convictions of my intellect hitherto were wrong. Whatever the idea of representation

occurred to the mind was seized by the same logical forceps, and served to illustrate the same truth; and that truth was that every opposition, among whatsoever things, vanishes in a higher unity in which it is based; that all contradictions, so-called, are of a common kind; that unbroken continuity is of the essence of being; and that we are literally in the midst of an infinite, to perceive the existence of which is the utmost we can attain. . . .

It is impossible to convey an idea of the torrential character of the identification of opposites as it streams through the mind in this experience. I have sheet after sheet of phrases dictated or written during the intoxication, which to the sober reader seem meaningless drivel, but which at the moment of transcribing were fused in the fire of infinite rationality. . . . Let me transcribe a few sentences:

What's mistake but a kind of take?
What's nausea but a kind of -usea? . . .
By George, nothing but othing!
That sounds like nonsense, but it's pure onsense!
Thought much deeper than speech! . . .

The most coherent and articulate sentence which came was this:

There are no differences but differences of degree between different degrees of difference and no difference.

But now comes the reverse of the medal. What is the principle of unity in all this monotonous rain of instances? Although I did not see it at first, I soon found that it was in each case nothing but the abstract genus of which the conflicting terms were opposite species. In other words, although the flood of ontologic emotion was Hegelian through and through, the ground for it was nothing but the world-old principle that things are the same only so far and no farther than they are the same, or partake of a common nature—the principle that Hegel most tramples under foot. At the same time the rapture of beholding a process that was infinite, changed (as the nature of the infinitude was realized by the mind) into the sense of a dreadful and ineluctable fate, with whose magnitude every finite effort is incommensurable and in the light of which whatever happens is indifferent. . . . A pessimistic fatalism, depth within depth of impotence and indifference, reason and silliness united, not in a higher synthesia, but in the fact that whichever you choose it is all one—this is the upshot of a revelation that began so rosy bright.[8]

---

8. James, "Effects," 186–208.

This marvelous piece of empirical research captures the two main objections that Hegel's critics will seize upon as they try to stop his Mighty Mediation Machine from consuming all of philosophy, history, and individuality: (1) that his tortured writing does not conceal any deeper meaning but is really just a lot of sound and fury that will only make sense if you are high; (2) that insofar as there is any real philosophy here it's actually quite perilous, like a very dangerous drug, because it contains a fatalistic vision of existence that swallows human individuality and freedom and along with them all possible meaning and value in life.

Arthur Schopenhauer (again)

Schopenhauer is important in the history of philosophy both as a critic of Hegel and for his own theory of everything: the single idea expressed in his ever-lengthening book *The World as Will and Representation*. We'll start with his criticism of Hegel, which was quite hilarious. Schopenhauer is 100 percent in the first camp of Hegel's critics: those who think that Hegel's philosophy is nothing but nonsense. He seems genuinely astonished that anyone could have ever taken Hegel seriously, and his astonishment was reinforced by the fact that he briefly taught at the same university as Hegel where he did his utmost to save the souls of the students by scheduling his own classes at the same time as Hegel's so that they would have a wholesome alternative to Hegel's hogwash and humbug. But this noble effort utterly failed: only a handful of students wandered into Schopenhauer's classes and they were mostly disappointed (perhaps because the theory Schopenhauer offered as an alternative to Hegel was probably the most pessimistic view of human life ever created, as we'll see shortly), and Schopenhauer quit his job as a philosophy professor after only a few unhappy semesters. Later he wrote several hilarious essays criticizing philosophy in the universities, but he reserved his most hilarious criticism for Hegel. Here are just a few examples:

> Anyone who, after all this, is still in doubt concerning the spirit and aim of university philosophy should consider the fate of Hegel's pretended wisdom. Has it in any way been discredited by virtue of the fact that its fundamental ideas were the absurdist fancy, a world turned upside down, a philosophical buffoonery, or by virtue of its contents being the hollowest and most senseless display of words ever lapped up by blockheads, and its presentation, as seen in the works of the author himself, being the

repulsive and nonsensical gibberish, recalling the rantings of a bedlamite? No, not in the least![9]

Let us look at the hideous example of Hegelry, that shameless pretended wisdom which for one's own careful and honest thought and investigation substituted as a philosophical method the dialectical self-movement of concepts and hence an objective *thought-automaton* that gambols on its own account freely in the air or in empyrean and whose traces and footprints are the scriptures of Hegel and the Hegelians. . . . And so let us contemplate the height and duration of this Babel-structure and reflect on the incalculable harm such a philosophy of absolute nonsense . . . was bound to do to the generation that grew up on it, and thus to the whole age. Are not innumerable minds of the present generation of scholars thoroughly distorted and deranged by it? Are they not crammed with corrupt views, and do they not accept hollow phrases, meaningless twaddle, and nauseating Hegel-jargon where thoughts and ideas are expected? . . . In fact, almost the whole of the younger set has been infected with Hegelry as it has been with venereal disease.[10]

Schopenhauer thinks Hegel is a menace because he tricks people into thinking he actually has something intelligible to say when in fact it's all just unintelligible babbling. Infected with this claptrap (as with a venereal disease) Hegel's followers completely lose their own ability to think independently, and thus real philosophy becomes impossible. It seems clear that Schopenhauer thinks the appropriate cure for this illness is laughter, so he aims his considerable powers of sarcasm at Hegel and lets him have it. (Later we'll see that Kierkegaard will also attempt to use humor to derail the Hegelian machine, but Kierkegaard will be motivated by the conviction that Hegel's philosophy is not incomprehensible, it's simply dangerous and wrong.)

In addition to his excellent jokes about Hegel, Schopenhauer was also a very influential voice in nineteenth-century philosophy because of his own theories. Earlier I proposed that this whole period be rebranded "The Age of Midlife Crises" using an argument from Schopenhauer that describes the phenomenon of a philosophical midlife crisis so well. The idea that philosophy will always be unpopular because it requires everyone to be willing at every moment to acknowledge that their whole life has been a mistake—this was quite a brilliant insight, and it also describes

9. Schopenhauer, "Universities," 144.
10. Schopenhauer, "Universities," 166–67.

marvelously the parade of midlife crises that make philosophy so much fun in this period. But according to the theory of everything that was Schopenhauer's own contribution to the history of philosophy on a deeper level everyone's life will always be a mistake because human existence itself is always a mistake. Explaining why this is so, and what we should do about it, was the project of *The World as Will and Representation*.

As noted earlier, Schopenhauer insisted there was only one big idea in this book, but the fact that he never stopped revising the book and made it longer every time suggests that it wasn't easy for him to express this one big idea. However, he did give us some excellent clues, and one of the best appears right off the bat in the preface to the first edition: that you'll be able to understand his theory better if you first study Eastern religions such as Hinduism or Buddhism. Since Buddhism is the Eastern religion that's easiest to summarize, and since I am lazy, I'll focus on it.

The basic principles of Buddhism were expressed succinctly by The Buddha (Siddhartha Gautama) himself in "The Four Noble Truths." These truths are:

1. Human existence is suffering.
2. Suffering is caused by desire.
3. The way to eliminate suffering is to eliminate desire.
4. The correct way to eliminate desire is the Middle Way (Dharma): an extremely patient set of practices including meditation, pacifism, and other disciplines that will gradually (probably many lifetimes will be required) eliminate all desire so that when you die you can finally cease to exist (Nirvana) and stop returning (through reincarnation) to this samsara existence.

"Samsara" means a world of illusions or dreams. According to Buddhism, we all live in such a world until we accept the Four Noble Truths and begin to practice Dharma so that we can progress toward enlightenment ("The Buddha" means "The Enlightened One"), which will ultimately extinguish all desire and make it possible to stop existing.

Buddhism provides an excellent way to get started in understanding Schopenhauer's philosophy, and that's exactly how he suggested that we use it, but it is of course a religion—albeit a very unusual religion compared to all Western religions since instead of starting with a creating God who should be worshipped and who provides a means of salvation it starts instead with a problem that needs to be solved (the fact that human existence is suffering) and offers a solution to that problem (ceasing to exist) in which Gods play no part. Schopenhauer agrees with many of these conclusions but presents his own arguments in the form of a philosophy: no meditation or other mystical experiences are required; all you have to do is follow the logic of a long book that keeps getting longer. Schopenhauer also doesn't propose anything like salvation or a solution to the problem of human suffering. The enlightenment of understanding the true nature of reality is all he offers, not a new religion or any sort of spiritual experience. "At least when you understand your life according to my philosophy you'll understand life correctly, so you won't need to throw your beliefs out and start over from the beginning," he says, and that's better than nothing.

Another way that Schopenhauer's philosophy differs from Buddhism is that it includes a far more elaborate metaphysical theory to explain exactly why existence is suffering. This theory is announced right in the title of *The World as Will and Representation*. There are two ways of understanding the world: as representation and as will, and roughly half of the book is devoted to each of these perspectives. When he argues that the world is our representation he basically extends and applies Kant's transcendental philosophy on a more existential level than Kant did, reminding us of Kant's argument that our experience is limited to phenomena, which are constructions of the mind's faculties, and we don't have unfiltered access to noumenal reality. But Kant insisted there still is a noumenal reality even if we can't access it directly, and it's impossible to make sense of our experience without this. Kant combines the elements of epistemology that rationalism and empiricism got right, and he thinks one thing that empiricism definitely got right was the conviction that knowledge requires the external, objective world to supply the raw material of cognition.[11] Kantian transcendental arguments start with what we actually experience and then reason backwards to the best possible explanation for what we experience, and Kant thinks it's impossible to explain our experience unless the ultimate cause of everything we experience is a noumenal reality that exists independently of us.

Schopenhauer agrees with Kant about the existence of an external noumenal reality, but he has very definite ideas about what that noumenal reality is. He argues that the best possible explanation of the world

11. Berkeley was the one empiricist who didn't agree with this principle, but Kant thinks that's why Berkeley went off the rails and found himself arguing that the very idea of an external, objective world is incoherent.

as we experience it (the world as we represent it to ourselves) is a very particular underlying noumenal reality which he calls The Will. This noumenal reality actually looks a lot like Hegel's Absolute Mind in some respects, which may be one reason Schopenhauer disliked Hegel so intensely: because he thought Hegel had stolen and then horribly distorted his own Big Idea. Like Hegel's Absolute Mind, The Will for Schopenhauer has all the puny individuals on Planet Earth in its clutches and sweeps all of us along toward its own end without bothering to inform us where it's taking us. But just as Hegel claims that one particular puny individual (named G. W. F. Hegel) managed to crack the code of Absolute Mind and is now able to give paid lectures on this subject, Schopenhauer likewise informs us that fortunately another puny human (named Arthur Schopenhauer) has figured out the true nature of The Will and can explain it to the rest of us even as we are all swept along by that same menacing, metaphysical power that's using all of us to further its own ends.

Just as Hegel gave us one very concrete example of his own very abstract theory when he applied that theory to human relationships in the "Master/Servant Dialectic," Schopenhauer also provided a very memorable and useful example when he applied his theory to sex. This sexy example (actually it's 100 percent anti-sexy, as we'll soon see), clarifies very effectively how The Will is a very sneaky and diabolical power. In chapters such as "The Metaphysics of Sexual Love" Schopenhauer argues that all the stories about romance we endlessly produce—from three-minute pop songs on the radio to epic novels and operas—are all just clever masks that conceal a simple and stark reality: the Will needs humans to keep having sex in order to preserve itself, and it will use any trick it can to convince us this is somehow in our own self-interest. In other words, even though we think of love stories as incredibly complicated and always about individuals they are in fact neither. Instead, all the "noise and fuss" of love is just a smoke screen The Will uses to conceal from us what's really going on: "love" is nothing more than camouflage for sex, and sex is just The Will perpetuating itself. This is one very specific consequence of Schopenhauer's philosophy that's easy to understand and tends to get everyone's attention: if his theory is right everyone should stop having sex immediately—including all those who are currently having sex, which may seem like a rather impolite interruption, but Schopenhauer says we should all be grateful for this philosophical *coitus interruptus* because it saves us from being used by a sinister metaphysical force. When Arthur Schopenhauer burst into the room and explained to us what was really going on we were rescued from this sinister metaphysical force, and for that we should all be grateful.[12]

The bottom line for Schopenhauer is that human existence is fundamentally an error, and that's why we would all be doing future generations a favor if we stopped having sex immediately and thus stopped bringing more unfortunate souls into existence.

> Let us for a moment imagine that the act of procreation were not a necessity or accompanied by intense pleasure, but a matter of pure rational deliberation; could then the human race really continue to exist? Would not everyone rather feel so much sympathy for the coming generation that he would prefer to spare it the burden of existence, or at any rate would not like to assume in cold blood the responsibility of imposing on it such a burden?[13]

This could be seen as a kind of preemptive nirvana: solving the problem of existence by preventing it from ever getting started. The fundamental error of human existence originates in the fact that The Will is using all humans to further its own being and doesn't care that humans are incapable of finding any meaning or happiness in their existence when they're used in this way. The impossibility of happiness is built right into our erroneous existence, as Schopenhauer explains in several passages that are hilarious even though the picture they paint of human life is truly bleak:

> That human existence must be a kind of error, is sufficiently clear from the simple observation that man is a concretion of needs and wants. Their satisfaction is hard to attain and yet affords him nothing but a painless state in which he is still abandoned to boredom. This, then, is a positive proof that, in itself, existence has no value; for boredom is just that feeling of its emptiness.[14]

> *Work, worry, toil, and trouble* are certainly the lot of almost all throughout their lives. But if all desires were fulfilled as soon as they arose, how then would people occupy their lives and spend their time? Suppose the human race were removed to Utopia

---

12. Schopenhauer himself did not follow this advice at all. He had numerous affairs throughout his life (Cartwright, *Biography*, 30–33)—one more example of the comical distance between ideals and actuality in the history of philosophy.
13. Schopenhauer, "Suffering," 300.
14. Schopenhauer, "Vanity," 287.

where everything grew automatically and pigeons flew about ready roasted; where everyone at once found his sweetheart and had no difficulty in keeping her; then people would die of boredom or hang themselves; or else they would fight, throttle, and murder one another and so cause themselves more suffering than is now laid upon them by nature. Thus for such a race, no other scene, no other existence, is suitable.[15]

Before leaving Schopenhauer we should remind ourselves of what he, along with every other author in philosophy's history, is trying to do. Though his account of The Will may seem like an attempt to create a truly terrifying science fiction story to frighten and entertain us, that isn't his objective. Schopenhauer, like Leibniz (who also created a philosophical theory that could be confused with science fiction), is completely committed to the principle of sufficient reason: that everything has a reason and everything can be explained, and he offers his theory as simply the best possible explanation for the very strange world in which we find ourselves. Yes, his explanation is pessimistic, but he would say that pessimism is just the result of trying to be honest and accurate in his account of human existence. He's not pessimistic just because he's in a bad mood, or for reasons he doesn't understand; he insists that it's based on principles that he understands very well, not just on feelings. He spent much of his life arguing for pessimism, giving reasons to support the conclusion that pessimism is the only reasonable worldview. If you were to ask Schopenhauer, "But why is the world so weird that it requires such a fantastic and pessimistic explanation?" he would likely respond: "If what you mean by 'fantastic' is 'truly awesome' then thank you very much and I concur! But if what you mean by 'fantastic' is 'thoroughly bizarre' I would say that I don't know why the world is so weird because I didn't make the world; I simply tried to give the best explanation for the world as I found it."

Søren Kierkegaard

Like Schopenhauer, Kierkegaard is important in the history of philosophy for his criticism of Hegel and also for his own philosophy, but in Kierkegaard's case it's a little harder to separate the two. While Schopenhauer thinks Hegel was just a pompous windbag who can be deflated and dispatched simply by pointing out that his so-called philosophy is

---

15. Schopenhauer, "Suffering," 293.

incomprehensible nonsense, Kierkegaard thinks the task is not quite so simple. Hegel seemed fully aware that his philosophy exceeded the mechanical limits of human language, but he thinks that's a problem with language, not his philosophy. Language is built on assumptions that are incorrect, such as the assumption that contradictions are incoherent, or that contradictions even exist, and he responds to these linguistic limits by simply writing and saying more—trying to break through the limits of language with brute force, because he sees no other alternative. So Hegel would not be embarrassed if someone pointed out that his writing doesn't make a lot of sense; he already knows that. But in spite of the clunkiness of his language Hegel's ideas are still quite simple, and one of those ideas is this one: it's impossible to disagree with the Hegelian System because that System says yes to everything. The dialectical machine that Hegel created was really quite powerful, and this is one of the reasons why his philosophy attracted so many admirers and imitators. But Kierkegaard looked at Hegel's Mediation Machine and thought it was something to be feared rather than celebrated because it consumes everything that gives human life meaning and value: individuality, freedom, and ethical choices, for example. The closing lines of the preface to *The Phenomenology of Mind*, in which Hegel advises us to stop trying so hard to be individuals and instead allow ourselves to be swept up in the larger reality of the Absolute Mind, are worth repeating here because Kierkegaard believes they are truly terrifying:

> For the rest, at a time when the universal nature of spiritual life has become so very much emphasized and strengthened, and the mere individual aspect has become, as it should be, correspondingly a matter of indifference, when, too, that universal aspect holds, by the entire range of its substance, the full measure of the wealth it has built up, and lays claim to it all, the share in the total work of mind that falls to the activity of any particular individual can only be very small. Because this is so, the individual must all the more forget himself, as in fact the very nature of science implies and requires that he should; and he must, moreover, become and do what he can. But all the less must be demanded of him, just as he can expect the less from himself, and may ask the less for himself.[16]

Kierkegaard thinks that this is a horrible prescription for how to live. He regards Hegel's philosophy as the epitome of everything that's wrong with

16. Hegel, *Mind*, 130.

the speculative nineteenth century, when so many people have forgotten that they exist as individuals and confuse themselves with abstractions. Hegel's System represents the high-water mark of abstraction and dishonesty, so he wants to derail this machine and restore life to its original difficulty.[17] "Life can only be understood backwards; but it must be lived forwards" as he wrote in his journal.[18] Life as we actually experience it is messy, fragmentary, incomplete, anything but systematic, and impossible to understand completely while we're living it, so we can't really understand our life in a complete and systematic way until we're dead; or more accurately: we'll never understand our life because when we're dead, sorry, it's too late. A system must be complete, but a human life is never complete until it's over. Hegel claims to comprehend everything: his own life, everyone else's life, all of time and history, as if he had somehow managed to step outside of life and time and history and gaze upon them from an external perspective. In brief, Hegel seems to have forgotten that he exists, and this is certainly unfortunate for him but it's even more unfortunate for all the other individuals who have absorbed his confusion and seem determined to follow him into oblivion.

For all of these reasons Kierkegaard views Hegel's philosophy as a dangerous drug and he wants to provide an antidote; but since the dialectical logic of Hegel's System absorbs all contradictions and disagreements it won't be enough just to stand up and say very loudly, "I disagree!" because the Hegelian Mediation Machine simply responds, "Thank you very much! This disagreement is also something we can use to fuel our progress toward the Absolute Mind!" Disagreeing with the Hegelian System without getting eaten by the Hegelian System is Kierkegaard's project. His philosophy is an attempt to identify and exploit the weaknesses in Hegel's logic so that the fraud Hegel is perpetrating against human existence is exposed and eliminated.

If you're now thinking, "This sounds a lot like existentialism," then I say, "Hats off to you!" because you're absolutely right. Existentialism as something like a brand name and a somewhat codified school of thought doesn't really emerge until the middle of the twentieth century, especially right after World War Two with writers such as Albert Camus, Simone de Beauvoir, and Jean-Paul Sartre, but a century earlier than this many of existentialism's key ideas were formulated by Kierkegaard. That's another

---

17. Kierkegaard, *Postscript*, 185–88.
18. Kierkegaard, *Journals 2*, 179.

thread we should hold onto as we piece together Kierkegaard's philosophy: that we're witnessing the birth of existentialism in his attempt to argue that the particularity of an individual human life can never be absorbed and synthesized into any so-called higher reality, including the abstraction called Absolute Mind.

To understand Kierkegaard's existential philosophy and his critique of Hegel a good place to start is with his criticism of another institution: Christianity. This may seem to have nothing to do with Hegel or with philosophy but it's actually a very good window into Kierkegaard's key ideas that will become central to existentialism. Kierkegaard only lived to be forty-two, and he spent the last year of his short life attacking official, institutional Christianity, in particular the Danish Lutheran Church which was (and still is) in Kierkegaard's native Denmark the official state church. These attacks took the form of many short pamphlets and articles, which were the last things that he wrote before he died. Kierkegaard was definitely very interested in religion but his version of religion was such a demanding and purely individual activity that he regarded the very idea of institutional religion as a contradiction. He argues that "Christendom" is something very different from "Christianity," and because everyone in a Christian country like Denmark is a Christian by default, Christianity has effectively been abolished.[19] You become a Christian when you're born, just like you become a Danish citizen, and almost no one gives either one of these much thought. His attack on Christendom was a philosophical project because it was all about rescuing individuals from the empty abstractions that might seem to be more real than individual existence, but actually have no reality at all.

For Kierkegaard religion is an example of a "subjective truth." In the nineteenth century (and still today for sure) many would argue that "subjective truth" is simply a contradiction in terms, but Kierkegaard thinks this is just one more symptom of the systematic illness that has overtaken the world. In a journal entry from 1835 (when he was twenty-two years old) he provides a good description of what he means by "subjective truth":

> The thing is to find a truth which is truth for me, to find the idea for which I am willing to live and die. And what use would it be in this respect if I were to discover a so-called objective truth. . . . What use would it be if truth were to stand there before me, cold and naked, not caring whether I acknowledged it or not, inducing an anxious shiver rather than trusting devotion? . . . That's

19. Kierkegaard, *Moment*, 188.

what I lacked for leading a completely human life and not just a life of knowledge, to avoid basing my mind's development on—yes, on something that people call objective—something which at any rate isn't my own, and to base it instead on something which is bound up with the deepest roots of my existence.[20]

The idea is not to deny the existence of objective truths, only to argue that objective truths are not the whole story. Subjective truths also exist, and anyone who ceases to care about subjective truths becomes comical, like Hegel: a human being who has forgotten that he exists.

Another text that clarifies very well why Kierkegaard believes subjective truth needs to be defended, and also many more important themes of his philosophy, is *The Present Age*. This essay is analogous to the pamphlets Kierkegaard wrote attacking "Christendom" except that here he's attacking the institutions and traditions of popular culture in general and not just those of establishment Christianity. The focus of this text is "macro" in that Kierkegaard applies his "micro" ideas about individuality and subjective truth to society as a whole, not just particular, single individuals. Here are some of the defining characteristics of the nineteenth century according to *The Present Age*, and I think you'll agree that many of them still apply quite well to the present, present age:

- Prudence: "If we had figures for the consumption of prudence from generation to generation as we do for the consumption of spirits, etc., we would be amazed to see what vast quantities are consumed nowadays.... Is there anyone who makes even just one tremendous blunder any more?"[21]

- Reflection: "Another hazard with reflection is not being able to tell whether it is a conclusion reached by deliberation that saves a person from evil deeds, or whether it is exhaustion brought on by the deliberation that saves him, by sapping his strength."[22] "That it is a prison that reflection holds both the individual and the age in, that it is reflection that does it and not tyrants or secret police, nor priests or aristocrats—is a view of things that reflection does all in its power to prevent."[23]

---

20. Kierkegaard, *Journals* 1, 19–21.
21. Kierkegaard, *Review*, 60.
22. Kierkegaard, *Review*, 68.
23. Kierkegaard, *Review*, 72.

- Levelling: "The self-establishing envy is levelling, and while a passionate age accelerates, raises and topples, extols and oppresses, a reflective, passionless age does the opposite—it stifles and impedes, it levels. Levelling is a quiet, mathematically abstract affair that avoids all fuss."[24]

- Individuals who allow themselves to be absorbed into abstractions: "For what the individual feared more than death would be reflection's judgment upon him, reflection's objection to his wanting to venture something as an individual. The individual does not belong to God, nor to himself, nor to his beloved, nor to his art, nor to his scholarship; no, just as a serf belongs to an estate, so the individual realizes that in every respect he belongs to an abstraction under which reflection subsumes him."[25]

- The public: "For levelling really to come about a phantom must first be provided, its spirit, a monstrous abstraction, an all-encompassing something that is nothing, a mirage—this phantom is the public."[26] "The public is a *corps*, more numerous than all the people together, but this *corps* can never be marshaled for inspection—indeed, it cannot have even so much as a single representative because it is itself an abstraction."[27]

- Talking about nothing: "What is it to chat? It is to have repealed the passionate disjunction between being silent and speaking. . . . Talkativeness gains in extensity: it has everything to talk about and goes on incessantly. . . . But chat dreads the moment of silence that would make the emptiness plain."[28]

- Knowledge without passion: "The present age is thus essentially sensible. Perhaps it knows more on average than any previous generation; but it is devoid of passion. Everyone is well informed; we all know what path to take, and what paths can be taken, but no one will take them."[29]

---

24. Kierkegaard, *Review*, 74–75.
25. Kierkegaard, *Review*, 76.
26. Kierkegaard, *Review*, 80.
27. Kierkegaard, *Review*, 81.
28. Kierkegaard, *Review*, 87.
29. Kierkegaard, *Review*, 93–94.

The "attack upon Christendom" and *The Present Age* are two good points of entry for understanding why Kierkegaard thinks Hegel's philosophical machine is so dangerous: because it destroys individuality; your life no longer matters because it's just one small moment in the larger reality of Absolute Mind. This is a serious problem, but since Hegel says yes to everything and thus consumes criticisms of his System for breakfast Kierkegaard chooses to attack Hegel's somber and serious theory with comedy, which he thinks is fundamentally different from every other event, idea, or individual that Hegel's System easily absorbs. Every individual human existence is unique and incommensurable, and comedy announces that incommensurability by surprising you and making you laugh, like the punch line in a good joke. Philosophy has a reputation for being somber, serious, and generally boring, but this is truly odd since the first real superstar of philosophy was Socrates and his basic technique was to make fun of people to demonstrate their ignorance. This proved to be so entertaining that Socrates attracted groupies, such as Plato, who followed him around every day just to watch the show. There was plenty of comedy in Socrates's philosophy, and after a while also plenty of drama too since he embarrassed so many people in Athens that his embarrassed victims got together and charged him with the ridiculous crime of "corrupting the youth," and managed to get him executed. So Socrates was both an excellent comedian and also a martyr for philosophy: funny and tragic at the same time. Philosophers since Socrates have mostly been highly allergic to comedy, probably because they were highly allergic to getting executed, but Kierkegaard is an exception to this rule. He believes the incongruity of comedy is one thing that Hegel's System can't consume or mediate into a higher synthesis. (In other words, he thinks Hegel's System can't bear to be laughed at.) Here are some of the methods of comedy that Kierkegaard employs to derail the Hegelian System:

- Writing in a deliberately unsystematic and fragmentary way. For example, Kierkegaard's longest book is called *Concluding Unscientific Postscript to the Philosophical Fragments* and it is in fact a postscript to another book called *Philosophical Fragments* (which can also be translated as *Philosophical Scraps* or—my favorite—*Philosophical Crumbs*.) But the postscript is about twenty times longer than the book for which it's supposed to be a mere appendix, and it is truly a scrappy book—unsystematic in every way just as the title promises. This book contains many arguments concerning the impossibility of any existential system, and it also performs those arguments with its fragmentary style. This is true for all of Kierkegaard's philosophical writing: it's deliberately crumby in both its form and its content in order to irritate and frustrate the machinery of Hegelian dialectic and also to demonstrate and celebrate the true nature of unsystematic human existence.

- A project he calls "indirect communication," which is an effort to force individual readers to think for themselves instead of blaming everything on the author. This is an attempt to make the author disappear, or to be an author without also being an author-ity. All of Kierkegaard's philosophy books were published under pseudonyms (who had suitably ridiculous names such as Hilarious Bookbinder, Nicolaus Notabene, and Constantin Constantius) so that it was impossible to assign either authorship or authority to Søren Kierkegaard, and all of these (nonexistent) authors also did everything in their power to remind their readers constantly that they (the readers) were responsible for their own interpretation and appropriation of the ideas in the books they were reading. This is always true of any text, even if it tries to communicate as directly as possible; but tactics of indirect communication (such as an author who deliberately contradicts herself, so that it becomes impossible to say what exactly the author's position is) make this fact more obvious and unavoidable for the reader. The goal of indirect communication is to get out of the way so that readers can create and accept responsibility for their own subjective truths.

- Presenting his ideas in an impish and impudent spirit that does not hesitate to poke fun at the somber seriousness of Hegel and any other systematic philosopher who has forgotten that human existence isn't systematic. To his everlasting credit Kierkegaard was willing to write philosophy books in a manner that was bound to get him censured and scolded by the powers that be in the philosophy world, both in the nineteenth century and still today, and by serious people who lack a sense of humor everywhere. Kierkegaard made it very easy for people to dismiss his ideas as immature and worthless simply because he wrote in a free-spirited and playful style, but anyone paying attention recognized that the comedy in Kierkegaard's philosophy was an essential part of the argument.

Schopenhauer and Kierkegaard are good representatives of those who thought that Hegel's philosophy was either completely nonsensical or else a clear and present danger to human life, but in the nineteenth century they were very much in the minority. The Hegelian dialectic was all the rage throughout most of the philosophy world, with many people tripping over each other in their eagerness to jump on the Hegel bandwagon and apply the Hegelian dialectic in some way that Hegel himself neglected to do. A great deal of this stampede to imitate Hegel was sound and fury that didn't end up signifying much, but one attempt to apply Hegel's ideas to economics and politics was hugely consequential, so much so that arguably no other philosophical theory has had as much impact on world events. This was the version of the Hegelian dialectic that Marx and Engels called "dialectical materialism."

Karl Marx & Friedrich Engels

Marx and Engels agree with Hegel that there is a dialectical logic to history and that history is moving toward a definite goal, but unlike Hegel they don't believe in Ghosts. The German word *Geist* is in fact the origin of the English word "ghost," and even though *Geist* can also be understood as "mind" they think even that is still too mystical and spooky. They love the dialectical part of Hegel's System but are not so wild about the idealistic or mystical part; so they take the idealism out of Hegel's philosophy and replace it with materialism. According to dialectical materialism, history is driven not by the thoughts of The Absolute Mind as it comes to know itself, but rather by the concrete, material, economic realities of human existence. Marx and Engels like the Hegelian System very much but they want to bring it down to earth where it can do some good. "Philosophers have hitherto only interpreted the world in various ways," Marx wrote. "The point, however, is to change it."[30] Dialectical materialism is an inverted, demystified version of Hegel's dialectic that undeniably did change the world.

Summarizing the full impact that Marx and Engels have had on politics, history, economics, and so many other areas of life is way beyond me since I'm very lazy and not particularly bright, so I will not even attempt to do this. It's clear, however, that philosophy was at the root of everything that Marx and Engels did accomplish and that they

---

30. Marx, "Theses," 109.

understood their work as fundamentally a philosophical project. But "Marxism" has certainly taken on a life of its own and now has a legacy way beyond philosophy that would no doubt surprise Marx and Engels if they could return to earth today and see what has been done in their names. Anyone who wants to study Marx and Engels as philosophers today will have to check a lot of baggage first if she wants to understand these authors on their own terms, because there are so many accumulated stereotypes and misconceptions about what they stood for. For example, in American politics if you call someone a "Marxist" or label some policy "Marxism" those are fighting words and in response you'll surely get an indignant denial or perhaps a punch in the nose. But try calling a politician a "Platonist" or a "Kantian" and see what happens: you'll just attract a few puzzled and pitying looks, as if you had just publicly announced you had lost your mind. The fact that "Marxist" and "Marxism" have ascended into the lofty realm of the most severe political insults, along with "not a dog lover" and "democrat," is a good indication that the ideas of Marx and Engels have traveled well beyond philosophy. (Most people who toss "Marx" and "Marxism" around as insults have never read a word of Marx's philosophy.)

A good place to begin to understand Marx and Engels as philosophers is with their arguments about alienation. Part of the inspiration for their thinking about alienation came from Ludwig Feuerbach, who argued in his book *The Essence of Christianity* that the Christian God is the self-alienation of humans: we create God in our own image, as a projection of ourselves and all of our highest values, and then we feel alienated from this God that we've created. That's a surprising result since religion claims to do just the opposite: it claims to connect and unify human life. Marx and Engels argue that something similar happens in the mundane world of working for a living. Within a capitalist economy work alienates us in four ways: we are alienated (1) from the objective world (both the products of our labor that we create and the natural world that we don't create), (2) from our time, (3) from ourselves, and (4) from others.[31] Capitalism turns everything on its head and alienates us from our own highest values and thus capitalism is like a really bad religion that does the exact opposite of what we want it to do: instead of connecting us with our highest ideals and aspirations it just gets in the way—it cuts us off from our most important values and condemns us to live like strangers in

---

31. Marx, *Manuscripts*, 69–84.

a strange land, forever alienated from our own nature. This is also a surprising result since capitalism promised everyone that a good job would do just the opposite: it would make you a complete and happy person, connected to the community and admired and respected by all.

According to dialectical materialism, alienation is one of the contradictions of capitalism that will be overcome in the higher synthesis of communism. For Marx and Engels, the dialectic of history is driven not by anything mystical or mysterious but instead by the very concrete and material facts of class conflict, and in the capitalist stage of history the fundamental class conflict is between the class of workers (aka the proletariat) and the class of capitalists (aka the bourgeoisie). The alienation that workers experience under capitalism is not just a mild sense of weirdness or confusion; it's more like a menacing, scary monster, like the monster in the many *Alien* movies that haunts the ship and makes it impossible for anyone to relax. Capitalism tries to conceal the alienation it creates, but that alienation will eventually and inevitably undermine this stage of history and lead to a higher synthesis of freedom in a communist utopia.

When Marx and Engels argued that history inevitably leads to this destination the announcement did not go unnoticed: many people and even entire countries bought tickets for this journey, and many other people and nations proclaimed that nothing was more important than stopping this train from reaching its destination—and since then many ideological battles (the kind fought with words) and even outright wars (the kind fought with guns and bombs) have been waged over this particular interpretation of Hegel's philosophy. But you already knew that, so perhaps all that's left to say about what Marx and Engels accomplished as philosophers is this: could anyone have asked for a better demonstration of how much impact a philosophical theory can have? I don't think so.

Jeremy Bentham, John Stuart Mill, and the other British utilitarians

Karl Marx lived the last part of his life in England and some of his most powerful writing describes the horrible conditions of the working class in London he observed in that time. All the philosophy that Marx and Engels created was motivated by a desire to improve the world by solving problems such as these: actual material problems like poverty, child labor, and other forms of human misery right here and now on Planet Earth. At the same time that Marx was in England theorizing about how to improve the world another group of philosophers in England were proposing an ethical theory they claimed could solve all the world's problems. Like the proponents of empiricism in the modern period, the advocates of this ethical theory were all British (for some reason), and like Bacon, Hobbes, Locke, Berkeley, and Hume these Brits for the most part didn't think being a philosophy professor was the best way to improve the world so they did all sorts of other things (the only exception being Adam Smith, who was a professor of moral philosophy, and yet today is remembered almost exclusively as an economist). Actually economics was an interest of all the members of this little club, which included James Mill, Jeremy Bentham, David Ricardo, Adam Smith, and John Stuart Mill (son of James), and the ethical theory they called "utilitarianism" had a big impact on economic theory as well.

Utilitarianism was a rebranding exercise, and all the utilitarians freely acknowledged this. They were trying to resurrect and revive the very old ethical theory called hedonism but they had the good sense to recognize that any ethical theory that trumpeted the value of pleasure right in its name would probably not sell very well in Victorian England. So they rolled up their sleeves and solved this problem by replacing the indecent and offensive word "pleasure" with the clever euphemism "utility" (a word so vague that almost no one will suspect that anything as sexy as pleasure might be hiding behind it); and then they mopped their brows and congratulated themselves because their work was done. They were convinced that nothing needed to be altered in the ancient ethical theory of hedonism except its name. It was, they thought, a modern scientific approach to ethics long before modern science, and so it was not appreciated in its own time and was quickly forgotten or misunderstood. (The current practice of giving the name "hedonism" to resorts where the main attraction is the complete absence of morality is a good example of the continuing confusion surrounding this ancient ethical theory.) The British utilitarians put all their energy into applying and marketing this very old theory in the modern world where there were so many obvious problems (such as those that Marx observed during his own time in England) since they truly believed that hedonism—whoops! I mean utilitarianism—could solve all of them.

That's essential to understand about the British utilitarians: they wanted to use their ethical theory to fix the world's problems, and they sincerely believed that utilitarianism could do that if it were systematically applied and effectively marketed so that everyone became convinced they should understand morality according to this system. In his book *Utilitarianism*, which was originally published as a series of articles in a popular magazine (a great example of the energy that was devoted to marketing this ethical theory to the masses) John Stuart Mill gives us a fine example of this utopian spirit:

> Yet no one whose opinion deserves a moment's consideration can doubt that most of the great positive evils of the world are in themselves removable, and will, if human affairs continue to improve, be in the end reduced within narrow limits. Poverty, in any sense implying suffering, may be completely extinguished by the wisdom of society, combined with the good sense and providence of individuals. Even that most intractable of enemies, disease, may be indefinitely reduced in dimensions by good physical and moral education, and proper control of noxious influences. . . . All the grand sources, in short, of human suffering are in a great degree, many of them almost entirely, conquerable by human care and effort.[32]

Mill and his buddies thought they could solve the world's problems with utilitarianism because this ethical theory makes it possible to turn morality into a science. Modern science has made impressive progress in just a few centuries and is universally admired for its ability to get everyone to agree, but ethical theory has made no progress at all after more than two thousand years and it's universally ridiculed for its inability to create anything other than words—words, words, words, words, words; but nothing ever gets done and none of the world's problems get resolved because no one can agree on anything. John Stuart Mill begins *Utilitarianism* by citing this embarrassing fact, and it's clear what the solution to the problem must be: ethics must adopt the methods of the sciences and then it too will be able to solve problems and improve the world just like science does. This is a remarkably bold proposal because it seems like utilitarians were proposing that the distinction between normative and positive (between facts and values) could be eliminated. But scientists are quite happy with the separation of facts and values, and one of the main reasons why the natural sciences have been able to make such rapid progress is because they have meticulously stayed on one side of this divide, avoiding all questions about values and focusing exclusively on facts: on

32. Mill, *Utilitarianism*, 15.

what is rather than what ought to be. So physicists, biologists, and chemists would probably not be pleased if a gang of utilitarians sauntered into their laboratories one day and suggested that the distinction between facts and values should be abolished. But these sauntering utilitarians could reassure the nervous scientists by explaining that the positive/normative distinction no longer matters only for their system of ethics—the true and living utilitarian system of ethics—but it continues to apply to all the other ethical theories out there, which will go on laboring in ignorance and darkness (like the blind leading the blind). Utilitarianism provides a way to turn values into facts, they could reassure the anxious scientists, and thus utilitarian ethics can become a science just like physics, biology, and chemistry, and so it ought to have its own laboratory in the same building as the rest of the natural sciences where it will figure out the objective, scientific facts of morality.

Utilitarianism claims it has turned ethics into a science by fixing the two defects in ethical theory that made it nothing but a noise-generating machine in the past: (1) the lack of clearly defined and understandable terms, and (2) the lack of measurable, quantitative results. The first defect is remedied by defining right and wrong in terms of pleasure and pain. In the past all discussions about ethics have led to nothing but confusion and misunderstanding because everyone had a different idea of good and bad and thus everyone was speaking a different language. "Good" and "bad" are such vague terms and are understood in so many different ways that agreement about them can never be reached; but as soon as these terms are defined simply as "pleasure" and "pain" all vagueness disappears and everyone knows exactly what they're talking about. Now, for the first time, everyone will be on the same page when discussing morality, speaking the same language and actually understanding each other instead of just making noise and talking past each other.

The second defect of traditional ethical theory is resolved by the fact that pleasure and pain are also quantifiable, so ethics can now employ mathematics as its basic, underlying, common language just like all the other sciences. We quantify our pleasure and pain every time we go to a doctor's office and are directed to a chart on the wall with a smiling face on one end and a screaming face on the other and the numbers 1–10 in between. "Please put a number on your pain," the doctor says, and we all do this quite easily. Unlike "virtue," "duty," "magnanimity," or any of the other hopelessly vague terms that have traditionally been used in discussions about ethics, pleasure and pain are quantifiable, and because of this the disagreements and debates of the past will all disappear since they will be replaced by some very simple math: add up the pleasure that an action will produce, then add up the pain, then compare the numbers: if the pleasure is greater than the pain the action is good, and if the pain is greater than the pleasure the action is bad—simple as that. Jeremy Bentham called this the "hedonic calculus" (apparently forgetting that the word "hedonic" was not to be uttered in public).

Since only simple calculations of pleasure and pain are required, and since everyone understands exactly what they're calculating instead of casting about blindly in a fog of abstractions and disagreements, utilitarianism transforms morality into an objective science that can actually solve problems and get things done. Hence the optimism reflected in the quote from Mill above, and hence the missionary zeal for marketing this theory: because the only thing standing in the way of solving all the world's problems is the fact that some people have not yet converted to utilitarianism and therefore continue to waste their time trying to make sense of ethics in unquantifiable terms. Once we all agree to speak the language of utilitarianism there will be no more ethical disagreements and ethics will finally be able to make progress and solve problems just like the sciences. There are no value judgments utilitarianism considers off limits: everything from disagreements with your roommates about cleaning your apartment to debates about the largest government programs are all governed by the same utilitarian principles. As Bentham puts it, the principles of morals are also the principles of legislation.

If you're looking for the perfect contrast to utilitarianism the most obvious candidate is Kant's ethical theory from the eighteenth century (also called "deontology," meaning an ethics of duty). These two approaches to ethics clash in every possible way, including all of the following:

- For utilitarianism the goodness or badness of an action is determined completely by its consequences, specifically by how much pleasure or pain the action produces (and thus utilitarianism is also called "consequentialism"). For deontology right and wrong are determined completely by obligations, which are discovered through logic and have nothing to do with consequences. Utilitarianism locates good and bad in the future (where an action's consequences are realized), and deontology locates good and bad in the past (since our ethical obligations existed before we figured them out; obligations are always already there, just waiting for us to discover them with logic).

- Since the consequences of any action in terms of producing pleasure and pain can vary dramatically, utilitarianism never says that any action is absolutely good or absolutely bad: it just depends on the context (the time, place, people involved, etc.). Deontology, on the other hand, insists that the Categorical Imperative gives us categorical results that are determined completely by logic and not by circumstances. Lying is a good example that shows this contrast. For deontology a lie is always wrong because the maxim behind it ("It's okay for me to lie to other people") is not one that we would ever be willing to universalize, since we never want other people to lie to us. But for utilitarianism a lie that in a given context produces more pleasure than pain is entirely a good thing. Each particular act has to be considered in its particular context, and only then can the calculations of the hedonic calculus be performed to determine what's good and bad.

- For deontology it's logic that makes an action good: applying the categorical imperative to the maxim of every action to determine if it can be consistently universalized, and logical reasoning takes place entirely in your head. This leads Kant to argue that the goodness of an action is entirely a matter of your intent or will: the will to be logical no matter what. Utilitarianism, on the other hand, does not care at all about your intent. Intend whatever you want, it says; we're not interested in the subjective thoughts in your head, only in the objective results in the world. As long as your actions end up producing more pleasure than pain, even if that wasn't at all what you intended, then they were good actions. (This is analogous to the economic argument advanced by Adam Smith—a member in good standing of the British Utilitarian Club—that the greed of capitalists is a good thing because it ends up benefiting everyone else in the economy indirectly. That isn't what the greedy capitalist intended, he just wanted to get rich; but it doesn't matter what his intentions were if his actions produce more pleasure than pain.)

William James and other American pragmatists

In the history of American philosophy there are two particularly famous moments: (1) the New England transcendentalists (Ralph Waldo Emerson, Henry David Thoreau, Nathaniel Hawthorne, Louisa May Alcott and the rest of her family, Margaret Fuller, and a few others who were in their orbit in the early nineteenth century); and (2) pragmatism, or the so-called "Golden Age" of American philosophy (C. S. Peirce, William James, John Dewey, and a few others who were in their orbit in the late nineteenth and early twentieth century). These two schools of American philosophy were very closely connected with each other since the epicenter of New England transcendentalism was Concord, Massachusetts (more specifically the home of Ralph Waldo Emerson at 28 Cambridge Turnpike, Concord, MA 01742) and the epicenter of American pragmatism was about fifteen miles away in Cambridge, Massachusetts (more specifically the Philosophy Department of Harvard University, which is now located in Emerson Hall; the Psychology Department is in William James Hall since William James was so important to the birth of psychology in the United States). The motley group of writers, thinkers, and experimenters who surrounded Emerson are generally all dropped into one big bucket labeled "the Concord transcendentalists." The activities and interests of this crowd, and what "transcendental" and "transcendentalism" meant to them, is a fascinating story, and philosophy is definitely part of that story, but it's not a story that this book will go into because there isn't time in this scrappy summary. The crumby overview of the history of philosophy that this book is presenting barely has time for philosophy's greatest hits, and for better or worse the transcendentalists didn't make a big enough splash as philosophers; more so as nature writers and advocates of thrift and self-sufficiency (Thoreau's *Walden* is probably the best known example of all three themes). But American pragmatism, which grew out of American transcendentalism, did present itself explicitly as a philosophy and it did make quite an impact worldwide as a philosophy, so I'll focus on that moment of American philosophy that, for better or worse, did get noticed. Since for the most part this school of thought developed within a roughly fifteen-mile corridor in eastern Massachusetts, if you wanted to give it an even more specific geographical tag you could call it "Bay State pragmatism" or even "straight outta the suburbs of Boston pragmatism," which definitely makes it sound much more edgy and exciting.

Pragmatism was an attempt to extend the principles of utilitarianism to every aspect of life, not just ethics. William James very explicitly asked everyone to see pragmatism in this way: as a continuation of what utilitarianism started. Here is the dedication James gave to the book he called simply *Pragmatism*, which was intended to summarize and defend this new philosophy as succinctly as possible:[33]

> To the memory of John Stuart Mill from whom I first learned the pragmatic openness of mind and whom my fancy likes to picture as our leader were he alive to-day.

Like utilitarianism, pragmatism has lost all patience with philosophy that doesn't get anything done. The British utilitarians thought that something was clearly broken in ethical theory if it never actually solved any ethical problems. The American pragmatists extended this idea to cover philosophy as a whole. If philosophy can't bring people to agreement, and if it can't solve real problems in the real world, then something is obviously broken—but have no fear because the Americans are here to repair this broken-down European car (picture a very rusty 1964 Fiat *Cinquecento* with a blown head gasket and four flat tires) and get it on the road again. One reason pragmatism has been recognized as "American philosophy" is because it very explicitly marketed itself in that way: as the young and energetic new world coming to the rescue of the jaded and exhausted old world, throwing it a lifeline and getting it back on track with an infusion of youthful Yankee energy and New England common sense.

Pragmatism takes the utilitarian paradigm that only results matter and extends it to every aspect of philosophy while also weakening and relativizing the standards for what counts as good and bad, success or failure. Utilitarianism claims it can solve problems and get results if everyone will adopt the same first principles: that pleasure is good and pain is bad. Pragmatism loves the idea of focusing on results and insisting that philosophy get something done, but it claims to be allergic to first principles. To make all of philosophy a productive and practical machine what's required, the pragmatists say, is a method that rejects the very idea of universally agreed upon first principles. Here is William James explaining how pragmatism is oriented in a completely different way than most philosophy:

> No particular results then . . . but only an attitude of orientation, is what the pragmatic method means. *The attitude of looking*

---

33. This book was assembled from a series of popular lectures that James gave, much like Mill's *Utilitarianism*, which was originally a series of articles written for a popular magazine. In both cases it's clear that Mill and James thought utilitarianism and pragmatism could change the world if more people understood and embraced these philosophies, so they made a great effort to proselytize on their behalf.

> away from first things, principles, "categories," supposed necessities; and of looking toward last things, fruits, consequences, facts.[34]

If you now hear suspicious voices in your head murmuring, "This insistence on renouncing all first principles sounds a lot like a first principle to me," then I think the voices in your head are quite intelligent and you should definitely listen to them. It would be more honest to say that rather than rejecting all first principles pragmatism wants to embrace one very specific first principle: that only results matter, and it also wants to leave the criteria for what counts as good or bad results completely up to individuals rather than stipulating universal standards that everyone should accept. Utilitarianism wanted everyone to speak the single language of quantifiable pleasure and pain, but pragmatism claims that the truly scientific method is to allow good and bad and true and false to be determined by individuals in terms of the results they are trying to achieve. This pragmatic theory of truth is the true scientific approach, James explains:

> Everywhere ... "truth" in our ideas and beliefs means the same thing that it means in science. It means ... nothing but this, *that ideas (which themselves are but parts of our experience) become true just in so far as they help us to get into satisfactory relation with other parts of our experience.* ... Any idea upon which we can ride, so to speak; any idea that will carry us prosperously from one part of our experience to any other part, linking things satisfactorily, working securely, simplifying, saving labor; is true for just so much, true in so far forth, true *instrumentally*.[35]

According to pragmatism if an idea or belief works with all our other beliefs (that is, if it gets along with all of them like a good co-worker and doesn't cause any disturbances or disruptions at the office), and if it also works in the sense that it does some useful work for us (that is, if it helps us realize our own projects and desires, whatever they may be), then it's perfectly appropriate to say that idea or belief is true. It is not an oversimplification to say that the pragmatic theory of truth is: whatever works (as long as "works" is understood in both of the senses just described). Claiming to renounce all first principles, pragmatism really enshrines a new, implied, and rather vague first principle: whatever works is true, and valuable, and legitimate.

---

34. James, *Pragmatism*, 47.
35. James, *Pragmatism*, 49.

This seems like a good time to return to the voices in your head to see if this theory of truth works for them. Is there any idea or belief that pragmatism could not justify as true according to its "whatever works" criteria? Probably not. Since truth is just another word for fitting in comfortably with the current beliefs and plans of some individual somewhere in the world it's hard to imagine any idea that could not find someone on Planet Earth whose web of beliefs would offer it a comfortable home. Pragmatism is happy to say yes to any belief as long as that belief can find a human sponsor who is willing to host it. Because pragmatism says yes to everything (not in the mystical and mysterious way that Hegel says yes to everything but instead in a very concrete and applied way), it does seem like it can definitely get a lot done. For any particular belief, practice, or tradition to be justified all pragmatism asks is: "Does it work for you?" If the answer is, "Yes, it does, it works great for me," then pragmatism approves of your blueprints and issues something like a building permit so that you can get to work and build something with your beliefs; so now you have no excuse not to get out there and get something done!

But maybe pragmatism approves a lot of building projects that never should be approved—like a new deck designed by a proud father-of-the-bride (who is full of enthusiasm and wants to construct this for his daughter's wedding but unfortunately knows nothing about building decks), which will almost certainly fall down as soon as all the invited guests are standing on it waiting for the bride and groom to finish reading their personalized vows, killing everyone and creating the worst wedding ever. The enthusiastic but uninformed and unskilled father said: "This idea works for me!" so pragmatism approved the idea as true, but maybe the idea didn't work so well for the wedding guests, who would have preferred the idea of a deck that doesn't collapse while they are standing on it. Perhaps the only reason pragmatism can be so productive is because it has effectively given up on philosophy and turned it into a rubber stamp that approves any idea people want to believe. Is pragmatism just a proposal not to ask or pursue philosophical questions anymore? Is this version of philosophy the antithesis of the approach that Schopenhauer said can never be popular, because it requires you to consider at every moment in your life the possibility that your whole life so far has been a mistake? (Pragmatism seems to urge you to do the complete opposite: to refuse to question the value of your life as long as it's working as you want it to work.) These are all questions that I urge you to ask the voices in your head that expressed some skepticism concerning pragmatism. Do all of these principles of pragmatism work for them? If not, then according to pragmatism's own rule book pragmatism isn't true.

Friedrich Nietzsche

Nietzsche died in 1900 so it's hard not to call him the last philosopher of the nineteenth century. It almost looks like he wanted that distinction since he hung on until just after the century ended even though he was quite unwell and generally regarded as mad for the last eleven years of his life. The fact that Nietzsche probably lost his sanity at the end of his life is just one of the things that has encouraged many people to dismiss his ideas as crazy and/or dangerous. Another thing that contributes to this dismissive attitude is the fact that his sister Elisabeth took charge of publishing her brother's writing during those last eleven years of his life (and for many years after that since she lived until 1935), and she tried quite hard and quite successfully to market his ideas to the emerging National Socialist movement in Germany (she even invited Adolf Hitler to the Nietzsche Archives that she created as a sort of shrine to her brother, and he accepted: there's a photo of him staring intently at a statue of Nietzsche as if he felt some deep kinship with the philosopher). Finally there's the fact that Nietzsche's thinking changed quite dramatically in his lifetime, and the fact that he adopted a style of writing to express his ideas—similar to what Kierkegaard called "indirect communication"—which compelled readers to sort through his disjointed, fragmentary, and changing arguments on their own rather than appealing to the author's intentions, since the author was carefully concealed under several layers of camouflage. For all of these reasons Nietzsche has been one of the most misunderstood and vilified philosophers in history and many people have not found it at all difficult to accuse him of being crazy, or a Nazi, or of espousing virtually any bizarre idea that they could think of—including Aryan supremacy and murder just for the fun of it[36]—and this has caused many to think there's no point in taking him seriously as a philosopher or even reading his supposedly insane books. Consequently anyone today who wants to read and understand Nietzsche's philosophy has to be willing to check all this accumulated baggage at the door, just as you must do if you want to understand Marx, but in Nietzsche's case

---

36. In the Leopold and Loeb murder trial in 1924 both of the murderers claimed that they were inspired to commit their crime (killing a fourteen-year-old boy simply to see what it felt like) by reading Nietzsche.

the challenges created by many historical accidents and accumulated misunderstandings are augmented by the author himself since he very deliberately wrote in a fragmentary and unsystematic style that seemed designed to make life more difficult for the reader rather than simplifying things. Nietzsche said that he only wanted readers who were willing to think for themselves, and he described such readers like this:

> When I imagine a perfect reader, I always think of a monster of courage and curiosity who is also supple, cunning, cautious, a born adventurer and discover.[37]

If you are a monster of courage and curiosity—as everyone who studies philosophy ought to be—the many misunderstandings that have accumulated around Nietzsche will not get in your way at all.

Two of Nietzsche's books are particularly good as introductions to his philosophy, so in this brief and scrappy overview I'll focus just on a few key arguments and a few stylistic features of these two books: *Twilight of the Idols, or How to Philosophize with a Hammer*, and *Thus Spoke Zarathustra, a Book for All and for None*. I recommend you start with *Twilight of the Idols*. This was one of the last things that Nietzsche wrote and it was the very last thing he published (in 1888, shortly before he collapsed on a street in Torino, Italy, in 1889, which apparently marked the beginning of his insanity).[38] In a letter to a friend he called this book "a summary of all my major philosophical heresies," and that does seem like quite an accurate and excellent description. *Twilight of the Idols* is a very accessible and playful summary of many of the most important ideas in Nietzsche's philosophy, and it's also a good introduction to the unique style that he used to present those ideas.

The book begins with a collection of short aphorisms called "Maxims and Arrows." This barrage of short, scrappy, disconnected, unsystematic aphorisms is a good introduction to all of Nietzsche's writing since really everything he wrote is aphoristic, even the longer pieces that look

---

37. Nietzsche, *Ecce Homo*, 103.

38. I keep saying "apparent madness" because no one really knows what happened to Nietzsche and it would be crazy to diagnose his condition more than a hundred years after the fact. After he collapsed in 1889 his behavior was certainly consistent with some form of mental illness, and he did not resist when first his mother and then his sister became his caretakers; but some suspicious souls have suggested that perhaps he was faking insanity as part of some grand experiment he was conducting. One consequence of his condition in the last eleven years of his life was that other people (especially his sister) appropriated his philosophy and marketed it to serve their own interests, but maybe this is exactly what he wanted.

more like essays or chapters such as all the other sections of *Twilight of the Idols*. These longer sections may be focused on a single idea or theme, but there's no attempt to unify all of these sections and all of their arguments into anything like a system. Nietzsche preferred to present his ideas in a scrappy, fragmentary style, and he explained one reason for this in "Maxims and Arrows" aphorism 26 when he wrote: "I mistrust all systematizers and I avoid them. The will to a system is a lack of integrity."[39] Nietzsche, like Kierkegaard, wrote only in fragments as part of a deliberate attempt to undermine or blow up systematic philosophy because he regarded any philosophical system as a dishonest distortion of human existence: a lack of integrity.

Aphorism 15 provides another useful key to understanding all of Nietzsche's writing: "Posthumous men—I, for example—are understood worse than timely ones, but heard better. More precisely: we are never understood—hence our authority."[40] This captures so perfectly how easy it is to hear Nietzsche but how hard it is to understand him. He is easy to hear because he is the rare (extremely rare!) philosopher who is also a good writer. He writes dramatic and funny phrases that are easy to hear but not necessarily easy to understand. For example, consider Nietzsche's most famous sound bite: "God is dead." These three words are dramatic and memorable so they are very easy to hear, but what do they mean? Perhaps the best known text in which Nietzsche uses the phrase "God is dead" is aphorism 125 of *The Gay Science*, so let's consider that in its entirety:

> *The madman.* Haven't you heard of that madman who in the bright morning lit a lantern and ran around the marketplace crying incessantly, "I'm looking for God! I'm looking for God!" Since many of those who did not believe in God were standing around together just then, he caused great laughter. Has he been lost, then? asked one. Did he lose his way like a child? asked another. Or is he hiding? Is he afraid of us? Has he gone to sea? Emigrated? Thus they shouted and laughed, one interrupting the other. The madman jumped into their midst and pierced them with his eyes. "Where is God?" he cried; "I'll tell you! We have killed him—you and I! We are all his murderers. But how did we do this? How were we able to drink up the sea? Who gave us the sponge to wipe away the entire horizon? What were we doing when we unchained this earth from its sun? Where is it moving to now? Where are we moving to? Away from all suns?

---

39. Nietzsche, *Twilight*, 159.
40. Nietzsche, *Twilight*, 157.

Are we not continually falling? And backwards, sidewards, forwards, in all directions? Is there still an up and a down? Aren't we straying as though through an infinite nothing? Isn't empty space breathing at us? Hasn't it got colder? Isn't night and more night coming again and again? Don't lanterns have to be lit in the morning? Do we still hear nothing of the noise of the grave-diggers who are burying God? Do we still smell nothing of the divine decomposition? Gods, too, decompose! God is dead! God remains dead! And we have killed him! How can we console ourselves, the murderers of all murderers! The holiest and the mightiest thing the world has ever possessed has bled to death under our knives: who will wipe this blood from us? With what water could we clean ourselves? What festivals of atonement, what holy games will we have to invent for ourselves? Is the magnitude of this deed not too great for us? Do we not ourselves have to become gods merely to appear worthy of it? There was never a greater deed—and whoever is born after us will on account of this deed belong to a higher history than all history up to now!" Here the madman fell silent and looked again at his listeners; they too were silent and looked at him disconcertedly. Finally he threw his lantern on the ground so that it broke into pieces and went out. "I come too early," he then said; "my time is not yet. This tremendous event is still on its way, wandering; it has not yet reached the ears of men. Lightning and thunder need time; the light of the stars needs time; deeds need time, even after they are done, in order to be seen and heard. This deed is still more remote to them than the remotest stars—and yet they have done it themselves!" It is still recounted how on the same day the madman forced his way into several churches and there started singing his requiem *aeternam deo*. Led out and called to account, he is said always to have replied nothing but, "What then are these churches now if not the tombs and sepulchres of God?"[41]

This is quite a memorable little story: very easy to hear but perhaps not as easy to understand. Nietzsche is always happy to blur the lines between philosophy and literature, to write in parables, stories, and jokes, but there are always philosophical arguments within his writing even though the method of presenting them may be unorthodox and indirect. So how should we make sense of the Madman's announcement that God is dead? The Madman says not only "God is dead" but also "We have killed him," and no one in the marketplace understands him even though the

---

41. Nietzsche, *Science*, 119–20.

Madman says, "And yet they have done it themselves." These are important details. If we understand "God" literally as the Lord God Almighty, Creator of Heaven and Earth, then the Madman is simply walking into town to make a personal announcement about his own religious beliefs rather than to give a philosophical argument (and it wouldn't be a very interesting announcement since it's just a declaration of atheism, which isn't anything new). But if Nietzsche is using the word "God" as a metaphor to explore a philosophical concept then there may be a far more interesting philosophical argument here, so let's see if we can interpret it in that way.

One way to understand the Madman's announcement of the death of God as a philosophical argument is suggested by the marvelous little section in *Twilight of the Idols* called "How the 'True World' Finally Became a Fable: The History of an Error."[42] This is a complete history of philosophy in less than one page, and the gist of the story is that the belief in a "true world" (a world above and beyond the world we actually experience; a stable and transcendent source of meaning for all the unstable and constantly changing events that fill the world as we actually find it) has gradually faded away until finally one day people woke up and realized that they didn't believe in this idea at all: it had become dead to them, a worthless idea that was no longer worth believing. This is a very important development, the Madman explains, because when we stop believing in a stable and transcendent source of meaning it's as if "we unchained this earth from its sun" and we no longer know how to orient ourselves: we don't know what's up, down, good, bad, etc.

This is why Nietzsche believes that his "revaluation of all values" project is necessary. Since we no longer believe in a transcendent source that dictates values to us we have to take responsibility for creating our own values; so it's high time that we sound out all the idols of the present and the past, tapping on them with a hammer as with a tuning fork to determine which of them are worth keeping and which of them are hollow and empty inside (this is the meaning of the book's subtitle: "How to Philosophize with a Hammer"). To use a slightly different metaphor, this can also be understood as a project of unmasking all the nihilists in the world who have been pretending to be something else. Nihilists almost never announce or acknowledge themselves; instead they wear a mask and pretend to be something completely different. They pretend

---

42. Nietzsche, *Twilight*, 171.

to believe in all sorts of noble and admirable things when in fact they believe in nothing.

> The Wisest men in every age have reached the same conclusion about life: *it's no good*. . . . Always and everywhere, you hear the same sound from their mouths—a sound full of doubt, full of melancholy, full of exhaustion with life, full of resistance *to* life.[43]

Nietzsche argued that many (perhaps even most) of the authors, ideas, and arguments that have been celebrated and idolized in the history of philosophy have actually just been various disguised forms of nihilism, and he worked to expose these imposters so that philosophy could finally become a creative and affirmative project and not just an endless repetition of the same old exhausted and enervated insistence that life has no meaning or value. This project of unmasking nihilism became his singular focus at the end of his life and it was his most important contribution to the history of philosophy. The "revaluation of all values" project is animated by these two convictions:

- It's simply a fact that we no longer believe in a transcendent source of meaning that serves as the anchor for all our earthly values, so we now need to take responsibility for creating our own values.
- Most of the values we've inherited are actually just masked versions of nihilism, so they need to be unmasked and revealed for the imposters that they are and then we can create our own authentic and genuine values to take their place.

It's worth noting that Nietzsche's revaluation of all values project was definitely informed by his own experience of idolizing a few famous wise men and then gradually deciding that his idols were empty inside—that they were just more nihilists repeating the same old song about life: *it's no good*. This may seem like a needless detour into Nietzsche's biography but it's actually quite relevant to the history of philosophy in the nineteenth century, because the first famous wise man that Nietzsche idolized was Schopenhauer. When he was a student Nietzsche stumbled upon *The World as Will and Representation* by chance when he was browsing in a bookstore, and when he read the book he fell head over heels in love with Schopenhauer's deeply pessimistic worldview. Not long after this he was introduced to the famous composer Richard Wagner and discovered

---

43. Nietzsche, *Twilight*, 162.

that Wagner too was a great fan of Schopenhauer, so the two of them formed a friendship that centered on their mutual love of Schopenhauer's worldview and shortly thereafter Nietzsche got a job as a college professor (teaching classics, not philosophy; he was a completely self-taught amateur in philosophy with no formal training) in Switzerland not far from where Wagner lived, and Wagner and his wife Cosima sort of adopted Nietzsche, who started spending much of his time at their house and was absolutely starstruck by this attention from one of the most celebrated musicians in the world at that time. Long story short, Nietzsche eventually went through a rather protracted and painful breakup with both Schopenhauer and Wagner as he gradually came to the conclusion that both of them were nihilists who, behind all the sound and fury of their music and their philosophy, were simply exhausted and weary of living. Since Nietzsche never really knew his own father (who died when he was four years old) it's tempting to imagine that he clung first to Schopenhauer and later to Wagner as something like father figures, which made breaking out of their orbit even more difficult. I won't venture to speculate any further on this aspect of Nietzsche's biography, but his experience of overcoming his own idolization of very distinguished nihilists was clearly the main earthquake in his life and the main impetus for the revaluation of all values project that became the focus of his philosophy after he broke free of their influence.

If you want to see a wonderful demonstration of how much Nietzsche's thinking changed when he stopped trying to repeat Schopenhauer's and Wagner's ideas like a ventriloquist, and instead learned to think for himself, read the preface that he wrote for the second edition of his very first book, *The Birth of Tragedy*. Nietzsche wrote this book in 1872 when he was twenty-eight years old and totally under the spell of both Schopenhauer and Wagner (the book begins with a "Foreword to Richard Wagner" that sounds very much like a love letter). Fourteen years later in a new preface that he titles "An Attempt at Self-Criticism" he looks back on the book and sees it in a very different light:

> I find it an impossible book today. I declare that it is badly written, clumsy, embarrassing, with a rage for imagery and confused in its imagery, emotional, here and there sugary to the point of effeminacy, uneven in pace, lacking the will to logical cleanliness, very convinced and therefore too arrogant to prove its assertions, mistrustful even of the *propriety* of proving things, a book for the initiated, "music" for those who were baptized

in the name of music. ... A *strange* voice was speaking here, the disciple of an as yet "unknown god" who concealed himself beneath the cowl of a scholar, beneath the ponderousness and dialectical disinclination of the Germans, even beneath the bad manners of a Wagnerite.[44]

I now regret very much that I did not yet have the courage (or immodesty) at that time to permit myself a *language of my very own* for such personal views and acts of daring. Laboring instead to express strange and new evaluations in Schopenhauerian and Kantian formulations, things which fundamentally ran counter to both the spirit and taste of Kant and Schopenhauer. ... And the same applies to current *German music*, which is romanticism through and through, and the most un-Greek of all possible forms of art; furthermore, as a ruiner of nerves it is in the first rank, a doubly dangerous thing amongst a people who love drink and who honor obscurity as a virtue, particularly for its dual properties as a narcotic which both intoxicates and *befogs* the mind.[45]

I mention these biographical details about Nietzsche coming to terms with his own idol worship only because they help to clarify the purpose of the revaluation of all values project which was his focus at the end of his life. The danger of falling under the spell of an empty idol that was really just another disguised version of nihilism was not an abstraction for Nietzsche: he lived through that experience himself, and this helps to explain the big shift in thinking that occurred late in his life and also the very unusual path that he followed to become one of the most provocative and misunderstood philosophers in history.

Thus Spoke Zarathustra is another book by Nietzsche that blurs the lines between philosophy and literature. Here's a brief summary of the "plot," such as it is, all of which is presented in the book's prologue.[46] Zarathustra just turned forty and he's been living alone in the mountains for the past ten years; now he wants to share his wisdom with others. He starts walking down the mountain in search of people and along the way encounters a "Saint," who, like him, has been living alone in the forest. "Why go back among the humans?" asks the Saint, and Zarathustra has an immediate answer: "Because I love mankind." He wants to give

---

44. Nietzsche, *Tragedy*, 5–6.
45. Nietzsche, *Tragedy*, 10.
46. Nietzsche, *Zarathustra*, 3–16.

mankind a gift, and later we'll see that he struggles to figure out how to give this gift but he is very clear right from the start about his motivation: he loves mankind. He leaves the Saint and as soon as he arrives at the very first town (which is called "The Motley Cow") he immediately begins teaching "the Overman," which seems like a very simple idea: "Human being is something that must be overcome. What have you done to overcome him?" But the townspeople just laugh at him and don't make any effort to understand his words; they treat him like a substitute teacher who will be gone tomorrow and can be safely ignored. It amazes Zarathustra that no one was moved by his excellent speech about the overman so he tries again with another speech, and in both speeches he uses tightrope symbolism ("mankind is a rope fastened between animal and Overman") apparently not noticing that overhead there is a real tightrope walker preparing to perform. The crowd responds to Zarathustra's second speech about the Overman just as they did to the first: with laughter and indifference, and now Zarathustra begins to get angry. So he tries a different approach in his third speech: he attacks the contentment and self-satisfaction of his audience. His third speech is all about the "last man," who is the opposite of the Overman and is meant to fill the crowd with disgust, but instead even before he can finish the speech the crowd interrupts him and says: "Give us this last man, oh Zarathustra." Now Zarathustra begins to have serious doubts about his future as a teacher, and while he contemplates this the tightrope walker (thinking that he has been summoned) goes to work—but when the tightrope walker reaches midway a jester emerges behind him on the tightrope, gives a hideous cry, and leaps right over him, causing him to lose his balance and fall to the ground where he dies right at Zarathustra's feet. The whole thing looks like a ridiculous parody of what Zarathustra has been trying to teach: mankind is something that must be overcome. It seems like maybe the Jester was the only one who understood Zarathustra's arguments about the Overman, and he understood them well enough to demonstrate how easy it would be to misunderstand and misrepresent them. As Zarathustra is carrying the dead tightrope walker out of town to bury him the Jester catches up with him and seems to say as much. He tells Zarathustra that he should leave town because all the good and the just people hate him since he asks them to reevaluate all of their values and to consider that perhaps they are not so good and just after all. Hearing this Zarathustra has an epiphany: instead of trying to teach everyone in a very direct and straightforward way, he decides to focus on a select group of people ("companions" or "disciples"), and to speak to them in a kind of code. He decides to make his teaching esoteric, so instead of just sort of hitting you over the head three times with his philosophy in a perfectly direct communication as he did at first, from this point on he will speak indirectly in parables and riddles and then leave it up to you to figure out what it all means.

And that's all the rest of the book is: eighty speeches by Zarathustra which are all coded, esoteric, indirect communications; riddles, parables, and strange little stories that blur the lines between philosophy and literature and require you the reader (a monster of courage and curiosity) to decode them. After striking out completely when he tried to teach the residents of The Motley Cow directly, Zarathustra decides that he will only teach his philosophy indirectly, and only to a group of people who are willing to be fellow "celebrators and creators" along with him. *Thus Spoke Zarathustra* is "a book for all and for none" because anyone who is willing to do the work required of a co-creator can find great meaning and value in this text, but for anyone who isn't willing to do that the book will be completely meaningless nonsense and they may as well throw it out the window right now. This adds up to a very strange philosophy book, perhaps the strangest ever, but also one of the most vibrant and living texts ever written. If Zarathustra wants his students to be co-creators that means his speeches are not finished: they need to be decoded and then continued (applied, expanded, questioned, celebrated) by you, the reader. You have to make a contribution to complete these speeches, and if you read *Thus Spoke Zarathustra* in this way the book comes to life and you become a co-creator of values who will contribute to the constant self-overcoming that the Overman ideal requires—and what could be more fun and fulfilling than that?

Ludwig Wittgenstein

Wittgenstein continues the parade of outsiders in nineteenth- and twentieth-century philosophy who were major disrupters, shaking up the complacent philosophical establishment in an entirely good way. Nietzsche was drawn to philosophy by Schopenhauer, but if he had remained just another Schopenhauer fanboy probably no one would remember him today; his philosophy only became truly innovative when he broke out of Schopenhauer's (and Wagner's) gravity field and struck out on his own. Wittgenstein, on the other hand, sort of backed into philosophy accidentally just because he wanted to study logic. In 1911, when he was twenty-two years old, Wittgenstein was in Manchester, England, studying aeronautical engineering and becoming intensely curious about the mathematics behind the engineering he was studying, which in turn led him to wonder about the possibility that logic is the foundation of all mathematics. He was advised that if he really wanted to learn about logic he should head southeast to Cambridge and talk to Bertrand Russell, who had been working for several years (along with Alfred North Whitehead) on an attempt to prove that all of mathematics could be derived from basic principles of logic. (They called their book *Principia Mathematica*. Eighty-six pages into volume 2 they had succeeded in proving that $1 + 1 = 2$.) So Wittgenstein went to Cambridge University where he showed up without warning in one of Russell's classes and afterward pursued him doggedly for days with deep questions about the foundations of mathematics and logic. Russell at first thought that his Austrian visitor might be mad but eventually decided that he was actually a genius; and since he was feeling burned out with logic himself and wanted to venture into other areas of philosophy he tried to make Wittgenstein his heir apparent to take over the work he had started on the foundations of logic and mathematics. With Russell as his sponsor Wittgenstein was welcomed into the academic and philosophical world at Cambridge, and eventually he was awarded a doctorate there (on the merits of the one and only book he ever completed: the *Tractatus Logico-Philosophicus*) and he also taught at the university for many years (with a few notable interruptions).

Wittgenstein didn't go to Cambridge to study philosophy; he just wanted to understand logic at its most fundamental level because he thought it was the basis of mathematics and that mathematics was the basis of everything that aeronautical engineers and everyone else in the world was doing. From Russell he learned, to his dismay, that logic was a branch of philosophy and that it was impossible to study logic on the deepest level without also wading into many other philosophical questions and debates, most of which remained unresolved after thousands of years. Apparently Wittgenstein found all of this to be quite annoying, and he resolved to clean up this mess: to finish philosophy once and for all and put it out of its misery. He formed the opinion that philosophy is a kind of disease that needs to be cured, and when he completed his very short and very influential *Tractatus Logico-Philosophicus* in 1918 he announced in the book's preface that he had succeeded:

> The book deals with the problems of philosophy, and shows, I believe, that the reason why these problems are posed is that the logic of our language is misunderstood. The whole sense of the book might be summed up in the following words: what can be said at all can be said clearly, and what we cannot talk about we must pass over in silence. . . . I am conscious of having fallen a long way short of what is possible. Simply because my powers are too slight for the accomplishment of the task.—May others come and do it better. On the other hand the truth of the thoughts that are here communicated seems to me unassailable and definitive. I therefore believe myself to have found, on all essential points, the final solution of the problems. And if I am not mistaken in this belief, then the second thing in which the value of this work consists is that it shows how little is achieved when these problems are solved.[47]

After he finished the *Tractatus* Wittgenstein took a job as an elementary school teacher in a remote Austrian village thinking that he, and the rest of the world, was done with philosophy forever and therefore it was time for all philosophers to find new jobs. Later he decided that this was a mistake, because the only way you can even try to kill philosophy is with . . . more philosophy. This led to a second act for Wittgenstein as a philosopher: he quit the elementary school job and went back to Cambridge to be a professor. But before we get to that second act we need to consider the *Tractatus* more carefully because this strange little book had a massive impact on philosophy even if it didn't succeed in euthanizing it, as its author had initially hoped it would. Here are some keys to understanding this book:

- Wittgenstein fell into philosophy through logic, and the *Tractatus* is very much a logic book. There are parts of the book that wade into technical formal logic and these will be easy to recognize because they look like math: words get replaced by logical symbolism. Those sections you can safely skim, but it's important to notice that logic is the engine that Wittgenstein thinks is powering this antiphilosophy machine.

---

47. Wittgenstein, *Tractatus*, 3–4.

- Officially the entire book consists of only seven propositions, although all of these except #7 have numerous supporting sub-propositions (2.1, 2.11, 2.151, etc.) so really there are 525 propositions in all. In logic "proposition" is a technical term that means "a use of language that has truth value." In other words, logical propositions are statements that are either true or false. For the most part Wittgenstein simply asserts that all of the 525 propositions in the *Tractatus* are true; he almost never argues for any of them. The numbering system for the propositions is meant to convey the idea that the book is a complete logical system and that none of these propositions are ambiguous or vague in any way: each proposition is in exactly the right place and its meaning is perfectly clear.

- Is it possible to imagine a more rigorously and systematically organized philosophy book? I don't think so. Wittgenstein insists that everything that needs to be said has been said in this book and that everything is in exactly the right place (as indicated by the number assigned to each proposition). The desire to create a complete philosophical system flourished especially in modern philosophy and peaked most obviously with Kant at the end of that period when he bequeathed to the world three *Critiques* which he claimed contained complete systems of epistemology, ethics, and aesthetics. In the nineteenth century there's a brief burst of system-building with authors like Hegel, Marx, and Schopenhauer, but it runs out of gas rather quickly and soon there are quite a few authors who write in a deliberately fragmentary and anti-systematic style such as Kierkegaard and Nietzsche. In his second act Wittgenstein will join the camp of the scrappy philosophers but first he wrote the *Tractatus*, which was perhaps the most carefully regimented and disciplined philosophy book ever.

- In spite of how hard Wittgenstein tried to nail each of his propositions into place there are parts of the book where they clearly got away from him. As the book nears the end, beginning especially with proposition 6.41—"The sense of the world must lie outside the world"—the book takes a decidedly mystical turn, leading up to the grand finale in the final two propositions:

> 6.54: My propositions serve as elucidations in the following way: anyone who understands me eventually recognizes them

as nonsensical, when he has used them—as steps—to climb up beyond them. (He must, so to speak, throw away the ladder after he has climbed up it.) He must transcend these propositions, and then he will see the world aright.

7: What we cannot speak about we must pass over in silence.[48]

And then the book is over; that's supposed to be the last word in the history of philosophy.

Many people did believe that these final words of the *Tractatus* had effectively silenced philosophy, or at least narrowed its scope drastically. Logical positivism was the most obvious consequence of this interpretation of the book (we'll get to that shortly). However not everyone agreed with the positivist interpretation of the book; even Wittgenstein himself came to reject it a few years later. So in addition to the reading of the *Tractatus* that makes it the last word in philosophy, there's also a long tradition of reading the book as a work that actually expanded philosophy because it gave it more material to work with and more life even though the author's intent was just the opposite.

Since Wittgenstein was not persuaded by his own announcement of the end of philosophy the *Tractatus* was not in fact his last word. In his second act as a philosopher he produced an enormous amount of writing but never published a word of it; the *Tractatus* was his one and only published work. But if you run to the library right now and start pulling all the books by Wittgenstein off the shelves you'll probably find ten or twenty or even more, depending on your library's budget; so—as they say in Cambridge—what's up with that? The explanation is that after Wittgenstein's death in 1951 there was such an appetite for his philosophy that all the scraps he left behind when he died (and there were a lot of them) were raided and turned into books. But it's important to note that Wittgenstein himself didn't finish or publish any of these books because he was never satisfied with the arrangement of his ideas. Perhaps the experience of trying so hard in the *Tractatus* to regiment all of his propositions into perfect military order and then witnessing how his ideas broke ranks and ran amok in spite of all his efforts left him gun shy. We've seen several examples of philosophers who preferred to write in fragments and scraps (for example, Kierkegaard and Nietzsche both chose that style), but the way Wittgenstein wrote in his second act is the

---

48. Wittgenstein, *Tractatus*, 89.

ultimate in scrappy philosophy. After he typed out his short, oracular fragments, he came back later with a pair of scissors and cut out each fragment so that he could move the scraps of paper around and experiment with creating different arrangements. Was he still trying to create something like the perfect system that the *Tractatus* aspired to, or was he trying to undermine the very idea of a system? No one knows, but this much is clear: he thought that the arrangement mattered and he was never satisfied, he never thought he got it just right, which is why he never published another book after the *Tractatus* but instead spent his time arranging and rearranging his many fragments, experimenting with different configurations. Everything that has been published from Wittgenstein's second act (including *Philosophical Investigations*, which is generally regarded as his second magnum opus) is something that Wittgenstein himself regarded as an unfinished work in progress—or perhaps not even a work at all but rather just a collection of scrappy ideas with which he was experimenting.

Given Wittgenstein's reluctance to publish any of his ideas after the *Tractatus* some of his students resorted to typing up their notes from his class lectures and sharing them with each other like bootleg recordings of Grateful Dead concerts; and after his death especially everyone who knew Wittgenstein was on the lookout for any stash of writing that he might have left behind. My favorite example of this is the collection of fragments that's now published under the title *Zettel*, which in German means "scraps of paper." Here is the editor's explanation of that 124-page book:

> We publish here a collection of fragments made by Wittgenstein himself and left by him in a box-file. They were for the most part cut from extensive typescripts of his, other copies of which still exist. Some few were cut from typescripts which we have not been able to trace and which it is likely that he destroyed but for the bits that he put in the box. . . . We were naturally at first rather puzzled to account for this box. Were its contents an accidental collection of left-overs? Was it a receptacle for random deposits of casual scraps of writing?[49]

Not knowing exactly how to interpret this box full of scraps of paper (after all it could have just been a box of rubbish that Wittgenstein forgot to take out to the curb on trash day), the editors decided to put them all into a book and send that book out into the world so that everyone

---

49. Wittgenstein, *Zettel*, v.

else could decide what to make of these fragments of philosophy. They are fascinating for sure, as is everything that Wittgenstein wrote in both his first and his second acts, but the contrast between the rigorously organized propositions of the *Tractatus* and the completely disorganized fragments of *Zettel* and all the other "books" that contain Wittgenstein's ideas after he decided that he had not succeeded in finishing philosophy, could not be more extreme, and this has led to extremely divergent interpretations of his ideas. Thus the philosopher who seemed most allergic to ambiguity has had perhaps the most profoundly ambiguous legacy of all, inspiring everything from logical positivism (that's next on the menu) to late-twentieth-century postmodernism (that will be the last course in this very large meal, so save some room).

Logical Positivism (starring A. J. Ayer)

The logical positivists were inspired by Wittgenstein's *Tractatus* but only because they engaged in a very selective reading of the text. Basically they ignored all the mysticism and ambiguity in the book, all the suggestions by Wittgenstein that even though language is limited—"everything that can be said can be said clearly" and "whereof one cannot speak thereof one must be silent"—there's still more to human existence than this, and it's possible to show this something-more even if it's not possible to say it. In a letter to a friend Wittgenstein explained how he personally understood the book in this way:

> You won't—I really believe—get too much out of reading it. Because you won't understand it; the content will seem strange to you. In reality, it isn't strange to you, for the point is ethical. I once wanted to give a few words in the foreword which now actually are not in it, which, however, I'll write to you now because they might be a key for you: I wanted to write that my work consists of two parts: of the one which is here, and of everything which I have not written. And precisely this second part is the important one.[50]

Wittgenstein's idea that what really mattered in the *Tractatus* was the unwritten part was so subtle that almost no one figured it out, especially not the logical positivists. They decided that just the visible, written part of the book was all they needed (thank you very much), and they

---

50. Monk, *Genius*, 178.

strategically ignored some of the rather mystical propositions that arrive mainly at the end of the book. This allowed them to cite Wittgenstein as one of the founding fathers of their movement, even though Wittgenstein didn't want the job. Clearly there are a lot of misunderstandings that separate Wittgenstein and logical positivism, even though the logical positivists claimed to be just working out the implications of his philosophy. In spite of the fact that Wittgenstein declined to be their sponsor the positivists were determined to do what Wittgenstein concluded he had failed to do in the *Tractatus*: to assassinate philosophy, or at least to give it the much-diminished role of language police, pointing out to everyone that they have said something nonsensical whenever they say something that can't be verified. The favorite word of all logical positivists is "meaningless," a word which they deploy like a referee throwing a flag or blowing a whistle: it's a way to declare that someone has just violated the rules of language and therefore must be publicly shamed. Logical positivism offers its services to clear up all the confusion in the world in this way, calling a penalty whenever anyone says or writes something that positivists think has no meaning because it can't be verified. According to positivism, almost everything we say or believe is nonsense, so there's a lot of whistle-blowing, flag-throwing, and cleaning-up to be done.

One of the most succinct explanations of the positivist project and worldview is the slim volume composed by Alfred Jules Ayer in 1935 called *Language, Truth and Logic*. This book has been widely regarded as something like the manifesto of the logical positivist movement. Ayer begins in the book's preface by trying to establish a respectable genealogy for this school of thought. Since Wittgenstein turned down their request that he be their daddy Ayer casts positivism as the natural offspring of British empiricism:

> The views which are put forward in this treatise derive from the doctrines of Bertrand Russell and Wittgenstein, which are themselves the logical outcome of the empiricism of Berkeley and David Hume.[51]

The idea that positivism is just a return to the good-old, common-sense empiricism of the modern period is interesting, especially since (as we saw in the last chapter) Berkeley and Hume left empiricism very effectively painted into a corner, denying that there is any empirical world at all or that there are any necessary connections between our ideas.

---

51. Ayer, *Language*, 31.

Nevertheless, Ayer decides to ignore the actual outcome of the empiricism of Berkeley and Hume and focus instead on the common-sense belief that there should be an empirical confirmation of any belief that's true. This leads to the "verification principle" which is the central tenet of positivism:

> I require of an empirical hypothesis, not indeed that it should be conclusively verifiable, but that some possible sense-experience should be relevant to the determination of its truth or falsehood. If a putative proposition fails to satisfy this principle, and is not a tautology, then I hold that it is metaphysical, and that, being metaphysical, it is neither true nor false but literally senseless. It will be found that much of what ordinarily passes for philosophy is metaphysical according to this criterion.[52]

In the rest of the book Ayer explains everything that will now be flagged as "literally senseless" according to the verification principle, and this list is a long one, including:

- Ethics (unless it's understood as nothing more than expressions of how someone feels, e.g.: "I personally don't like dishonesty, theft, murder, genocide, etc.")
- Aesthetics (unless, again, it's understood as nothing more than expressions of how someone feels, e.g.: "I personally do like Westerns staring Clint Eastwood, short stories by Tolstoy, songs by the Beastie Boys, sunsets on the beach in Malibu, pasta alla carbonara, etc.")
- Any beliefs about selves or (God forbid) souls; and speaking of God—
- Actually don't speak of God, because anything you say about religion or theology can be nothing but nonsense.

Positivism repeats Hume's call (in the final paragraph of the *Enquiry Concerning Human Understanding*) to run through all the libraries making havoc, committing to the flames all the volumes which contain nothing but sophistry and illusion (which is most of them); but now instead of "Sophistry and Illusion!" the battle cry of these library wreckers is "Nonsense!" because positivism claims to have added logic to empiricism—to have made empiricism logical, so now it's possible to say that any claims in the censored areas above are just completely senseless and incoherent, like the word which I will now write: "Xrwphtarggggh."

---

52. Ayer, *Language*, 31.

Logical positivism did catch on in the mid-twentieth century in many parts of the world, especially in England and America where philosophers seemed particularly attracted to the job of being language referees and calling a foul whenever anyone said something nonsensical. There are, however, a few glitches in its machinery that positivism has had difficulty overcoming. One is the fact that the verification principle itself clearly cannot meet the requirements of the verification principle. There's no empirical evidence that every belief must be supported by empirical evidence; that first principle has to be an act of faith for positivism just as it was for empiricism throughout the modern period, but that's rather embarrassing for a philosophy that has so confidently proclaimed all faith is nonsense. Another thing that has proven troubling for positivism has been its attempt to present the empiricist tradition as if it were a glorious and unmitigated success story, but as you know very well that wasn't the case at all. Empiricism seemed like a perfectly reasonable and commonsense explanation of how knowledge is possible when it began so promisingly with Bacon, Hobbes, and Locke, but by the time Berkeley and Hume are done with it common sense is receding very quickly in the rearview mirror. When logical positivism presents itself as the child of modern empiricism it seems determined to ignore all the weird stuff that's in its family history; but that history is still there and the strange results that empiricism leads to do not vanish just because we decline to look at them.

Martin Heidegger

If you're now in the mood for some philosophy that would make a logical positivist thoroughly exasperated and perhaps collapse in exhaustion from shouting "Nonsense!" at the top of his lungs, then your timing is perfect because it's time to talk about Martin Heidegger. Like Wittgenstein, Heidegger's philosophy has two distinct stages, and in his case the Second World War was the great earthquake that divided the two. The magnum opus of Heidegger's early philosophy was *Being and Time*, which was published in 1927, so we'll start with that book.

The overall project of *Being and Time* is to reveal the true nature of Being (*Sein* in German), and Heidegger proposes to do this by using the being of an individual person, a particular human existence (*Da-sein* in German which means "existence" or more literally "being there") as the means of accessing the larger truths about Being in general. Consequently most of *Being and Time* is taken up with what Heidegger calls "the existential analytic of *Dasein*" and this makes it very easy to read *Being and Time* as a work of existentialism; but Heidegger insisted that wasn't what he intended. He wanted the book to be understood as a work of "fundamental ontology": an attempt to reveal the true nature of all Being, Being in general, and therefore not really interested in human being at all. "Ontology" is just another word for "metaphysics" but it places greater emphasis on the study of being in particular rather than just the study of reality in general. (The Greek root *ontos* means "being.") Since the only access we have to Being in general is through our own particular human being, Heidegger says he had no choice but to spend most of the book analyzing human being; but that was meant to be understood as just a means to the end of revealing the nature of Being in general. That this way of understanding *Being and Time* was lost on most readers probably has a lot to do with the fact that Heidegger never finished writing the book. What was published as *Being and Time* was supposed to be just the first two sections of a book with six sections in all, but those last four sections never got done (and perhaps the rise of National Socialism in Germany followed by World War Two had a lot to do with this, as we'll see later).

So *Being and Time* ended up being a very influential book, but the influence it had was mostly a disappointment to its author who thought that almost everyone had misunderstood it. Like Wittgenstein, Heidegger thought that the unwritten part of his book was the most important part; but this was such a subtle and cryptic interpretation that almost no one else understood the book in this way. This leads to the distinction now commonly made between Heidegger's early philosophy and his later philosophy. The early philosophy was dominated by the single book *Being and Time*, while the later philosophy is scattered among many different essays, letters, lectures, and courses that are challenging to piece together into anything approximating the very systematic presentation of *Being and Time*. In this respect, and also in terms of their style (the later philosophy is presented in a much more poetic and obscure manner) and their subject matter, the early and the later philosophy seem miles apart. Heidegger might have understood everything he wrote as one big, interconnected project, the master plan for which he announced at the beginning of *Being and Time*, but in this brief introduction I'll follow the convention of distinguishing between early and later Heidegger simply because it seems like the best way to get a foot in the door of the House of Being. (The meaning of the excellent joke in the previous sentence will become clear shortly!)

Being and Time attracted a lot of attention, including from one Jean-Paul Sartre: a high school philosophy teacher in France. Sartre was drafted into the French army in 1939 and captured by the Germans in 1940. While he was in a German prison camp he got his hands on a copy of the German philosophy book *Being and Time* and liked it so much that he was inspired to start writing his own book which he called *Being and Nothingness* in a clear homage. In 1941 Sartre was allowed to leave the camp and return to his teaching job in Paris where he continued writing *Being and Nothingness* and then published the book in 1943 while France was still occupied by the German army. Shortly after World War Two ended the philosophy of *Being and Nothingness* (which Sartre called existentialism) became an extremely hot commodity throughout the world and he became an international superstar. Sartre's existentialism borrowed heavily from many previous authors including Hegel, Kierkegaard, Nietzsche, and of course Heidegger—the most obvious catalyst for *Being and Nothingness*. However Heidegger was not flattered by this attention and wanted nothing to do with existentialism even though *Being and Time* had done so much to inspire it, so after the war he renounced this theory that he had inspired and went off to his rustic cabin in the Black Forest to compose the many obscure lectures and essays that constitute his later philosophy. He officially disowned existentialism in a 1946 essay called "The Letter on Humanism" which was a response to the famous lecture that Sartre gave in 1945, shortly after the war ended, called "Existentialism is a Humanism." Even though Heidegger wanted nothing to do with existentialism *Being and Time* was undeniably an important part of its development, so I'll consider that part of Heidegger's legacy even though he would prefer that everyone forget about it.

Whether you read *Being and Time* as a work of fundamental ontology (as Heidegger would prefer), or as a work of existentialism (which annoys Heidegger very much), it's essential to understand the method he follows in this book, which he calls "existential phenomenology." (This is also important for understanding Sartre's existentialism since he uses exactly the same method in his book *Being and Nothingness*.) "Phenomenology" can mean many different things but the basic idea is always a reconceptualization of what should count as evidence; a new perspective on what the real phenomena are. For Hegel the phenomenology of mind requires us to reconceptualize the events of history as epi-phenomena which are just side effects of the real phenomena—the phenomena that really matter—which are the stages in the Absolute Mind's coming to know itself. Existential phenomenology, on the other hand, argues that subjective experience, which is treated as irrelevant and even somewhat obscene by the modern scientific world, is actually exactly what you need to study if you want to answer questions like "What is the true nature of being?" or "Are humans really free?" Every version of phenomenology in the history of philosophy presents itself as a new and improved form of empiricism, a sort of super-sexy empiricism, that gets better results because it looks for the right empirical data in the right places. The natural sciences practice traditional, old-fashioned, not-very-sexy empiricism according to which the truth is out there in the world and scientists go out looking for it, and the facts they discover are objective, empirical facts in the world that are revealed directly to the five physical senses. Then along comes Heidegger and he says, "I'm going to alter traditional empiricism in two ways":

- "I'm going to observe and analyze phenomena that have mostly been ignored because they were considered boring, uninteresting, embarrassing, or obscene." Existential phenomenology does empirical observations of average, everyday experience, especially the boring and embarrassing stuff, which no one thought was worth studying before.

- "I'm going to expand the definition of empiricism to include consciousness. I'm going to observe and study our experience of the world as we actually experience it: in our consciousness, since that will get us closer to the true nature of the world." The phenomenological descriptions that Heidegger gives in *Being and Time* are descriptions of consciousness. "This," he says, "is what our conscious experience of the world looks and feels like, and I'm going to do a close and careful analysis of these phenomena because they are the only access we have to the world."

The basic paradigm shift that has to take place for existential phenomenology to work is this: instead of treating average, everyday experience as boring, irrelevant, embarrassing, or pointless and incapable of teaching us anything at all, do just the opposite. Instead of going out into the world to do research and gather evidence that is scientifically respectable, redirect your attention within your own consciousness, put every moment of lived experience under a microscope, and analyze it intensely, because when you do this you can discover deeper truths that are inaccessible in any other way. All of us are very conditioned to treat our own subjective experience as unworthy of close and careful analysis, and certainly inappropriate for public conversation (like sex, politics, and religion); but if you want to be a good phenomenologist you have to stop feeling embarrassed and embrace your subjectivity as the only access we have to the truth of human being.

When Heidegger does this in *Being and Time* it results in many phenomenological descriptions of the average, everyday experience of *Dasein* that are startling in their simplicity and insight. "Analysis" usually means taking something apart, but Heidegger's existential analysis does just the opposite. The hyphen, which normally gets to relax on the bench in its warm-up jacket watching the rest of its punctuation teammates run up and down the court, is suddenly called into the game quite often to explain the many aspects of Dasein's Being-in-the-world, which include: Being-ready-to-hand, Being-present-at-hand, Being-alongside, Being-one's-self, Being-already-alongside, Being-a-sign-for, and Being-present-at-hand-along-with.[53] Heidegger explains right at the outset that this is simply what an honest account of the empirical data of our conscious experience looks like.

> The compound expression "Being-in-the-world" indicates in the very way we have coined it, that is stands for a *unitary* phenomenon. This primary datum must be seen as a whole. But while Being-in-the-world cannot be broken up into contents which may be pieced together, this does not prevent it from having several constitutive items in its structure.[54]

The "several constitutive items" in the overall structure of Dasein's Being-in-the-world that Heidegger explores include: the worldhood of the world (a report of our lived experience of the physical world); the many phenomena of Being-with (relationships with others and with ourself); the many states of mind that constitute our Being-in (such as fear, ambiguity, and anxiety); care as the Being of Dasein (care means mainly anxiety for Heidegger); and finally a long exploration of our experience

---

53. The poor, exhausted hyphen only gets this workout in English. In German no hyphens are necessary since a neologism such as "Being-present-at-hand-along-with" can be created just by mashing words together to create *Mitvorhandensein*.

54. Heidegger, *Being*, 78.

of temporality, which is fundamentally Being-toward-death and which can be either authentic or inauthentic.

In addition to being a heavy-user-of-hyphens, Heidegger is also a great fan of adding emphasis (mostly with italics, and sometimes boldface type) to his writing to make sure that the reader doesn't miss the words and phrases that matter the most. (If you think of italics as the typographical equivalent of shouting there's a lot of shouting in *Being and Time*; some in almost every paragraph.) Near the end of the book the following paragraph is italicized in its entirety, except for the words in boldface type (an even louder shout), so apparently this is a very important paragraph which ought to be reprinted here:

> *Only an entity which, in its Being, is essentially* **futural** *so that it is free for its death can let itself be thrown back upon its factical "there" by shattering itself against death—that is to say, only an entity which, as futural, is equiprimordially in the process of* **having-been**, *can, by handing down to itself the possibility it has inherited, take over its own thrownness and be* **in the moment of vision** *for "its time." Only authentic temporality which is at the same time finite, makes possible something like fate—that is to say, authentic historicality.*[55]

Reading a paragraph like this, to which Heidegger gave as much emphasis as the limits of typography allowed, it's not hard to see how *Being and Time* was understood by almost everyone as a sort of instruction manual for authentic being, and therefore a quintessential work of existentialism.

After *Being and Time* was published in 1927 Heidegger's thought seems to shift rather dramatically. In the "Letter on Humanism" he asserts that this shift was part of his master plan right from the start, but he also acknowledges that readers might have missed this because he never finished writing the rest of *Being and Time*. In the final words of the introduction to *Being and Time* he announced that the whole book, when it was finished, would look like this:

Part 1
1. The preparatory fundamental analysis of Dasein;
2. Dasein and temporality;
3. Time and Being

---

55. Heidegger, *Being*, 437.

Part 2
1. Kant's doctrine of schematism and time, as a preliminary stage in a problematic of Temporality;
2. The ontological foundation of Descartes's "*cogito sum*," and how the medieval ontology has been taken over into the problematic of the "*res cogitans*";
3. Aristotle's essay on time, as providing a way of discriminating the phenomenal basis and the limits of ancient ontology.[56]

What was published as *Being and Time* is just the first two sections of part 1. Starting with section 3, "Time and Being," Heidegger planned to make a major shift or turn, as he explained in the "Letter on Humanism":

> The adequate execution and completion of this other thinking that abandons subjectivity is surely made more difficult by the fact that in the publication of *Being and Time* the third division of the first part, "Time and Being," was held back. Here everything is reversed. The division in question was held back because thinking failed in the adequate saying of this turning and did not succeed with the help of the language of metaphysics.[57]

Just in this short excerpt from 1947 you can see how Heidegger has become highly allergic to any mention of individual, existing, human subjects. He doesn't say, "I, Martin Heidegger, didn't finish writing my book because I couldn't come up with ideas and then put those ideas into words"; instead everything is expressed in a passive voice as if human subjects were not involved: "the rest of the book was held back; thinking failed to think the necessary thoughts; language got in the way because it was contaminated by metaphysics, etc." In his later philosophy Heidegger turns to language itself to reveal the truth about Being, rather than human existence, because (as he declares in the first paragraph of the "Letter on Humanism")

> Language is the house of Being. In its home man dwells. Those who think and those who create with words are the guardians of this home.[58]

The shift in style and focus from the early philosophy (an intense existential analytic of human being) to the later (no human beings at all please, since they scare away Being, which must be allowed to reveal itself in

---

56. Heidegger, *Being*, 64.
57. Heidegger, "Humanism," 231.
58. Heidegger, "Humanism," 217.

language) is about as stark as it could possibly be. This shift/turn could have been totally planned out in advance by Heidegger as a sort of throw-away-the-ladder-after-you've-climbed-up strategy (to borrow an analogy from Wittgenstein), but it's also possible that Heidegger's experiences in the war had something to do with this shift. Heidegger went all in on National Socialism in the 1930s, most notably in 1933 when he was appointed Rector of the University of Freiburg (roughly the equivalent of university president) and quickly leveraged that position to implement Nazi policies throughout the university. He only lasted one year in the job because he was apparently quite disappointed by the individual humans who were running the Nazi machine. In a 1935 lecture he expressed this sentiment concerning the politics of his day:

> The works that are being peddled about nowadays as the philosophy of National Socialism but have nothing whatever to do with the inner truth and greatness of this movement—have all been written by men fishing in the troubled waters of "values" and "totalities."[59]

Heidegger seems to be saying that National Socialism had something profound and wonderful that aligned with his own philosophy, but unfortunately humans who didn't understand these deep truths got in the way with all their "values" and other subjective nonsense. From this experience he apparently learned the lesson that it was best to avoid the troubled waters of human existence when fishing for the deep truth of Being, and instead look for it in the quiet dwelling of language—the house of Being—instead.

Both Heidegger's early and later philosophy have been very influential, but in very different ways. While *Being and Time* was a major catalyst in the development of postwar existentialism, his writing from the 1930s on (after the turn) has inspired many critiques of technology and modernity. When Heidegger shifted to looking for the meaning of Being within language he also became one of the main targets of the logical

---

59. This lecture was published in 1953 as "An Introduction to Metaphysics." In the published version (p. 199) Heidegger added a parenthesis (italicized below) that was not part of the original lecture in 1935:

> The works that are being peddled about nowadays as the philosophy of National Socialism but have nothing whatever to do with the inner truth and greatness of this movement (*namely the encounter between global technology and modern man*)—have all been written by men fishing in the troubled waters of "values" and "totalities."

positivists, who criticized him for leaving all his logic in the car when he checked into the House of Being. For example, fellow German Rudolf Carnap, one of the founders of the Vienna Circle and the logical positivist movement, singled out Heidegger's "Introduction to Metaphysics" as his prime example of "metaphysical pseudo-statements" (aka NONSENSE!) in his essay "The Elimination of Metaphysics through the Logical Analysis of Language."[60] So Heidegger managed to make at least three different groups of people very happy if you include the logical positivists, who were very grateful to him for giving them so many examples of language that they regarded as completely meaningless.

Jean-Paul Sartre

If there were a contest for most successful philosophical packaging and marketing Sartre's version of existentialism should probably win first prize. In *Being and Nothingness*, which he published while the war was still raging in 1943, Sartre brought together ideas that many other authors had left scattered throughout the history of philosophy, added some original spin of his own, and then fused the whole concoction into a philosophical theory that was not difficult to understand and that responded very deftly to the questions about meaning and value that so many people were asking at the time. Especially when the war ended there was a huge appetite for a theory that could make sense of a world that suddenly seemed senseless, and Sartre was definitely in the right place at the right time with a theory that was profound and inspiring but at the same time immediately applicable to every moment of daily life. Of course Sartre was just trying to make sense of the world he fell into, like every philosopher who preceded him, but he did have a particular genius for bringing together ideas and arguments that no one else had thought to combine and for expressing big ideas in clear and memorable language.

A good example of Sartre's talents, and also the explosion of interest that existentialism enjoyed right after the war, is the public lecture he gave in October 1945 (about five months after the war officially ended in France) which was later published under the title "Existentialism Is a Humanism." A standing-room-only crowd showed up for this philosophy lecture, and Sartre began his talk by informing his audience that

---

60. Carnap, "Analysis," 69–73.

existentialism had already become so popular that it was badly misunderstood, so he was going to clear up all the confusion by distilling the principles of existentialism down to a few key ideas which were presented with very memorable soundbites, such as the following:

- "Existence precedes essence." This formula applies only to human being, or what he refers to in *Being and Nothingness* as being-for-itself. It simply means that humans exist before they have any meaning, because any meaning and value that a human life has can only be created by the existing individual after she already finds herself in existence, and it's entirely possible (quite easy really) that an entire life can be lived from beginning to end without ever having any meaning or value because the person living that life failed to create them. This differs from the mere objects or things in the world that Sartre calls being-in-itself which have an essence or a meaning even before they exist. He gives the example of a paper cutter: before it came into existence the essence of its existence was planned and determined in advance: the materials that would compose it; the function it would perform; the price it would sell for; etc.

- Humans are "condemned to be free"—condemned because no one chooses to be born (that's the one thing no one can choose) but once you're thrown into existence you're necessarily free and no circumstances can take your freedom away. If, for example, you happen to live in a country that goes to war or if you're taken prisoner during that war, of course you didn't choose those circumstances but within those circumstances you still have an infinite range of possible free choices, and you always retain the ability to say "no" in the midst of any circumstances. ("No" seems to be the first word that all children learn, and it is a very powerful concept.) Sartre argues that "facticity" (the totality of facts that make up our lives and our history beginning with our birth, when we were thrown into a set of circumstances that we didn't choose) never eliminates "transcendence" (our ability to make free choices among the range of options that our factical circumstances make available).

- "If God does not exist then everything is possible." Actually he borrowed this line from Dostoevsky in order to declare that existentialism makes this principle something to affirm rather than something to fear. Like Nietzsche, Sartre is using "God" here not in a literal religious sense but rather as metaphorical shorthand for something like "a transcendent source that creates objective values for humans here on Planet Earth." In other words, the argument behind this memorable soundbite is that all values are subjective, and that we should embrace this fact rather than run from it in terror.

Sartre reportedly spoke without any notes when he gave this lecture, giving a very spontaneous and off-the-cuff summary of the main ideas from *Being and Nothingness*; but it's notable that he limited his summary to roughly just the first half of that book, focusing mainly on the theory of limitless individual freedom which became existentialism's most famous and most well-received collection of ideas. What came to be recognized and consumed as existentialism was basically just the first part of *Being and Nothingness*. The second half of the book, which presents an utterly despairing and profoundly pessimistic theory of human relationships (being-for-others), succinctly summarized by the most famous line in Sartre's play *No Exit*: "Hell is other people," was almost always left out of the version of existentialism that was popularized after the war, and Sartre didn't say a word about it in this speech. What Sartre did very effectively in this lecture, and in *Being and Nothingness* generally, was to organize an assortment of ideas that developed especially in the nineteenth and early twentieth centuries into a philosophy that explained how humans could always create meaning and value in their lives through their own free choices regardless of the circumstances that were obviously not in their control, such as wars or other catastrophes. Many of these ideas can be traced all the way back to classical stoicism, but twentieth-century existentialism brings them all together and makes them very obviously relevant to the present age.

The main disease that Sartre wants to diagnose and cure with his philosophy is self-objectification. This is the strangest disease ever because we inflict it on ourselves. Everyone has been objectified—treated like an object, a mere thing, rather than a subject who is much more than just a thing in the world. If you've ever been admitted to a hospital you've experienced some degree of objectification: your body was broken in some way and the medical staff focused on fixing this broken thing, not unlike how an auto mechanic focuses on fixing your car when you take it in to be repaired. This objectification is necessary and understandable, but no one ever enjoys it; on some level we all feel deeply offended when we are objectified. Therefore it's really amazing that we are immediately indignant whenever someone else objectifies us, yet we very casually and thoughtlessly objectify ourselves all the time. Existentialism is meant to cure the disease of self-objectification, which we inflict upon ourselves every time we deny our own freedom.

The importance of the phenomenological method that Sartre borrowed from Heidegger is especially apparent in the evidence he gives to prove that humans are free. Arguments for determinism were readily available in the 1940s when Sartre wrote *Being and Nothingness* and they have only become more common since then. You certainly could argue that humans are not free because we are controlled by psychological conditioning, or our DNA, or the purely mechanical chemistry and electrical activity of our brains, or many other objective and external features of our bodies or our physical surroundings, but Sartre would argue today just as he argued in 1943 that all proposed explanations of how humans are not free are based on the wrong evidence. They are all looking for evidence in the wrong place: in the external, objective world of facts and objects instead of the internal, subjective world of our consciousness and lived experience.

The primary phenomenological evidence of freedom is our experience of anxiety (or "anguish" as it's often translated), which Sartre (following Kierkegaard) argues is fear of our own freedom:

> First we must acknowledge that Kierkegaard is right: anguish is distinguished from fear in that fear is fear of beings in the world whereas anguish is anguish before myself. Vertigo is anguish to the extent that I am afraid not of falling over the precipice, but of throwing myself over. A situation provokes fear if there is a possibility of my life being changed from without; my being provokes anguish to the extent that I distrust myself and my own reactions in that situation.[61]

To extend the vertigo example: if you go hiking in the mountains there are numerous aspects of the being-in-itself physical world that are dangerous which it is reasonable to fear (severe weather, rockslides, snakes, bears, etc.); but you can take precautions against all of these with good training (knowledge of the terrain, hiking experience, physical fitness, etc.) and good gear (sturdy boots, snakebite kit, bear spray, etc.), and thereby diminish or even eliminate your fear. But honest phenomenological analysis of your consciousness reveals that no amount of training or gear can eliminate your fear of your own freedom because you realize

---

61. Sartre, *Nothingness*, 65.

that you're capable at any time of doing something you'll regret, such as spraying yourself with your own bear spray or throwing yourself off a cliff, and you are legitimately anxious about this all the time. Anxiety (or anguish) is a constant reminder of our constant ability to do something stupid, something we don't want to do, something we will regret; and the fact that we have such anxiety is the best proof that we are in fact free. Any argument for determinism ignores this phenomenological evidence of freedom because it's looking for evidence in all the wrong places.

> This determinism, a reflective defense against anguish, is not given as a reflective *intuition*. It avails nothing against the *evidence* of freedom; hence it is given as a faith to take refuge in, as the ideal end toward which we can flee to escape anguish. This is made evident on the philosophical plane by the fact that deterministic psychologists do not claim to found their thesis on the pure givens of introspection. They present it as a satisfying hypothesis.[62]

In other words: yes determinism can work as a possible explanation of human behavior, but it's an explanation that's based simply on faith that humans really are not free beings rather than on the actual phenomenological evidence that we are free, and this evidence is available to everyone in the form of the constant anxiety we feel, which is the recognition of our own freedom.

At this point if you say that actually you don't feel constantly anxious, Sartre has an explanation for that: you're not being honest with yourself; you're living in bad faith. A truly honest phenomenological accounting of our consciousness, he argues—especially those moments of our consciousness that we're most inclined to ignore or conceal because they seem embarrassing, indecent, or just boring—reveals that anxiety is the authentic condition of human existence because we know that we are completely free, and also that values only exist because we create them. Thus the phenomenon of anxiety brings together the two great themes of existentialism: that we're always already free regardless of the circumstances we fell into, and that all values are subjective creations:

> It follows that my freedom is the unique foundation of values and that *nothing*, absolutely nothing, justifies me in adopting this or that particular value, this or that particular scale of values. As a being by whom values exist, I am unjustifiable. My

---

62. Sartre, *Nothingness*, 79.

freedom is anguished at being the foundation of values while itself without foundation. It is anguished in addition because values, due to the fact that they are essentially revealed to a freedom, cannot disclose themselves without being at the same time "put into question," for the possibility of overturning the scale of values appears complementarily as *my* possibility. It is anguish before values which is the recognition of the ideality of values.[63]

Sartre's existentialism goes about as far as it's possible to go in arguing that humans are free at all times and in all places, and that absolute freedom entails the absolute responsibility of creating all our own values and recognizing that we might decide later that we created the wrong values, which is definitely cause for anxiety.

Sartre wrote several other philosophy books before and after *Being and Nothingness*, and to his everlasting credit he also attempted to bring philosophical ideas and arguments alive in many other forms and media. He wrote novels and short stories, several plays (which he also produced and directed), an autobiography for which he won the Nobel Prize in literature (he turned it down), a few screenplays, many essays of social and political criticism, and when he died in 1980 he was still at work on a multivolume critique of the writer Gustave Flaubert called *The Idiot of the Family* that had already reached three volumes and over three thousand pages. When existentialism became a hot commodity after the war Sartre quit his job as a high school teacher and embraced the role of public intellectual with gusto. In 1945 he helped to found a new journal called *Modern Times* (the name was borrowed from a Charlie Chaplin film) dedicated to writing that engaged with contemporary cultural, social, and political issues. Sartre's partner throughout his life in all these ventures was someone he met in 1929 when they were both college students preparing for careers as high school philosophy instructors: Simone de Beauvoir.

Simone de Beauvoir

The relationship between Beauvoir and Sartre had many different dimensions, but fundamentally it was an intellectual partnership. It was also a romantic partnership that was quite unconventional, and this attracted considerable attention in the postwar period when Sartre and Beauvoir

---

63. Sartre, *Nothingness*, 76.

were sort of the king and queen of existentialism in the public imagination. After they met as college students they both agreed they would pursue romantic and sexual relationships with other people without any limits but they would remain intellectually faithful to each other throughout their lives, which meant they would share with each other all the details of their various other relationships, and also all of their other ideas regarding philosophy, politics, and everything else. The idea of a relationship that combined intellectual monogamy with sexual promiscuity captured the public imagination, especially the sexual promiscuity part; but in terms of understanding the philosophy that Beauvoir and Sartre created what really matters is the fact that their ideal of intellectual monogamy meant they always shared all their philosophical ideas with each other (along with the details of their latest romantic adventures). They published whatever they wrote (philosophy books, novels, plays, social commentary, etc.) under their individual names, but they always shared all their ideas with each other first and each of them read and commented on everything the other wrote. Consequently the line between Sartre's ideas and Beauvoir's ideas is probably not so easy to draw and Beauvoir probably deserves a lot more credit for theories and arguments that have been attributed solely to Sartre. The postwar existentialism that made Sartre especially famous is probably better understood as a collaborative project to which both he and Beauvoir contributed, along with many others: just one of the intellectual babies which was created by their intellectual partnership.

As we near the end of the twentieth century and therefore the end of this last chapter on the history of philosophy you've no doubt noticed that even though the modern period ended on such a promising note when Mary Wollstonecraft summarized the essential philosophical arguments for feminism, in this chapter on nineteenth- and twentieth-century philosophy Beauvoir is the first woman to make an appearance. This is mainly because I've followed a quantitative approach to the history of philosophy in this book, focusing just on the authors who had the most influence and impact, and for better or worse those authors continue to be mostly men throughout most of the nineteenth and twentieth centuries. But things are definitely starting to change by the middle of the twentieth century, and Simone de Beauvoir's story illustrates this well. Sartre and Beauvoir met in 1929 because they were both on the same academic and career track: studying to become high school philosophy instructors. When Beauvoir and Sartre both took the competitive exam that would qualify them to be teachers the exam readers wanted to give first place to Beauvoir, but gave it to Sartre instead because he had failed the test the year before and because they were simply uncomfortable awarding first prize to a woman. So Beauvoir got second place based on extremely dubious reasoning, but at least women were finally getting access to the same philosophical education as men and their ideas were being taken a seriously as men's (or almost, anyway). Beauvoir's education enabled her to become a high school philosophy instructor, like Sartre, and like him she also published numerous works of philosophy, including several novels and autobiographical memoirs. Her 1947 book *The Ethics of Ambiguity* works through many of the ethical implications of existentialism that were not at all obvious in *Being and Nothingness*, and it also demonstrates how thoroughly involved she was in postwar existentialism—that it wasn't just Sartre's baby.

Beauvoir's most famous and influential work of philosophy was *The Second Sex*, which was published as a complete book in 1949 after first appearing serially in *Modern Times* (the journal she edited with Sartre and others). In this exploration of the philosophical assumptions behind sex and gender Beauvoir deepens the arguments for the fundamental feminist principle that there are no essential differences between women and men, and she also offers a theory to explain how it was that women became the second sex—the Other defined by its opposition to the essentially human, which has long been regarded as male.

> One is not born, but rather becomes, woman. No biological, psychic, or economic destiny defines the figure that the human female takes on in society; it is civilization as a whole that elaborates this intermediary product between the male and the eunuch that is called feminine. Only the mediation of another can constitute an individual as an *Other*.[64]

This argument—that gender is a social construction with a long and complicated genealogy, and not a simple physical and material fact like sex—may seem rather obvious today, but as in the case of Wollstonecraft's arguments at the end of the eighteenth century that's a measure of how successful these arguments have been. *The Second Sex* can be understood as a very focused work of applied existentialism. It applies one of the core ideas of existentialism—that there is no predetermined or preestablished essence for any human being, that this always has to

---

64. Beauvoir, *Second*, 283.

be created—to questions of sex and gender in order to demonstrate that most of what has been understood as facticity is actually transcendence (or at least could be transcendence, if we allowed it to be). The arguments in this book helped to establish feminist criticism as an accepted and essential part of philosophy from this point onward.

More healthy, revitalizing philosophical midlife crises at the end of the twentieth century: Michel Foucault

This chapter, and this whole section on the history of philosophy, is about to come to a screeching halt as we approach the end of the twentieth century. This isn't because philosophy itself came to a screeching halt at the end of the century (obviously), but only because the approach to the history of philosophy that I've followed has been primarily a quantitative approach that regards the "classics" of philosophy as the theories which have had the most impact and influence, and that approach requires some time to pass in order to see which ideas resonate and leave a lasting legacy and which ideas do not. I think enough time has passed that we can confidently include the postwar feminism and existentialism of Beauvoir and Sartre among philosophy's classics, but for most philosophy that came after that it's still too early to tell. In spite of this I'm going to throw caution to the wind and include one more author in this chapter mainly because his thinking embodies so perfectly the vision of nineteenth- and twentieth-century philosophy as The Age of Midlife Crises which I've tried to present in this chapter, and which I love so much. As the twentieth century neared its end Michel Foucault demonstrated philosophy's ability to reinvent itself in a burst of creativity, which is the best possible kind of midlife crisis—and that's a perfect note on which to end this chapter so how could I resist?

To be more specific, there are two reasons why Foucault's philosophy makes the perfect last scene for this last chapter on the history of philosophy. The first is that we see in his thinking a joyous return to the idea that philosophy is the love of all wisdom, without any boundaries. This was the vision of philosophy that animated all of the first philosophers, and the vision that's built right into the word they chose to describe what they were doing: *philosophia*, the love of all wisdom. In the period of philosophy's infancy no one did this better than Aristotle, who studied everything he could in both the human world of ethics, politics, rhetoric, etc., and the natural world of animals, plants, weather, etc., and regarded all of it as philosophy. Since Aristotle's time the terrain where he and his fellow peripatetic philosophers wandered freely has been subdivided and fenced off into numerous specialized fields and disciplines, like gated suburban communities that carefully guard their borders and defend their turf—and not without reason because each of these disciplines really does require a lifetime of disciplined and focused study before anyone can pretend to know much about them. Leibniz, at the very end of the seventeenth century, was perhaps the last human being who had any shot at being competent in nearly every intellectual pursuit on earth, and he was so overwhelmed when he attempted this that he almost never completed any of the projects that he started as he bounced from one field to another, leaving behind an enormous trove of unfinished writing that testified to how quickly human knowledge was expanding and effectively warning everyone else: "Don't even think about trying this; you'll just give yourself a nervous breakdown."

Then almost three hundred years after Leibniz along comes Michel Foucault, a philosopher who doesn't seem at all interested in staying within the little plot of ground that has been fenced off for him. He starts writing books that seem to wander cheerfully all over the carefully surveyed and subdivided neighborhoods of academia as if nothing had changed since Aristotle did this in the fourth century BC. These books include *The Birth of the Clinic* (a history of the concepts of health and medicine); *Madness and Civilization* (a history of the concept of mental illness); *Discipline and Punish* (a history of concepts of control and discipline and their implementation in prisons and schools); and *The History of Sexuality* (a three-volume history of the many ideas that have circulated around sex and sexuality). Foucault also wrote other books that looked more like standard philosophy books such as *The Order of Things* and *The Archaeology of Knowledge*, but it's obvious from the four books listed above that he didn't think he was obligated to stay in his lane as a philosophy professor and he was happy to trespass into the domains of other academic disciplines where he couldn't claim to be an expert.

That's an important point to make about Foucault's philosophy books that wander into other neighborhoods such as history, anthropology, psychology, sociology, criminology, etc., and it's a point that I think he would be happy to acknowledge: that in those fields he was an amateur and a dilettante who couldn't pretend to have the same expertise as people who had devoted their lives to the study of history, anthropology, psychology, sociology, criminology, etc.; so of course it's up to the experts in those fields to decide if he made any useful contributions to those disciplines and I'm certainly no expert in any of those areas so I won't presume to say. But from a philosophical perspective I will say that I think Foucault's willingness to venture into other academic neighborhoods as an amateur and a dilettante—not claiming to be an expert in those fields himself as perhaps Aristotle or Leibniz once could—is a marvelous and wonder-ful return to the idea that philosophy begins in wonder and in love for all wisdom without any deference to borders or boundaries. Part of the motivation for Foucault's trespassing (or transgression, as he liked to call it) was simply the idea that since philosophy is focused on the ultimate nature of all reality, knowledge, and values, and since these questions are relevant to every discipline, there's no reason for it not to attempt to make a contribution in other fields as long as it remains humble and recognizes its status as an amateur and a visitor when it ventures out of its own neighborhood.

Another part of Foucault's motivation for these transgressive books was the idea he got from Nietzsche that every idea has a genealogy that's just as complicated, messy, and potentially surprising as every person's family genealogy. Nietzsche argued that ideas never fall from the sky fully formed, they always have twisted and tormented family histories just like all of us. Much like studying your own family history will inevitably reveal lots of surprises, Foucault explores the genealogy of ideas we now consider completely normal and "common sense" (for example, conventional notions about what it means to be sane or self-controlled) and demonstrates that there are always some weird and embarrassing relatives hidden away in their past. Nietzsche directed his own genealogical research primarily at the concepts and traditions that constitute morality and he wrote a complete book on this topic (*On the Genealogy of Morality*) to demonstrate what his genealogical method looked like. Foucault borrowed Nietzsche's method and applied it to medicine, madness, punishment, and sex, and if he had had more time there's no doubt that he would have kept going (he was still at work on volume 3 of his *History of Sexuality* when he died).

The second reason I can't resist ending this chapter with Foucault is because in addition to transgressing not just the boundaries between philosophy and other disciplines he was also happy to transgress the many customs and conventions that had taken root in philosophy now that it had reached the age of (roughly) 2,500. No one can live that long without developing a few bad habits that need to be criticized. In the nineteenth and twentieth centuries, philosophy definitely became more established and institutionalized and even somewhat respected, and all of this middle-aged comfort made it easy to relax into merely repeating or rearranging the ideas of its youth and no longer trying to create anything new. Foucault was quite allergic to anything repetitive or boring. He recognized the value of a midlife crisis—and not just one but as many as possible—and he challenged philosophy not to relax as it neared its 2,500th birthday but instead to reinvent itself so that it wouldn't descend into contentment and complacency. Foucault's attempts to reinvigorate philosophy with the midlife crises that it needed got labeled all sorts of things: post-structuralism, post-modernism, anarchism, and of course nonsense (because there were still logical positivists who walked the earth), but he himself didn't care much about these labels. In 1970 when he was offered a job at the Collège de France, which is the top of the academic anthill in France, he called himself "Professor of the History of Systems of Thought," and that title does seem to capture very accurately the focus on the genealogy of ideas that permeated everything he did while at the same time leaving everyone scratching their heads about what bucket to put him in. (Analytic? Continental? Modern? Postmodern? Philosopher? Historian? Something-completely-new-that-didn't-have-a-label-yet?)

In a truly excellent prank that he managed to pull off shortly before he died in 1984, Foucault submitted a review of his own philosophy for the *Dictionnaire des Philosophes* (*Dictionary of Philosophers*) writing under the pseudonym "Maurice Florence." In this review he writes of himself:

> If Foucault is indeed perfectly at home in the philosophical tradition, it is within the *critical* tradition of Kant, and his undertaking could be called *A Critical History of Thought*.[65]

In another essay that he wrote just before he died in 1984 Foucault also made a very deliberate effort to connect his own philosophy to Kant's. He called the essay "What Is Enlightenment?" which is exactly the same title that Kant gave to an essay he wrote two hundred years earlier in 1784. Kant was the quintessential modern philosopher and given the way that he closed out the nineteenth century with a fusillade of *Critiques* before finally exiting Königsberg and also this mortal plane shortly after the century ended no one has tried very hard to challenge him for that role. But by 1984 most people were inclined to think that philosophy had

---

65. Foucault, "Foucault, Michel," 314.

moved way beyond boring old Kant and his tedious *Critiques*. Given the reputation that Foucault had acquired for doing highly-experimental and super-sexy philosophy (he literally wrote a three-volume work on the history of sexuality; what could be more sexy than that?) it's quite surprising that in multiple essays at the end of his life he tried very hard to tell everyone that his philosophy was just a continuation of what Kant had started two hundred years earlier. He did this again in his own "What Is Enlightenment?" essay. He also made it clear in this essay that he wouldn't be offended at all if anyone described his philosophy as "modern" (as opposed to "postmodern" or some other label that was even more *avant garde*), because he thought the project of modernity (which is also the project of enlightenment) was a project that would never be finished, and he was happy to make his own humble contribution to this ongoing work.

> I know that modernity is often spoken of as an epoch, or at least as a set of features characteristic of an epoch; situated on a calendar, it would be preceded by a more or less naïve or archaic premodernity, and followed by an enigmatic and troubling "postmodernity."
>
> Thinking back on Kant's text, I wonder whether we may not envisage modernity rather as an attitude than as a period of history. And by "attitude," I mean a mode of relating to contemporary reality; a voluntary choice made by certain people; in the end, a way of thinking and feeling; a way, too, of acting and behaving that at one and the same time marks a relation to belonging and presents itself as a task. A bit, no doubt, like what the Greeks called an *ethos*. And consequently, rather than seeking to distinguish the "modern era" from the "premodern" or "postmodern," I think it would be more useful to try to find out how the attitude of modernity, ever since its formation, has found itself struggling with attitudes of "countermodernity."[66]

So what exactly is enlightenment/modernity, according to Foucault? What is this ongoing project of battling against attitudes of "countermodernity" that he thinks will never end?

> This philosophical ethos may be characterized as a *limit-attitude*. . . . Criticism indeed consists of analyzing and reflecting upon limits. But if the Kantian question was that of knowing what limits knowledge has to renounce transgressing, it seems

---

66. Foucault, "Enlightenment," 39.

to me that the critical question today has to be turned back into a positive one: in what is given to us as universal, necessary, obligatory, what place is occupied by whatever is singular, contingent, and the product of arbitrary constraints? The point, in brief, is to transform the critique conducted in the form of necessary limitation into a practical critique that takes the form of a possible transgression.[67]

This critique will be genealogical in the sense that it will not deduce from the form of what we are what it is impossible for us to do and to know; but it will separate out, from the contingency that has made us what we are, the possibility of no longer being, doing, or thinking what we are, do, or think. It is not seeking to make possible a metaphysics that has finally become a science; it is seeking to give new impetus, as far and wide as possible, to the undefined work of freedom.[68]

That's quite an awesome statement of what philosophy has always been about in every moment of its history regardless of whatever labels have been applied to its different stages and schools. I couldn't ask for a better conclusion to these four chapters on the history of philosophy, and it's also a fine introduction to the next chapter which is about the philosophy of the future, so I should stop talking now because there's nothing I can say that will improve on these words from Foucault shortly before he died.

This concludes the final chapter on the history of philosophy in this book, but of course that history isn't over and in fact will never end. That's the only defect in the PIJLAO2500YOPGTPAUSOLMFMSOTHOP model of the history of philosophy that I've been using, which is otherwise completely flawless and perfect in every way: philosophy, unlike any given human being, doesn't have to die; it's possible for it to continue forever. But philosophy's continuing existence is not a given, not a *fait accompli* (as they say in Idaho); it depends entirely on you, the person reading this book right here and right now, so please turn the page and read about the next stage in philosophy's history—which is entirely up to you.

---

67. Foucault, "Enlightenment," 45.
68. Foucault, "Enlightenment," 46.

Chapter 7

Philosophy in the future, which is completely up to you!

(The joyous art of creating new concepts, new theories, and new meanings for the very strange thing called human existence)

I am going to insist that people finally stop mistaking philosophical laborers and scientific men in general for philosophers—that here, of all places, people be strict about giving "each his due" and not too much to the one, and much too little to the other. In the course of his education, the genuine philosopher might have been required to stand on each of the steps where his servants, the philosophical scientific laborers, have come to a stop—have had to come to a stop. Perhaps the philosopher has had to be a critic and a skeptic and a dogmatist and historian and, moreover, a poet and collector and traveler and guesser of riddles and moralist and seer and "free spirit" and practically everything, in order to run through the range of human values and value feelings and be able to gaze with many eyes and consciences from the heights into every distance, from the depths up to every height, from the corner onto every expanse. But all these are only preconditions for his task: the task itself has another will— it calls for him to create values. The project for philosophical laborers on the noble model of Kant and Hegel is to establish some large class of given values (which is to say: values that were once posited and created but have come to dominate and have been called "truths" for a long time) and press it into formulas, whether in the realm of logic or politics (morality) or art. It is up to these researchers to make everything that has happened or been valued so far look clear, obvious, comprehensible, and manageable, to abbreviate everything long, even "time" itself, and to overwhelm the entire past. This is an enormous and wonderful task, in whose service any subtle pride or tough will can certainly find satisfaction. But true philosophers are commanders and legislators: they say "That is how it should be!" they are the ones who first determine the "where to?" and "what for?" of people, which puts at their disposal the preliminary labor of all philosophical laborers, all those who overwhelm the past. True philosophers reach for the future with a creative hand and everything that is and was becomes a means, a tool, a hammer for them. Their "knowing" is creating, their creating is a legislating, their will to truth is—will to power. Are there philosophers like this today? Have there ever been philosophers like this? Won't there have to be philosophers like this?[1]

Nietzsche wrote many aphorisms that have become well-known (though not necessarily well-understood). This particular aphorism (number 211 out of 296 that are collected in the weird and wonderful book called *Beyond Good and Evil*) is not one of those. It has been almost completely ignored, but it deserves careful consideration because it contains a truly insightful vision of what philosophy is trying to accomplish. What could possibly be more exciting and adventurous than the vision of philosophy presented here? There are three aspects of this vision, three big ideas that are worth underlining and celebrating.

First of all, philosophy embraces and affirms everything. It says "yes" to every aspect of human life and human experience, and "no" to nothing. Life is, as the cool kids today agree, all good. And philosophy doesn't just tolerate the full diversity of possible human experience, it values and celebrates all of it so much that it insists one can't really become a philosopher in the fullest sense of the word without first experimenting with everything else that life has to offer.

> Perhaps the philosopher has had to be a critic and a skeptic and a dogmatist and historian and, moreover, a poet and collector and traveler and guesser of riddles and moralist and seer and "free spirit" and practically everything, in order to run through the range of human values and value feelings and be able to gaze

1. Nietzsche, *Beyond*, 105–6.

with many eyes and consciences from the heights into every distance, from the depths up to every height, from the corner onto every expanse.

There's a very simple idea at work here, so simple that it's easy to overlook how profound and powerful it is. Philosophy should grow and develop out of life, and it should always remain connected to life. It doesn't stand above life and gaze down upon it with a superior or suspicious gaze; it isn't something different from life; it's the result of life, the product of experiencing and experimenting with every part of life. That's the first step in the process of becoming a philosopher: Go and live your life to the fullest, and in the process try to experience everything—and what could possibly be more life-affirming or more fun than that? According to this vision of philosophy, experiencing everything that can be experienced is a requirement for becoming a philosopher.

This requirement of extreme living is one necessary but not sufficient condition that prepares the way for real philosophy to get started. Trying to experience everything that can be experienced in life will not in itself make you a philosopher, and similarly Nietzsche points to one other form of life that may help to prepare the way for philosophy and is also easily and often confused with philosophy, but still is not philosophy. This is the work of what he calls "philosophical laborers" who diligently organize and reorganize the ideas, arguments, and theories that other people created. This is, he says, "an enormous and wonderful task in whose service any subtle pride or tough will can certainly find satisfaction," but it isn't yet philosophy because philosophy doesn't just rearrange ideas that already exist, it creates new ideas. That's the essential and startling conclusion of this vision of what philosophy ought to be: true philosophy must always create something new. Diligently trying to experience everything that can be experienced—"in order to run through the range of human values and value feelings and be able to gaze with many eyes and consciences from the heights into every distance, from the depths up to every height, from the corner onto every expanse"—is an essential prerequisite for creating philosophical ideas of one's own. Arranging and rearranging the ideas that people other than you have created is also valuable labor that can assist in the overall work of philosophy, but philosophy doesn't really begin until one begins to create something new. Nietzsche insists that philosophers must create values, and values are certainly a good and (ahem) valuable thing to create, but philosophical creation isn't limited just to values. Values, concepts, ideas, arguments, theories, possibilities, meanings: philosophy creates all of these things and more. These creations should be derived from a life fully and completely lived that seeks out every possible perspective from every possible experience, and once they have been created they can be ordered and reordered endlessly by philosophical laborers to shift and rearrange the conceptual kaleidoscope that the history of philosophy has left for us, but philosophy is the act of creating ideas, not just rearranging them.

This is the vision of philosophy that I hope you'll remember after you close this book and put it back on the bookshelf—or throw it out the window, or launch it into the sky with a homemade catapult, or light it on fire, or use it as a coaster for your favorite cold drink, or whatever it is that you do with your books after you finish reading them: philosophy is a creative activity, a creative art, that is meant to create concepts, meanings, and values for the very strange and wonderful thing called human existence. Philosophy is just as creative as any other art, science, sport, performance, or any other creative activity that humans engage in. In this act of creation philosophy is guided by extremely high and lofty ideals, perhaps the highest ideals that can be imagined, because the goal is nothing less than figuring out the ultimate truth of reality, knowledge, and values by means of purely independent and creative thinking and then sharing those discoveries with the world in a way that allows everyone to evaluate them with their own independent thinking. The ideals of philosophy are so high that the actual practice of philosophy—the creation by mere mortals of new values, concepts, ideas, arguments, theories, possibilities, and meanings for their lives—is bound to fall short in rather comic fashion, and that's why philosophy has always been and always will be so good at generating comedy. I hope this part of the book has given you a sense of how much comedy there is in the history of philosophy and also why philosophy is so good at creating it; and I hope it has also persuaded you that every moment of comedy in philosophy's history is something we should be proud of and something we can celebrate as the philosophical project of creation continues into the future.

Act Two

Philosophy is a very awkward business that has always been on the verge of going out of business

Chapter 8

Why all philosophy professors are sophists even though Socrates—the closest thing there is to a founding father or a saint in the history of philosophy—despised sophists and declared that he would sooner die than become one himself

Socrates was the first to recognize the comic incongruity between the ideals of philosophy and the practice of teaching philosophy for a living. The targets of his ridicule were the sophists. "Sophist" and "sophistry" come from the Greek word *sophia* which just means "wisdom," so when the ancient Greeks called someone a sophist it was intended as praise. Today "sophistry" has taken on a decidedly shameful meaning, and this is entirely due to the effectiveness of Socrates's derision, so no philosophy professor would ever call himself a sophist; but in fact all of us undeniably are sophists. The most fundamental fact of sophistry, which is the focus of all of Socrates's sarcasm, is this simple fact: sophists want to get paid to share their *sophia*. Socrates, on the other hand, went to work every day trying to teach the people of Athens but never asked to be paid for this work. Socrates was a philosophy teacher because he was convinced that the Gods wanted him to be a philosophy teacher, and he was still getting out of bed and going to work every morning at age seventy-one even though almost everyone in Athens found his teaching to be extremely annoying and wanted him to stop.

In 399 BC the Athenians decided that since no one was paying Socrates to teach philosophy, and therefore he couldn't be fired, the only way to get him to stop was to charge him with a crime. The charges were: "Socrates is guilty of wrongdoing in that he busies himself studying things in the sky and below the earth; he makes the worse into the stronger argument, and he teaches these same things to others."[1] Clearly it was only the third charge that mattered. No one would have cared if seventy-one-year-old Socrates had busied himself studying things in the sky and below the earth and making the worse argument into the stronger if he had just kept it to himself. What the Athenians found unendurable was the fact that he refused to stop trying to teach them philosophy: he refused to retire from what they considered to be a job. In his trial Socrates explained that he couldn't retire because he actually didn't have a job. He was a philosophy teacher, and that was a vocation—a calling from the Gods—not a paid profession. "If you have heard from anyone that I undertake to teach people and charge a fee for it, that is not true," he insisted,[2] and he went on to explain that the only way the Athenians could get him to stop teaching philosophy would be to put him to death.

So that's what they did. The execution of Socrates made him a hero forever, a martyr for the cause of teaching philosophy, but it inspired exactly no one to follow his example. Even Plato, who reported all the noble arguments that Socrates gave for teaching-philosophy-until-you-die-without-ever-getting-paid-even-one-drachma, and who called Socrates "a man who, we would say, was of all those we have known the best, and also the wisest and the most upright,"[3] never considered the possibility of teaching philosophy for free. Plato did just the opposite: he started the world's first university, thereby becoming the world's first university administrator. Plato created college. Plato clearly concluded that the Socratic ideal of teaching-philosophy-for-free-until-people-can't-stand-it-any-longer-and-decide-to-execute-you was more idealism than even he could stand, so he decided to throw his lot in with the sophists and find a way to teach philosophy and get paid at the same time. Plato turned teaching philosophy into a business, thereby creating the job of philosophy professor that sophists have held ever since.

1. Plato, *Apology*, 19c.
2. Plato, *Apology*, 19e.
3. Plato, *Phaedo*, 118a.

There is nothing necessary about the fact that all philosophy professors have been sophists ever since Plato created The Academy. This is not a logical, or epistemological, or moral necessity. It's simply the consequence of everyone considering what happened to Socrates and deciding they didn't want that to happen to them. The day Socrates was executed there was nothing he could say to his wife Xanthippe when she asked him how she was going to take care of their three children now that he was about to die, leaving them with no money. All Socrates could do was turn to one of his buddies and ask him to give Xanthippe and the kids a ride home.[4] No teacher wants to die like that, leaving behind an angry spouse and three hungry children who need new shoes. Ever since Plato started offering philosophy teachers steady employment no philosophy teacher needed to sacrifice like Socrates did ever again. This created the career track that philosophy professors have followed ever since. Aristotle, for example, arrived as a student at Plato's Academy and quickly decided he never wanted to leave, so when he graduated he got a job as a philosophy professor so that he could stay at The Academy, and when he eventually got fired from that job he created his own university so that he could once again get paid to teach philosophy.

The best way to make the best of this less-than-ideal reality—the fact that every philosophy professor on earth is a sophist—is to look the comedy of this situation right in the eye. In other words, what is needed is more funny stories about philosophy professors. That is why I have selflessly and very nobly devoted myself to this very important work, and that is why I wrote the next chapter.

---

4. Plato, *Phaedo*, 60a.

Chapter 9

Ten philosophy departments reinvent themselves to make philosophy a more marketable commodity

Ever since philosophy departments went into business in the fourth century BC they have been threatened with going out of business, and so from the beginning every philosophy department has felt the need to reinvent itself. However, it's not at all clear what it means to reinvent philosophy and this is itself a philosophical problem, so every philosophy department that has tried to reinvent itself (which, by now, is all of them, without exception) has done it differently. Here are ten examples.

(1)
One philosophy department, which was composed entirely of faculty who wanted to get a better job at a more famous and prestigious university and who therefore reflexively mined every situation in which they found themselves for a possible journal article that would make them hot commodities in the job market, immediately sensed an opportunity when they were informed that their department needed to reinvent itself. What this calls for, they realized, is a new theory: a philosophy of philosophy departments. They all had this idea simultaneously but they didn't say a word about it to each other; instead they all scurried back to their offices to begin writing papers on this topic before someone else got to it first. The project of reinventing the philosophy department where they were currently employed (but, they all hoped, not for long) became

entirely a thought experiment and a research project. They continued to teach their classes since unfortunately that was contractually required, but all of their classes, regardless of the title of the class or the ostensive topic, were transformed into classes about the philosophy of philosophy departments. Students, who were already quite unhappy and confused in their classes, became even more depressed, but their instructors were undeterred and pressed forward resolutely with their research.

At the end of the semester—which passed in a frenzied blur for the faculty but seemed like an endless death march to their students—they all sent their papers off to prestigious journals and anxiously prepared themselves for the job offers which they hoped would follow. All of their papers had essentially the same title: "The philosophy of philosophy departments: a new field of philosophical research which was completely ignored until I wrote this essay," and all of these papers were accepted and appeared in print at the same time, which caused all the professors in the department to be suspicious of each other, but they immediately stopped caring when they were all offered new jobs at more famous and prestigious universities; so they all departed to assume their endowed chairs in the new field of philosophy of philosophy departments, which they had created, and the university that had previously employed them saw this as the perfect opportunity to close its philosophy department entirely, thus solving decisively the problem of how to reinvent philosophy.

(2)
Another philosophy department decided that their future depended on connecting philosophy to popular culture. They quickly replaced their entire curriculum with "Philosophy and ___" classes where the "and ___" is instantiated by whatever happens to be popular and selling well at the time. All of their boring old courses in logic, metaphysics, and the history of philosophy were thrown out and replaced with much more exciting classes such as these: Philosophy and TikTok; Philosophy and The Masked Singer; Philosophy and Lady Gaga; Philosophy and the Kardashians; Philosophy and Instagram; Philosophy and The Lego Movies; Philosophy and Grinder; Philosophy and The Bachelor; Philosophy and Sponge Bob Square Pants; Philosophy and Game of Thrones; Philosophy and Fortnite; Philosophy and Pokemon; etc.

This department quickly discovered that the shelf life of popular culture is extremely short when no one at all showed up for the Philosophy and Lady Gaga class they offered, and while the Philosophy and

Fortnite class was very popular the first time they offered it, when they offered it the following semester it too attracted no students at all. So they hired several work study students to keep them informed on what was currently popular among college students, but this only confirmed their worst suspicions because the students revised their lists of popular things sometimes on a daily basis. The faculty, therefore, felt like they were always behind the times, always chasing a pop culture caravan that they would never be able to catch. They did not give up, however, diligently creating new "Philosophy and ___" courses every semester, and often revising a course multiple times within the same semester so that a class that began the semester as "Philosophy and Facebook" might morph into "Philosophy and Spider Man" and then finally "Philosophy and *Fast and Furious 7* (or 8 or 9 or 10 . . .)."

Through their relentless revisions the professors in this department did manage to keep philosophy fresh, young, and hip, but they became so harried, anxious, and exhausted in the process that while their courses remained eternally young and fresh the professors teaching these classes visibly aged before everyone's eyes. Soon they all died *en masse* of exhaustion and stress, and the university administration instructed the campus police to cordon off the department until they could investigate what killed all of their philosophy professors. They did this with a great show of solidarity and sympathy for their fallen comrades, but at the same time they also seized the opportunity to suspend all philosophy classes with no intention of ever restarting them in the future, which is something they had wanted to do for years. The fact that philosophy had literally killed an entire department only confirmed their suspicion that it is highly dangerous and best avoided.

(3)
Another philosophy department decided that the way to make philosophy popular is to kill philosophy. They came to this conclusion after taking seriously the suggestion from students, which was so often repeated on end-of-semester course evaluations: that the best way to improve this philosophy class would be to "stop teaching philosophy." So this department decided to reinvent itself as the Department of Anti-Philosophy. All of their classes were revised to focus on what was wrong with philosophy, how philosophy was a disease, and how philosophy deserved to die. This proved to be quite a popular approach, and their classes attracted many

students who had taken philosophy classes in the past and didn't like them, which was quite a few.

But then a clever undergraduate pointed out that even arguments against philosophy can't help but be philosophical arguments, so the Department of Anti-Philosophy might as well rename itself the Department of Anti-Anti-Philosophy. All the anti-philosophy professors in the Department of Anti-Philosophy agreed that the logic of this argument was flawless, and so they changed their name one more time to the Department of Anti-Anti-Philosophy.

The Department of Anti-Anti-Philosophy proved to be even more successful than the Department of Anti-Philosophy. Students flocked to Anti-Anti-Philosophy classes because they assumed it must be some kind of postmodern performance art and they didn't want to miss the chance to receive college credit for witnessing what must be a fresh and hot new thing. Since all the professors in the Department of Anti-Anti-Philosophy were required to take at least one formal logic class in grad school they knew that any doubly-negated proposition is truth-functionally equivalent to a proposition that isn't negated at all, so they now felt comfortable just teaching philosophy again exactly as they did before they became the Department of Anti-Philosophy. Their classes remained very popular, however, because students who registered for an Anti-Anti-Philosophy class expecting to witness avant-garde art were unwilling to confess publicly that they didn't get it when the class turned out to be just about Leibniz or business ethics; and so after taking an Anti-Anti-Philosophy class they would tell everyone who asked that it was deep and profound and of course they totally got it.

(4)
Another department decided to kill philosophy in a more literal and dramatic fashion: with a public execution. They decided the best way to do this was to recreate the death of Socrates with a professor playing the part of Socrates drinking actual hemlock and expiring in front of a class. All the tenured professors agreed that tenure obviously includes protection against death by hemlock, and therefore it was only rational that the one and only untenured professor in the department should be the one to play the part of Socrates; and this assistant professor confessed that this was both a valid and a sound argument so he had no choice but to drink hemlock and die.

The department's plan was to kill philosophy once and for all by killing Socrates one more time, and this time making sure that philosophy stayed dead by immediately canceling all future philosophy classes and closing the department. The remaining, non-hemlock-drinking professors were content with this plan because they all planned to go home afterward and write a book called *Killing Socrates: This Time We Really Got Him*, which they expected to be a bestseller that would provide them with a comfortable retirement. But to their surprise immediately after their young untenured colleague drank the hemlock and died—to spectacular applause—students surrounded the remaining faculty and demanded to be registered in whatever philosophy classes were available next semester. The students did this because they truly enjoyed watching a professor die and considered it the highlight of their college experience, but the philosophy professors (blinded by their own vanity) imagined that the students were thirsty for their wisdom. So the department decided to stay in business after all and their classes were well-enrolled from that point on, buoyed by the hope that still flourishes among students at this university that if they take a philosophy class they may get to watch a professor drink poison and die right before their eyes.

(5)
Another philosophy department decided that the appropriate response to their declining enrollments was to argue stridently that everyone else was wrong: every other department that was attracting students was wrong, and also immoral, because of the damage they were causing to philosophy by being successful departments that are not philosophy departments. These other departments should have realized that since philosophy is the oldest and most distinguished discipline it must be respected and honored by all the other younger and less distinguished disciplines, like an aged grandparent should be honored and respected by his many grandchildren. All of these departments should immediately apologize and stop being successful, because it's everyone else's duty to make sure that philosophy flourishes.

The department quickly drafted a manifesto to this effect, finding it very easy to write since the arguments were obviously self-evident, and they sent this manifesto via email to every department and every administrator on campus. When they received no response to this email they dispatched their work study student to nail a copy of the manifesto to every department's door, and the professors in this department also carried a copy with them at all times and read some of their favorite passages at every faculty meeting, party, or chance encounter from that moment on, which made them even more unpopular than they already were. The manifesto made them feel confident and even proud of their superiority as a department, and when the number of students in their classes continued to decline every semester this only served as more evidence in support of the impeccable logic of their argument, so it added to their feeling of satisfaction.

(6)
Another philosophy department decided to purify their curriculum of any authors who had ever harbored any beliefs or attitudes that were less than enlightened with regard to women, children, people of color, non-European countries, animals, plants, colonialism, religion, war, art, or culture. They carried out this purification with gusto and then realized that the only authors still available for class readings were Hypatia and Mary Wollstonecraft. They did not let this deter them, however. They revamped all of their courses, building every class—from formal logic to metaphysics to business ethics—around readings exclusively from Hypatia and Mary Wollstonecraft. In practice this meant there were often very few readings, or even none at all (in a class on nineteenth-century German idealism, for example), and really only in the feminist philosophy class was there any significant assigned reading; so students avoided the feminist philosophy class and instead flocked enthusiastically to classes where the professors were compelled to do imaginative reenactments of what Hypatia or Mary Wollstonecraft might have said about the topic if they had ever given it any thought, such as classes on the ethics of engineering or computer science. Buoyed by high demand for these classes the department flourished.

(7)
Another philosophy department decided that if they did not have any shame at all (which they did not) they could make their enrollments soar simply by taking advantage of something that every college professor figured out long ago, probably on the first day of their first semester: students will flock to any class that involves watching movies or TV shows. What this meant, effectively, is that they would transform their department into the department of watching movies and TV shows, but they were fine with that because, as I mentioned, they didn't have any shame.

So they hastily printed large posters explaining that in all of their classes next semester, from introduction to philosophy to advanced meta-ethics, students would watch the following movies and TV shows (which were then listed in great detail and at such length that prospective students quickly deduced that nothing else would be happening in these classes except watching movies and TV shows; and they were correct). The curriculum for a class on Hegel, for example, consisted of watching every episode of all five seasons of *Breaking Bad*, and after every episode the professor would call out to the students—as they were rushing out of the classroom and completely ignoring her, high-fiving each other and celebrating their enormous good fortune because that had found a way to get college credit for watching TV—"What we watched today was totally relevant to Hegel's philosophy . . . ." But no one heard her because they had long ago stopped paying attention to the person who showed up every day to turn the TV on and off, and in fact they weren't even sure who she was.

This reinvention of philosophy was hugely successful in terms of increasing enrollments, but it also had the effect of making philosophy itself completely irrelevant. After a few years even the professors in this department could not recall what "philosophy" meant. "Something about the love of wisdom," they thought, "or maybe it was the love of movies and TV shows; we can't remember."

(8)
Another philosophy department decided they should capitalize on something they had all noticed in their classes for years: that students seemed to find anything that appeared on their phones to be far more interesting than the professors's lectures; so all they had to do was make their lectures appear on the screens of those phones. They all agreed the best way to accomplish this would be to ask the university's massive IT department—which seemed to have unlimited resources and was always more than willing to throw an enormous pile of money and machinery at any pedagogical problem, believing that every problem could and should be solved with technology—to construct a broadcast booth in all the classrooms where philosophy classes were taught and staff those booths with a camera operator and also someone to run the control room. The professor would then enter the classroom, perhaps tip his hat to the students (who would not notice him because they would be looking at their phones) and then enter the broadcast booth and lecture on Plato's

theory of idealism, or Aristotle's four causes, or Descartes's arguments for rationalism, or Kant's theory of the categorical imperative—or whatever he was going to lecture on anyway because the content of their classes did not change at all; but now the lectures were relayed directly to the screens of the students's phones via a dedicated YouTube channel. The IT Department agreed immediately to spend several million dollars to build and staff these broadcast booths; the professors loved the arrangement because now they could simply talk nonstop for the entire class, entertaining themselves with their witty banter and feeling no obligation to interact with the students in any way (which is the kind of teaching they preferred); and the students came flocking back to philosophy classes, where they spent every class period staring intently at their phones.

It was clearly stated in the syllabus for each class that students were required to watch only their professor's lecture during class, and every student earnestly promised to do so. One professor felt some concern when, after her course on modern philosophy which included nine truly excellent lectures on Kant's three *Critiques*, most of the students could not answer even one question on the exam about who Kant was, and the one answer from a student which did make some sense seemed to be a verbatim repetition of a video on YouTube called "Kant in Three Minutes." But she dismissed these concerns when she considered how enrollment in her department had soared and how even Kant would surely appreciate that every Copernican Revolution in philosophy necessarily brings with it some growing pains.

(9)
Another philosophy department decided that the key to reversing their enrollment decline was to take advantage of the fact that studying philosophy has always been used by undergraduates to frighten and anger their parents. "We know that at least half of our current students are studying philosophy just because it makes their parents unhappy," they said to each other, "and we got those numbers without any marketing campaign—these students figured out completely on their own that taking philosophy classes is the single best way to make their parents miserable. If we actively market philosophy as a way to get even with Mom and Dad we can easily triple those numbers." So the department created a marketing campaign focused completely on the fact that taking philosophy classes—or even better, majoring in philosophy—will make your parents furious. The posters featured pictures of parents pulling out

their hair, gnashing their teeth, and weeping. "Want to settle a score with your parents?" the caption asked. "Then take philosophy classes and soon your parents will be very unhappy!" Everyone in the department agreed that this marketing campaign was unethical and disgraceful, so they were confident that it would work very well.

And it did work extremely well. Philosophy classes were soon completely full of angry students intent on making their parents regret paying for their college education, and professors discovered that their students seemed to love their classes the most whenever they emphasized the uselessness of philosophy, so they began to do that a lot. It soon became a very safe bet that any student taking a philosophy class had some serious parental issues that were far from resolved; and every day the philosophy faculty gave thanks to the United States Congress for creating the FERPA statute which makes it not just optional but actually ILLEGAL to speak to parents when they call.

(10)
Another philosophy department decided there was no reason to think of philosophy as merely a way to exact revenge upon your parents, because really almost everyone is offended by philosophy, not just your parents. They decided to focus on this singular characteristic of philosophy and the unique power it entails in their marketing campaign. If you study philosophy (they pointed out in their advertising) you will offend almost everyone in the world, and this is very easy to demonstrate: just notice that when you tell someone that you're taking a philosophy class you'll instantly provoke this incredulous and even somewhat angry response: "What are you going to do with that?" If you major in philosophy you will spend the rest of your life responding to that question. Even after you have been employed for decades, perhaps even as a philosophy professor, people will continue to ask you: "What are you going to do with that?" There's no other subject you can study that will provoke such a powerful response of shock and indignation, as if you had just walked up to a total stranger and punched her right in the liver. You could see this as something negative (because perhaps you would prefer not to spend the rest of your life shocking and offending people), but on the other hand just think of the power this will give you! All you have to do is take an interest in understanding the nature of this very strange world that we all fell into and you'll offend most people more than if you decided to spend the afternoon standing completely naked on a busy street corner shouting

insults at everyone who passes by. That would only provoke laughter, but daring to ask questions about the true nature of reality, knowledge and values will (for some reason) make most people feel deeply and personally offended.

However, there will always be a small and perverse band of humans who delight in doing this, so this philosophy department decided to market itself explicitly to them. When it did this it attracted just enough students to stay in business, and so the study of philosophy survived for one more generation.

Act Three

Philosophy is something that makes
almost everyone write very badly

Chapter 10

Six different forms of bad philosophical writing, which clarify six important aspects of philosophy (so all this bad writing is actually a good thing!)

Almost all philosophy is in fact very badly written, but badly written in at least six different ways, and these six different forms of bad writing contain six important insights into what philosophy is, what it's trying to accomplish, and how you can enjoy reading philosophy and learning from its insights in spite of how badly it's written. The nature of the philosophy game causes most people to write very badly, but that bad writing is still worth reading because it contains so many very good ideas.

To make this chapter a more useful resource here's the complete list of the six forms of bad philosophical writing this chapter explores. If you ever feel confused or stymied by the writing of a particular work of philosophy I hope you'll return to this chapter for a quick glance at this index to see if the bad writing you've just encountered falls into any of the six types discussed here, and if it does hopefully a quick review will allow you to return to the text that frustrated you with a greater understanding of why the writing is bad, why the text is still worth reading, and how to read it in a way that reveals its most valuable ideas and arguments.

1. Philosophy is a project many people will always regard as very weird and nearly crazy, and therefore many people will judge all philosophical writing to be bad writing just because they think

philosophy is nuts. (This is a completely superficial prejudice that no intelligent person—such as you—would ever fall for.)

2. Bad writing that results from the fact that philosophy can be surprisingly hard work that leaves people exhausted.
3. Bad writing caused by trying to say something new and therefore pushing language to the point that it breaks and possibly even blows up.
4. Bad writing by authors who are trying to make themselves disappear because they take seriously the idea that philosophy is about thinking for yourself, so they try to erase their own author-ity.
5. Bad writing that results from trying not to anger your employer when your employer isn't paying you to write philosophy books.
6. Bad writing due to a lack of good ideas, because philosophy is an amateur sport and there's never any guarantee of quality.

(1)
Philosophy is a project many people will always regard as very weird and nearly crazy, and therefore many people will judge all philosophical writing to be bad writing just because they think philosophy is nuts. (This is a completely superficial prejudice that no intelligent person—such as you—would ever fall for.)

Philosophy tries to discover the ultimate nature of things, the most basic truth or reality in the three areas we care about the most, the three questions that we most want answered: What is real? What is true? What is valuable? If you want to use technical, elitist, Greek terminology (and who doesn't?) questions about the ultimate nature of reality constitute metaphysics; questions about the ultimate nature of truth and knowledge make up epistemology; and questions about the ultimate nature of value comprise axiology, or more specifically, ethics (value judgments about human choices and human behavior) and aesthetics (value judgments about beauty or the lack thereof). These three questions just happen to be the most fundamental questions we're capable of asking, and so every human occupation, activity, obsession, hope, dream, worry, fear, habit, tradition, reform, or regret—any human project whatsoever is ultimately based on assumptions that are metaphysical, epistemological, or axiological in nature.

Philosophy didn't arbitrarily stipulate or demand that these three questions are the most important; they just are the most basic questions we can ask, the questions we care about the most and the areas where we make assumptions that make everything else we do possible. This is just the world as we all found it and if you want to know why the world is this way I would say in response, like the Amazing Bone in William Steig's eponymous story, "I don't know, I didn't make the world"[1]—and I would also point out that the very question you just asked ("Why does philosophy consist of metaphysics, epistemology, and axiology?") is itself motivated by a desire to understand the nature of reality (What really are the most basic areas of human life, and what really are the most basic areas of philosophy, which claims to study the most basic areas of human life?), the nature of truth (Is it really true that the most basic areas of human life are metaphysics, epistemology, and axiology? Why should I believe this?), and the nature of value (Are metaphysics, epistemology, and axiology really the most important questions we can ask? Why should I care about them?)—and therefore your question is itself evidence that metaphysics, epistemology, and axiology are in fact the most basic areas of human life, the areas where we make assumptions that guide everything else we care about and everything else we do. So congratulations! Just by asking this question you effectively answered it, and you demonstrated exactly the curiosity and the wonder that motivates philosophy.

Clearly what philosophy is trying to do is something many people will always consider very close to crazy. First of all, the many institutions and authorities that have already staked a claim to exactly the territory that philosophy wants to explore (which includes all the religions of the world, along with every government, and culture, and tradition) will be deeply annoyed to discover that some philosopher is poking around in what they regard as exclusively their domain. "Excuse me," they will say, "you are trespassing. This is our property and you're an intruder here; you're not authorized to say anything about the ultimate nature of things since that is our property, so now we're going to call the police and have you arrested." Secondly you will also annoy your friends and family for sure, and also every single human being who doesn't want to be bothered with thinking about the assumptions behind every single thing they do and every single belief they have about why their life is valuable and important. "Excuse me," they will say, "you're a very irritating person, a real

---

1. Steig, *Amazing Bone*, 7.

pest, like a mosquito or a fly, always buzzing around with your annoying questions about the meaning of this and the truth of that. We don't want to stop and analyze everything we do because that takes all the fun out of life. Who invited you to this party anyway? That was a big mistake because you're a deeply unpleasant person who sucks the joy out of everything; so now we're going to make a completely transparent excuse so that we can slip away from you and go talk to someone else over there on the opposite side of the room, as far away from you as possible, and in the future we'll make a point of staying as far away as possible from you and all your bothersome questions."

This is the reception you can plan on whenever you try to ask a question about the ultimate nature of anything: those who consider themselves authorities on such things will accuse you of criminal trespassing and everyone else will run from you because they don't want to think about such things. In addition to these practical difficulties which will make your life unpleasant, purely as a matter of principle it seems likely that it's just not possible to figure out the ultimate nature of things with any kind of certainty or completeness. There's good reason to believe this is simply more than humans can handle, more than we can comprehend, and the history of philosophy only seems to confirm this suspicion because after more than 2,500 years no one has yet found an answer to any ultimate question that has satisfied everyone. The history of philosophy suggests that philosophy itself is perhaps impossible simply because that history never ended: philosophers are still asking the same three questions they started asking over two thousand years ago.

To all these obstacles and objections every philosopher in human history has said: "Yes, you're right, but it's still worth it. It's true that I may never get to the bottom of metaphysics, epistemology, or axiology, and it's true that I'll annoy a lot of people in the process, but it's still worth it. I'm willing to be regarded as odd and even dangerous, and I'm willing to devote myself to a pursuit that I understand may very well be ultimately impossible because I believe that's the best way to live. Just getting closer to the truth, even if I never actually reach the ultimate truth, makes the whole thing worth it. As Socrates said a long time ago, just before he was put to death by his fellow Athenians for asking them questions they thought were annoying: 'an unexamined life is not worth living.'"[2] The examined life that Socrates said was the only life worth living has always

---

2. Plato, *Apology*, 38a.

been, and always will be regarded by many people as a completely crazy way to live, and therefore philosophical writing has often been judged to be bad writing for this reason alone: because it seems like the writing of a crazy person about questions that no sane person would try to answer.

This is the first form of bad philosophical writing that we need to consider, which comes from the judgment that (obviously) all philosophy is badly written because (obviously) the whole enterprise is just a crazy waste of time. As we'll see shortly there's no shortage of truly bad writing in the history of philosophy, but the narrow-minded prejudice that makes many people allergic to philosophy prevents them from experiencing philosophy's full, wonderful catalogue of bad writing because they refuse even to read it. That's unfortunate, because anyone who is willing to get past the traditional prejudices against philosophy can discover a whole world of truly bad writing—but in every case there's something valuable to be learned from this bad writing about the nature of philosophy itself, and so we should all rejoice and be grateful for all of it. We'll begin our tour of some of those truly bad forms of philosophical writing now.

(2)
Bad writing that results from the fact that philosophy can be surprisingly hard work that leaves people exhausted

Even though philosophical research is generally done while sitting in a chair, or perhaps even lying in bed with your eyes closed, and thus is difficult to distinguish from doing nothing at all, or sleeping, it does have its own peculiar form of athleticism. Philosophy is a sport in its own way, and here are the rules:

> Rule 1. Try to discover the truth about the most basic areas of human life, the most basic questions that humans are capable of asking.
>
> Rule 2. Do this yourself, with your own independent thinking; don't let anyone else supply the answers for you and don't defer to anyone who claims to be an authority.
>
> Rule 3. Write down your discoveries and present them to the world so that everyone else can decide for themselves if you're right.

Playing the game by these rules, many philosophers repeat the example set by Pheidippides, the first marathoner: they finish the race and then they drop dead. Or maybe they don't literally expire, but they're so thoroughly exhausted that they collapse at the finish line and only manage to stammer a few nearly incomprehensible words before surrendering to their exhaustion and falling into a deep and well-deserved slumber. Poor Pheidippides had to run all the way to Sparta and back (about three hundred miles), and then he was immediately dispatched to run to Marathon and return with news of the battle there (another fifty miles or so). When he made it back to Athens after running nearly 350 miles he apparently spoke in such a garbled and incoherent fashion that there was widespread disagreement about what exactly his final words were, but the general consensus was that it was something along the lines of "We won!" And then he collapsed and died. Many philosophers too emerge from the battle of trying to figure out the ultimate nature of things so exhausted that they barely have any energy left to write down what they learned. Consequently there are no doubt many profound and even potentially world-altering philosophical insights that never got written down and are therefore lost now because the philosophers who made these discoveries were too tired; or else if they did write them down they wrote in a sort of dream-language that almost no one could comprehend, like a child mumbling something haunting and mysterious just before falling asleep that her parents can't understand, though it sounded fascinating and profound.

At this point you would probably like to raise your hand indignantly and say: "Excuse me but I've read a few philosophy books and I've noticed that most of them are actually quite long—much too long in almost every case, by which I mean the author says essentially the same thing seven, eight, or even nine times when just once would be more than enough. So it hardly seems like philosophy leaves everyone too exhausted to write anything at all. Clearly not everyone collapses at the finish line; many seem to keep running forever." This is a good point, so I should clarify that the difficulty of philosophical research has two consequences: it results in both writing too little (or perhaps nothing at all in the case of the truly exhausted), and also in writing too much. Fatigue plays a part in both cases. A philosopher who writes an extremely long and repetitive book often does so in a state of extreme exhaustion, like someone determined to drive across the country without sleeping because she doesn't want to spend a single dime on a motel. She drives erratically and dangerously from coast to coast in a nearly delirious condition: almost hitting a flock of geese racing on their little legs to cross the highway outside of Gary, Indiana; narrowly avoiding a collision with a tired looking family repacking a U-Haul trailer on the side of the road surrounded by endless fields of corn sixteen miles west of Council Bluffs, Iowa; drifting across several lanes of traffic at 3 a.m. just before the off ramp for North Platte, Nebraska, under the light of a nearly full moon; almost driving completely off the road too many times to count on the empty, windswept plains of Wyoming while greatly exceeding the 80 mph speed limit. The result may be many pages of words (obviously too many pages) but none of those pages are written with style or grace, or anything approximating coherence. Thus in philosophy both under-writing (or not-writing) and over-writing are often caused by fatigue.

Gilles Deleuze and Felix Guattari are two philosophers who are generally thought to have written too much. The books they wrote together, especially *Anti-Oedipus* (400 pages) and *A Thousand Plateaus* (610 pages) strike most readers as overwrought and in need of a good editor. At the end of their career they tried to explain what they had been doing in these strange and excessive books by finally answering the question, "What is philosophy anyway?" Their answer emphasizes philosophy's difficult and exhausting nature. They argue that philosophy, like art and science, must struggle to bring order out of chaos while at the same time battling with mere opinions or beliefs which attempt to shield us from chaos by simplifying or simply denying the disorder that surrounds us. This battle on two fronts is exhausting work:

> We require just a little order to protect us from chaos. Nothing is more distressing than a thought that escapes itself, than ideas that fly off. . . . We constantly lose our ideas. That is why we want to hang on to fixed opinions so much. We ask only that our ideas are linked together according to a minimum of constant rules. . . . That is all we ask for in order to *make an opinion* for ourselves, like a sort of "umbrella," which protects us from chaos. . . . But art, science, and philosophy require more. . . . Philosophy, science, and art want us to tear open the firmament and plunge into the chaos. . . . The philosopher, the scientist, and the artist seem to return from the land of the dead. . . . It is as if one were casting a net, but the fisherman always risks being swept away and finding himself in the open sea when he thought he had reached port. The three disciplines advance by crises or shocks in different ways, and in each case it is their

succession that makes it possible to speak of "progress." It is as if the *struggle against chaos* does not take place without an affinity with the enemy, because another struggle develops and takes on more importance—the *struggle against opinion*, which claims to protect us from chaos itself.[3]

Philosophy, art, and science venture into chaos ("the land of the dead") so they can bring back the kind of order we truly want: order that continues to be energized and animated by chaos. This means genuine philosophy, art, and science will always be somewhat risky, messy, and chaotic. These are signs of the authenticity and value of these disciplines. On the other hand, opinion seems perfectly safe, stable, and still, which makes it both attractive and dangerous.

The greatest works in the history of philosophy were written by people who were willing to defy their own laziness and do the hard work of investigating the ultimate truth of reality, knowledge, and values themselves. They did this work sitting down at a desk, or maybe lying down in bed, so when people asked, "What are you doing?" and they replied, "I'm working," everyone was confused. They sat, or reclined, and then they thought long enough and hard enough that they wrestled new ideas and new concepts from chaos; and then they tried to write down these new ideas and concepts but they probably did so very badly because by then they were very tired.

(3)
Bad writing that results from trying to say something new and therefore pushing language to the point that it breaks and possibly even blows up

Most of the breakthrough texts in the history of philosophy belong in this category. They are badly written not just because the authors are trying to do something that many people regard as rather crazy, and perhaps they're also thoroughly exhausted, but also because those authors are trying to say something fundamentally new: something that had never been said before. This will inevitably push language right to the breaking point and perhaps even cause it to blow up or break down, like a machine that has exceeded its mechanical limits. Just as it's difficult to explain to others that philosophical research is actually hard work since it appears that you're just sitting in a chair doing nothing, it's also very difficult to

---

3. Deleuze and Guattari, *What Is Philosophy*, 200–203.

explain the results of this research in any existing language and in a way that everyone will understand if what you're trying to express is a fundamentally new idea. It shouldn't be surprising that when philosophers attempt to write down what they have learned from their research—from plunging into chaos and trying to extract some order from it, while also trying to avoid the temptation to merely paint over chaos with opinion or belief—they often sound like they've invented a completely new language. In effect they have invented a new language: they broke an existing language into pieces and used the scraps to build something new. A truly revolutionary theory will often (as engineers say) test language to the point of failure.

Consequently any genuinely new philosophical theory will often be expressed in language that's awkward and strange, definitely not beautiful and definitely not pleasant to read. No one would ever call this language elegant or graceful, nor should they. But the inelegance and awkwardness of the language are necessary consequences of something radically new being born. With time and practice any idea can be explained with style and grace, but the classics of philosophy are the first attempts to put an idea into words so they stammer like infants who are struggling to learn how to speak. This is bad writing in the same way that an infant's first words are bad speaking, but it would be churlish to hold this against the infant or against the philosopher: both of them are doing the best they can. A truly ground-breaking, revolutionary theory will often be written in a broken language, and to appreciate the meaning and value of such a theory the reader has to learn to look past the broken machinery of language to see the insights of the writer who did everything in her power to put her strange new ideas into words.

When philosophy itself was in its infancy there were many excellent examples of infantile writing. The pre-Socratic philosophers who first figured out the rules of philosophy were doing something profound and revolutionary when they began proposing theories about the ultimate nature of things based entirely on their own independent thinking, but their written accounts of their new theories can easily be confused with the babbling of infants. The pre-Socratics are easy and obvious examples of infantile writing since they were writing in the period when philosophy too was an infant, but this form of bad writing didn't stop with them. Lest anyone think that philosophers got any better at expressing their strange ideas in human language without doing violence to the language in the process, here are a few modern examples.

Fast-forward from the fifth century BC in Greece to nineteenth-century Germany and Georg Wilhelm Friedrich Hegel. It's impossible to say anything about Hegel (or at least it should be impossible, and also illegal) without citing his last words: "Only one man understood me; and he did not understand me." Inevitably there's some controversy about whether or not Hegel actually said these words, but they are the ideal last words for Hegel since they perfectly summarize his philosophy so I hope this is exactly what he said just before he left this mortal plane. Strictly speaking these words express a simple contradiction ("one person understood me; that same person did not understand me"), so by the rules of ordinary logic and language they're just incoherent nonsense. But Hegel spent his life arguing that the rules of ordinary logic and language are mistaken. There are no contradictions, according to Hegel. Everything that appears to be a contradiction is actually resolved in a synthesis on a higher level of consciousness or mind. Hegel says yes to everything and no to nothing; there's nothing that's simply false (except the claim that anything is simply false). If Hegel had been willing to take a few questions from you before he expired the conversation might have gone like this:

You: "So only one man understood you?"

G. W. F. Hegel: "Yes."

You: "And that same man also did not understand you?"

G. W. F. Hegel: "Yes."

You: "It seems like you just broke rule 1 in the rule book for how to use a human language: don't contradict yourself, because a contradiction is nonsensical. How is this not a simple, nonsensical contradiction?"

G. W. F. Hegel: "I'm actually dying right now so I don't have time to answer your question. I did write several books on the subject so you might take a look at those. All the books I wrote are horribly written because my philosophy causes any human language to blow up, like what would happen if you drove a 1971 Ford Pinto in the 24 Hours of LeMans. I hope you enjoy reading my badly-written books! Now I'm dead!"

If you did take Hegel's admonition to heart and turned now to his writing to discover the meaning of his gnomic last words you could open at random any book he wrote and immediately find an example of almost perfectly unintelligible writing that embodies his principle of non-non-contradiction, aka Just-Say-Yes-To-Everything; but here's one passage that's particularly good (by which I mean bad):

> Dealing with something from the perspective of the Absolute consists merely in declaring that, although one has been speaking of it just now as something definite, yet in the Absolute, the A = A, there is nothing of the kind, for there all is one. To pit this single insight, that in the Absolute everything is the same, against the full body of articulated cognition, which at least seeks and demands such fulfillment, to palm off its Absolute as the night in which, as the saying goes, all cows are black—this is cognition reduced to vacuity.[4]

Although Hegel was quite a superstar in his time a few people did have the temerity to suggest that his writing was not particularly good. By far the most hilarious criticism came from Schopenhauer, who made no effort to hide his disgust for Hegel's writing and his philosophy. Here are a few delightful examples:

> Let us overcome our reluctance and turn over the pages of the nauseating rubbish, for no man can be expected to read it! Then let us consider and calculate how much time, paper, and money the public must have wasted on these bungling works in the course of half a century. . . . For the writer who has nothing clear and definite in his mind heaps words on words and phrases on phrases; and yet he says nothing because he has nothing to say, knows nothing, and thinks of nothing. Yet he wants to talk and so chooses his words not in accordance with how they express his ideas and judgments more strikingly, but with how they more skillfully conceal the lack of them. . . . I refer to the artful trick of writing abstrusely, that is to say, unintelligibly; here the real subtlety is so to arrange the gibberish that the reader must think he is in the wrong if he does not understand it, whereas the writer knows perfectly well that it is he who is at fault, since he simply has nothing to communicate that is really intelligible. . . . No one has practiced this same trick so boldly and to such an extent as has Hegel.[5]

---

4. Hegel, *Spirit*, 9.
5. Schopenhauer, "Universities," 161–62.

> Hegel's followers are accordingly quite right when they assert that their master's influence on his contemporaries was immense. To have completely paralysed mentally a whole generation of scholars, to have rendered them incapable of all thought, indeed to have brought them to such a pass that they no longer know what thinking is, but regard as philosophical thinking the most wanton, as well as the most absurd, playing with words and concepts, or the most thoughtless rubbish on the stereotyped themes of philosophy with fabricated assertions, or with propositions wholly devoid of sense and even consisting of contradictions—all this has been the boasted influence of Hegel.[6]

When he's criticizing Hegel's writing as a menace to society Schopenhauer writes with style and grace, using language artfully and sounding very much like a grown-up. Therefore it's fascinating to note that when Schopenhauer attempts to write his own philosophy he too pushes the language past its limits and causes it to stammer like an infant.

Schopenhauer had, by his own account, exactly one big philosophical idea, and this idea is contained succinctly in the title of the book he worked on throughout his life: *The World as Will and Representation*. The idea expressed by those six words seems simple enough, yet Schopenhauer wrote well over a thousand pages trying to explain it and was never satisfied that he had succeeded. In the first edition of the book published in 1818 he began by apologizing for the fact that he found it necessary to write an entire, rather lengthy book in order to express a single thought. "I should have been able to explain my idea in fewer words," he says in the preface, "and I really don't understand why I couldn't. Sorry about that. Oh, and by the way you should plan on reading this book very slowly and patiently and at least twice."[7] But things only got worse. Twenty-five years later in 1844 Schopenhauer released a second edition of the book which more than doubled its length, adding an entire second volume that was longer than the first. Effectively he wrote a second book, though he insisted that it was just a continuation of the effort that started twenty-five years earlier to explain his one and only philosophical idea. "Now it's complete," Schopenhauer assures us in the preface to the second edition; however, this proved not to be accurate since fifteen years later in 1859 he found it necessary to release a third edition which added another 136 pages.

---

6. Schopenhauer, "Universities," 173–74.

7. That was my paraphrase, not Schopenhauer's words, in case it wasn't completely obvious.

If Schopenhauer hadn't died one year after the third edition was published there's every reason to believe that there would have been a fourth edition, and then a fifth, sixth, and seventh edition, and if he had somehow managed to find a way to live forever (which according to his philosophy would be the worst possible thing that could happen to anyone) then he would have kept adding words and pages to *The World as Will and Representation* forever. The "single thought" this book sought to communicate exceeded human language, so the closest approximation of the idea that he could produce within language was an ever-expanding, infinite book. Schopenhauer clearly found human language quantitatively inadequate to express his one idea. There simply are not enough words in any language, and there never will be, to express the true and complete metaphysical reality that he claims to have discovered: that the world really is nothing but will and representation. Consequently Schopenhauer too, like Hegel whom he so mercilessly criticized, ends up pushing the machinery of language past its mechanical limits until it blows up before our eyes. The only philosophy book Schopenhauer can imagine is an infinite book. Here we have run up against the most obvious limitation of any human language, and also any human life: both of them are finite. A book that only gets larger and longer is a rather inhuman, unnatural, and frightening book: a book that will kill you and outlive you, like a cancerous tumor or a virus. This is one more example of language being made to stammer and stutter because it's driven too hard and too fast—pressed into service beyond its mechanical limits.

(4)
Bad writing by authors who are trying to make themselves disappear because they take seriously the idea that philosophy is about thinking for yourself, so they try to erase their own author-ity

Philosophical writing is often obscure because philosophy is hard work that leaves you exhausted and causes language itself to stammer, and philosophers who produce this sort of bad writing are happy to apologize for it. "The last thing I wanted to do was write something unclear, uncertain, and difficult to read," they will all explain, in sincere embarrassment. "I did my best to make my writing clear and distinct and easy to understand, but it was very hard work and it made me very tired, and also it seemed like when I tried to put my hard-won and exhausted thoughts into words I managed to break the whole language in the process. Sorry about that; it was the best I could do." These apologetic writers did not aspire to obscurity, nor were they born obscure; they had obscurity thrust upon them.

But there are other writers in the history of philosophy who write with deliberate obscurity. This tradition began with a bang—albeit a very obscure bang, which almost no one understood—when Heraclitus wrote his one and only book, the title of which was so obscure that no one even bothered to write it down or make any effort to remember it. Heraclitus was also known as "Heraclitus the Obscure" and "Heraclitus the Riddler," and apparently he was quite happy with both titles. He was the first of a motley collection of authors in the history of philosophy who deliberately wrote in a way that was unclear, enigmatic, cryptic, and confusing so that the reader would have to work hard to decode the meaning of the text on her own—and then would have to accept responsibility for the interpretation that she created. The writers in this tradition believe it would be a disservice, and even an insult, to make their ideas easy to understand. "Nature and the truth both love to hide," Heraclitus said,[8] because it's good for us to make the effort required to find them.

To his everlasting credit Heraclitus figured out the differences between philosophy, religion, and business very early in the period of philosophy's infancy when so many other writers were not fully clear about these distinctions. He understood that philosophy was all about thinking for yourself, unlike religion, which instructs you to follow the guidance and commandments of some other authority, and he also understood that if you're really thinking for yourself—really trying to make sense of your own experience and your own life—you're never going to end up with a theory or an idea that someone else wants to buy so there's no point even trying to turn philosophy into a business because no one will be buying what you'll be selling. Understanding these differences between philosophy, religion, and business Heraclitus concluded that a philosophy book should be a kind of anti-book: a book that deliberately repels every potential reader; a book that effectively reaches out and pokes you right in the eye when you open it up and try to read it; a book that runs away from you and forces you to chase it down and then wrestle with it—creating a public spectacle that will leave every onlooker shocked and puzzled when they walk past this scene on a busy street, where you finally caught up with Heraclitus's book and tackled it to the ground. If philosophy is thinking for yourself then the only way anyone

---

8. DK 22B123.

can teach you something about philosophy is by finding a way to provoke you to think for yourself. Just handing you some philosophical truth, like a waiter delivering drinks and *hors d'oeuvres* to your table, contradicts the very idea of philosophy and therefore causes the whole enterprise to derail right at the start. This is the pedagogical theory that motivated Heraclitus, and everyone else who followed in his obscure footsteps, to write in a deliberately enigmatic and mysterious way.

This is bad writing in the same sense that any code is bad writing: it's clumsy and cumbersome and difficult to read, and it strives to make your life more difficult by forcing you to do some hard work, which everyone finds offensive. This is writing so bad it doesn't even want to exist. It's goal is to disappear and leave no trace; it wants to erase itself, make itself vanish for the sake of the reader, so that the reader will have to think for herself. Authors like Heraclitus tie themselves into knots to prevent themselves from becoming author-ities for any reader.

(5)
Bad writing that results from trying not to anger your employer when your employer isn't paying you to write philosophy books

We arrive now at the most difficult and delicate question that has always been foremost in the minds of every philosopher throughout history: "How can I get someone to pay me to do this?" "Philosophy is great fun, and also I have no other skills, so I would like to spend the rest of my life doing this," every philosophy major in the history of the world has thought to herself shortly before graduating; "however I also like money quite a bit because it's useful for buying shoes and pizza and fashionable pants and gasoline for my Humvee. Ergo I need to find a way to get money so that I can survive while I spend my days writing philosophy books. I could steal money, but that would be difficult and physically demanding and also perhaps it's not ethical; so it looks like that option is off the table. What's left? How is it possible to get paid to be a philosopher?"

There have always been exactly five possible answers to this question:

1. Get a patron to support you or inherit money so that you don't have to work for it. (But this will require extraordinary luck or personal charm, and most philosophers have neither.)

2. Write books which are so popular everyone will want to buy them and you can live off the profits. (But since these are philosophy

books this will be nearly impossible, because almost no one likes philosophy books.)

3. Get paid to do something else, such as grinding lenses or traveling with an army, and then write philosophy books in your spare time. (But then you might die of inhaling glass particles, or you might get shot by another philosopher who works for an opposing army, so this is not preferable.)
4. Claim that you're not really a philosopher because you have turned yourself into something else (a theologian, for example, or a priest) and get paid for doing that job while actually continuing to be a philosopher on the sly.
5. Persuade the world that studying philosophy is essential to being a good and complete person, and therefore every parent should send their children to college to take philosophy classes (which you will teach, in exchange for money).

A few people have managed to make options 1, 2, or 3 work for them, and for the past century or so option 5 has been the go-to method for getting paid, but there was a time in the history of philosophy when opportunities to make a living via option 4 were abundant. This was the golden age of the philosophy job market which ever since then has only constricted. Employment in category 4 had only one unique requirement: you had to be willing to lie to your employer. You could get a job doing whatever, and promise to do that whatever faithfully, but secretly spend your time writing philosophy books, articles, pamphlets, and manifestos. Since you want to keep your job (because you like money) any philosophical writing you do under these fraudulent conditions will have to be carefully concealed. Though you're writing philosophy you'll have to make what you write look like something else, and this act of concealment and fraud will necessarily result in some very bad writing.

This type of bad writing was especially abundant during the Middle Ages, which was actually the best time by far for someone with a philosophy degree to get a job as long as they were willing to engage in a small subterfuge: promise to use your philosophy training in the service of theology and religion. "Yes," many medieval philosophers said very solemnly in their job interviews, "we promise to make philosophy the servant and handmaiden of religion," and then they accepted excellent jobs as employees of (primarily) the Catholic Church. In the Middle

Ages it was business, marketing, psychology, and communication majors who were routinely ridiculed and who made their parents feel ashamed and anxious. Whenever someone asked what their major was and they had to confess they were studying business, marketing, psychology, or communication they knew that without fail the next question that would be hurled at them was: "What on earth are you going to do with that!" Everyone laughed at those majors in the Middle Ages because there were no jobs in those fields except teaching, so those students were all competing to replace their teachers (which of course made their teachers very suspicious of them). If you really wanted to guarantee yourself a good job you majored in philosophy because the richest and most powerful business in the world at the time (the Catholic Church) could not get enough philosophy majors. Philosophy flourished for the nearly 1,300 years of the Middle Ages because many philosophers were willing to commit this small act of fraud and promised to use philosophy only as a righteous tool in the service of the greater good of theology and religion. (This was definitely a sin, but I'm confident that God has forgiven them.)

Speaking of "God," one thing that these sneaky medieval philosophers discovered very quickly is that if you just use that word a lot in your writing you could usually get away with anything. Anyone who suspected that you might be writing a work of philosophy instead of doing your job as an employee of the Church would quickly forget their suspicions as soon as they saw the frequency with which you used the word "God" in your writing. "I truly do not understand what this treatise is about," your boss might say, "but I did notice that on page 23 alone you use the word 'God' sixty-seven times, and on page 43 the word occurs fifty-one times, and indeed there is no page in your treatise in which the word 'God' does not appear at least seven times; ergo I conclude that this must be a work of theology dedicated to the greater good of God, since you have so much to say about God. Well done; I'm going to recommend you for a raise."

Since one of the basic rules of philosophy is that you can't defer to any other authority, including God, medieval philosophy is all terribly written since every medieval philosopher constantly claims to be deferring to The Lord. To understand medieval philosophy as philosophy you have to remind yourself that it is, in addition to being a work of philosophy, also a work of fraud. If you don't allow for that fraud then philosophy disappears from the earth for about 1,200 years. But all it takes to see that philosophy did not take a 1,200-year break is to recognize that philosophers too are happy to commit fraud in order to stay employed—and really who could pass up all the great jobs that were available to philosophy majors in the Middle Ages! That period really was the golden age of philosophy in terms of job prospects. You had to be a very clever and cunning monk, priest, or bishop to make this gig work, and you had to be willing to write very badly, but those were sacrifices that philosophers have always been happy to make in order to survive.

(6)
Bad writing that results from the lack of good ideas, because philosophy is an amateur sport and there's never any guarantee of quality.

So far we've only considered ways in which good philosophy can be badly written; but of course we must acknowledge that not all philosophy is good philosophy. Sometimes bad philosophical writing is just the result of the authors not having anything interesting or coherent to say; not having any ideas that were worth writing down. This can happen because philosophy is entirely an amateur, do-it-yourself activity. Since one of the founding principles of philosophy (rule 2 in the philosophy rule book) is that you must think for yourself and not defer to any other person, institution, or tradition that claims to be an authority, there can't be any sort of certification process or accreditation agency or any rules or standards whatsoever beyond the three minimal rules I already mentioned. Rule 2 in the philosophy game basically says: "This is all the rules you get; there can't be any additional rules about what qualifies as philosophy and what doesn't because no one has the authority to make such rules." Unlike dentists, tugboat captains, accountants, civil engineers, physical therapists, comptrollers, paralegals, airplane pilots, kindergarten teachers, cardiac surgeons, tax attorneys, long-distance truck drivers, lion tamers, plumbers, and almost every other occupation on Planet Earth, there is no degree that must be completed or test that must be passed before you're allowed to practice philosophy.

So if you were to call a philosopher to fix your philosophical problems, just as you might call a plumber to fix your plumbing problems, there's no guarantee that the person who shows up will have any competence whatsoever. If this happens it would be like calling a plumber to fix a clogged toilet at your house and the plumber who arrives insists that all the plumbing in the house should be removed and thrown away so that it can never get clogged again, or that all the pipes should be replaced with ideas or concepts of pipes, or that the very idea of plumbing is fundamentally flawed and in need of a paradigm shift and before such a conceptual revolution is completed no plumbing work can be done in good conscience. To such a plumber you would rightly say: "You are a terrible plumber and your license should be revoked immediately. You shouldn't be able to call yourself a plumber because at best that just wastes everyone's time and at worst you could do some real damage if anyone ever allowed you to work on their plumbing." You would be completely right, and you should definitely report that rogue, incompetent plumber to the plumbing police. But in the case of a philosopher there's no license to revoke and no police to call. Anyone who wants to practice philosophy can do so. Anyone bold enough to want to explore the nature of reality, knowledge, or value can just dive right in and start exploring, and then they can write up their ideas in books that have very impressive and memorable titles, and are thousands of pages long and filled with impressive terminology and paragraphs that continue for several pages, that have an elaborate architectonic and a thoroughly developed system and perhaps even charts and graphs—however, there is no guarantee that these books will be anything but nonsense, thousands and thousands of pages of nonsense: the equivalent of a plumber who has no idea what a pipe is or thinks that physical sinks, bathtubs, and toilets should all be replaced with purely conceptual sinks, bathtubs, and toilets.

Like a plumber who is completely incompetent, an incompetent philosopher will at best waste your time but at worst can do a lot of damage—much more damage than a rogue plumber if you decide to throw out all the assumptions and concepts that structure your life and follow a philosophy that's completely nuts and therefore bound to ruin your existence. Wouldn't it be nice if there were some sort of certification process which prevented this from happening by guaranteeing that you will never waste your time and perhaps even destroy your life when you start reading a philosophy book? A world in which there are no incompetent plumbers or philosophers would probably be preferable to most of us, but in the case of philosophy that's simply a logical impossibility because philosophy is, by definition, an activity that requires everyone to think for herself and therefore there never will be any authorities to appeal to except for the authority of a good idea.

Since almost all philosophy is badly written it can be hard to tell the difference between writing that's bad for good reasons (such as the fact that profound new ideas can stretch language to the breaking point) and writing that's bad just because the ideas are stupid. On the surface they may both just look like bad writing, and they may both look infantile, like they were scribbled in crayon by the unsteady hand of a small child. It's certainly possible to make a mistake either way: to mistake idiotic philosophy for something profound and therefore treat such writing with respect and admiration even though it only deserves to be laughed at and then ignored; or to mistake truly profound and insightful philosophy for the writing of an idiot, and therefore laugh at and then ignore a brilliant but necessarily badly written work—badly written profound new ideas that are pushing language past its limits, and not because the author is an incompetent idiot who happens to have written another idiotic philosophy book that can be added to the enormous heap of idiotic philosophy books that humans have so far managed to write. Many philosophers who were rejected as idiots in their own lifetimes later came to be understood as very profound.

For example, only a few hundred copies of Nietzsche's *Thus Spoke Zarathustra* were sold during his lifetime, so apparently most people thought this was a book about an idiot (Zarathustra seems to be off his rocker at many times in this book) that was also written by an idiot. But then after Nietzsche died in 1900 the book became a bestseller, and today no self-respecting angry teenager, intent on tormenting his parents, would ever be seen without a copy. The rediscovery of *Thus Spoke Zarathustra* really took off during World War I when for some reason the book came to be regarded as some sort of guidebook for Aryan warriors and 150,000 copies of a specially durable edition of the book were issued to German soldiers as they headed off to war.[9] As Robert Pippin notes: "it is hard to imagine a book less suitable for such a purpose than Nietzsche's *Thus Spoke Zarathustra*" since it's hard to picture a soldier being inspired by the book's "Fellini-esque title character, himself hardly possessed of a 'warlike nature,' chronically indecisive, sometimes self-pitying, wandering, speechifying, dancing about and encouraging others to dance, consorting mostly with animals, confused disciples, a dwarf, and his two mistresses."[10] So first this philosophy book was rejected as infantile nonsense, and then it was embraced as a masterpiece based on a truly breathtaking misunderstanding of the book, and perhaps the book still is venerated for all the wrong reasons based entirely on a misunderstanding. Clearly the mistake can go the other way too: perhaps some

---

9. Aschheim, *Nietzsche Legacy*, 135.
10. Nietzsche, *Zarathustra*, xi.

philosophers we now regard as important and profound actually have nothing truly important or valuable to say.

Perhaps this very afternoon someone will knock at your door and proclaim: "Greetings! I've written a philosophy book and you should read it because it contains profound and interesting insights that will make you wise and improve your life dramatically! It's only $9.99 and I take cash, checks, and credit cards." Perhaps you'll say to yourself, "Why not? I have $9.99 right here in my pocket. What have I got to lose?" So you buy the book but when you sit down to read it you say to yourself: "This is certainly terrible, truly awful writing, and it also seems like complete nonsense—like a book that was written by an idiot, full of sound and fury but signifying nothing." Before you run out of the house to chase down that bold entrepreneurial philosopher to demand a refund of your $9.99 you should consider that, while it's certainly possible the book is complete idiocy written by a philosopher who is utterly incompetent and has no profound and interesting insights whatsoever in spite of what he promised in his excellent sales pitch, and that reading this book will be at best a complete waste of your time and at worst your life may be utterly wrecked if you take seriously any of the ideas in this idiotic book—while all of this is possible, it's also possible that you're holding a truly profound book in your hands that could make you wise and improve your life dramatically, and therefore $9.99 was a bargain; but perhaps you can't see the value of the book now because you haven't decoded the writing yet so at the moment it just looks like infantile gibberish. You could be holding a book by a young Nietzsche; or maybe it's just another philosophy book written by another idiot, because absolutely anyone can write a philosophy book (though it won't necessarily be a good philosophy book).

And now this philosophy book is over. I hope it was a good book and you learned something from it, but of course that's entirely up to you to decide.

Appendix

Some of the authors and texts that were left out of the four history of philosophy chapters

(an incomplete list, but better than nothing I guess)

THE HISTORY OF PHILOSOPHY is very much a work in progress and no doubt the understanding of who the most important philosophers were will change in the years to come. Fifty years from now when I am dead perhaps my granddaughter Piper or my grandson Gabriel will write the second edition of this book and the philosophers they choose to include in the history chapters will be very different. Here's a list of some people they might want to consider—some philosophers I left out because there wasn't space for everyone and also because I'm just not very bright and I didn't write a very good book. It would not surprise me if fifty years from now many of these authors are thought of as far more important; and of course there are no doubt many others who remain to be discovered. (Good luck, Gabriel and Piper! I'm sure you will write an excellent book!)

Chapter 3: Ancient philosophy

Aspasia
Diogenes
Diotima

Hypatia
Plotinus
Pyrrho
Seneca
Sextus Empiricus

Chapter 4: Medieval philosophy

Albertus Magnus
Avicenna
Catherine of Siena
John Duns Scotus
John Scottus Eriugena
Pico della Mirandola
Saadia Gaon
William of Ockham

Chapter 5: Modern philosophy

Anton Wilhelm Amo
Pierre Bayle
Margaret Cavendish
Anne Finch Conway
Christine de Pisan
Denis Diderot
Desiderius Erasmus
Pierre Gassendi
Hugo Grotius
Catharine Macaulay
Nicolo Machiavelli
Damaris Cudworth Masham
Michel de Montaigne
Montesquieu (Charles Louis de Secondat)
Thomas More
Jean-Jacques Rousseau
Mary Shepherd
Anna Maria van Schurman
Voltaire (François-Marie Arouet)

Chapter 6: Nineteenth- and twentieth-century philosophy (p.s. no one who is still alive was considered eligible for this list— nothing but dead philosophers here)

Jane Addams
Hannah Arendt
Walter Benjamin
Henri Bergson
Auguste Comte
Albert Camus
Frantz Fanon
Johan Gottlieb Fichte
Edmund Husserl
Thomas Kuhn
Emmanuel Levinas
Harriet Taylor Mill
Iris Murdoch
Friedrich Schelling
Friedrich Schiller
John Rawls
Simone Weil

Chapter 7: Philosophy in the future

(Insert your name here)

Bibliography

FOR CLASSICAL SOURCES WHICH have an established referencing system I've cited those numbers in the footnotes but included here in the bibliography the English translations I used.

- Stephanus numbers for works of Plato, and the English translations are taken from *Plato, Complete Works*, edited by John M. Cooper. Indianapolis: Hackett, 1997.
- Bekker numbers for works of Aristotle, and the English translations are taken from *The Complete Works of Aristotle*, edited by Jonathan Barnes. Princeton: Princeton University Press, 1984.
- Diels Kranz numbers for all pre-Socratic fragments, and the English translations are taken from *A Presocratics Reader*, edited by Patricia Curd. Indianapolis: Hackett, 2011.
- Book and paragraph numbers for selections from Diogenes Laertius, *Lives of Eminent Philosophers*, and the English translations are taken from the translation by R. D. Hicks. Cambridge: Harvard University Press, 1925.

FOR ALL OTHER WORKS I cite the page number from the texts listed below.

Abelard, Peter, and Heloise d'Argenteuil. *The Letters and Other Writings*. Translated by William Levitan. Indianapolis: Hackett, 2007.
Al-Ghazali, Abu Hamid Muhammad. *The Incoherence of the Philosophers*. Translated by Michael E. Marmura. Provo, UT: Brigham Young University Press, 2002.
Anselm. *Monologion and Proslogion: With the replies of Gaunilo and Anselm*. Translated by Thomas Williams. Indianapolis: Hackett, 1996.

Aquinas, Thomas. *Summa Theologica*. Translated by the Fathers of the Dominican Province. Notre Dame: Christian Classics, 1981.

Aschheim, Steven. *The Nietzsche Legacy in Germany, 1890–1990*. Berkeley: University of California Press, 1992.

Augustine. *Confessions*. Translated by R. S. Pine-Coffin. New York: Penguin, 1961.

Aurelius, Marcus. *Meditations*. Translated by Gregory Hays. New York: Modern Library, 2003.

Averroes. *The Incoherence of the Incoherence*. Translated by Simon Van Den Bergh. Edinburgh: Edinburgh University Press, 2008.

Ayer, Alfred Jules. *Language, Truth, and Logic*. New York: Dover, 1952.

Bacon, Francis. *The New Organon*. Edited by Lisa Jardine and Michael Silverthorne. Cambridge: Cambridge University Press, 2000.

Beauvoir, Simone de. *The Second Sex*. Translated by Contance Borde and Sheila Malovany-Chevallier. New York: Vintage, 2011.

Bentham, Jeremy. *The Principles of Morals and Legislation*. New York: Prometheus, 1988.

Berkeley, George. *The Principles of Human Knowledge*. In *The Works of George Berkeley*. London: Thomas Tegg, 1843.

———. *Three Dialogues between Hylas and Philonous*. In *The Works of George Berkeley*. London: Thomas Tegg, 1843.

Boethius. *The Consolation of Philosophy*. Translated by P. G. Walsh. Oxford: Oxford University Press, 2002.

Bonaventure. *The Journey of the Mind to God*. Translated by Philotheus Boehner. Indianapolis: Hackett, 1993.

Burke, Edmund. *Reflections on the Revolution in France*. Edited by J. G. A. Pocock. Indianapolis: Hackett, 1987.

Carnap, Rudolf. "The Elimination of Metaphysics through the Logical Analysis of Language." In *Logical Positivism*, edited by A. J. Ayer, 60–81. New York: Free Press, 1959.

Cartwright, David E. *Schopenhauer: A Biography*. Cambridge: Cambridge University Press, 2010.

Critchley, Simon. *The Book of Dead Philosophers*. New York: Vintage, 2009.

Davies, Norman. *Europe: A History*. Oxford: Oxford University Press, 1996.

De Botton, Alain. "The Schopenhauer Method." *New York Times Magazine*, February 13, 2000, section 6, page 58.

Deleuze, Gilles, and Felix Guattari. *What Is Philosophy?* Translated by Hugh Tomlinson and Graham Burchell. New York: Columbia University Press, 1994.

Descartes, René. "Correspondence with Elisabeth, Princess of Bohemia." In *Modern Philosophy: An Anthology of Primary Sources*, translated by Roger Ariew, 93–99. Indianapolis: Hackett, 2019.

———. *Discourse on the Method*. In *The Philosophical Writings of Descartes*, vol. 1, translated by John Cottingham, 111–76. Cambridge: Cambridge University Press, 1985.

———. *Early Writings*. In *The Philosophical Writings of Descartes*, vol. 1, translated by John Cottingham, 2–5. Cambridge: Cambridge University Press, 1985.

———. *Meditations on First Philosophy*. In *The Philosophical Writings of Descartes*, vol. 2, translated by John Cottingham, 1–62. Cambridge: Cambridge University Press, 1985.

Epicurus. "Principal Doctrines." In *The Epicurus Reader*, translated and edited by Brad Inwood et al., 32–36. Indianapolis: Hackett, 1994.

Epictetus. *Handbook*. Translated by Nicholas White. Indianapolis: Hackett, 1983.

Foucault, Michel. "Foucault, Michel, 1926–." Translated by Catherine Porter. In *The Cambridge Companion to Foucault*, edited by Gary Gutting, 314–19. Cambridge: Cambridge University Press, 1994.

———. "What Is Enlightenment?" In *The Foucault Reader*, edited by Paul Rabinow, translated by Catherine Porter, 32–50. New York: Pantheon, 1994.

Greenblatt, Stephen. *The Swerve: How the World Became Modern*. New York: Norton, 2011.

Heidegger, Martin. *Being and Time*. Translated by John Macquarrie and Edward Robinson. New York: Harper, 1962.

———. *An Introduction to Metaphysics*. Translated by Ralph Manheim. New Haven, CT: Yale University Press, 1959.

———. "Letter on Humanism." In *Basic Writings* edited by David Farrell Krell, 213–66. New York: Harper, 1993.

Hegel, G. W. F. *The Phenomenology of Mind*. Translated by J. B. Baillie. New York: Harper, 1967.

———. *The Phenomenology of Spirit*. Translated by A. V. Miller. Oxford: Oxford University Press, 1977.

Hesiod. *Works and Days; Theogony*. Translated by Stanley Lombardo. Indianapolis: Hackett, 1993.

Hobbes, Thomas. *Leviathan*. Edited by Richard Tuck. Cambridge: Cambridge University Press, 1991.

Hume, David. *Enquiry Concerning Human Understanding*. Oxford: Oxford University Press, 1975.

———. *A Treatise of Human Nature*. Oxford: Oxford University Press, 2000.

James, William. *Pragmatism*. New York: Meridian, 1974.

———. "Subjective Effects of Nitrous Oxide." *Mind* 7 (1882) 186–208.

Kant, Immanuel. *Critique of Pure Reason*. Translated by Norman Kemp Smith. New York: St. Martin's, 1965.

———. *Groundwork of the Metaphysics of Morals*. Translated and edited by Mary Gregor. Cambridge: Cambridge University Press, 1997.

———. *The Metaphysical Elements of Justice*. Translated by John Ladd. Indianapolis: Library of Liberal Arts, 1965.

———. *Prolegomena to Any Future Metaphysics That Can Qualify as a Science*. Translated by Paul Carus. La Salle, IL: Open Court, 1902.

Kierkegaard, Søren. *Concluding Unscientific Postscript to Philosophical Fragments*. Translated by Howard Hong and Edna Hong. Princeton: Princeton University Press, 1992.

———. *The Corsair Affair and Articles Related to the Writings*. Edited and Translated by Howard Hong and Edna Hong. Princeton: Princeton University Press, 1982.

———. *Johannes Climacus; or, De Omnibus Dubitandum Est*. Translated by Howard V. Hong and Edna H. Hong. Princeton: Princeton University Press, 1985.

———. *Kierkegaard's Journals and Notebooks*. Vol. 1, *Journals AA–DD*. Edited and Translated by Niels Jørgen Cappelørn et al. Princeton: Princeton University Press, 2007.

———. *Kierkegaard's Journals and Notebooks*. Vol. 2, *Journals EE–KK*. Edited and Translated by Niels Jørgen Cappelørn et al. Princeton: Princeton University Press, 2008.

———. *Kierkegaard's Journals and Notebooks*. Vol. 11, pt. 2, *Loose Papers, 1843–1855*. Edited and translated by Niels Jørgen Cappelørn et al. Princeton: Princeton University Press, 2020.

———. *A Literary Review*. Translated by Alastair Hannay. New York: Penguin, 2001.

———. *The Moment and Late Writings*. Translated by Howard Hong and Edna Hong. Princeton: Princeton University Press, 1998.

Leibniz, Gottfried Wilhelm. "The Principles of Philosophy, or, The Monadology." In *Philosophical Essays*, translated by Roger Ariew and Daniel Garber, 213–25. Indianapolis: Hackett, 1989.

Locke, John. *An Essay Concerning Human Understanding*. In *The Works of John Locke in Ten Volumes*. London: Thomas Tegg, 1823.

———. *Two Treatises of Government*. Edited by Peter Laslett. Cambridge: Cambridge University Press, 1988.

Lucretius. *On the Nature of things*. Translated by Martin Ferguson Smith. Indianapolis: Hackett, 2001.

Maimonides, Moses. *The Guide of the Perplexed*. Translated by Chaim Rabin. Indianapolis: Hackett, 1995.

Marx, Karl. *The Economic and Philosophic Manuscripts of 1844; and The Communist Manifesto*. Translated by Martin Milligan. New York: Prometheus, 1988.

———. "Theses on Feuerbach." In *The Marx-Engels Reader*. Translated by Robert C. Tucker, 107–9. New York: Norton, 1972.

Mill, John Stuart. *Utilitarianism and the 1868 Speech on Capital Punishment*. Edited by George Sher. Indianapolis: Hackett, 2002.

Monk, Ray. *Ludwig Wittgenstein: The Duty of Genius*. New York: Penguin, 1990.

Nietzsche, Friedrich. *Beyond Good and Evil*. Translated by Judith Norman. Cambridge: Cambridge University Press, 2002.

———. *The Birth of Tragedy*. Translated by Ronald Speirs. Cambridge: Cambridge University Press, 1999.

———. *Ecce Homo*. In *The Anti-Christ, Ecce Homo, Twilight of the Idols*, translated by Judith Norman, 69–152. Cambridge: Cambridge University Press, 2005.

———. *The Gay Science*. Translated by Josefine Nauckhoff. Cambridge: Cambridge University Press, 2001.

———. *Thus Spoke Zarathustra*. Translated by Adrian Del Caro. Cambridge: Cambridge University Press, 2006.

———. *Twilight of the Idols*. In *The Anti-Christ, Ecce Homo, Twilight of the Idols*, translated by Judith Norman, 152–230. Cambridge: Cambridge University Press, 2005.

Pascal, Blaise. *Pensées and Other Writings*. Translated by Honor Levi. Oxford: Oxford University Press, 1995.

Peirce, Charles S. "How to Make Our Ideas Clear." In *Charles S. Peirce: Selected Writings*. New York: Dover, 1958.

Russell, Bertrand. "The Value of Philosophy." In *Philosophic Classics from Plato to Derrida*, edited by Forest E. Baird, 1078–89. New York: Prentice Hall, 2011.

Sartre, Jean-Paul. *Being and Nothingness*. Translated by Hazel E. Barnes. New York: Washington Square, 1993.

Schopenhauer, Arthur. "Additional Remarks on the Doctrine of the Suffering of the World." In *Parerga and Paralipomena*, vol. 2, translated by E. F. J. Payne, 291–305. Oxford: Oxford University Press, 1974.

———. "Additional Remarks on the Doctrine of the Vanity of Existence." In *Parerga and Paralipomena*, vol. 2, translated by E. F. J. Payne, 283–90. Oxford: Oxford University Press, 1974.

———. "On Philosophy and Its Method." In *Parerga and Paralipomena*, vol. 2, translated by E. F. J. Payne, 3–20. Oxford: Oxford University Press, 1974.

———. "On Philosophy at the Universities." In *Parerga and Paralipomena*, vol. 1, translated by E. F. J. Payne, 137–98. Oxford: Oxford University Press, 1974.

Spinoza, Baruch. *Ethics Demonstrated in Geometrical Order*. Translated by G. H. R. Parkinson. Oxford: Oxford University Press, 2000.

Steig, William. *The Amazing Bone*. New York: Farrar, Straus and Giroux, 1976.

Stern, Karl. *The Flight from Woman*. New York: Farrar, Straus and Giroux, 1965.

Tolstoy, Leo. *Anna Karenina*. Translated by Richard Pevear and Larissa Volokhonsky. New York: Penguin, 2004.

Whitehead, Alfred North. *Process and Reality*. New York: Free Press, 1978.

Wittgenstein, Ludwig. *Culture and Value*. Translated by Peter Winch. Chicago: University of Chicago Press, 1980.

———. *Tractatus Logico-Philosophicus*. Translated by D. F. Pears and B. F. McGuinness. London: Routledge, 2001.

———. *Zettel*. Translated by G. E. M. Anscombe. Berkeley: University of California Press, 1967.

Wollstonecraft, Mary. *A Vindication of the Rights of Woman*. New York: Penguin, 2004.

Index

Abelard, Peter, 86–94
Absolute Mind, 197–200
Agathon, 51
Alcibiades, 53
Al-Ghazali, 94–96
Alienation, 219–20
Allegory of the Cave, 53
American pragmatism, 225–30
American Revolution, 117, 119
Anaxagoras, 35–36, 195
Anaximander, 30–31
Anaximenes, 30–31
Anselm, Saint, 100–103, 105
Anxiety as evidence of freedom, 259–61
Apology, The 41, 278, 283–84
Aquinas, Saint Thomas, 103–7
Aristophanes, 51
Aristotle, 5, 6, 15, 44–46, 54–63, 108; on logic, 57; on ethics, 57–58; political theory, 58–59; psychology, 59–60; metaphysics, 60–63; influence on Islamic philosophy, 94–95; influence on Aquinas, 104–7
Atomism, 34–35, 167
Augustine, Saint, 77–86; on the problem of evil, 80–84; on time, 84–85; on pessimism, 85–86
Averroes, 94–96
Ayer, Alfred Jules, 245–48

Bacon, Francis, 137–38
Being and Nothingness, 250, 256–61
Being and Time, 248–56

Bentham, Jeremy, 221, 224
Berkeley, California, 151–52
Berkeley, George, 145–52, 207, 246, 248
Beyond Good and Evil, 270–73
Boethius, 108–10
Bonaventure, Saint, 98–99
British empiricism, 136–57
British utilitarianism, 220–25
Buddhism, 206–7
Burke, Edmund, 119–20, 177, 187–88

Calamities of Peter Abelard, The 89–90
Camus, Albert, 212
Candide, 166
Categorical Imperative, 184–86
Christendom, 213
Cicero, 68
City of God, The 85–86
Cogito ergo sum, 129
Comedy as a key to philosophy, xv–xvi, xxiii, 70, 279, 280–89
Concluding Unscientific Postscript, 216–17
Confessions, 78–84
Consolation of Philosophy, The 108–9
Critique of Practical Reason, 181–86
Critique of Pure Reason, 157–65
Crumby approach to the history of philosophy, 25–28, 69–71, 264, 269

De Anima, 59–60
De Beauvoir, Simone, 212, 261–64
Deleuze, Gilles, 299–300
Democritus, 34–35, 167

Descartes, René, 120–37
Diotima, 51–52
Direct argumentative essays, 11–14
Discourse on Method, 123–24

Elisabeth, Princess of Bohemia, 134–36
Emerson, Ralph Waldo, 225–26
Empedocles, 35, 38–39
Engels, Friedrich, 202, 218–20
Enlightenment, 266–69
Enquiry Concerning Human Understanding, 152, 156
Epictetus, 66–68
Epicureanism, 63–69
Epicurus, 63, 67–68
Eryximachus, 50–51
Essay Concerning Human Understanding, 138–45
Ethics Demonstrated in Geometrical Order, 170–76
Euthyphro, 84
Existential phenomenology, 251–54, 259–61
Existentialism, 212–13, 248–64

Feuerbach, Ludwig, 219
Foucault, Michel, 264–69

Gorgias, 42
Gorgias, 42–43
Greek religion, 28–29
Guattari, Felix, 299–300
Guide for the Perplexed, 96–97

Hedonic calculus, 224
Hedonism, 63–69, 220–25
Hegel, Georg Wilhelm Friedrich, 192–93, 195–205, 216–17, 218–20, 302–3
Hegelian Dialectic, 196
Heidegger, Martin, 248–56
Hellenistic philosophy, 63–69
Heloise, 86–94
Heraclitus, 32–34, 306–7
Hesiod, 29
Hildegard of Bingen, 99–100
Hippias, 39
Hobbes, Thomas, 114–16, 138, 177

Hume, David, 152–57, 180–81, 246–48
Hypatia, 285
Hyperbolic doubt, 126–36

Idealism, 36–38
Incoherence of the Incoherence, The, 94–96
Incoherence of the Philosophers, The, 94–96
Indirect communication, 217, 239
Indirect philosophical arguments, 14–17
Innate ideas, 140–41
Intellectual blind spots, 7–10, 69–71, 100
Islamic philosophy, 94–96

James, William, 202–4, 225–30
Jewish philosophy, 96–97
John from Cincinnati, 169

Kant, Immanuel, 121, 157–65, 181–86, 192, 207, 224–25, 267–69
Kierkegaard, Søren, 47, 202, 205, 210–18, 243, 259

Language, Truth and Logic, 246–47
Leibniz, Gottfried Wilhelm, 165–69, 210
Leucippus, 34–35, 167
Leviathan, 114–16, 138
Locke, John, 116–19, 138–47, 177
Logical positivism, 245–48

Maimonides, Moses, 96–97
Manichaeism, 81–82
Marcus Aurelius, 66–68
Marx, Karl, 202, 218–20
Master-servant dialectic, 201, 208
Medieval mysticism, 97–100
Meditations on First Philosophy, 124–37
Meditations, 66–67
Metaphysics, 60–63
Mill, John Stuart, 220–25, 227
Mind's Journey into God, The 98–99
Mind-body dualism, 93–94, 133–36
Modern political philosophy, 114–20
Monadology, 166–69

Monism, 32–34, 35–36, 171–76, 195

Natural law theory, 58–59, 106–7
New Organon, The 137–38
Newton, Isaac, 166
Nietzsche, Elisabeth, 230
Nietzsche, Friedrich, 230–39, 243, 266, 270–73, 312–13
Noumena, 160–63, 200, 207–8
Nous, 35–36, 195

On Interpretation, 57
On the Nature of Things, 167

Parerga and Paralipomena, 194
Parmenides, 32–34
Pascal, Blaise, 178–80
Pausanias, 50
Peirce, Charles Sanders, 196, 226
Pensées, 178–80
Peripatetic philosophers, 54
Personal identity, 144–45, 154–55
Phaedrus, 46
Phaedrus, 50
Pheidippides, 298
Phenomena, 160–64, 200
Phenomenology of Mind, The 195–204, 211
Phenomenology, 195–204, 251–54
Plato, xxii, 15, 44–53, 78–84, 94, 99, 108
Platonic dialogues, xvi–xvii, 48–49
Platonic Idealism, 46, 51–53, 79–80, 99
Platonic love, 51–53, 99
Pragmatism, 227–28
Present Age, The 214–18
Pre-Socratic philosophers, xxii, 30–44, 301
Primary and secondary qualities, 142–44
Principle of sufficient reason, 210
Problem of evil, 80–84, 109, 131
Prodicus, 39
Proofs for the existence of God, 100–103, 104–6, 130
Protagoras, 39
Pythagoras, 36–38

Quantitative approach to the history of philosophy, 25–28, 69–71, 264, 269

Raphael, "The School of Athens," 44–47, 56, 79
Reductio ad absurdum, 32–33
Reflections on the Revolution in France, 119–20
Republic, 58
Russell, Bertrand, 240

Sartre, Jean-Paul, 212, 250, 256–61
Scholasticism, 56
Schopenhauer, Arthur, 194, 202, 204–10, 235–36, 303–5
Scientism, 5
Second Sex, The 263–64
Second Treatise of Government, The 116–19
Siddhartha, 206–7
Smith, Adam, 221
Social contract theory, 114–20
Socrates, 39–53, 277–79, 283–84
Sophistry, 36, 39–44, 277–79
Spinoza, Baruch, 170–76
State of nature, 114–19
Stoicism, 63–69
Subjective truth, 213–14
Summa Theologica, 103–7
Symposium, 49–53, 79–80, 99

Teresa of Avila, Saint, 99–100
Thales, xxii, 30–31
Thoreau, Henry David, 225–26
Three Dialogues between Hylas and Philonous, 147–51
Thus Spoke Zarathustra, 237–39, 312–13
Tractatus Logico-Philosophicus, 240–45
Transcendental philosophy, 157–65
Treatise of Human Nature, 152–55, 180–81
Twilight of the Idols, 231–36

Utilitarianism, 220–25, 226–27
Utilitarianism, 222

Verification principle, 247–48
Vindication of the Rights of Woman, A, 70, 186–89
Virtue ethics, 57–58

Wissenschaft, 198
Wittgenstein, Ludwig, 239–45

Wollstonecraft, Mary, 70, 186–89, 262, 285
World as Will and Representation, The 194, 206–10, 235–36, 304–5

Xanthippe, 279

Zeno, 32–34

www.ingramcontent.com/pod-product-compliance
Lightning Source LLC
Chambersburg PA
CBHW032047220426
43664CB00008B/897